ISLAM
AND THE
DESTINY
OF MAN

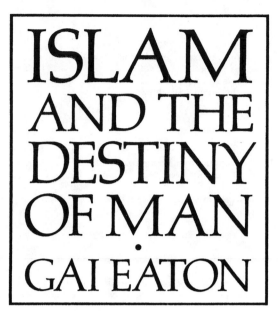

ISLAM
AND THE
DESTINY
OF MAN

GAI EATON

Published
in association with
The Islamic
Texts Society

STATE UNIVERSITY OF NEW YORK PRESS

THE ISLAMIC TEXTS SOCIETY

Iranian Garden Carpet C. 1800
cover photograph courtesy of Metropolitan Museum of Art,
Gift of William R. Pickering, 1967.
Title letterforms courtesy Marjorie Corbett;
Cover design by Sushila Blackman.

First published in U.S.A. by State University of New York Press,
Albany, 1985

For information, address:
State University of New York Press
State University Plaza
Albany, N.Y. 12246

Library of Congress Cataloging-in-Publication Data

Eaton, Charles Le Gai, 1941–
Islam and the destiny of man.
(SUNY series in Islam)
"Published in association with the Islamic Texts Society."
Includes index.
1. Islam   I. Title   II. Series.
BP161.2.E27   1985   297   85-14877
ISBN 0-88706-161-3
ISBN 0-88706-163-X (pbk.)

ACKNOWLEDGEMENTS

I have relied principally upon *The Glorious Koran* (Muhammad Picthall, published by Allen & Unwin) and *The Message of the Qur'ān* (Muhammad Asad, published by Dār al-Andalus) for translations of Quranic verses quoted in this book, and upon *Mishkāt al-Masābih* (translated by James Robson, published by S. Muhammad Ashraf, Lahore) for many of the *ahadīth*. I am indebted to the late Eric Schroeder's remarkable collection of early texts, *Muhammad's People* (published by The Bond Wheelwright Company, Portland, Maine in 1955), for many of the anecdotes quoted in Chapters 7 and 8.

SUNY series in Islam
Seyyed Hossein Nasr, Editor

At a time when so much attention is concentrated upon the role of Islam on the stage of contemporary history, it is important to focus upon the roots and sources of Islam and the spirituality which has infused it over the ages and which has been and remains its perennial fountainhead of energy and rejuvenation. In this series, under the general editorship of Seyyed Hossein Nasr, works of a scholarly nature which at the same time treat the spiritual aspects of the Islamic tradition will be made available to the English-speaking public. Some of these books concern the Islamic religion itself, others its inner dimension as contained in Sufism, and yet others the intellectual teachings of those schools which have been intertwined with and are inseparable from islamic spirituality and which in fact represent a most important expression of this spirituality. It is hoped that in this way the series will provide a more in depth knowledge of Islam and the Muslim peoples at a moment when broad and yet profound knowledge of the Islamic tradition has become so necessary for the contemporary world.

CONTENTS

Introduction   *page*   1

Part I   AN APPROACH TO THE FAITH
  1   Islam and Europe   9
  2   Continuity and Contrast   31
  3   Truth and Mercy   52

Part II   THE MAKING OF THE FAITH
  4   The World of the Book   73
  5   The Messenger of God   96
  6   The City of the Prophet   112
  7   The Successors   130
  8   The Way of the World   144

Part III   THE FRUITS OF THE FAITH
  9   The Rule of Law   163
 10   The Human Paradox   181
 11   Art, Environment and Mysticism   203
 12   Other Dimensions   223

INTRODUCTION

Religion is a different matter.

Other subjects may lend themselves, in varying degree, to objective study, and in some cases personal commitment serves only to distort what should be a clear and balanced picture. Religion is a different matter because here objectivity only skims the surface, missing the essential. The keys to understanding lie within the observer's own being and experience, and without these keys no door will open. This is particularly true of Islam, a religion which treats the distinction between belief and unbelief as the most fundamental of all possible distinctions, comparable on the physical level to that between the sighted and the blind. Believing and understanding complement and support one another. We do not seek for an adequate description of a landscape from a blind man, even if he has made a scientific study of its topography and has analyzed the nature of its rocks and vegetation. In Islam every aspect of human life, every thought and every action, is shaped and evaluated in the light of the basic article of faith. Remove this linchpin and the whole structure falls apart.

For the unbeliever this article of faith is meaningless and, in consequence, nothing else in the life of the Muslim makes sense. Even for the faithful Christian the 'sublime' and the 'mundane' relate to different dimensions, and he is disturbed by any confusion between the two. Islam does not recognize this division. For the Muslim, his worship and his manner of dealing with his bodily functions, his search for holiness and his bartering in the market, his work and his play are elements in an indivisible whole which, like creation itself, admits of no fissures. A single key unlocks the single door opening on to the integrated and tight-knit world of the Muslim.

That key is the affirmation of the divine Unity, and of all that follows from this affirmation, down to its most remote echoes on the very periphery of existence, where existence touches on nothingness. Islam is the religion of all or nothing, faith in a Reality which allows nothing to have independent reality outside its orbit; for if there were such a thing, however distant, however hidden, it would impugn the perfection and the totality of that which alone *is*.

It follows that one cannot speak of Islam without adopting a specific point of view and making that point of view quite explicit. This book is written by a European who became Muslim many years ago, through intellectual conviction and within the framework of a belief in the transcendent unity of all the revealed religions. The word 'convert' implies the rejection of one religion in favour of another, but mine was an act of acceptance which carried with it no corresponding act of rejection other than the rejection of the secular, agnostic world of thought in its entirety.

One who enters the community of Islam by choice rather than by birth sinks roots into the ground of the religion, the Qurān and the traditions of the Prophet; but the habits and customs of the Muslim peoples are not his. He lacks their strengths and is immune from their weaknesses; immune, above all, from the psychological 'complexes' which are the result of their recent history. He does not become a mimic Arab, since he knows that Islam, as a world religion, owes both its endurance and its rich fabric to the entry, century after century, of outlanders: Persians, Berbers, Mongols, Turks, Indians, Malays, Africans. These outlanders often broke the mould cherished by the Arabs, but they vivified the religion, and with it the culture and society that are stamped with its mark. Islam has created an immediately recognizable design for human living, but the way in which this design has been filled out and coloured has differed widely from one region of the *Dār-ul-Islām* (the 'House of Islam') to another; the peacock's tail has been spread over the world.

The European or American who has come to Islam in this way stands astride the oldest frontier in the world, the frontier that has separated Islamic civilization, first from Christendom and later from the post-Christian world, for some thirteen centuries. This is in many ways a strange position to occupy because the frontier runs between two areas of reciprocal incomprehension, and to be at home in both is, in a sense, to commute between different planetary systems. The Westerner's inability to understand the Muslim is matched by the Muslim's incapacity to understand the Westerner. Those who stand astride the frontier find themselves obliged to act as interpreters between two different languages and must themselves speak both with adequate fluency.

The Western Muslim does not change his identity, though he changes his direction. He is dyed with the colour characteristic of the culture into which he was born and which formed him; he asks the questions which this culture asks; he retains a sense of tragedy and of the world's ambiguity, with which the European tradition is imbued but which is strange to the traditional Muslim, and he is still haunted by the ghosts of Europe's past. Ancestral voices familiar to his kind are not silenced, but he has distanced himself from them.

The Semitic mind and temperament are legalistic by nature and a certain literal-mindedness is characteristic of the Muslim. The European, on the other hand, is more concerned with the spirit than with the letter of the law, and he inevitably brings something of this bias with him into Islam. This may even be the most useful contribution he can make to his adopted faith in an age of change and fluidity, in which the outworks of religion are eroded by the times so that it is necessary, as never before, to establish what are the essentials of the Faith and to hold fast to them. To say this is not to suggest that any part of the total structure is unimportant, but only to emphasize that when a castle is under siege, and alien forces have scaled the outer battlements, one must be ready to man the inner defences.

This book is written for those whose minds have been shaped by

Western culture. Given that the contemporary world, as it now exists almost universally, is entirely a product of that culture, I write as much for those of my co-religionists who have received a 'modern' education as I do for non-Muslims. Among the former there are already quite a number who have rediscovered the religion into which they were born as a result of seeing it through foreign eyes; no longer convinced by the traditional arguments of their Faith, which sufficed while Islam was a closed system, they have had to dive deep and travel far in order to return to their origin. They will assess this book in the light of their knowledge of the religion. But the non-Muslim who has an interest in understanding Islam, but who lacks the time and the inclination to read and compare a number of books, has every right to ask whether what he is told is authentic and, in a general sense, 'orthodox'.

No simple answer can be given to this question. It is difficult to provide a universally acceptable definition of Muslim 'orthodoxy', a term for which there is no precise equivalent in the Arabic language. There is no ecclesiastical hierarchy in Islam (whatever may be the appearances in Shi'a Islam as we find it in Iran), no ultimate doctrinal authority other than that of the Book itself, the Qurān. What I believe or what the next man believes, provided we stay within the framework of the religious Law, is largely a matter of personal insight, so long as we do not depart too far from the consensus of the community (assuming that such a consensus exists, and this is an open question today).

If, however, we borrow what is essentially a Christian term, it can be said that Sunni orthodoxy emerged in the tenth century AD, taking shape over the next two hundred years; and that it emerged as a consensus following a middle way between conflicting points of view, which threatened to tear the community apart. Leaving room for wide variations of opinion, it was achieved in reaction against narrow and exclusive views of what constituted orthodoxy and of what entitled a man or woman to belong to the *Ummah*, the sacred community of Islam. A Muslim, by this definition, is anyone who is able to make the confession of faith in sincerity; to say seven words, and to mean them. *Lā ilāha illa 'Llāh*; *Muḥammadun rasūlu' Llāh*: 'There is no divinity but (or 'if not') Allah: Muhammad is the messenger of Allah'. And since human beings cannot read the secrets of hearts, the judgement as to sincerity rests only with Allah.

In practice few would accept that this suffices, unless it is taken to include all the consequences which flow from the simple affirmation of faith. The Muslim believes in One God, who is all-powerful and has no partner; believes in His messengers, sent to mankind for their guidance from the beginning of time; believes that Muhammad closed the cycle of messengers and that there can be no further revelation of the divine Law after him; believes that the Qurān is the Word of God, unaltered and unalterable, and believes in the obligation to conform to the 'Five Pillars', which are the confession of faith, the five daily prayers, payment of the poor-due, the fast of Ramadan, and performance of the Pilgrimage to Mecca by those physically and financially able to undertake it. A Muslim may neglect one or more of the pillars (except the first) and still be counted as a believer, but if he denies their necessity he has placed himself outside the community.

The Qurān itself offers a broad definition: 'The messenger believes in that which has been revealed to him from his Lord, as do the believers. Each believes in Allah and His angels and His scriptures and His messengers – We make no distinction between any of His messengers – and they say "We hear and we obey. Forgive us, O Lord. Unto Thee is the journeying". A further condition, however, follows from this. If membership of the community of believers requires acceptance of the Qurān as the revealed Word of God, then denial of any part of the Qurān or of any statement made in the Book may be assumed to call belief into doubt. This is so, and yet we have here an area of ambiguity. Certain verses, particularly those relating to matters of law, are plain enough, but there are many parts of the Qurān which lend themselves to a variety of interpretations; and indeed it is said that, in principle, every single verse contains layer upon layer of meaning. It is natural that there should have been wide variations in interpretation, variations which have, on the whole, been accepted, provided they did not contradict the literal meaning.

This is why the common sense which has constantly re-asserted itself against the passions and follies of fanaticism throughout the history of Islam inclines towards the broad definition of 'orthodoxy', leaving the final word with the consensus of the community. But the battle for tolerance and the broad definition has never been finally won, and this is particularly clear at the present time when for various reasons, including what may be called an 'identity crisis', many Muslims have taken refuge in narrowness and literalism. Since each particular group holds to its own narrow corridor, the *Ummah* as a whole is troubled by bitter and unnecessary conflicts of opinion. The Muslim who writes or speaks about Islam today may expect to be accused of *kufr* (unbelief) or *bid'a* (innovation) by one group or another, not unlike the Christian who, in former times (when religion was still a matter of life or death, salvation or damnation), walked a tightrope over the abyss of 'heresy'. He accepts these accusations with as good a grace as he can muster, detecting in them symptoms of weakness rather than strength.

So far as 'innovation' is concerned, it would in fact be very difficult to introduce any new element into Muslim thought – even supposing that one wished to do so – but it is easy to re-introduce much that has been forgotten or overlooked in the course of time. It happens often enough that, flushed with what we take for some new insight into the religion, we find that this very idea was put forward by such-and-such a Muslim thinker a thousand years ago; and this is as it should be.

While on the one hand the Western Muslim's 'orthodoxy' may be questioned by the more hidebound among his co-religionists, he is likely, on the other, to be accused by non-Muslims who have had some contact with the Islamic world of 'idealizing' Islam and presenting a view of the Faith which is contradicted by the perceived facts. These facts, however, relate to practice not to principles, and he is under no obligation to defend or to attempt to justify the manner in which the religion is practised in a particular period of history by those of its adherents who catch the light and attract attention. Where human beings are concerned, good men and good women are by no means thick on the ground, but vice always pays its tribute to virtue by masquerading behind the mask of religion or – more recently – of some political ideology, and both wickedness and stupidity walk the streets more confidently when decently clothed.

It would be foolish and, to say the least, counter-productive to seek arguments to excuse divisions within the *Ummah*, wars between Muslim states, the brutality and hypocrisy of certain national leaders, the corrupt practices of the rich or the hysteria of zealots who have forgotten the fundamental law of Mercy and the binding obligation to make use of the gift of Intelligence. We live in an age of *fitnah*. This term is usually translated as 'civil commotion'. An alternative translation might be 'fermentation', and it is a characteristic of the process of fermentation that the scum rises to the surface.

At the same time it must be borne in mind that, despite the fairly recent division of the *Ummah* of Islam into nation states, Muslims still tend to identify a man in terms of the religion into which he was born rather than in terms of his nationality or racial origin. Since they find it difficult to grasp the fact that there are people in this world who do not even profess to believe in God – any God – they habitually refer to all Europeans and Americans as 'Christians' (it is quite common to hear the late Adolf Hitler cited as an example of how wickedly Christians can behave). By the same token, everyone who happens to have been born into the Islamic world calls himself a 'Muslim'. Westerners take this designation at its face value, and shabby little tyrants who are as distant from Islam as was Hitler from Christianity are seen as 'Muslims'; the religion as such is judged – or misjudged – in terms of their behaviour.

Beneath the surface, however, and invisible to the casual observer, there exist a vast number of simple men and women who remain exemplary Muslims and who redeem Islam today as they did in the past, as do the mystics, whose selfless thirst for God reduces the sins of the mighty to little more than a rude irrelevance. Islam is not always discoverable in the hands or the hearts of its leaders or of its official spokesmen, but those who seek it will find it.

They will find it expressed in many different forms. The central theme of any serious study of Islam must be unity in diversity. Muhammad was an Arab and the Qurān is quintessentially an Arabic scripture, expressed in a language which contains within its own structure an implicit view of reality. From this point of view every Muslim is in a certain sense 'Arabized', but although this has created a recognizable pattern in the various textures of Islamic civilization, it has not extinguished a rich cultural diversity shaped by racial and historical differences. The principles of the religion and of the law derived from it are simple, but no limit can be set to the variety of their applications.

In what follows I hope, God willing, to show what it means to be a Muslim, and to consider doctrine, history and social life in the light of the Revelation which is the source of the Faith, as it is of the civilization and culture constructed by human beings, good and bad, wise and foolish, out of the materials crystallized from that source. But the whole, which reflects the divine Plenitude, cannot be caught in any net of words. To every statement I would gladly add a formula of great significance in the Islamic context, a formula which means that God knows best, that He alone knows, and that those who speak or write must always keep in mind their relative ignorance and the limitations of their perspective, just as the living must always keep death in mind. *Wa Allāhu ā'lam.*

PART I

An Approach to the Faith

Chapter 1

ISLAM AND EUROPE

With the fading away of imperial power, which had made it possible for the West to despise other cultures, interest in Islam has revived recently, and the economic influence of oil-rich Muslim states has provided, for the first time in 250 years, a practical motive for seeking to understand the Muslim world. There is no lack of information available, and library shelves are heavy with books on Islam; but whether this spate of information has provided the keys to understanding – and to the empathy without which understanding can only be superficial – is another question. In any case, those of us who see a need to build bridges across the frontier are never satisfied. An affirmation is nothing if the signal which carries it is weak or distorted, and although it may be that all such signals, by their very nature, lack strength and clarity, the attempt must be made, repeatedly, to find the right words and the most effective means of communication.

Between Islam and Christianity, as between Islam and post-Christian culture, communication has been hampered by very particular difficulties. Occidental[1] writing about Islam – what we would now call the work of the orientalists – has only too often been rooted in the bitter polemics of the Middle Ages. From the time when Christianity came into possession of the Roman Empire until the seventh century it would have been reasonable to suppose that nothing could stop the universal expansion of the Christian message. In the seventh century Islam stopped it. From then on nothing short of a piety capable of withstanding the severest shock could save Christians from the unthinkable thought that God had made a dreadful mistake. Palestine and other lands of the Near East, together with Christian Egypt, had been devoured by a monster which appeared without warning out of the Arabian sands; the foundations of the world had been shaken and the shadow of darkness had come down upon the heart of Christendom, the Holy Land.

Since Islam was strong in arms and Christendom was weak, words were the only available weapons against what was seen first as a 'heresy' and later as a false religion of satanic origin, and all the resources of language were pressed into the service of a propaganda campaign which might have

---

[1] In common usage the term 'Western' refers to Western Europe and the Americas, contrasted with the socialist 'East'. It seems best, therefore, to use the term 'occidental' when referring to the white man's civilization as a whole, and this has an added advantage if it serves to remind us that Marxism is as much a product of European culture as is parliamentary democracy.

brought a blush to the cheeks of the late Doctor Goebbels. One can still catch its echoes in our time. Pope Innocent III had identified Muhammad as the Anti-Christ; almost 700 years later the explorer Doughty described him as 'a dirty and perfidious Arab'. In his *History of Europe*, published in 1936 and a standard work in schools for many years after, H. A. L. Fisher called him 'cruel and crafty, lustful and ignorant' and made reference to the 'crude outpourings of the Koran'.

The contemporary Muslim, however, is often less troubled by books which show an open and clear-cut bias, whether this arises from a narrow denominational point of view or as part of a generalized attack on traditional religion, than he is by works which are sympathetic (or condescending) in intention, but which in practice undermine the foundations of his faith. To take the most obvious example, many writers who might be considered well-disposed work on the unspoken assumption that Muhammad was the 'author' of the Qurān. To suggest that the Qurān had a human author, even if it is admitted that he was 'an inspired genius', is to do away with the religion of Islam. These authors refer readily to the 'greatness' of the Prophet; like sympathetic schoolmasters, they find in him much to admire, and they are astonished by his magnanimity to his enemies. They rebut charges that he was anything but sincere, brave and honourable and are shocked by the scurrilous charges brought against him by earlier writers. At the same time there emerges, quite unconsciously, that note of amiable condescension which – ever since the end of Empire – Europeans have adopted towards the 'backward' or 'developing' peoples of the Third World.

There is a certain ambiguity in many of these books, as though their authors were unable to decide whether Islam is or is not a truly revealed religion. Even the British Islamicist, W. Montgomery Watt, appears to be a victim of such indecision. In his assessment at the end of *Muhammad: Prophet and Statesman* he remarks in passing that 'not all the ideas that he proclaimed are true and sound, but by God's grace he had been able to provide men with a better religion than they had had before'. One suspects a slip of the pen here, since the author is a Christian, and Christianity came before Islam; but the ambiguity is apparent if one asks, first, why 'God's grace' should have been only partially effective in Muhammad's case, and secondly, in terms of what absolute criterion of truth some of these ideas were true and others less so. Transpose this to the Christian context and it might reasonably be asked how a believing Christian would respond to the statement that 'not all Jesus's ideas were true and sound', but that Christianity represented an advance on Greek and Roman religion.

Where Christian writers are concerned certain limitations are appropriate and acceptable. One does not expect them to be untrue to the principles of their own faith, and the fact that they are themselves believers gives them an understanding of religion as such which opens doors and may, on occasion, lead to the very heart of things; and there are some who understand very well that to speak of another religion with courtesy is not only a gesture of respect to its adherents but is also a courtesy to God in the face of the mysteries of divine Self-revelation. This was well expressed by the Catholic Islamicist, Emile Dermenghem, in his *Life of Mohamet*[1], when – writing of 'the barriers which must be destroyed' – he said that 'the sense of true relativity does not destroy the sense of the Absolute', adding that, 'The divine Revelation comes from the mouths of human beings, adapting itself to times and places ... What seems to us contradictory is only the refraction of the eternal ray in the prism of time'.

Even Dermenghem, despite the deep love for Islam which led him to end his life in Algeria, demonstrates that there are sticking points beyond which the Christian cannot go and perspectives which he cannot share. Many Muslims, out of a natural suspicion of a related but rival religion, distrust all Christian writing on Islam and prefer the supposedly objective works of agnostics. In this they are mistaken. Faith speaks to faith, even in dispute, while the unbeliever is dumb. And, so far as objectivity is concerned, it is not to be found in this quarter. The more closely one considers the typical Western liberal-agnostic (child of a particular culture at a particular moment in its history) from the other side of the frontier, the more unmistakably he identifies himself as a 'godless Christian'. He may close himself to faith, but if he reacts against Christianity this is in the name of principles indirectly derived from the Christian religion, just as Asians and Africans have reacted against colonialism in the name of principles derived from their colonial masters. The open prejudices of the Christian writer are, on the whole, preferable to the hidden ones of the agnostic.

In theory the limitations of books on Islam by non-Muslims should be of little consequence. Few people, seeking a proper understanding of Christianity, would turn to non-Christian authors. Cannot Muslim writers satisfy the need that undoubtedly exists?

Most Muslim scholars seem to agree, at least in private, that there has been a singular failure to communicate across the cultural frontier. The actual means of communication – the way in which religion needs to be presented nowadays – have been forged, not out of Islamic materials, but in the West. The Muslim writer finds himself obliged to work with instruments which do not fit comfortably in his hand. Moreover, traditional Muslims, who have escaped the influence of 'modern', that is to say, occidental education have no understanding of the occidental mind, which is as strange to them as it would be to a Christian of the Middle Ages. Since the Renaissance, European man has ventured out beyond the barriers set up by traditional civilizations against all such straying. In doing so he may have done irreparable damage to himself, but he has become sophisticated in a way that makes other cultures seem naive in comparison. There was a time when it was otherwise. Plato could call the orientals 'old' in comparison with the innocent youthfulness of the Greeks; now it is the Europeans who are 'old', having seen too much, and being burdened with intolerable memories.

The traditional Muslim writes with authority and conviction, but he does not know how to answer the questions which dominate Western thought in the religious context. These questions seem to him unnecessary

[1] (London: Routledge), 1930.

if not actually blasphemous, and at heart he feels that his task is super-fluous. The truth of the Qurān is, for him, so compelling and so self-evident that, if it does not convince the unbeliever, his poor efforts are hardly likely to do so.

For the most part, however, it is Muslims who have been through the modern educational machine who write the books which circulate in the West. The works they produced in the late nineteenth and early twentieth century cannot now be read without embarrassment. These men were the 'Uncle Toms' of Islam. Their defence of the religion depended, they thought, on proving that it contained nothing incompatible with the best contemporary fashions of thought and accorded perfectly with the moral and philosophical norms of European civilization. They scoured the libraries for any favourable references to Islam in the works of the 'great philosophers' (such as H. G. Wells), but were often reduced to quoting long-forgotten journalists who had found a good word to say for the Prophet or for Muslims as such. The idea that the civilization they admired so blindly might be open to radical criticism in terms of Islamic norms scarcely crossed their minds.

The situation has changed in recent years, though the 'Uncle Toms' are still with us (thinly disguised as modernists). Contemporary Muslim writers cannot be accused of taking no pride in Islam, indeed this pride is sometimes expressed in strident tones, and no one could claim that they are uncritical of Western 'decadence', though their criticism tends to miss the mark, focusing on symptoms rather than on causes. They have not, however, escaped a different kind of subservience to occidental norms. They tend to be deeply concerned with *al-Naḥdah*, 'renewal', the 'Islamic Renaissance', which they readily compare with the Renaissance in Europe. Yet the European Renaissance was, from the religious point of view, a rebirth of the paganism which Christianity had supplanted, and it was the source of that very 'decadence' which Muslims perceive in Western life and thought. Their inherent hostility to Christianity blinds them to the fact that forces and ideologies which destroyed one religion may as easily destroy another; or, if they do see this, they believe that Islam's inherent strength and its capacity to absorb and Islamicize alien elements will protect it from subversion. This is, to say the least, a dangerous gamble.

Those who have close contact with Muslims will be accustomed to hearing, with monotonous regularity, the parrot-cry: 'We will take the good things from Western civilization; we will reject the bad things'. It is strange that any Muslim should imagine this to be possible. Islam itself is an organic whole, a *gestalt*, in which everything is interconnected and in which no single part can be considered in isolation from the rest. The Muslim above all others should understand that every culture has some-thing of this unity and should realize that the modern civilization created in the West, even if it seems constantly to change shape as in a kaleido-scope, forms a coherent pattern in terms of cause and effect. To draw one fibre from it is to find that this is attached, by countless unseen filaments, to all the rest. The small fragment of 'good', lifted from the pattern, brings with it piece after piece of the whole structure. With the light come the shadows; and with everything positive come all the negative elements which are related to it either as cause or as effect.

Seyyed Hossein Nasr, who is almost unique among Muslim writers in his understanding both of traditional Islam and of the forces of subversion at work in the West, makes this point: 'Words and expressions have been used by many [of these writers] in such a way as to betray the state of cultural shock and often the sense of inferiority *vis-à-vis* the West from which they suffer. Their writings reveal most of all a slavery of the mind to the norms and judgements of Western civilization. Moreover, these norms are usually hidden under the veil of an "Islam" of which there often remains little more than a name and certain emotional attachments, an Islam which has become devoid of the intellectual and spiritual truth which stands at the heart of the Islamic revelation.'[1]

The view first put forward by more or less hostile orientalists that Islamic civilization became decadent, 'stagnant' and 'sterile', from the moment it no longer produced scientists (as the term is now understood), that is to say around the thirteenth century of the Christian era, is uncritically accepted by modernists and 'fundamentalists' alike. This is compensated by a passionate faith in the present or imminent 'renaissance', and they do not see that decadence (if the word has any application) is greatly to be preferred to deviation. Decadence is a symptom of weariness and laxity, whereas deviation takes the form of a malignant activity or dynamism directed towards false goals. Better a sleeping giant than a mad or demonic one.

The inclination of many contemporary Muslims to turn their backs on a thousand years of historical and cultural development has its roots in the eighteenth century, before the West had made its impact upon Islam. There were at that time twelve particularly influential 'reformers' teaching and preaching in the *haramain* (the 'two sanctuaries', Mecca and Medina). They called for the purification of the religion from every element that could not be traced directly to the Qurān or to the sayings and practice of the Prophet, and they condemned *taqlīd* (blind adherence to the opinions of earlier scholars), much as Protestants in the Christian world had preached a return to scriptural sources some 350 years earlier.

Muslim scholars have always been great travellers, at home everywhere in the 'House of Islam', and only five of these men were Arabs, the others being of Indian, Moroccan and Kurdish origin. Pilgrim-scholars from every corner of the world would stay in the *haramain* for a year or two to study under them before returning home, and in this way their views were swiftly disseminated. But, with hindsight, the most important of the eighteenth century reformers was Muhammad Ibn Abdu'l-Wahhāb (1703–1792). He had studied in the *haramain* and travelled widely before returning to his village in a remote part of the Arabian peninsula, there to ally himself – with momentous historical consequences – with a tribal chieftain named Saud, whose descendants now rule over the greater part of the peninsula. Appalled by the contrast between the Islamic ideal and the Muslim world discovered in the course of his travels, he concluded that

[1] *Islam and the Plight of Modern Man* (Longman), p. 122.

few of the Muslims of his time had any right to call themselves Muslims; with passionate conviction and great eloquence he preached a simple and uncompromising doctrine of pure transcendence and of unquestioning obedience to the revealed Will of the Transcendent; there was no place in this doctrine for mysticism, the allegorical interpretation of the Qurān, syncretism or adaptation. This was true monotheism and everything else was false, damnable and un-Islamic.

Time has passed and the cult of simplicity has only too often degenerated into a cult of banality, a process which has been hastened by the experience of Western domination. Islam, we are told, is so simple and straightforward, so easy to understand and to follow, that it has no need of explanation or interpretation. God is King. Man is His slave. The King has issued His orders. It is for the slave to obey these orders or be damned. All would have been well – the 'Christians' would never have triumphed – had not the pure religion been overlaid in the course of the centuries by a web of theological speculation, mystical extravagance and complex philosophy, with the result that the Muslims allowed their inheritance to slip from their grasp, until the decadent civilization of the West was able to overcome and dominate 'the best of nations'. All that is required to reverse this lamentable situation is a return to the Qurān and to the *Sunnah* of the Prophet. 'Throw the books away' has become something of a slogan. We have the Scripture, and that should suffice any man.

It is indeed true that the essentials of Islam are clear and simple. As the final revelation of God's Guidance to His creatures it presents a stark confrontation: Man stands naked before his Maker, without any intermediary and with nothing to blur the immediacy of this encounter. The rules governing personal life and social life have been set out with a clarity which leaves no room for misunderstanding; and, when all is said and done, the divine Mercy compensates for human weakness. No doubt this would suffice if human nature contained no complexities and no fissures, and if we had not been endowed with a searching intelligence which must analyse before it can achieve synthesis. The rich development of Muslim thought and religious speculation over so many centuries is sufficient proof that this is not enough.

Islam has been described by Europeans who have lived and worked in the Arab world as a 'Boy Scout religion', and it is precisely in this way that many of its spokesmen present it; an image that bears no relation to the splendours of the Baghdad Caliphate, Muslim Spain, the Sassanids in Iran, the Timurids in Central Asia, the Ottomans at the height of their power, and the host of philosophers, mystics and artists who were the glory of these various crystallizations of Islamic civilization. Boy Scout precepts do little to answer the questions we ask or to assuage the soul's anguish. They satisfy neither Westerners nor educated Muslims, and the only reason that more of the latter have not drifted away from the religion is that, on the one hand, they have been able to interpret it as a political ideology (in an age obsessed with political 'solutions') and, on the other, they have nowhere else to go. The European or the American who turns his back on Christianity is still heir to a rich culture and has no reason to feel that he has become a 'non-person'. The child of Islam who turns away has empty hands and no longer knows who he is. Islamic culture is neither more nor less than an aspect of the religion; there is no secular culture whatsoever. Moreover, the community is still essentially a religious community, and to quit the religion is to leave the community.

However, it is not only contemporary Muslims who question the need for profundity, the need for theology and for a metaphysical approach to religion. Many Christians do the same, to the great impoverishment of Christianity. God has chosen to create in certain men and women a type of intelligence which, by inner necessity, asks far-reaching questions about the nature of reality. This is a divine gift, though not without its dangers, as is the case with all gifts; it has, therefore, certain rights, including the right to receive answers to the questions which arise spontaneously within it. In a sense these questions are posed by God Himself so that He may answer them and thereby enrich our understanding, and we are assured that He never gives us a genuine need without providing for its satisfaction. Questioning minds may always and everywhere be in a minority, but it is precisely these – the questioners – who are the ultimate formers of opinion. What the intellectuals doubt today will eventually be doubted by simple people.

Ideas which, on their first appearance, seem most abstract and farthest removed from the affairs of ordinary men and women have a way of percolating through the whole fabric of society, though they often suffer distortion in the process. Given the very nature of modern civilization (and the nature of its origins), the ideas current in our time are destructive of religious faith unless this faith is protected by an intellectual armour – and intellectual weapons – suited to the conditions of the late twentieth century. The traditional arguments in support of faith are no longer entirely effective, and it no longer seems 'natural' to believe in God and to believe in states of being beyond this present life. Since the Qurān addresses itself specifically to 'those who think' and who 'meditate' and, in effect, commands us to make full use of our mental faculties, Muslims are under an obligation to deepen and develop the intellectual bases of their faith and have no excuse for relying on unthinking obedience and emotional fervour to protect it against the searching questions of our time.

The cult of simplicity or of platitude is expressed not only in expositions of Islam as a way of life but also in modern interpretations of the Qurān. One need only compare a popular modern commentary, sentimental or banal, with the great medieval commentaries, those of the rationalists, whose intellectual instruments were derived from Greek philosophy, those of the Sufis, who plumbed the depths of meaning beneath the surface of the text, and those of the grammarians, who analysed subtle shades of meaning behind every word and phrase, to see what an impoverishment has taken place.

This might best be illustrated by direct quotation, but it would be unkind to ridicule the efforts of sincere and pious men to communicate their love for the Book in this way; the point can be made just as effectively by means of a parody or pastiche without identifying the original from which, in fact, it departs very little. This commentary is on the opening verses of *Sūrah* 91: 'By the sun and its radiance; by the moon which reflects it; by the day which reveals [the earth], and by the night which enshrouds it . . .'. The medieval commentators discovered profound significance in these simple lines, interpreting their symbolism with astonishing subtlety and speculative daring. The modern commentary runs something like this: 'The oath refers first to the sun's rising, and how beautiful this is! The sun is at its clearest when it rises and it shines with a pure light. It is the source of our physical life, and how generous God is to give us life! Then there is the moon with its beautiful light, whispering to the human heart and inspiring poetic thoughts. How nice it is to sit in the moonlight! Then comes the oath by the day, when the sun shines and the earth is lit up; but when night covers the earth it is the opposite to what happens in the day. The sun no longer shines. Everything is concealed from our sight and we are in darkness. How incomparably the holy Qurān describes all this and how inspiring these verses are!' And so on, weaving words together to fill page after page, with the best of intentions but little meaning.

Sincerity and good intentions do not guarantee effective communication, but the failure of most contemporary Muslim writers to express themselves in what is really an alien idiom merely reflects the extraordinary situation of Islam in the post-colonial period and in a world shaped entirely by occidental values and by ideologies which originate in the *Dar-ul-Ḥarb* (the 'House of Conflict', the world beyond the frontiers of the Faith). It could be said that the Muslims 'awakened' (if, for convenience, we use this dubious term) to find themselves on a planet occupied by their enemies, obliged to imitate these enemies in everything if they were to survive their rude awakening. To understand just how extraordinary this situation is from the Muslim point of view, it is essential to understand something of the history of the confrontation between these two civilizations.

Within a century of the Prophet's death in 632 of the Christian era the Muslim Empire stretched from the borders of China to the Atlantic, from France to the outskirts of India, and from the Caspian Sea to the Sahara. This astonishing expansion had been achieved by a people who, if they were known at all to the great world beyond the Arabian peninsula, had been dismissed as ignorant nomads. They had overrun something above four-and-a-half million square milies of territory and changed the course of history, subordinating Christianity to Islam in its homelands in the Near East and in North Africa and Spain, forcing the Roman Empire of Byzantium onto the defensive and converting the Empire of the Persians into a bulwark of Islam. Human history tells of no other achievement comparable to this. Alexander had dazzled the ancient world by his conquests, but he left behind him only legends and a few inscriptions. Where the Arabs passed they created a civilization and a whole pattern of thought and of living which endured and still endures, and they decisively determined the future history of Europe, barring the way to the rich lands of the east and thereby provoking – many centuries later – the voyages of exploration to the west and to the south which were to nurture European power.

By the year 720 the Muslims had crossed the formidable barrier of the

Pyrenees and all Western Europe lay open before them. They were defeated by the Franks in a battle between what are now the cities of Tours and Poitiers, but it is doubtful whether this battle was in any sense decisive, and in any case the eastern wing of the army was already penetrating the Swiss Valais. It seems more likely that the dark forests which lay ahead appeared uninviting, and the bitter chill of the so-called temperate lands must have seemed like the chill of death itself; and no doubt the great wave of expansion had, for the time being, exhausted itself and reached its natural limit. A few miles more and the story would have been very different, with a Sultan on the throne of France, his Emir in a palace by the Thames, and Europe's offspring populating North America under the banner of Islam.

The rapidity with which Islam spread across the known world of the seventh to eighth centuries was strange enough, but stranger still is the fact that no rivers flowed with blood, no fields were enriched with the corpses of the vanquished. As warriors the Arabs might have been no better than others of their kind who had ravaged and slaughtered across the peopled lands but, unlike these others, they were on a leash. There were no massacres, no rapes, no cities burned. These men feared God to a degree scarcely imaginable in our time and were in awe of His all-seeing presence, aware of it in the wind and the trees, behind every rock and in every valley. Even in these strange lands there was no place in which they could hide from this presence, and while vast distances beckoned them ever onwards they trod softly on the earth, as they had been commanded to do. There had never been a conquest like this.

In the centuries which followed the abortive expedition into France the threat to Western Europe was never far removed. Islam was the dominant civilization and Christendom was confined to an appendix to the Euro-Asian land mass, closed in upon itself and never really safe except in those periods when the Muslims – so often their own worst enemies – were divided among themselves. The Crusaders came to Palestine and were, in due course, driven out, and in the thirteenth century the Arab world was devastated by the Mongol hordes; but the Mongols were converted, to become champions of Islam, as were the Turks. Constantinople fell in 1453, and soon the Ottomans took up the challenge represented by the European enclave. Belgrade was captured in 1521 and Rhodes in the following year. Sulayman the Magnificent entered Hungary and won a great victory at Mohács, and in the 1530s the French King, Francis I, sought his support against the Hapsburgs and encouraged Ottoman plans for the invasion of Italy. A few years later it was the Protestant princes who negotiated for Muslim help against the Pope and the Emperor, and the Sultan made his preparations to enter Germany.

The threat may have been an empty one, for by then Europe was overtaking the Muslim world in effective power, chiefly owing to technical improvements in firearms and shipbuilding; but it echoed the age-old threat which, through almost nine centuries, had shaped the European's perception of the world. The 'menace of Islam' had remained the one constant factor amidst change and transformation and it had been branded on the European consciousness. The mark of that branding is still visible.

The tide, however, was turning. In 1683 the Ottomans besieged Vienna for the last time. They were already a spent force, and this fact was acknowledged in the Treaty of Carlowitz, signed in 1699. The world of Islam, if it could still be called a 'world', had already been on the defensive for some years, and the defences were cracking. The British were in India and the Dutch in Indonesia, and the Russian capture of Azov brought to the Balkans the Muslims' most implacable enemy, then as now.

Almost a thousand years separated Carlowitz from the Muslim advance into Southern France; less than three hundred separate us from Carlowitz, three hundred years in which Europeans could, at least until very recently, try to forget their long obsession with Islam. It was not easily forgotten. 'The fact remains', says the Tunisian writer Hichem Djaït, 'that medieval prejudices insinuated themselves into the collective unconscious of the West at so profound a level that one may ask, in terror, whether they can ever be extirpated from it.'[1]

Certainly, the years of imperial power were years of forgetfulness. Writing in the late eighteenth century, Edward Gibbon had thought it necessary to devote nine of the seventy-one chapters of *The Decline and Fall of the Roman Empire* to Islam. European historians of the following century could ignore it. And yet we do not have to search far to find the familiar note of fear and detestation making itself heard again, even while the glories of Empire were still undimmed. John Buchan's *Greenmantle*, published in 1916 and probably read by every English schoolboy over the following twenty years, dealt with a threat to civilization more terrible than all the Kaiser's troops, the threat of 'resurgent Islam'.

As so often in previous centuries, the children of Europe were encouraged to go to bed with nightmares of the green-turbaned hordes crying '*Allāhu akbar!*' and descending upon civilization to reduce it to cinders. To change public opinion and popular beliefs is uphill work but to reinforce them is easy. Buchan would not have written *Greenmantle* had he felt obliged to argue his case against Islam, but there was no need to do so.

The nightmares, however, were all on one side. Throughout the greater part of their history, Muslims had no cause to be obsessed with Europe and, except during the relatively brief episode of the Crusades, could afford to ignore it. During the Middle Ages Muslim scholars, preachers and traders travelled throughout the world of Islam between Spain and Indonesia, their passport the declaration of faith – *Lā ilāha illa 'Llāh* – and their adventuring made easy by the fact that hospitality and assistance to the wayfarer are a religious duty. The scholar from Muslim India was at home in Morocco, and some of the early mystics travelled so far and so widely that one wonders what possible means of transport they can have used, other than the legendary magic carpet.

Many, particularly the traders, travelled beyond the *Dār-ul-Islām*. A traveller from Cairo could cash his notes of hand in Canton. But they kept to the civilized world and did not venture into darkest Europe – where they would almost certainly have been killed – although they must have gained some knowledge of the region from the Christian scholars who came to the great universities of Muslim Spain in search of education. An early writer

---

[1] *L'Europe et l'Islam* (Paris: Collection Esprit/Seuil), p. 21.

argued, with much good will, that the white man (contrary to popular belief) was no less intelligent than the black man of Africa; but on the whole medieval Europe beyond the Pyrenees appeared to be a region of squalor and barbarism. The Europeans who invaded Palestine as Crusaders, savage in warfare, without respect for women and children, and dirty in their habits, can have done little to alter these prejudices. The Muslims could not be aware of the secret spiritual life of Christendom, hidden from their sight in monasteries and hermitages, just as the modern European knows little of the secret spiritual life of the Muslims, seeing only the outward masquerade.

Even before the Crusades, a certain Sa'id Ibn Ahmad of Toledo had written a book on the 'categories of nations', dividing humanity into two kinds, those concerned with science and those ignorant of it. The first group included Arabs, Persians, Byzantines, Jews and Greeks; the rest of mankind consisted of the northern and southern barbarians – the whites and the blacks. The idea that Frankish religion and philosophy might be of some interest occurred to no one. Writing at the end of the fourteenth century Ibn Khaldūn, one of the greatest historians of all time, ignored Western Europe except for mentioning that he had heard reports of some development in the philosophic sciences in that region of the world. He added, 'But God knows best what goes on in those parts!' This was at the height of the European Middle Ages and less than a century before Europe broke bounds and 'discovered' the Americas. While a considerable number of works had been translated into Arabic from Greek, Persian and Syriac, there is only one known case of the translation of a Latin work before the sixteenth century.

There was, no doubt, another reason for this lack of concern. Whereas the very existence of Islam was an intolerable affront to Christianity, Muslims had no problem in accepting the existence of these 'people of the book'. A Christian who confessed to believing that Muhammad had received a true message from God would have been a heretic, ripe for the stake. In total contrast to this, the Muslim is obliged to accept the authenticity of Jesus, while believing nonetheless that the Christian message was not the last word. The Qurān makes it clear that the denial of any bearer of a divine message is equivalent to a denial of all the messengers and their messages, including the Qurān itself. 'Whosoever believes all that he is bound to believe,' says a well-known credal statement, the Fīqh Akbar I (attributed to Abū Hanīfa), 'except for saying, "I do not know whether Moses and Jesus (Peace be upon them) are – or are not – among the messengers [of Allah]", he is an infidel'.[1] Muslim acceptance of Jews and Christians, particularly in Spain while it was part of the *Dār-ul-Islām*, was not a question of 'tolerance' in the modern sense of the term but of religious obligation; equally mandatory was the

---

[1] Muhammad is reported to have said: 'If anyone testifies that there is no deity other than Allah, who has no partner, and that Muhammad is His servant and His messenger, [testifies also] that Jesus is Allah's servant and messenger – His Word which He cast into Mary and a spirit from Him – and [testifies] that Paradise and hell are real, then Allah will cause him to enter Paradise whatever he may have done'.

Christians' insistence, when they conquered Spain, that Jews and Muslims must either convert or be put to death.

While the Muslim world enjoyed a security which must have seemed destined to last for ever, extraordinary things were happening in the region which Ibn Khaldūn had dismissed as 'those parts'. Ironically, it was from Islam that the 'barbarians' had received the books of Greek philosophy and science, now translated from Arabic into Latin, and a process of fermentation had been started. Unable to integrate the 'new learning' into its structure on a selective basis, as Islamic civilization had done, Christendom – as an integral whole, sufficient unto itself, embracing every aspect of life and answering all the questions that a Christian had the right to ask – began to disintegrate; what had previously been no more than hairline cracks were forced upon by ideas which the structure could not contain and European man, bursting all bonds, developed in directions never before tried or taken by humanity.

Just as the process of decomposition releases explosive gases – or just as water, running downhill, generates energy – so the Christian world, in the process of fission, generated immense material power. The Church of Rome could no longer impose restraints on the development of this power, which obeyed its own logic and its own laws, and with the coming of the industrial revolution, and the uncontrolled growth of applied science, the energies which had been released possessed the instruments which could be effectively exercised in conquest and exploitation.

Now inward-looking, and perhaps over-confident, the Muslims had scarcely noticed what was happening. While the peripheral regions of the *Dār-ul-Islām* came under alien rule, the heartland remained closed in upon itself, forgetting that the world changes and that worldly dominion is, as the Qurān teaches, a transient thing. The shell which had protected the heartland proved to be no more than an eggshell. It was broken by Napoleon when he arrived in Alexandria in July 1798, with plans for marching on Mecca and some talk of himself becoming a Muslim. The Egyptians could do nothing to stop him; it was the Englishman, Nelson, who destroyed his dreams of a new Islamic empire with himself at its head. From then on there was no effective resistance. There were heroic episodes – the Emir Abdu'l-Qādir in Algeria, Shamyl in the Caucasus, Dipo Nagaro in Indonesia, the 'Mahdi' in the Sudan – but by the end of the First World War almost the whole Islamic world was under foreign domination.

The impossible had not merely become possible, it had happened; and no great insight was required for the Muslims to see that they themselves were at least partly to blame, so that guilt was joined to the humiliation of defeat and subjection. Despite Western superiority in armaments, technology and administrative skills, disaster could not have fallen so swiftly or so totally had the Islamic world remained true to its faith and to the obligations of its faith. No matter what had been accepted in practice – men being what they are – Islam cannot in principle be divided into separate and mutually hostile units without self-betrayal. An Islamic world united from the Atlantic coast of Morocco to the outer islands of the Indonesian archipelago and from the Aral Sea to the Sudan would have been no easy prey. Just as the disunity and internal rivalries of the *Ummah* had made possible the temporary triumph of the Crusaders in Palestine, so now these vices had laid it open to total subjection and would, in the 1980s, still frustrate all high ambitions.

What had occurred was not simply a matter of physical conquest. Those who had previously made their impact upon the Muslim world had either been militarily strong but culturally weak (as were the Mongols) or *vice versa*. Now, in their encounter with Western power, the Muslims met physical force joined to cultural dominance. Had the experience of colonialism been one of savage oppression the wound would have been relatively shallow, leaving only a superficial scar. The dead are soon buried, and massacres are forgotten. But this was, for Islam as for the rest of the non-European world, an experience of tutelage to well-intentioned masters who thought it their moral duty to instruct and improve the 'natives', and who showed polite contempt for the deepest values by which these 'natives' lived; and polite contempt for a creed or a deep-rooted tradition is far more deadly than persecution. These masters destroyed, not bodies, but souls – or at least the nourishment upon which human souls subsist.

Although the conquerors called themselves Christians, they were not, for the most part, men of religion in any sense familiar to the subject peoples, for they alone were not totally possessed by the religious idea and by the sense of the sacred. They were – or appeared to be – people indifferent to the essential but devoured by the inessential and therefore immensely skilled in dealing with inessentials. Like Mussolini in a later period, they knew how to make the trains run on time. There was no way in which they could understand or be understood by people for whom the sacred took precedence over everything else.

The Europeans withdrew, but left their sting behind. Except in Algeria and Indonesia, it cannot be said that they were driven out. Their empires collapsed from a lack of will, from self-doubt and from weariness following on two great wars, as well as from economic factors; but in abdicating they still tried to do their duty by imposing upon the newly independent natons entirely inappropriate systems of government and administration. There may indeed have been no alternative, since traditional patterns of rulership and of social life had, to a large extent, been destroyed; but nowhere was there any question of restoring the *status quo ante*, and in recent years we have seen in Uganda (a particularly striking example) the results of the deliberate undermining of the traditional authority on the eve of independence.[1]

The independence movements in the colonies and protectorates came into being, not through a return to indigenous values on the part of those concerned, but through the absorption of occidental ideas and ideologies, liberal or revolutionary as the case might be. The process of modernization

---

[1] Sir Andrew Cohen's well-intentioned and liberal-minded destruction of the Kabaka had results which might not have been achieved by deliberate malevolence. The Kabaka, he thought, stood in the way of 'progress' and 'democracy'; for these two terms we are now forced to substitute 'chaos' and 'barbarism' so far as Uganda is concerned. There are today many educated Muslims who share Cohen's contempt for traditional patterns of rulership. They too may prove to have been agents of darkness.

– a euphemism for Westernization – far from being halted by this withdrawal, was in fact accelerated. The enthusiasm of the new rulers for everything 'modern' was not restrained, as had been the enthusiasm of their former masters, by any element of self-doubt. The irony implicit in this whole situation was tragically apparent in the Vietnam war, when the people of that country fought, not to preserve their own traditions or to gain the right to be truly themselves, but under the banner of a shoddy occidental ideology and for the privilege of imitating their former masters in terms of nationalism and socialism. The West was at war with its own mirror image in a vicious Dance of Death.

It is often said that although only thirty years have passed since Europe (with the exception of Russia) shuffled off its imperial burden, it is no longer possible to imagine a state of mind, a state of inner self-confidence, which took the imperial role for granted. How could those red-faced sahibs have been so sure of their own righteousness? The young find pictures of viceroys and governors strutting under the palm trees in peculiar hats hilariously funny. And yet there has been no fundamental change. Western values remain the standard by which all are judged and most accept to be judged. Much of the self-confidence which enabled the sahib of an earlier generation to keep a crowd of natives in order with only a swagger-stick in his hand persists, since it is taken for granted that the rest of the world must play by the rules which Western civilization has laid down, rules which are the product of European history. The European powers are a small minority in the United Nations, but a glance at the Charter of that organization is enough to show that it contains not one principle derived from any other source, and the same is true of international law as it is at present understood. The opinions, prejudices and moral principles of the former colonial masters remain as powerful as were European arms in the past, and the only escape attempted has been down a blind alley, the Jewish-European doctrine – or pseudo-religion – of Marxism, with its mixture of Christian heresies, Judaic Messianic dreams and dubious science.

The key-word is 'civilization'. One may be a Muslim, a Hindu, a Buddhist or, for that matter, an Eskimo *shaman*; there is just one condition that is obligatory for all – one must conform to 'civilized values' on pain of being condemned as 'backward'. Frithjof Schuon has defined 'civilization' as 'urban refinement in the framework of a worldly and mercantile outlook', hostile both to virgin nature and to religion,[1] and in origin the word means no more than living in cities (commonly regarded in the past as places of spiritual corruption and physical dirt). It is nonetheless a very potent word and even the most ardent revolutionary, in the Muslim world as elsewhere, fears being described as 'uncivilized'. Anti-colonialism on the political level has proved to be a kind of opium of the people, preventing them from noticing that what matters most is the way in which their minds have been colonized.

The consequent traumas, which afflict the greater part of the non-European world, have been intensified among the Muslim peoples by

---

[1] *Light on the Ancient Worlds* (Perennial Books), p. 9.

special circumstances and affect almost every public manifestation of Islam today, on the intellectual level as also on the political one. In the attempt to beat the West at its own game, alien ideas and ideologies are adopted and 'Islamicized' overnight, simply by tacking the adjective 'Islamic' on to them, and one should not be surprised if this results in an acute attack of indigestion. Politically, defiance of the West is seen as the most effective way of re-asserting 'Islamic values', regardless of how deeply these values may have been corrupted, and regardless of the fact that hysterical behaviour in response to insults – or imagined insults – is totally contrary to the spirit and ethos of Islam. It becomes almost impossible for the observer, unless he possesses a touchstone within himself, to disentangle what is truly Islamic from what is merely a convulsive reaction to the traumatic experience through which the Muslim world has passed; nor are the majority of contemporary Muslims sufficiently self-analytical – or sufficiently self-critical – to make this distinction.

This would suffice to explain much of what is happening now in the world of Islam, as it does many of the crises occurring in the Third World in general, but for Muslims there is an additional factor which keeps old wounds open; as they see it, Western military and political power is still firmly established in the midst of the *Dār-ul-Islām* under cover of the state of Israel.

The Palestine question is so fraught with emotion that one would be glad to escape the necessity of mentioning it. Necessity, however, cannot be escaped, and the existence of the state of Israel in Palestine (the first territory beyond the Arabian peninsula to be conquered by Islam) is the key to the political orientation of the vast majority of educated Muslims in our time, the cause of most of the troubles which have afflicted the Arab world over the past forty years and a constant factor of instability in the Middle East. There are those who would add that it is also, potentially, a trigger for nuclear conflict. The United States and the European Community might be less inclined to indulge in wishful thinking on this issue if they understood a little more about the Muslim perspective.

In the first place, Muslims do not in general share the occidental obsession with 'race'. Europeans and their American cousins, even when they are quite free from any hostile prejudice, automatically identify people in terms of their racial origin. The Muslim, on the other hand, identifies and judges a man or a woman primarily in terms of their religion. A 'Jew' is a faithful adherent of Judaism just as a Muslim is an adherent of Islam, even if his grandfather happened to be a Jewish Rabbi (as is the case with an eminent contemporary writer and scholar, Muhammad Asad); as it happens a surprisingly high proportion of European and American converts to Islam over recent years have been of 'Jewish origin', no doubt on account of the strong affinities between these two religious perspectives.

What the West sees in Israel is the establishment of a homeland for the Jewish 'race', just recompense for centuries of persecution at the hands of Europeans. Whether or not the citizens of the new state happen to be individually 'religious' seems quite irrelevant. The Nazis did not inquire into a man's piety before sending him to the gas chamber.

What the Muslim sees in Israel is European and American settlers established in a Muslim country with the support of the former imperial powers, maintained there by American arms and apparently determined to extend their territory still further into the *Dār-ul-Islām*. A 'secular' Jew is, for him, a contradiction in terms. So far as he can judge, most Israelis, particularly those in the ruling group, are not Jews at all. They look like Europeans, they talk like Europeans, they think like Europeans and – most important of all – they exhibit precisely those characteristics of aggressiveness and administrative efficiency which the Muslim associates with European imperialism.[1] The parallel with the Crusades is painfully obvious. Westerners have again come to Palestine; they again occupy the Holy City of Quds (Jerusalem). The misfortunes of the Jews as a 'race' – the pogroms and the holocaust itself – were certainly not the fault of the Muslims. Europe's guilt is Europe's business, and they do not see why they should be expected to suffer for it. 'Why do you not give the Jews some of the choicest lands of Germany?' King Abdu'l-Aziz Ibn Saud asked President Roosevelt. He might as well have suggested, no less reasonably but no more profitably, that the Americans, if they felt so strongly on this subject, could quite well spare one of their own forty-eight states (Texas perhaps) as a home for the Jews. The 'white man', as the Arabs see it, is more inclined to give away other people's territory than his own.

Many Muslims are convinced that Western support for Israel can be ascribed quite simply to hypocrisy. They believe that Europe and the United States created Israel as a means of ridding themselves of their Jewish populations. However absurd this accusation may seem to Europeans and Americans the fact remains that Zionism arose as a reaction to anti-Semitism and, in the view of its founders, 'needed' anti-Semitism. Theodor Herzl himself was not afraid to say that 'the anti-Semites will become our surest friends and the anti-Semitic countries our allies'. Precisely because, in his time, prejudice against people of Jewish origin was diminishing and the process of assimilation accelerating, it was all the more necessary to emphasize that Jews were 'different' and did not really 'belong' in the countries of their adoption, an opinion in which the anti-Semites heartily concurred. Herzl was warned by a friend, the President of the Austrian parliament, that this emphasis upon the 'separateness' of the Jewish people would eventually 'bring a bloodbath on Jewry'. Fifty years later it was the holocaust and the sense of guilt prevailing in Europe and the United States (which could have saved so many lives by an 'open door' policy towards Jewish refugees) that made possible the establishment of the state of Israel.

This was made easier by the Palestinians' self-identification as 'Arabs'. It was – and still is – assumed by many people in the West that this is an indication of their racial origin. In Islam the term 'Arab' is applied to anyone whose first language is Arabic; it tells us nothing about his

[1] It is true that the oriental Jews, the *Sephardim*, now outnumber the 'Westerners', the *Ashkenazim*, in Israel and are beginning to exercise decisive influence on government; but in politics appearances are more important than facts. The impression that Israel is a Western colonial enclave is reinforced by public attitudes in Europe and America. It is interesting, for example, to note that Israel is the only non-European country to participate in the annual Eurovision Song Contest, watched by an estimated 500 million viewers, yet no one finds this peculiar.

ancestry. In fact the Palestinians are descended from the ancient Canaanites, to whose 'blood' (if one must speak in racialist terms) a dozen invading peoples added their quota: Philistines, Hebrews, Greeks, Romans, Persians, Arabs and Turks, to name but a few. The only point to be made is that the Palestinians are not a people who took possession of the land by force; they were 'always' there.

Finally, Muslims – with their first-hand experience of colonialism – can see plainly enough that the notion of settling people from elsewhere in a Third World country against the wishes of the indigenous inhabitants could only have arisen in the context of colonialism and as a manifestation of the colonialist mentality. Here again the public statements of the founding fathers of Zionism seem to them to support this view. The Zionist pioneers were necessarily men of their time, and their time was the high noon of 'imperialism'; they shared with their fellow-Europeans a set of values and beliefs which justified and even glorified the colonization of Asia and Africa in the worthy cause of bringing civilization to the 'natives'. It is little wonder, for example, that Aaron Aaronsohn, addressing an audience of French *colons* in Tunisia in 1909, should have drawn attention to the fact that Jewish immigration into Palestine began in the same year as the French colonization of Tunisia, 1882, and compared the Jewish settler in Palestine to the French settler in Tunisia.

For educated Muslims who identify with the Palestinians, the humiliation of being treated as 'natives' who could be pushed aside to make room for white men and women was intensified by the failure of superior Arab forces to dislodge these 'settlers'. At the very time when Western imperial power was making a discreet withdrawal elsewhere in the world, they were again forced to recognize their own impotence in the face of this power. Humiliation begets rage, and this rage has now sunk deep roots even in the more distant outposts of the Muslim world, most particularly among the young. Turbulent emotions are not easily analysed but one has the impression that these young people reserve their most bitter resentment, not for the Israelis, but for the Americans. To some extent they understand that the Israelis act as they themselves might act under similar circumstances; they cannot, however, forgive the nation but for whose support the state of Israel could not survive in its present form.

This has resulted in a distortion of history which, if it is not soon corrected, may have the most bitter consequences for all of us. However 'decadent' the United States may appear in Muslim eyes, this might be seen as a lesser blemish in comparison with the aggressive atheism of the Soviet Union. For the first time since the Prophet's triumphant return to Mecca, Islam has come face to face with a power determined to eradicate the religion as such and to convert Muslims from faith to infidelity. Were it not for the Palestinian question – the Palestinian trauma – this, surely, would be the overriding concern of contemporary Islam. Some 45 million Muslims live under Soviet rule in Central Asia and the Causasus. For sixty years they have struggled to preserve their faith, and to preserve the principles and customs of Islam, despite almost constant persecution. In all this time they have received no effective support from the worldwide community whose right to call itself the *Ummah* depends upon fulfilling the primary duty of aiding those of its members who are persecuted for their faith.

The unqualified support given by the United States to Israel has persuaded a great number of Muslims that the Soviet Union represents a lesser evil. Since they can only maintain this view if they blind themselves to the facts, ignore the plight of their co-religionists victimized by Soviet imperialism and misunderstand the nature of the modern world, they now live in the midst of political fantasies which bear no relation to the realities of the situation.

Although Europeans and Americans have recently – and largely for economic reasons – recognized the need to understand the Muslim world, it cannot be said that much progress had been made. The obstacles are, as we have seen, formidable, but the survival of that sector of humanity which still acknowledges that religious faith has a right to exist may yet depend upon these obstacles being overcome. A reconciliation with Islam, on the political as well as the religious level, is now essential to the future of the West and should be amongst its highest priorities. Precise figures cannot be established, but it seems likely that there are now at least one billion Muslims and this represents, to say the least, a decisive weight to be placed in the scales of the balance of power. The *Ummah* is divided by national boundaries and national rivalries but, at the grass-roots from Morocco to Indonesia, the sense of unity and of common interest has survived the vicissitudes of history and is still the primary focus of the peoples' loyalty.

'Thus have we appointed you,' says the Qurān, 'a middle nation' (or 'a community of the middle way'), 'so that you may bear witness to the truth before mankind ...' (Q.2.143). Islam is a 'middle nation' even in the purely geographical sense, spanning as it does the centre-line of the planet; a 'nation' which is the heir to ancient and universal truths, and to principles of social and human stability (often betrayed but never forgotten) of which our chaotic world has desperate need; a nation which witnesses to a hope that transcends the dead ends against which the contemporary world is battering itself to death.

In the midst of a humanity polarized between East and West, North and South, Islam represents both a connecting link and a centre of gravity. Division, defeat, subjection and political confusion have not entirely destroyed the Muslims' sense of priorities. 'In a world of materialism, hedonism and techology,' wrote a Jesuit priest recently in *The Times* of London, 'the Islamic masses still contrive to make God and not technology the central certainty of their lives ... Meanwhile, between Marxism and Americanism, the choice must sometimes seem a poor one to people who decided long ago, and have seen fit to stand by their decision, that man cannot live by bread alone...'[1]

Everywhere today we see the dislocation produced by the impact of the modern West upon beliefs and cultural patterns which could not survive the encounter; whole peoples now exist in a spiritual and psychological vacuum. The world of Islam was shaken, if not to its foundations, at least

[1] 'Examining the root cause of Islam's present discontents', Francis Edwards, S. J., *The Times*, 26 January 1980.

throughout its structure, but it has survived relatively intact – in this case one might speak of an irresistible force having come up against an immovable object – and provides us with the only fully surviving exemplar of a different way of living, a different way of thinking, a different way of doing things. Its link with the past has not been broken. 'From Indonesia to Morocco,' writes Seyyed Hossein Nasr, 'for the overwhelming majority, Islamic culture must be referred to in the present tense and not as something in the past. Those who refer to it in the past tense belong to a very small but vocal minority which has ceased to live within the world of tradition and mistakes its own loss of centre for the dislocation of the whole of Islamic society'.[1] The Muslim attitude to time itself is different from that of the Christian. History, for the Muslim, is never something dead and buried. The Companions – and the Prophet himself – together with the great and pious men of earlier ages, seem to keep company with the living, and in a sense the *Ummah* includes them, though they are in Paradise and we are encapsulated in this present time. Modern man lives in futile and illusory dreams of the future; for the Muslim, the past is not merely *there* but also, in a certain sense, *here and now*.

The medieval Christian would have understood the Muslim very well if he had allowed himself to do so. Modern man cannot even understand his own forebears, having become over recent centuries a type of creature never before seen on earth, governed by beliefs which correspond to nothing in the traditional and religious heritage of mankind. If he could understand the Muslim he might begin to understand himself before he blunders into self-destruction.

For the 'average man', secular, agnostic (or quite simply unaware of religion as a reality on any level) and rootless, Islam may open the door to a whole universe of discourse, familiar to his ancestors but strange to him; for the Christian, there is the experience of a closely related religion which has taken a completely different path to Christianity and has maintained its role as the dominant force in a whole civilization, intellectually, culturally, and socially. But, in considering the differences between Christian and Muslim, one must distinguish between those that are essential and those that are peripheral. The place in which the religions meet is, as it were, a secret chamber in which man, stripped of his temporal dress, is alone with God, or in which the relative is seen as no more than a shadow of the Absolute. From this centre the radii diverge, to be differentiated in terms of theology, moral law, social practice and, finally, in terms of human 'climate'.

On the one hand there are the differences between the religions as such (in the way they perceive Reality) and, on the other, the differences between societies and individuals moulded by a particular tradition; and, in the latter case, the most significant factor is what people take for granted, what appears to them self-evident. What counts on the periphery is the 'flavour' of the religion and of the culture it has shaped, or the spiritual and human 'climate' within which its adherents live out their lives and interpret their experiences.

[1] Seyyed Hossein Nasr, op. cit., p. 135.

It is important to know what a religion is in itself, but one should also be aware of what it is thought to be and how it is expressed in the prejudices and instinctive assumptions of ordinary people. The modern Westerner, persuaded that he has a right to 'think for himself' and imagining that he exercises this right, is unwilling to acknowledge that his every thought has been shaped by cultural and historical influences and that his opinions fit, like pieces of a jigsaw puzzle, into a pattern which has nothing random about it. Statements which begin with the words 'I think...' reflect a climate created by all those strands of belief and experience – as also of folly and corruption – which have gone to form the current state of mind and to establish principles which cannot be doubted by any sane and reasonable man in this place and at this point in time.

The climate in which the ordinary Muslim lives has been at least partly determined by the environment into which the religion was providentially projected and in which it developed: the desert and, so far as the Turks and Mongols were concerned, the steppes of Asia; in other words, the 'open' – open space and clear horizons at the end of the world – and this is the polar opposite of the human world of cities and cultivated fields and, ultimately, of the man-made antheap. Frithjof Schuon has remarked that the genesis of a new religion amounts to 'the creation of a moral and spiritual type'. 'In the case of Islam,' he says, 'this type consists of an equilibrium – paradoxical from the Christian point of view – between the qualities of the contemplative and the combative, and then between holy poverty and sanctified sexuality. The Arab – and the man Arabized by Islam – has, so to speak, four poles: the desert, the sword, woman and religion.' The sword, he adds, represents death, 'both dealt and courted', while woman represents 'love received and love given, so that she incarnates all the generous virtues, compensating for the perfume of death with that of life. ... The symbiosis of love and death within the framework of poverty and before the face of the Absolute constitutes all that is essential in Arab nobility...'[1]

This nobility is still to be found, though not always among public figures in the Arab world or among those who have appointed themselves the official spokesmen of Islam; but what of the mass of the people conditioned by the Islamic climate? For the most part inarticulate, they cannot speak for themselves, and we are obliged to rely upon neutral observers. Such an observer is Paul Bowles, an American novelist who has lived for many years in Morocco. He might be described as 'neutral' because his interest has been solely in the people around him; he has had no concern with religion, except as he has seen it exemplified in their daily lives and habits of thought, and in an essay entitled 'Mustapha and Friends' he summed up his observations in a fictional portrait of a typical Moroccan boy whose Western equivalent would live only for football and discotheques. This makes his 'Mustapha' a kind of test case for comparison between the social periphery of Islam on the one hand and, on the other, the contemporary Western world.

It must be admitted that many Muslim academics and leaders of opinion

[1] *Islam and the Perennial Philosophy* (World of Islam Publishing Company), p. 91.

would condemn this portrait and identify Bowles as just another foreigner ill-disposed towards the 'Arab nation' and towards 'resurgent Islam'. They could not deny a certain authenticity to the portrait, but they would see 'Mustapha' as representing something that is to be overcome in a return to the pure faith, a survivor from a past that is better forgotten. Unlike Christianity, they might say, Islam is a religion of this world, a religion of social responsibility and political idealism; 'Mustapha' must be disciplined and taught true Islam so that he can parade with other, more worthy, young men under a revolutionary banner shouting 'Death to So-and-so!' and 'Down with the corrupt servants of imperialism!'

This is a matter of opinion. Poor 'Mustapha' does not know much about imperialism, but then he is free from the complexes and inner torments which afflict his more educated brothers, and he is not aware that the religion he takes for granted must be used as a means to re-establish the pride of the Arab nation. No doubt he could be described as feckless; but 'Mustapha' is one of 'the people' (in whose name the slogans are coined) and, throughout Islamic history, while rulers have murdered each other, while doctors of law and theology have argued, and while reformers have reformed, the people have gone their way and taken little note of what the great men thought or did. It may even be that 'Mustapha' and his friends will outlive the great men; the Prophet, curiously enough, seems to have had a few 'Mustaphas' around him, whom he treated with an amused kindness and tolerance which has not always been imitated by the religious authorities of later times.

'Mustapha,' says Bowles, 'may have little education, or he may be illiterate, which is more likely. He may observe his religion to the letter, or partially, or not at all, but he will always call himself a Moslem. His first loyalty is towards fellow Moslems of whatever country... The difference between Mustapha and us is possibly even greater than it would be were he a Buddhist or a Hindu, for there is no religion on earth which demands a stricter conformity to the tenets of its dogma than that supra-national brotherhood called Islam. Even the most visionary and idealistic among us of the Western world is more than likely to explain the purpose of life in terms of accomplishment. Our definition of that purpose will be a dynamic one in which it will be assumed desirable for each individual to contribute his share, however infinitesimal, to the total tangible or intangible enrichment of life. Mustapha does not see things that way at all. To him it is slightly absurd, the stress we lay upon work, our craving to "leave the world better than we found it", our unceasing efforts to produce ideas and objects. "We are not put on earth to work," he will tell you, "We are put here to pray; that is the purpose of life..." Such social virtues as a taste for the "democratic way of life" and a sense of civic responsibility mean very little to him.'

Mustapha is 'the adventurer *par excellence*. He expects life to have something of the variety and flavour of *The Thousand and One Nights*, and if that pungency is lacking he does his best to supply it. A whole-hearted believer in dangerous living, he often takes outrageous chances', due, says Bowles, to a 'refusal to believe that action entails result. To him, each is separate, having been determined at the beginning of time, when the inexorable design of destiny was laid out ... It is the most monstrous absurdity to fear death, the future, or the consequences of one's acts, since that would be tantamount to fearing life itself. Thus to be prudent is laughable, to be frugal is despicable, and to be provident borders on the sinful. How can a man be so presumptuous as to assume that tomorrow, let alone next year, will actually arrive? And so how dare he tempt fate by preparing for any part of the future, either immediate or distant?

'The wise man is complete at every moment, with no strings of hopefulness stretching out towards the future, entangling his soul and possibly making it loath to leave this life. Mustapha will tell you that the true Moslem is always ready for death at an instant's notice ... He has a passion for personal independence. He does not look for assistance from others ... since all aid comes from Allah. Even the gift of money a beggar has managed to elicit from a stranger in the street will be shown triumphantly to a friend with the remark: "See what Allah gave me" ... It has never occurred to him that a man might be able to influence the course of his own existence. His general idea about life is that it is a visit: you come, stay a while, and go away again. The circumstances and length of the stay are beyond anyone's control, and therefore only of slight interest.'[1]

This portrait, despite certain distortions of perspective, is rich in implications and may perhaps indicate more clearly than any amount of theorizing the gulf which separates those whose minds have been formed in an Islamic climate from the 'common man' of the Occident. The social and educational strata of contemporary Muslim society are sharply separated, and the gulf must be bridged on more than one level if understanding is ever to be achieved.

[1] *Their Heads are Green*, Paul Bowles (London: Peter Owen), pp. 83–89.

Chapter 2

CONTINUITY AND CONTRAST

An ancient tradition tells us (and God knows best the truth of it) that Adam, the first man and the first prophet, was commanded to make a great journey. Having fallen from Paradise to the dusty earth he was only a shadow of his former self, diminished in stature and in vision, yet he was still one of those to whom God speaks from behind the veils of time and mortality.

So his Lord spoke, saying: 'I have a sanctuary directly beneath my Throne. Now go and build Me there a House, and go around it in the way you have seen the angels circling my Throne.' Then Adam set out for the holy place, which lies at the axial point of every circle. There the heavenly centre had cast its reflection in the form of a temple roofed with one great ruby, supported on columns of emerald and sheltering a white stone which was luminous beyond any other earthly light. This stone was like the human soul in its primordial perfection, as yet undarkened by the passage of time.

He travelled far, guided by an angelic power, till he passed through the deserts of the Hejaz and stood at last in a valley ringed by mountains, a place of rock and sand seemingly even more remote from remembered Paradise than the fragrant land where he had first broken his fall. There he encompassed the heavenly vision with an earthly house made from stones taken, so it is said, from Mount Sinai, the Mount of Olives, Mount Lebanon and a fourth mountain, sometimes called el-Jūdī, on which, long afterwards, Noah's ark would come to rest. His task accomplished, he performed the prescribed rites and then departed, as all creatures must whether they live for a day or for a thousand years; and for a great period of time silence descended upon this holy place and windblown sand covered the temple Adam had built.

After the passage of the ages (and only God knows how long this was) two strangers came over the desert to the Meccan valley, bringing with them a small child: a tall man, already in his eighties, Abraham by name (and a prophet by destiny), with Hagar, the lovely Egyptian maid-servant who had borne him the son of his old age, Ishmael. Beside the mound which covered the sacred House, Abraham abandoned Hagar and their child to the divine mercy, leaving with them but a few dates and a skin of water.

Distraught and thirsty, Hagar left the child in a sheltered place and followed a track that led through the hills. From Safā she saw no spring nor sign of habitation, and from Marwa she saw none. Seven times she ran between these two hillocks, calling upon God's mercy, and then she heard the sound of a voice and hastened back to her son. Beside him stood an angel who now struck the earth with his wing so that sweet water gushed forth. This was the spring called Zamzam, from which the pilgrims in their millions drink today. Here it was that she reared Ishmael, ancestor of the Arab race, joined eventually by wanderers from the north, and here she died.

The boy had grown to manhood by the time Abraham returned and together they set about rebuilding the House of God, the Ka'ba, repeating Adam's task as all men must in one way or another, being of Adam's flesh and blood. Ishmael brought the stones on his back while his father set them one upon another without mortar: 'And when Abraham and Ishmael raised the foundations of the House they said: Our Lord, accept this [service] from us, for truly Thou art the All-Hearing, the All-Knowing' (Q.2.127). And when he left the Hejaz, never to return, Abraham blessed the valley of Mecca and prayed: 'Our Lord, I have settled a part of my progeny in a barren valley close to Thy sacred House...' (Q.14.37); and he prayed also: 'Our Lord, raise up in their midst a Messenger from amongst them, who shall recite to them Thy revelations and teach them the Scripture and Wisdom, and purify them' (Q.2.129).

Many centuries passed before Abraham's prayer was answered. The luminous stone was blackened by men's sins and the water of Zamzam grew brackish. Once again the holy place was a forgotten sanctuary, known only to a scattered nomadic people of whom history took no account, awaiting re-discovery and awaiting the advent of a reminder to mankind; until, the time being ripe, there was born from Ishmael's seed, among the Arabs, from the tribe of Quraysh and the clan Hāshim, a Messenger of God, the last Prophet of Adam's lineage: Muhammad, 'the Glorified'.

That is one way of putting it. Perhaps the best way, for explanations are always second-best compared with the imaginative images they elucidate; and such images are not to be dismissed as mere subjective fancies. The divine Imagination, in which all things have come into being, both overshadows and inspires the human imagination, so long as it is receptive to inspiration; but the manner in which this tale is interpreted is a matter of individual vocation, for such tales contain a multitude of meanings.

What emerges most obviously from this traditional account of the founding of the Ka'ba in Mecca and the coming of Muhammad is the sense of continuity which binds all sacred history together and which characterizes every manifestation of Islam. It could not be otherwise. The religion of unity and unification must necessarily be the religion of continuity, which allows no break with the past and refuses to allow time to disperse the interrelated elements of the perennial Truth. Had the message of the Qurān been something entirely 'new' it would have disrupted the pattern, cut the thread of continuity and cast doubt upon the divine Wisdom, which is by its very nature unchanging. The Qurān itself confirms this unambiguously: 'Nothing is said unto thee [Muhammad] other than what was said to all the messengers who preceded thee' (Q.41.43). Had God chosen to contradict what He had said in the past one might legitimately ask why He had denied this guidance to the people of earlier times, or why He had waited so long to say what needed to be said.

An important point of contrast between the perspectives of Christianity and Islam also emerges from the story. For Christians, nothing less than the sacrificial death of the God-man Jesus could redeem Adam's sin and restore the cosmic balance disturbed by that sin. In the Islamic version of the Fall, Adam was forgiven and his sin blotted out, so that it counted for nothing (although its consequences were not, as such, abolished; Adam was not restored to Paradise). In the Muslim view, what was required of Jesus, as also of Muhammad, was not an act of universal redemption but simply the repetition, in a form appropriate to these later times, of the age-old message given to Adam, and man's sin is therefore primarily one of forgetfulness. If we were not by nature forgetful, and if we were not so readily inclined to idolatry (preferring illusions to reality), there would have been no need for either. This is why it is said that Islam is neither more nor less than a restoration of the primordial religion of mankind, the 'perennial philosophy'. 'He hath ordained for you that religion which He enjoined upon Noah and which We have revealed unto thee, and which We enjoined upon Abraham and Moses and Jesus, so that you should make firm the religion and not be divided therein' (Q.42.13). This religion, this wisdom, is as much a part of the total human situation as the winds and the tides and the earth itself. A man has two eyes, two ears and so on; and, unless his heart is sick, he has – as man – this God-given wisdom, which is a part not merely of his heritage but of his nature. Even in those who seem most ignorant, most unenlightened, the pilot-light still burns; but for this, they would not qualify as human beings.

Islam takes its stand immovably upon the nature of things, not as they might be but as they are; in the first place, upon the transcendent Reality beside which every other light is dimmed, and secondly, upon the palpable (but contingent) realities of the world and of human experience. Perhaps Napoleon was more Muslim than might be supposed, for he said once: 'My master is the nature of things.' One of the great weaknesses of contemporary Islam is the eagerness which which Muslims ignore facts and lose themselves in dreams, contrary to the example of the Prophet, who was a realist in every possible sense of the term. Realism is by nature serene, because it cannot be surprised or disillusioned, and it is in this spirit of serenity that the Muslim is required to observe and endure the vicissitudes of time and history, fortified by a quality of stillness and of timelessness which is at the heart of his faith. Everything around him moves and changes, but he must remain rooted in stillness; and this is one reason why Muslims claim that all other religions have been, in one way or another, corrupted and altered by the passage of time, whereas Islam, in accordance with God's solemn promise, remains and will always remain what it is.

The follower of Islam is required to hold fast to the human norm, *fiṭrah*, the dignity and integrity of the human creature as he issues from the hand of God: 'So set thy face toward the religion in uprightness – the *fiṭrah* of Allah – in which He hath created man' (Q.30.30). It could even be said that the primary aim of Islam is to persuade man to be truly man at every level of his being, and woman to be truly woman at every level of her being, and to hold them back from the abyss of limitless multiplicity in which – tossed to and fro by the storms which rage there – they risk losing both dignity and integrity and, eventually, losing themselves. The perfect Muslim, standing upright in the presence of his Maker, at once proud and submissive, free from all illusions and from any bias in dealing with his fellow men, exemplifies *fiṭrah*. He is both perfect master and perfect servant.

Within the planetary system of monotheism Christianity broke the ritual forms and sacred law of Judaism in favour of spiritual freedom and inwardness. After this – as Muslims see the matter – the divine purpose required that the balance should be restored, and that the last Word should be spoken in the form of a synthesis or summing-up. It is for this reason that Islam has to contain such rich diversity within its unified structure, as though it were a direct manifestation of the divine Name, *al-Wāsi* ('the Vast' or 'the Capacious'), preserved from fragmentation by three factors: the revealed Law, which governs social behaviour as it does the rites of the Faith; the Pilgrimage, which draws all Muslims towards the sacred House, the Ka'ba in Mecca; and the weight given to the consensus of opinion among pious and informed believers. The Law does not invade the privacy of man's inwardness, the relationship of the human soul to God, nor is it concerned with the way in which each individual interprets the basic spiritual teachings of the religion (deepening them in terms of a truth that is both outwardly apparent and inwardly real), provided this does not express itself in behaviour contrary to the interests of the community, but it provides a framework of social and psychological equilibrium within which each individual can follow his particular vocation.

Christianity operated, as it were, from the opposite end of the spectrum. Having no *Sharī'ah* – no God-given Law for society – it concerned itself with man's inward relationship with God through Jesus as intermediary; the outward Law was assembled over the course of time from the elements of two very different traditions, the Judaic and the Roman, and in modern times it has readily adapted itself to the changing currents of secular opinion. For the people of Christ, the inward landscape was mapped in detail by a rich and complex theology; Islamic theology, on the other hand, has never been in a position to claim magisterial authority over the Muslim's spiritual life. It may be used to illuminate points of doctrine or it may be ignored; a tool which is, for the most part, left on the workbench. So far as his spiritual life is concerned, the Christian depends upon his priest or upon the abbot of his monastery. Since Islam has no priesthood and no monasticism, the Muslim is inwardly alone with God, face to face with the absolute Reality without meditation.

Whereas the Christian is for ever reaching out towards the distant goal with a longing that can be both noble and tragic, the Muslim does not seek to go elsewhere – though great efforts are demanded of him if he is to re-establish within himself the human norm – for all is here and all is now.

It is precisely in the light of this perspective of return to the norm and to essentials that Islam presents itself as the synthesis of all that came before. The final brick has been put in place in the great edifice of divine Revelation and, for this very reason, the Muslim must expect his truth to be confirmed in other religions.

Muhammad said: 'Wisdom is the believer's straying camel; he takes it from wherever he can find it and does not care from what vessel it has issued.' It is common enough for occidental writers, when considering the different forms which Islam has assumed among different peoples, to say that it has failed to eradicate 'pre-Islamic ideas'. The religion of the Qurān did not come into this world to eradicate such ideas, unless they had been twisted by human passions and falsified by human one-sidedness, for it is the heir to the spiritual treasures of the past. Nothing true is alien to it. Many streams have been absorbed into this river over the course of time; it still flows towards the sea.

'Truly We have sent messengers before thee [Muhammed]. We have told thee concerning some of them; concerning others We have not told thee" (Q.40.78). Unlike Judaism and Christianity, says Martin Lings, Islam, from 'its stronghold of finality as the last religion of this cycle of time can afford to be generous to other religions. Moreover, its position in the cycle confers on it something of the function of a summer-up, which obliges it to mention with justice what has preceded it or at least to leave an open door for what it does not specifically mention;'[1] and in this context Dr Lings quotes the following verse from the Qurān: 'Truly the believers and the Jews and the Sabians and the Christians – whosoever believeth in God and the Last Day and doeth deeds of piety – no fear shall come upon them neither shall they grieve' (Q.5.69).

The profound bond which unites one particular religion with other God-given messages is, in fact, a clear sign of its orthodoxy in the most universal sense of this term; and unless we possess a touchstone by which to judge the orthodoxy of the religions, we have no means of passing judgement on the false prophets and vicious cults which have surfaced in this century, exemplified by the late Mr Jones of Jonestown in Guyana, who led his followers in an act of mass suicide, thereby demonstrating – perhaps providentially – the true nature of all such heresies. But this basic orthodoxy is balanced (though never destroyed) by the differences between one set of outward forms and doctrinal formulations and another. A square and a triangle are quite different figures, but they may nonetheless be related to a single geometrical centre.

The comprehensiveness of the Faith as such cannot entirely offset a tendency to exclusiveness which is inherent in human nature, and the question is frequently asked whether Muslims accept Christianity (and the other traditional religions) as ways to 'Salvation' and manifestations of the Truth. There is no simple answer to this. Opinions have differed and still differ on this point and one sometimes hears it said that the adherents of other faiths escape condemnation only if they have never had the opportunity to convert to Islam. The fact that in practice Islam, when it was

---

[1] 'With all thy Mind', published in *Studies in Comparative Religion* (Winter, 1976).

dominant, accepted without any difficulty the presence of Jews and Christians in its midst is significant, but a number of theologians and jurisprudents have taken the view that this final and conclusive revelation of the divine Will entirely superseded all other revelations and that there can be no valid excuse before God for clinging to an earlier religion. They claim to find support in the following Quranic verse: 'Whosoever follows any other religion than *al-islām*, it shall not be accepted of him, and in the Hereafter he shall be among the losers' (Q.3.85).

Since the word *islām* means 'self-surrender (to God)', it is in this sense that most commentators and translators understand the verse, acknowledging that the surrender of heart and will and mind to God is a basic principle of every authentic religion. According to Zamaksharī (12th century AD) the Qurān bears witness here as elsewhere to the transcendent unity of all the revealed religions based upon belief in One God, despite the differences between them 'in statutes and practices enjoined for the benefit of the various communities in accordance with their conditions'. There are however many believers, within the community of Islam as in other communities, who appear to derive profound satisfaction from the notion that they alone are on the right track and everyone else is astray. The conviction that theirs is the only true Faith, nourished by the human tendency to exclusiveness, finds support in the fact that the different religions must necessarily have firm outlines if they are to be clearly distinguished one from another.

The ordinary believer, the 'common man' in the community of his Faith, is likely to be confused rather than enlightened when told that religions other than his own are effective ways of approach to God. This may seem to him to threaten his certainties and undermine the foundations of his happiness and security; and to undermine simple faith, even when it seems to us both narrow and naive, is indeed a grave matter if we have nothing to put in its place – nothing, that is, that would make sense to the simple-minded. In any case, faith without zeal is a poor thing and we should pause before disturbing those whose zeal depends upon a narrow perspective.

In the extraordinary conditions of the late twentieth century, however, the pause should not be prolonged. In earlier times reciprocal intolerance between, for example, Muslims and Christians may have served to preserve the integrity of different religious 'worlds', each of them spiritually self-sufficient.[1] As the Qurān assures us, it is in accordance with the divine Will that such different 'worlds' should co-exist within a single humanity, and it was natural enough that each should raise a protective wall around its territory to exclude ideas which did not accord with its particular perspective. But in recent times the human situation has changed so radically that there are those who see in this transformation a sign that our time is nearing its end and that the shadow of the Last Judgment, at which all the religious communities will stand before the One God, has already

---

[1] 'Needless to say our ancestors were aware of the existence of other religions beside their own; but, dazzled and penetrated as they were by the great light shining directly above them, the sight of more remote and – for them – more obliquely shining lights on the horizons could raise no positive interest nor did it create problems'. Martin Lings, *Ancient Beliefs and Modern Superstitions*, Unwin Paperbacks–Mandala Books, London 1980, p. 70.

fallen across the world. Be that as it may, the religions meet today in uneasy confrontation and questions which did not arise in the past now force themselves upon us.

These questions can no longer be avoided by the believer once he has encountered the adherents of other Faiths, and religious exclusiveness – no longer protective – becomes a factor of weakness and vulnerability. The Muslim or the Christian who has habitually regarded all others as infidels is compelled (assuming that he has a modicum of intelligence) to ask himself whether he can continue to believe in a God who has apparently chosen to mislead the majority of His creatures throughout the ages by permitting them to follow false religions and who chooses to send them to hell for worshipping Him sincerely but in the wrong way. Are we to suppose that He mocks sanctity when it is achieved by methods other than our own and are prayers unheard unless (from the Christian point of view) addressed to Him in the name of Jesus or (from the Muslim point of view) within the framework of the Islamic creed? To rest one's faith upon such suppositions is, in the words of Martin Lings, 'to think ill of Providence' and, according to Ibn 'Arabī, the common believer who refuses to acknowledge the divine Self-manifestation in religions other than his own and recognizes his Lord only in the form known to his own religion is guilty of showing bad manners towards God.

In fact, as soon as these questions are posed and their implications fully perceived, exclusive faith is under threat. If other men and women of good sense and good intent have been so easily misled then – sooner or later – this believer asks himself whether he too might not be the victim of a grand deception. If so many others were and still are mistaken, then it is a statistical probability that he too is living an illusion; at the end of the day the doctrine in whose name all others were condemned is itself fatally undermined. 'What is sauce for the goose is sauce for the gander', as the British say.

Over the past century this has been one of the most potent factors in the destruction of religious faith in the West.

The believer now faces alternatives to which his ancestors were never exposed. Either all the religions are false, irreconcilable fictions devised by the human animal as a refuge from a meaningless universe and a life without purpose, or else each is valid in its own way and represents a particular perspective in relation to a Truth which cannot be fully expressed in any single formulation.

If he is able to accept this second proposition, despite the apparent contradictions between the Faiths, then he faces a further alternative. On the one hand he may accept, in a spirit of humility, the principle that the ways of God are beyond his rational understanding because the Infinite escapes all finite categories. In this context the Muslim is fortunate in possessing in the text of the Qurān itself indications of the universality of the Truth which transcends every formulation. 'For each of you We have appointed a divine Law and a way of life. Had Allah so willed He could have made you one people; but so that He might try you by that which He hath bestowed upon you (He willed otherwise). Therefore compete in doing good. Unto Allah ye will all return, and He will enlighten you concerning that wherein ye differ' (Q.5.48). The Muslim may then wait peacefully for this ultimate enlightenment, sure that his religion will prove to have been the best of all. The Christian faces more formidable difficulties in making this act of acceptance. Surely it is only through Christ that we come to God? He may however find it possible to follow the example of a pre-Conciliar Pope who was by no means renowned for his ecumenicalism. Speaking to the delegate he was sending to Libya some sixty years ago, Pope Pius XI said: 'Do not think that you are going among infidels. Muslims attain to Salvation. The ways of God are infinite'.

On the other hand the believer may, if such is his vocation, embark upon the path of metaphysics and of intellectual intuition until he understands that 'the God of the Faiths' (to use Ibn 'Arabī's term) is not God-as-such, not the Absolute. He will see then that God-as-such is beyond all definitions – transcending every concept and every form – and therefore beyond worship. We cannot pray to the utterly unknowable. For this very reason He enters into the limitations which the human worshipper imposes upon Him and allows Himself to be known and loved as we are by nature inclined to know Him and love Him. He owes us no less since it is He who has given us this nature, imposed upon us these limitations and revealed Himself to us in a variety of manifestations. Once satisfied that the different forms are indeed veils assumed by the One Reality, the believer can then return to his own religious perspective and follow, with a free mind and a heart at ease, the manner of worship and the moral prescriptions which relate to this perspective.

According to the great *mujāhid* (the 'warrior in the path of Allah'), the Emir Abdu'l-Qādir, 'our God and the God of all the communities opposed to ours are in truth One God ... despite the variety of His manifestations ... He has manifested Himself to Muhammad's people beyond every form while manifesting Himself *in* every form ... To Christians He has manifested Himself in the form of Christ ... and to the worshippers of whatever form it may be ... in the very form of this thing; for no worshipper of a finite object worships it for its own sake. What he worships is the epiphany in this form of the attributes of the true God ... Yet that which all the worshippers worship is one and the same. Their error consists only in the act of determining it in a limitative manner'.[1] Abdu'l-Qādir fought the Christians who invaded his land, Algeria, because he was a Muslim. Exiled in Damascus, he protected the Christians against massacre by taking them into his own home because he understood. Those who would challenge him or accuse him of heresy should be prepared to face his sword and accept death from its blade since small men risk their necks when they challenge great ones.

No Muslim denies or ever could deny that the Qurān is the sacred ground in which the doctrines and the practice of his religion are rooted but when this is taken to mean that only what has been specifically spelled out in the Scripture can be accepted as truly 'Islamic' – all else being *bid'ah*, innovation – then the universality and comprehensiveness to which the

[1] Quoted from Mawqif 236 in the *Mawāqif of Abdu'l-Qadir* (French translation by M. Chodkiewicz published by Editions du Seuil, Paris, 1982).

Scripture itself bears eloquent witness is denied. It is more in accordance with the spirit of Islam to say that when the Qurān calls to mind certain ancient truths found in earlier traditions or in mythologies dating from before the dawn of history or, perhaps, in metaphysical doctrines such as Neoplatonism, then it has performed one of its essential functions as a 'rope of salvation' for men and women of every kind and of every persuasion. It has reminded us of a universal truth or of an aspect of the primordial truth as such – the *dīn ul-fiṭrah* – Adam's truth. It has reminded us also that God did not deceive the people of earlier times nor did He leave them without guidance.

The Word of God, projected into human categories and human language, does not necessarily dot every 'i' and cross every 't', nor does it exempt us from spiritual, intellectual and imaginative effort. Those who insist that no opinion is acceptable unless supported by a relevant quotation from the Qurān (or at least from an approved *ḥadīth*) think that they are protecting the purity of the Faith, but they are in fact limiting the universality of Islam and, in the long run, reducing it to the status of one cult among others.

However unwilling they may be to admit it, they have been deeply influenced by those very 'orientalists' whom they so fiercely condemn. The idea that Islam, in the course of the centuries, 'borrowed' elements from other traditions, thereby changing its whole character, originated in the West; and what the orientalists really meant was that the religion of the Qurān was too 'primitive' to have given rise to a great culture, rich in art, mysticism and philosophy. Incredibly, Muslim puritans – or perhaps 'purists' would be a more appropriate term – have accepted this idea uncritically and made it their own. 'Purify Islam from alien elements and all will be well' is an enticingly simple answer to the problems of the Muslim world, even if it means denying that religion develops, just as a plant develops the possibilities contained in its seed or tuber. And because illogical attitudes are seldom consistent, the very same people who call for the 'purification' of the religion from alien 'superstitions' and from 'un-Islamic practices' are ready enough to borrow from occidental ideologies, swallowing the ordures of modernism with a good appetite (often on the grounds that Islam would have developed along the same lines had it not been 'corrupted') and welcoming secular and scientific ideas which are rooted in the denial of God, characterized by indifference to the sacred and built upon the assumption that human life has no ultimate meaning. It is no coincidence that many so-called 'fundamentalists' are attracted by political ideas which have their origin in Marxism.

It is perfectly legitimate for Muslims to 'borrow' from other religions what is in fact already theirs by right – their 'straying camel' – but nothing that has its roots in secularism and agnosticism can be incorporated into Islam without poisoning the whole system. The sacred is one, in that it reflects the One in inexhaustible variety; there is no danger of corruption in admitting that a particular truth inherent in the Qurān may have been well and effectively expressed in Christian theology, in the Jewish Kabbalah or in Hindu Vedanta, but this is anathema to Muslim purists. The trivialities of Western secular philosophy, on the other hand, are treated with respect.

The question as to what can or cannot be assimilated into Islam without danger both to the Faith and the community presses hard upon Muslims today and admits of no easy answers. It is not only a matter of determining whether a particular idea or practice is *ḥalāl* (permissible) or *ḥarām* (forbidden) in the light of Qurān and *ḥadīth*, but also of judging, by means of an inward touchstone, whether it accords with the spirit – or climate – of Islam, and this spirit is more easily experienced than defined. In making this judgement, learned men well versed in the letter of the Law may go astray, while simple and uninstructed believers, relying upon an instinctive sense of what is fitting and harmonious, may provide the right answers.

Emile Dermenghem, choosing to live in an Islamic climate though himself a Catholic, caught something of this spirit in a striking passage written almost forty years ago. Islam, he wrote, offers 'the possibility of real and effective liberty and of equilibrium between society and the individual, a sense of justice, of equality in variety, of tolerance even in war, of spiritual poverty even within the most ostentatious cities, of dignity even in wretchedness, of rite and ritual purity, of the conviction that nothing matters beside the Absolute, with the corollary that every-thing which exists does so only by participation in the Absolute, that is to say, that everything is "priceless" in the double sense, that all that happens is "adorable" (as Leon Bloy said) and that nothing is of any importance outside this participation in Reality'.[1] These are qualities the loss of which would empty Islam of its content even if the letter of the Law were still strictly observed.

Two particular sayings of the Prophet are significant in this context. 'God has created nothing more noble than intelligence,' he said, 'and His wrath is on him who despises it'; and here intelligence might be defined as the capacity to perceive and assimilate the truth on every level, on the one hand distinguishing between the Absolute and the relative, and on the other, perceiving that two and two make four. He said also: 'God is beautiful and He loves beauty.' This relates closely to the concept of *fiṭrah*, for the human norm is one of beauty of spirit, beauty of soul, beauty of comportment and, finally, the beauty of those things with which we choose to surround ourselves – home, dress, utensils and so on. Anger, condemned in Qurān and *ḥadīth* on moral grounds, is condemned also because it disfigures the human countenance. An ugly building is un-Islamic, however functional it may be, as is everything cheap and tawdry. The true and the beautiful, therefore, belong to this final faith in a very special way.[2] Stupidity and ugliness have no place in it.

---

[1] 'Témoignage de l'Islam', published in *Les Cahiers du Sud*, 1947.

[2] Those who have observed only the moralistic, 'puritanical' aspect of Islam may dismiss this view as untypical. Two remarks made to the author by Muslims from opposite ends of the educational spectrum suggest otherwise. The first remark was made by a mosque servant, an Algerian who had spent most of his working life at sea. 'Why,' he asked, 'do learned people argue so much? Islam is simple. Islam is to love the beautiful things in the world.' The second was made by an Egyptian professional man working in London: 'Shall I tell you my concept of God? I can put it in one word – Beauty! If I go into a shop and see a fine pair of shoes, perfectly crafted, I realize that they are beautiful because they are perfect, and that brings God to mind. His beauty is the beauty of Perfection!'

Each of them differently shaped yet serving the same purpose, the religions are ships built to carry a multitude across the turbulent seas of existence, in which they would otherwise drown. But for the divine mercy there would have been no such ships to support men who had forgotten how to swim. 'And a sign for them is that We carried their seed in a laden ship, and We have created for them the like thereof wherein they travel, and had We so willed We might have drowned them, with none to answer their cry, nor are they saved except as a mercy from Us and enjoyment of life for a while' (Q.36.41). The framework of each ship is divinely ordained to bring the human person to a safe landfall, driven by that same wind to which Islam ascribes creation itself, the Breath (*nafas*) of the Merciful. But no ship is alone upon the waters; the oceans are wide and the heavens are wider still, and those carried in the ship will hear the whisper of other messages and windborne fragments of other prayers, which they will understand (or fail to understand) according to their greatness of heart.

Islam has been principally concerned with the ships closest to it on the ocean, the religions descended – as it is itself – from the undifferentiated monotheism of Abraham. Precisely because these three faiths (unlike, for example, Hinduism or Buddhism) express themselves in similar terminology, their differences of perspective stand out very clearly; and yet what they have in common outweighs these differences.

Jews, when they come into contact with informed Muslims, are frequently astonished by the extent of this common ground. Many aspects of Islam which seem alien to the Christian – such as the revealed Law – present no problem to the Jew, who finds in the Qurān many echoes of his own faith, as he does in the Muslim's characteristic attitude to life. As has often been observed, the Torah – the Pentateuch – never employs any Hebrew term corresponding to the word 'religion', since it does not recognize any separate compartment of personal or public life which could be described as 'profane'; if religion encompasses everything, then the word itself becomes redundant, and in Judaism – as in Islam – all the normal and regular acts of human living, down to the most 'mundane', are sanctified. Either there is a God or there is not. If there is, then it follows that nothing can be beyond His dominion and His concern. For the same reason, there are many Muslims who object to the translation of the Quranic term *dīn* as 'religion', preferring 'way of life', with all the inclusiveness that this phrase implies.

There is, moreover, the matter of racial affinity. The word 'Semitic' is a dubious one, since the Levant – that part of Asia which borders the Mediterranean – has been a melting-pot of races, probably to a greater extent than any other part of the world; and as the Jews lay claim to a Palestinian origin they are obliged to acknowledge their close kinship with the Arabic-speaking people of the Levant.

It is hardly surprising that only a hundred years ago the opponents in Britain of Disraeli's Eastern Policy attacked the Prime Minister on the grounds that, as a Jew, he was bound to be pro-Muslim (and, by implication, anti-Christian). Jews held positions of great eminence in the Muslim world of the Middle Ages and were respected for their integrity. It is only recently, under the impact of Zionism, that this sense of kinship has been destroyed.

The Qurān, however, blames the followers of Judaism (it must be emphasized that we are speaking, not of a race, but of the adherents of a particular faith, many of them – in the Prophet's time – of Arab ancestry) on two counts: first, that they betrayed the sacred mission entrusted to them and, uniquely privileged as they were by a wealth of prophetic revelation, scorned many of their prophets (including Jesus); secondly, that they plotted against Muhammad when he had treated them with trust and friendship. Seen through a quizzing glass of one colour, Islam has more in common with Judaism than with Christianity; seen through a glass differently tinted, the situation is reversed, and it is with the followers of Jesus that Muslims appear to have the closest affinity.

'Thou wilt find the strongest of mankind in enmity to the believers to be the Jews . . .' says the Qurān; 'and thou wilt find the closest in affection to the believers [to be] those who say: Behold! We are Christians. This is because there are among them priests and monks, and because they are not arrogant. For when they recognize the truth of what has been revealed to this messenger, thou seest their eyes overflow with tears' (Q.5.82/83). Here, quite apart from the applications of this passage to events in the time of the Prophet, the pride and hypocrisy of the scribes and the Pharisees is contrasted with the devotion and self-sacrifice of priests and monks, dedicated to the worship of God; and their sin of *shirk* (ascribing divinity to Jesus) is mitigated, according to Muhammad Asad, by the fact that it 'is not based on conscious intent, but rather flows from their "overstepping the bounds of truth" in their veneration of Jesus'.[1] His quotation is from a verse in the preceding sura: 'O People of the Book, do not overstep the bounds [of truth] in your religious beliefs, and do not say of Allah anything but the truth. Christ Jesus, son of Mary, was but a messenger of Allah and His Word, bestowed on Mary, and a spirit proceeding from Him; so believe in Allah and His messages . . .' (Q.4.171).

Jesus and his Virgin Mother are, according to the Qurān, a sign or symbol of divine grace, and the Prophet said that all men and women were marked at birth by the devil's claw, except for these two alone. One of the sternest reproaches made by Islam against the Jews is for their calumnies against Mary. 'Allah has chosen thee,' the Angel of the Annunciation told her, 'and exempted thee from all stain. Thou are the preferred amongst women' (Q.3.42); and she is a reminder to mankind of the divine mercy and bounty. According to the Qurān, Zachariah, whenever he came to seek her in the prayer-niche of the Temple, found her supplied with food (the symbol of inexhaustible spiritual nourishment). He would ask her then: 'O Mary, whence came this unto thee?' and she would reply: 'It is from Allah; truly Allah giveth beyond measure to whom He will' (Q.3.37). This verse is frequently inscribed above the prayer-niches in mosques, and the Marian message ('Allah giveth beyond measure to whom He will') occurs a number of times in the Qurān, indicating an overflowing generosity to which no human limits can be set. The incomparable Lady

[1] *The Message of the Qurān*, p. 160, note 97.

who presides over what might be called the feminine aspect of Islam is also the link between Islam and Christianity.

In Dermenghem's view, when the Qurān mentions the Incarnation and the Trinity, what it really condemns is not so much these dogmas in themselves as their heretical interpretation: it blames Monophysitism, Eutychianism, Collyridism and other more or less aberrant forms of Christianity rather than the orthodox idea.[1] This is perhaps an over-simplification, but when Muslims and Christians are at loggerheads over the doctrine of the Incarnation (probably the single most unacceptable element in Christianity as Muslims see it) one sometimes wonders whether they are arguing about anything more than the meaning of words. Christians themselves have interpreted this dogma in many different ways, and these are regions of conceptualization and discourse in which every-thing depends upon how one understands a particular term.

The two religions drew further apart in the course of time as they developed in accordance with their own inherent logic; but, as Hichem Djaït has pointed out, one of the historical effects of the rise of Islam was the triumph of Western Christianity over Eastern Christianity.

In the time of the Prophet, Christianity was primarily a religion of the Near East, exemplified today by the Coptic and Maronite Churches. Eastern Christianity, however, became politically subject to Islam, and it was the 'barbarians' of the West who were to carry the torch and give the religion its Latin (and later Germanic) colouring. The bitter arguments which took place regarding the doctrines of the Trinity and the Incar-nation were to some extent, according to Montgomery Watt, disputes between Greek-speaking Christians and oriental Christians who spoke Syriac, Armenian or Coptic. 'The formulations that were eventually accepted as orthodox,' says Montgomery Watt, 'represented a compro-mise between the Greek-speaking and the Latin-speaking; it proved impossible to find formulations which would satisfy the orientals as well, and they were therefore excluded from the Church as heretics.'[2]

It was this exclusion which led the oriental Christians to welcome their Muslim conquerors as liberators, and they were indeed liberated from persecution at the hands of their fellow Christians. This had far-reaching historical consequences. From Alexander's conquest of Persia in 330 BC until the coming of Islam, the Levant, together with Egypt and North Africa as a whole, had been part of the Western world, and as a province of the Roman Empire, it was integrated into a political, economic and cultural pattern which also included Britain and Gaul. Islam inherited the Graeco-Roman culture of the area, and it was not until the Muslim capital was transferred from Damascus to Baghdad that the dividing curtain finally descended between East and West.

From then on it was the differences between these two faiths which were emphasized − or, in the case of the Christian polemicists, exaggerated − and opportunities for fruitful contact diminished. It is these differences, together with those between Islam and Judaism, which chiefly concern us here, in so far as they serve to clarify the particular characteristics of each

[1] *The Life of Mahomet*, p. 111.
[2] *Islam and the Integration of Society*, W. Montgomery Watt, p. 268.

religion and to draw in broad strokes the geometrical figures – square, circle, triangle – by which each might be represented, without losing sight of the fact that their common centre is the divine Unity, the One God, and their common origin the faith of the patriarch Abraham.

In the Muslim view, Judaism 'nationalized' monotheism, claiming it for one people alone, while in Christianity the person of Jesus as it were eclipsed the Godhead, as the sun is eclipsed by the moon; or again, Judaism stabilized this monotheism, giving it a home and an army, but at the same time confiscated it; Christianity universalized the truth, but diluted it; Islam closed the circle and restored the purity of the faith of Abraham, giving to Moses and to Jesus positions of pre-eminence in its universe and seizing upon the quintessential nature of monotheism, single-minded worship of the One, and upon the reflection of the divine Unity in personal and social equilibrium – a balance between all contrary forces and between the different levels of human experience. Ibn Taymiyyah (d. AD 1328) maintained that Islam combined the Mosaic law of justice with the Christian law of grace, taking a middle way between the severity of Judaism and the mercy of Jesus; and he said that while Moses had proclaimed God's Majesty and Jesus His Goodness, Muhammad proclaimed His Perfection. In the same context, it is said that Jesus revealed what Moses had kept hidden, the secrets of the divine Mercy and the richness of the divine Love, and that Islam finally brought everything into perspective in the light of total Truth.

It has been said also that Judaism is the religion of Prophecy, Christianity the religion of a Person, and Islam the religion of God; in the words of Massignon, Israel is rooted in hope, Christianity is vowed to charity, and Islam is centred upon faith. The latter is, of course, a Christian view of this triune diversity; Muslims would say that the Jews confined the true faith to a single people and the Christians limited it a single manifestation, whereas Islam proclaims that it cannot be limited or possessed in any way, or exhausted by any historical manifestation. At the very heart of Islam lies an almost ruthless determination not to impose human standards – or the categories of human thought – upon God or to confine Him within any definition. By the same token, human likes and dislikes can have no relevance to the objective truth, and the idea that we, His creatures, might judge God in terms of our own interests seems, to the Muslim, a monstrous presumption. What Muslims reject in Christianity is the way in which God appears to suffer in the process of history, thereby ceasing to be totally independent and wholly self-sufficient, as the Qurān describes Him, uninvolved in the reflections of His power and benevolence which shine through every fragment of His creation.

As Muslims see it, Christians have been so possessed and overwhelmed by the splendour of their prophet, Jesus, as to compromise the divine transcendence; and in their cultivation of personal piety, they have allowed human society to slip away from righteousness, leaving the conduct of worldly affairs to secular forces indifferent to the priority of the eternal norms. It had become necessary to redeem the situation, not because there were shortcomings in the message brought by Jesus (or in the message brought by Moses), but because of what men had made of these revelations in the course of time and the manner in which the balance characteristic of every divine message had been disturbed. A final and unambiguous statement of the truth was therefore added to what had gone before, delivered by a messenger of God who would interpret it and live it with undeviating precision. Moreover, the community shaped by this divine intervention was to preserve the message with scrupulous care and to carry it to the ends of the earth, without any possibility of error or distortion. It is for this reason that Muslims have so profound a horror of anything that savours of *bid'ah*, 'innovation', including what modern Christians would regard as necessary adaptations of religion to the changing times. Man's function in the scheme of things, his destiny and his duties, have been declared with unprecedented clarity; since all that needed saying has been said, there can never again be any need for a 'reminder' to mankind. If men and women fall once more into forgetfulness, or if they again distort the God-given truth, then there can be no hope for them.

It is not always easy for Christians to grasp or live with the seemingly 'abstract' truth which lies at the heart of monotheism. The miraculous coming of Jesus and the sublimity of the example which he sets dazzle them, so that truth itself becomes personal rather than objective. In Islam God does not Himself descend into the human matrix or convert by miracles. He makes known what He is and what He wishes, and this leaves at least some part of the task of 'redemption' – which, for the Christian, falls with an all but crushing weight upon Jesus – to man as the vice-regent and earthly representative of God.

Islam takes man as he is and, on that basis, teaches him his duties and guides him to his goal. It is able to do so because it rejects the Christian dogma that human nature is corrupted in its very substance. Man is weak, foolish and forgetful, but his centre is uncorrupt and he does not need a miracle to save him. Christianity, on the other hand, locates the core of sin and deviation in the heart of every man and woman born; moreover the natural world as a whole is seen to have participated in the Fall, each leaf and each flower stained by the primal sin; a view which, in a secularized world, has made possible the brutal exploitation of nature to satisfy human appetites.

We are told in the book of Deuteronomy that 'the Lord thy God is a consuming fire', and this element in the Judaic revelation lives on in Christianity through the Old Testament. The fire of love and the fire of sacrifice liquefy the hardened heart, and the Christian seeks warmth even as the Muslim seeks space, the 'open'. If we associate fire with Christianity it is possible to summon up the image of snow in connection with Islam, although – for obvious reasons – the Qurān does not mention this particular 'sign of God'; Islam has something of the quality of a vast, pure blanket of snow which covers even ugly and unseemly objects with its cool luminescence. Coolness and sobriety relate to the same religious perspective. Conversion to Christianity, says Frithjof Schuon, 'seems in certain respects like the beginning of a great love which makes all a man's past life look vain and trivial – it is a "rebirth" after a "death"; conversion to Islam is, on the contrary, like an awakening from an unhappy love or like sobriety after drunkenness, or again like the freshness of morning after a troubled night. In Christianity the soul is "freezing to death" in its congenital egoism, and Christ is the central fire which warms and restores it to life; in Islam, on the other hand, the soul is "suffocating" in the constriction of this same egoism, and Islam appears as the cool immensity of space which allows it to "breathe" and "expand" towards the boundless'.[1]

In all such comparisons between the religions what concerns us is not dogmatic theology but differences in 'climate', differences which affect not only ways of thought but also imagination and sensibility. The rays of the sun which, in the southern deserts, kill men and beasts are filtered in northern latitudes to create not only a different climate but also a different landscape. The fact remains that there is but one sun in our planetary system.

The circumstances of human life present us on every side with alternatives and with the necessity for making a choice between them. We cannot be in two places at once or adopt two quite different perspectives simultaneously, even if both seem equally desirable; this is the most obvious reason for the complete impossibility of creating some kind of universal religion out of the 'best elements' of each. It is in the way the different religions see the major forces and episodes of human life that they provide the most illuminating clues to their essential character, and it is in their attitudes to human sexuality that their perspectives are defined with particular clarity. This is especially so when we contrast Islam with Christianity, and no other aspect of their long, enduring confrontation has given rise to more persistent misunderstandings. Until the 'permissiveness' of recent years infiltrated the churches (reversing the situation, in so far as Muslims now reproach Christians for the laxity of their sexual morals), nothing in Islam horrified – and fascinated – Christians more than what was seen as the 'licensed sensuality' of the Muslim; Muhammad was condemned as much for being a 'voluptuary' as for being a 'false prophet'. Even to this day, jokes about the 'harem' are good for a snigger; and in response to the Christian polemic, Muslim apologists have gone to absurd lengths, trying to suggest, in tones of coy puritanism, that the Prophet himself made love to his wives only from a sense of duty.

Attempts have been made to classify the religions of the world by distinguishing between those that are 'life-affirming' and those that are 'life-denying'. This has led to gross over-simplifications, but it may be one way of expressing the ambiguity characteristic of creation as a whole and indeed of all that is – or appears to be – 'other-than-God'. On the one hand the world is a divine creation, a creation which, according to Genesis, God found to be 'good'; and Islam teaches that creation flows from the divine Mercy, to which all its joys and all its beauties bear eloquent witness.

On the other hand, this world is marked by separation from its source; its 'fissures' – death, suffering and the disappointment of human hopes – mark only too painfully the extent of this separation. It is so close to

[1] *Gnosis: Divine Wisdom*, F. Schuon (John Murray, London, 1957) p. 15.

nothingness – to the blackness of the void – that everything in it is ephemeral, emerging briefly out of the Unseen and disappearing into it once again.

In other words, creation as such is both centrifugal and centripetal. Through it God projects outwardly and brings back inwardly, so that the world may be seen either as a road which leads away from the light of heaven or, quite literally, as a *Sharī'ah*, a road back; or it may be seen as both at once. There are many Quranic passages which speak of how God both 'misleads' and 'guides' His creatures, and it is as though the great wind of creation carries the individual essences out to the edge of the abyss and then, provided they have not cut themselves off completely and forgotten their origin, the magnetism of the divine Centre draws them back again.

It has been said, and not only by Muslims, that everything in the world – every object, every energy, every event – has two faces, the one light and the other dark; the one turned towards God and inseparably related to its origin, the other turned towards nothingness and fatally condemned to disintegration; the one transparent, the other opaque. Al-Ghazzali (d. AD 1111) said that everything has 'a face of its own and a face of its Lord; in respect of its own face it is nothingness, and in respect of the face of its Lord it is Being'. Both faces exist: the whole question is to which of them we attach ourselves.[1]

Traditional Christianity, because it posits man's corruption through original sin, must assume that his natural inclination will be to choose the dark face. Islam, being realistic, cannot take an entirely opposite point of view, but it bases its perspective on the assumption that, rightly guided and controlled, man is capable of choosing the light one and of perceiving, through phenomena, the Face of God.

The ambiguity of creation is crystallized in the feminine and in sexuality as such. It is here that the contrast between the 'transparency' of phenomena and their 'opaqueness' is most significant. For Islam it is the quality of transparency that takes precedence, since all things are, according to the Qurān, 'signs of God'; they show Him, they express Him, and through them He can be found. Christianity does not deny this transparency in principle, but it doubts whether human beings are capable of profiting from it and tends to regard phenomena – and particularly sexuality – as temptations. It is important to be clear about this difference, neither exaggerating it nor underrating it. Islam disapproves of casual promiscuity as does Christianity; but the Muslim takes it for granted that when a man sees a beautiful woman he will desire physical union with her, and that when a woman sees a man who appeals to her she will be drawn to him, and this mutual desire is seen as flowing directly from the nature of things as willed by God. It is in itself an unqualified good, however much it may need to be hedged about with restrictions.

This difference of perspective may be illustrated by two quotations. The first is from St Thomas Aquinas, who said that marriage becomes 'more

[1] This point, which is one of the essential keys to understanding the human situation, was perfectly expressed by Rumi in his *Mathnawi*. 'Every existent [thing] that has emerged from non-existence is poison for one person and sugar for another' (M. 5.4236); and, 'Each and every part of the world is a snare for the fool and a means of deliverance for the wise' (M.6.4287).

holy *sine carnale commixione*', in other words when sexual desire is absent; and although in traditional Christianity, sexual intercourse is permitted for the sake of procreation, this permission is granted, as it were, with regret, and sexual intercourse for its own sake is condemned.

The second quotation is from Ibn 'Arabī, the Spanish mystic and philosopher sometimes known as the Shaykh al-Akbar, the 'greatest of spiritual masters'. 'The most intense and perfect contemplation of God,' he said, 'is through women, and the most intense union is the conjugal act.' If we come to the present day, Pope John Paul II has spoken of the evils of 'lust' even within marriage, whereas a contemporary Muslim writer remarks in passing: 'On the marriage night when two people come together Allah forgives them all their previous sins, so much does He like marriage.' The Prophet said that marriage is 'half the religion', and he astonished his companions by telling them that there is a reward in heaven for every act of intercourse between a man and his wife; he said on another occasion: 'When a husband and wife hold each other by the hand, their sins pass out through their finger tips ...'.[1] Nothing shocks Christians more than the tales (whether apocryphal or not is irrelevant) of the Prophet's sexual potency. 'We used to say,' reported his companion Anas, 'that the Prophet was endowed with the potency of thirty men.' At least among simple Muslims, unaffected by the embarrassment of modern academics, this *ḥadīth* only increases the force of the divine Message and the prestige of the messenger.

No less shocking to the Christian are the Quranic references to the wide-eyed maidens of Paradise, of whom it is said (in the traditions) that were one of them to let down her scarf upon the world, the whole earth would be perfumed. How can this be reconciled with Jesus's statement that there is no marrying or giving in marriage in heaven? It is a question, surely, of what might be described as divine expediency: since people will always be inclined to take images of Paradise in too narrow and too earthly a sense, they must be told that 'it is not like that at all'; but since nothing that is good or beautiful or dear to us on earth can be absent from Paradise, we may take these as foretastes of heavenly joy, while trying to understand how inadequate such images are. Christianity emphasizes their inadequacy; the Qurān, on the other hand, 'speaks in terms of the pleasure of the senses, because these direct pleasures are in fact the earthly projections or shadows of the Paradisal archetypes which it is seeking to convey. Having their roots in these archetypes, the sensations have power to recall them, for the "tether" which attaches the symbol to its reality not only traces the path by which the symbol came into existence but can become, in the opposite direction, a vibrating chord of spiritual remembrance'; and while reminding the soul that Paradise is intensely desirable, these descriptions serve also 'to re-endow life on earth with a lost dimension'.[2]

Here again we encounter the ambiguity inherent in our experience, the fact that the symbol represents an otherwise indescribable and unknowable reality, and the fact that it is not, in itself, the reality in question. The things of this world are both shadowy images of heavenly things and at the

---

[1] *Mercy Oceans*, Sh. Nāzim Qibrisi, p. 147.

[2] *What is Sufism?*, Martin Lings, (Allen & Unwin, London 1975) p. 55.

same time false and misleading, in so far as they are thought to have any independent reality. Expediency determines which of these opposite points of view should be adopted in a given context.

One reason why Ibn 'Arabī chose to emphasize the importance of sexual union is that, for the Muslim, nothing of such power and intensity could come from anywhere other than from God. Not only is it among the greatest of His gifts, but it is also a ravishing away of all that we are in our petty everyday selves; an image, therefore, of that ravishing by the Spirit which is the goal of religion. Christianity sees first and foremost the binding quality of this experience, as it does the binding quality of all earthly beauty (condemned, as such beauty is, to corruption as soon as it has caught our fancy). Islam regards its carnal and ephemeral character as no more than a veil, and by insisting upon the 'greater ablution' – washing from head to toe – after intercourse, chose a means of washing away what is earthly and mortal in the act, leaving behind all that savours of the eternal Beauty.

It is evident, in any case, that the beauty of a human body is a radiance that has fallen upon this poor flesh from elsewhere, and awareness of this radiance is itself a form of contemplativity. In certain extreme sexual perversions one may observe a desperate effort to grasp and possess what can never be grasped or possessed. Islam concerns itself with the 'transparency' of phenomena, that is to say it seeks to find their Creator through them; the Christian tendency, as Schuon has said, is to 'rend the veil' upon which phenomena are woven, casting it aside in order to reach the light behind. We do not need to beat our heads against a wall or to argue from set positions as to which point of view is 'right' and which is 'wrong'; both correspond to the realities of human life and to our situation within the matrix of reality.

It is significant that in the Biblical account of the Fall, Eve was the instrument of Adam's transgression, and woman as 'temptress' is central to the occidental imagination. This element plays no part in the Quranic account of the Fall, in which it is 'Iblīs' – the satanic force – who alone brings down the first couple. Christianity was obliged by its 'mythology' to adopt a stern and suspicious attitude to women as 'vessels of wrath', and it is perfectly logical that Christians should be said to 'fall' through their sexuality, and that on the popular level sexual humour merges readily into the scatological. It is as though the Christian and his secular heirs experienced their mortality most acutely through their sexual nature, and they find it incomprehensible that a Muslim ascetic who eats the minimum to keep body and soul together, who spends half his nights in prayer and vigil, denies himself even legitimate pleasures and is, so far as the world is concerned, 'like a dead man walking', should none the less marry – and perhaps marry more than one wife. The occidental, whether believer or unbeliever, feels that celibacy would be more in accordance with such a vocation. The Muslim, on the other hand, rejoices that this holy person has not removed himself from the human community but takes pains to follow in the footsteps of the Prophet.

There is a further cultural factor which conditions the Christian (and post-Christian) view of human sexuality. Christianity was obliged, in terms of its whole perspective, to react against the naturalism of the classical world which it was destined to transform, a naturalism that had lost its sacred character and become trivial and profane. Occidental man regards nature, if not as an enemy, at least as something to be conquered and dominated. He cannot approve of being subjected to the laws and requirements of the natural world, whether beyond him or within himself; laws and requirements which, for the Muslim, are divine in origin and sacred in character.

The Christian and his heirs hold moral heroism in high esteem and sometimes see advantages in being surrounded by temptations, which offer an opportunity for exercising control and discipline over their natural instincts. The Muslim is inclined to believe that man has something more important to do than engage in a wrestling match with temptation, which he sees as a distraction from his principal business, the constant awareness of God. Since he also believes what the Qurān tells him about human weakness, he thinks it unlikely that men and women will resist temptation when it is offered and therefore takes measures to remove occasions for temptation, hence the rules concerning the segregation of the sexes and feminine dress. It is even taken for granted in some communities that if a man and a woman are left together in privacy for a short time, they are as sure to come together as are iron filings brought close to a magnet. Not for nothing has God created the two sexes and inspired in them a passion to unite, and this is a cause for wonder rather than for reproach. According to certain authorities, when the Prophet accidentally saw Zainab (his freedman's wife, whom he himself later married) in a state of disarray, he exclaimed: 'Praise be to Allah who transforms our hearts and does with them as He pleases!'

It is precisely because Islam goes so far in accepting the natural instincts, and in sanctifying them, that it is obliged to 'draw the line' so firmly and to punish with such severity departures from the norm and excursions beyond the limits established by the religious Law. The requirements of social and psychological equilibrium, the need to protect women and the security of children are the motives that determine this Law, and, since the whole social structure is anchored in the family, its infringements threaten society as a whole and are punished accordingly. As a civilization and a 'way of life' Islam stands or falls in terms of the delicate balance maintained between order and liberty, as also between society and the individual.

Among the orientalists some have described Islam as individualistic', while others have seen it as 'collectivist'. It is both. Standing shoulder to shoulder in straight lines in the communal prayer, the Muslims form a single block, an indivisible army of God in which the individual is merged into the sacred community; and yet one man praying alone in the desert, isolated from all others, represents in himself the fullness of the community and exercises the divine authority on earth; the rest might have died, yet Islam is present where he is present. The same may be said of those who follow the example of the Prophet in rising to pray in the still hours of the night; the world sleeps, but the *Ummah* is awake and stands before its Lord. Even in the midst of the community, the individual recognizes no ultimate authority, spiritual or temporal, but that of God, which is one reason why the Qurān tells us that if we kill a single man unjustly it is as though we had 'killed all mankind' (Q.5.32).

In this, as in all the particular characteristics and points of emphasis which distinguish Islam from other religions, the essential confession of faith – *lā ilāha illa 'Llāh* – determines every element in an integrated pattern, and the principle of Unity is reflected in the single individual, complete in himself and conforming to the human norm, as it is in the community united in prayer and in obedience to the Law.

Chapter 3

TRUTH AND MERCY

To those who find it difficult to believe in any deity, let alone a multitude of gods, and who think of idolatry as a primitive cult – as remote from rational people as cannibalism – the Credo of Islam, 'I bear witness that *lā ilāha illa 'Lhāh*' – 'There is no divinity but God' – seems meaningless, particularly if they are unaware that the whole Qurān could be described as a commentary on these four words, or as an amplification of them. Yet both Jews and Christians have, in their own tradition – the Torah or Pentateuch – a comparable statement. Speaking to Moses from the burning bush, God describes Himself in these words: 'I am That I am'.[1] Perhaps this too is meaningless to many of those whose Scripture is the Bible; they ask to be told what 'That' is, although 'That' is – by definition – beyond all definitions.

The first *Shahāda* – witnessing to the divine Unity – is the fountainhead of all Islamic doctrine, as it is of all Muslim practice. 'No divinity but God' indicates that nothing is absolute beside the sole Absolute; nothing is entirely real other than that Reality which is One and indivisible; for how could things which come and go in time – like pictures flashed briefly upon a screen, here today and gone tomorrow – be considered 'real' in the full sense of the term? It follows that nothing which exists, whether for millennia or for a fraction of a second, does so except by participation in the One or, to use a different imagery, by the will of God, who 'says unto a thing "Be!" and it is.' When its time comes, the peopled earth with all its ornaments disappears like a puff of smoke: 'everything thereon perishes except the Face of thy Lord of Majesty and Bounty' (Q.55.27). *Lā ilāha illa 'Llāh*: God *is*, He is because He is, having no cause. 'Say: He is Allah, One, the Totally Self-Sufficient Uncaused Cause, He begets not neither is He begotten, and there is no thing that is like unto Him' (Q.112).

It follows also that there is no power but the Power, no love but the Love, no mercy but the Mercy, no helper but the Helper; and, on the darker side of human experience, there is no slayer but the Slayer, and no avenger but the Avenger; and it follows, again, that He alone uplifts and He alone casts down, gives prosperity or withdraws it, makes happy or makes sad. He alone is the Agent and He alone is the Cause. Let a thousand men come against me, armed to the teeth, they cannot touch me unless He so wills. Let my enemies plot till they sweat venom, they are impotent unless He wills otherwise.

[1] *'Eheyeh asher eheyeh'* (Exodus III. 14).

The *Shahādah* distinguishes between other-than-God and God Himself, and it brings the former – all that appears to be 'other' – back to its origin and its true identity. Perfect incomparability means that nothing can be set beside the Incomparable. According to a *ḥadīth qudsī* (one of the directly inspired sayings of the Prophet), 'Allah was, and there was nothing beside Him'; to which 'Alī is said to have added: 'And He is now even as He ever was.' But this extreme remoteness (*tanzīh*) implies or contains its complement. Since nothing can be opposed to the One – for it would then be a 'divinity' in its own right – every contingent reality must be a reflection of the one Reality, and every meaning we might give to the word 'divinity' is transposed *in divinis*.

Islām means submission to the One and, as the Qurān tells us, there is nothing that does not submit, 'willingly or unwillingly,' at every moment – as also in its origin and in its end – to the God other than whom there is nothing; no thing, no being, no light, no word, no breath. 'Say: Who provides for you from the heavens and from the earth; who is the owner of hearing and of sight ...?' (Q.10.31). We cannot speak; He speaks. We cannot see; He sees. We cannot hear; He hears. We cannot taste; He tastes. We cannot enjoy apart from Him, for joy is His alone. He lends us these powers, through his mercy, but their root remains in Him. To quote one of Muhammad's favourite Quranic sayings: *Lā ḥawla wa lā qūwata illa bi 'Llāh*, 'there is no strength and no power except with Allah'.

God is sometimes described as *al-Bayyin*, translated as the Evident, the Apparent; but such tepid words cannot convey the force of meaning inherent in the word. To a man in the desert the sun is more than simply 'apparent'; it is blazingly and undeniably present, and he cannot escape it; such is the actuality of the Divine for the Muslim. Frithjof Schuon speaks of the nomads 'scorched by the ever present and ever eternal Divine Sun'. 'In the face of this Sun, man is nothing: that the Caliph 'Umar should conquer a part of the ancient world or that the Prophet should milk his goat amounts to more or less the same thing; that is to say, there is no "human greatness" in the profane and Titanesque sense, and thus no humanism to give rise to vain glories; the only greatness admitted is the lasting one of sanctity, and this belongs to God.'[1]

There can be no mystery about something so overwhelmingly clear.[2] In the climate of Islam one might reasonably say: 'God is plain and evident. I am obscure and hard to discern.' Mystery lies in the shadows and in all the ambiguities of the human world, ambiguities inherent in relativity precisely because it is relative, not absolute. It may happen that the longer a man lives the more aware he becomes of the complexities of human subjectivity, and of the encounters between human subjectivities, until he turns away from sorting out such tangled skeins to seek and face that which is alone clear and unambiguous.

The *Shahādah* may be analysed in various ways, always with the object of impressing it the more deeply upon our minds and our hearts. It can, for example, be divided into two parts, a denial and an affirmation: 'No

[1]*Dimensions of Islam*, Frithjof Schuon, p. 69.

[2]According to the Persian poet Mahmūd Shabistārī: 'the Absolute is so nakedly apparent to man's sight that it is not visible.'

divinity' relates to the world and reduces it to nothingness, in so far as it is separated – or envisaged as separated – from its source; 'if not Allah' relates to Truth, and having said 'No' to a world (or an ego) which presumes to set itself up as a little god, the *Shahādah* says 'Yes' within this same framework and restores the world (or ego) to an existence which is qualified by its total dependence upon the One.

Again, the formula may be considered word by word, and this too helps us to assimilate its meaning. *Lā*, 'No', when spoken by an Arab has an almost explosive force, and here it is the explosive negative which destroys all illusions, shattering multiplicity as a self-sufficient universe of objects and selfhoods. Everything in our experience can be treated – and, at one time or another, is treated – as though it had a separate existence, as though it were a 'divinity' in competition with Allah, and the word *ilāha* therefore stands for anything and everything that is so treated. The third word of the formula, *illa*, is a contraction of *in lā* ('if not'); it is sometimes called the 'isthmus' (*barzakh*) between negation and affirmation – the link – and beyond this stands the true Reality, *Allāh*; and all that has been denied is restored to its true identity in God.

There is no end to the ways in which these words may be illuminated, but a particularly striking one is in terms of light; for according to the Qurān, 'Allah is the Light of the heavens and the earth,' and Islamic doctrine accounts for the existence of what appears separated from Him in terms of the 'veiling' of that light by veils beyond number. According to this teaching, *lā* represents the veils in so far as they conceal the light, being entirely opaque; *ilāha* is the reflection of the light, separated from its source; *illa* indicates the transparent veil which communicates the light, and *Allāh* is Light as such.

The knowledge that *lā ilāha illa 'Llāh*, though given outwardly through revelation as a 'reminder', can be regarded as inherent in the deepest layer of human nature; but harsh measures may be required to bring it into consciousness. 'On the Day when the deniers are exposed to the Fire [they will be asked]: Is not this *real*? They will say: Yea, by our Lord!' (Q.46.34). This is the encounter with Reality in the manner to which we are predisposed by our nature – and destined through our actions – to encounter it. Face to face with Reality in its most compelling manifestation, the 'denier' is unavoidably a 'believer', and he says: 'Yea, by our Lord!'[1] Only in dreams can the Lord be denied, only through self-deception can Reality be entirely veiled. 'As for the deniers, their actions are like a mirage in a desert. The thirsty one taketh it for water, till he cometh to it and findeth it nothing, and findeth in its place Allah, who payeth him his due ...' (Q.24.39). 'Wheresoever thou turnest, there is the Face of Allah' (Q.2.115). On every horizon, at the end of every road and in every secret chamber, there is the Face, inescapable in its omnipresence; and we have to be careful that the road we take leads to the Face of Mercy and not to that of Wrath.

---

[1] When the screens, with their innumerable pictures and patterns (their landscapes, events and people), are torn away by the termination of a world or of an individual existence, then there is but one possible cry: 'Can ye see yourselves when ... the Hour cometh upon you, crying unto other than Allah? ... Nay, but unto Him ye will cry ... Forgotten will be all that ye [formerly] associated with Him' (Q.VI.40–41).

That which, for the philosopher, is Reality or the Absolute is, for the ordinary man or woman immersed in their everyday business, power. It is as 'power' that we encounter Reality in our normal experience; and it is in the language of normal experience that the Qurān speaks to mankind. The *Shahādah* is not only doctrine, it is also practice – or the key to practice. Its truth is something to be assimilated and lived, which is why, when we speak of the Islamic Credo, we are speaking, not of an abstraction, but of the way in which men and women order their whole lives, their waking and their sleeping, their work and their rest, the words they use in speaking to one another and the gestures they make in loving one another, the planting of a seedling and the reaping of a crop, the turning on of a tap from which water flows and its turning off, and the life and the death of all creatures.

To understand how decisive this formula is one must observe the place it occupies in the life of the ordinary Muslim, who will pronounce these words in every crisis and at every moment when the world threatens to overwhelm him, as he will when death approaches. A pious man, seized by rage, will appear suddenly to have been stopped in his tracks as he remembers the *Shahādah* and, as it were, withdraws, putting a great distance between himself and his turbulent emotions. A woman crying out in childbirth will as suddenly fall silent, remembering; and a student, bowed anxiously over his desk in an examination hall, will raise his head and speak these words, and a barely audible sigh of relief passes through the whole assembly. This is the ultimate answer to all questions.[1]

It follows that there can be no graver sin for the Muslim than *shirk*, the 'association' of other 'gods' with God; in other words, idolatry or polytheism. 'Indeed Allah forgiveth not that a partner should be ascribed unto Him. He forgiveth [all else] except that to whom He pleaseth . . .' (Q.4.48). Idolatry and polytheism are seen, not as simple errors about the nature of reality, but as the final stage of a process of corruption or dissocation in which the human will plays a major role.

Now that naive theories concerning the 'evolution' of religion, current in the last century, have been put to sleep, it is generally recognized that polytheism arises when divine 'energies', originally seen as aspects of the one supreme Deity, take on a life of their own and are worshipped as though they were independent entities. The motives behind this process can always be attributed to worldliness in one form or another; and this scenario may be observed in the religion of ancient Greece, in African tribal religion and in 'popular' Hinduism. The Qurān bears witness to just such a development among the Arabs, before the advent of Islam as a 'reminder' of what they had chosen to forget. They were not unaware of *Allāh*, but they had ascribed to Him 'sons' and 'daughters' – and sundry

---

[1] A friend of the author's, driving with his wife and two small children in a remote and seemingly uninhabited part of East Africa, swerved into a ditch. All efforts to start the car having failed, he stood aside and exclaimed: *lā ilāha illa 'Llāh*. Immediately a number of Muslim villagers, who had been watching in concealment, emerged from the bush, righted the car and then entertained the family with the best that their meagre resources could provide.

'partners' – convenient, comfortable and serviceable deities who were easy to deal with and made no demands on their adherents.

Idolatry is, in essence, the worship of symbols for their own sake, whether these take the form of graven images or subsist only in the human imagination. 'In the "classical" and "traditional" cases of paganism,' says Frithjof Schuon, 'the loss of the full truth and of efficacity for salvation essentially results from a profound modification in the mentality of the worshippers and not from an ultimate falsity of the symbols ... A mentality once contemplative and so in possession of a sense of the metaphysical transparency of forms had ended by becoming passional, worldly and, in the strict sense, superstitious. The symbol through which the reality symbolized was originally clearly perceived ... became in fact an opaque and uncomprehended image or an idol ...'[1]

The Meccans of Muhammad's time had, however, taken a further step on the downward slope which leads from the worship of uncomprehended symbols to the worship of man-made dolls and toys, idols which represent nothing (like signposts pointing nowhere). The Muslim's fierce suspicion of anything that savours even remotely of idolatry – as, for example, the sculpting of human or animal figures – may be attributed to the fact that when human beings have lost the capacity to 'see through' images of the Divinity, perceiving what lies behind them, and see them only as material objects, then it is but a short step to treating any and every material object as though it were self-existent and worshipping it for its own sake.

Polytheism and idolatry might be described as institutionalized *shirk*, but *shirk* can also take more subtle and more universal forms. It is not difficult to see that the modern scientist, not as an observer and recorder but as a theorist, is a *mushrik* (one who is guilty of 'association'), since he regards the forces of nature and all causative agencies as independent powers rather than as the instruments of a single omnipotent Will. So is the man who sets his heart upon some worldly prize – power or wealth, for example – in forgetfulness of the only prize worth seeking, and so too is anyone who wants to possess some object for its own sake more than he wants to please God; from this point of view every act of disobedience to the divine commands has the smell of *shirk* about it and we are all, in one way or another, guilty. 'If Allah were to take mankind to task for the ill they do [on earth] He would not leave upon it a living creature; yet He grants them respite for an appointed time ...' (Q.16.61). It is usual to add to the *Shahādah* the words *lā sharīka lahu*, 'no partner hath He,' and there are a million different ways in which – whether in thought or action – we can ascribe partners to the One who has no partners. Were it not for the intervention of the divine mercy and the overflowing of the divine forgiveness none would escape the trial by fire. Moreover, the ultimate 'false god', the shadowy presence behind all others, is the human ego with its pretensions to self-sufficiency.

Somewhere along the road which leads from light to darkness, *shirk* merges into *kufr*, the denial of God, atheism[2] or agnosticism. The word

---

[1] *Understanding Islam*, Frithjof Schuon, p. 55.

[2] Atheism as an active 'anti-faith' is rare in the West – a lazy indifference to religion is more common – but it is the official creed of the Soviet Union, and it arouses in the Muslims

kāfir is usually translated as 'unbeliever' or 'infidel', which will serve so long as one recognizes in this term an active, voluntary element; a corruption of the will as much as of the intellect. Muhammad Asad translates it as 'one who denies the truth', and the fact that 'unbelief' is something much more than a simple intellectual inability to accept a given proposition is clear from the root meaning of the word. A *kāfir* is 'one who covers', as a farmer covers (*kafara*) the seed he has sown with earth, or as the night 'covers' the visible world in darkness. 'In their abstract sense,' says Asad, 'both the verb and the nouns derived from it have a connotation of "concealing" something that exists or "denying" something that is true. Hence, in the usage of the Qurān ... a *kāfir* is "one who denies" (or "refuses to acknowledge") truth in the widest spiritual sense of this latter term; that is, irrespective of whether it relates to a cognition of supreme truth — namely the existence of God — or to a doctrine or ordinance enunciated in the divine Writ, or to a self-evident moral proposition, or to acknowledgment of, and therefore gratitude for, favours received.'[1]

This should in fact be obvious as soon as one recognizes that the truths in question are inherent in human nature, though 'forgotten', as the Qurān asserts again and again. It is not a matter of being unable to accept something we are told, but rather of refusing — from self-interested motives — to admit something we already know. The act of concealing something, even from oneself, is an act of the will. The demerit of unbelief, says Frithjof Schuon, 'lies in the passionate stiffening of the will and in the worldly tendencies which bring about this stiffening. The merit of faith is fidelity to the supernaturally natural receptivity of primordial man; it means remaining as God made us and remaining at his disposition ...'[2] What is commonly called 'realism' is closely related to this stiffening and this worldliness, because belief in the total and self-sufficient reality of this world is what persuades us to pile things, objects and dreams upon the inwardly known and outwardly revealed truth.

'Nay, but what they have done is rust upon their hearts. Nay, but truly on that Day they will be covered from [the mercy] of their Lord' (Q.83.14/15). Here again the factor of wilfulness is emphasized, but this time what concerns us is not a single and definitive act of denial, but rather the cumulative effect of a whole series of small actions which carry with them an implied denial of God; the sinner has in effect behaved as though God did not exist and as though he were free to act exactly as he pleased, that is to say as a little god in his own right. And if, as the Sufis say, the divine mercy is present as an inexhaustible spring in the heart of every human being, then he may be said to have covered over this immanent mercy and isolated himself from it.

The practical distinction between believer and unbeliever (or 'denier') is

---

subjected to its impact a searing contempt. 'To the Muslims a real atheist is not deemed to be a romantic rebel or a superior philosophical free-thinker, but a subhuman of limited intellect ... degraded to the level of bestiality, if not below.' *The Islamic Threat to the Soviet State*, Alexandre Bennigsen and Marie Broxup (Croom Helm, 1983).

[1] *The Message of the Qurān*, Muhammad Asad, p. 907, note 4.
[2] *Logic and Transcendence*, Frithjof Schuon, p. 200.

inevitably simplistic. It is immensely important as an indication of a man's primary orientation – the direction in which he faces spontaneously as a result of what he is and all that he has done – but it takes no account of the ambiguities and inconsistencies of human nature, or of the question mark which has to be placed after every judgement we make concerning our fellow men and women; nor does it allow for our incapacity to see ourselves as others see us and the corresponding incapacity of others to see into our hearts and assess our deepest motives. People are not always what they say they are – or even what they think they are. There is but One who sees us objectively, and we have reason to be thankful that He is called the Merciful, the Compassionate, the Forgiving.

Every man and woman is inwardly a city in which there are many factions, one gaining the upper hand today, another tomorrow. The only people in whom this warfare of the factions is appeased are, on the one hand, the saints, those wholly integrated beings who have brought all such contrary forces under the control of the highest principle, and on the other, those who have surrendered entirely to the most powerful and brutal faction in their make-up and so enjoy an illusion of peace worse than any warfare.

Between these two extremes lies a battlefield. The fact that there are many people who live quiet lives of routine, looking neither to right nor to left, neither upwards towards the heavens nor downwards into the abyss, is misleading, for there are forces lurking within everyone which may remain dormant so long as no great prize is within reach or so long as no great danger threatens. When a man turns to religion these forces are awakened, whether for good or ill, and – if for ill – may try to seize hold of it and use it for their own purposes.

No ego is more inflated than the one which feeds upon religion and justifies its greed and its fury in religious terms; it can even happen that the inhibitions which restrain murderous impulses in those who live only for this world are released when the opportunity arises to murder in the name of God. Those who seek Paradise walk a tightrope over hell; the greater the prize, the greater the risk.

But light is light; by its very nature it shows up things we might prefer to keep hidden; it reveals and exposes, as does that Judgement to which we must all finally submit. The agnostic has a very curious notion of religion. He is convinced that a man who says 'I believe in God' should at once become perfect; if this does not happen, then the believer must be a fraud and a hypocrite. He thinks that adherence to a religion is the end of the road, whereas it is in fact only the beginning of a very long and sometimes very rough road. He looks for consistency in religious people, however aware he may be of the inconsistencies in himself.

The fact that we do expect consistency of others – and are astonished by their lack of it – is sufficient proof of our awareness that the human personality ought to be unified under one command. Perhaps the most difficult of all the requirements of religion is simplicity, for the simple man is all of one piece; he does not leave bits of himself scattered all over the landscape of his life. He is, so to speak, the same all through, whichever way you slice him, and it has been said that only the saint has a right to say 'I'; the rest of us would do better to confess 'My name is legion'. This inward multiplicity – the multiplicity of the 'factions' – is like an echo within the human personality of outward polytheism; on the one hand many persons within a single envelope of flesh, on the other many gods in a fragmented universe. Monotheism is not only a theology; it is also a psychology. As is the *Shahādah – lā ilāha illa 'Llāh*.

The agnostic also has difficulty in understanding that those who are capable of belief and assent to a faith may believe quite different and irreconcilable things at different levels of their personality. A striking illustration of this inconsistency was given by the writer and diplomat Conor Cruise O'Brien, in a recent newspaper article. He quoted an Irish priest in a remote parish who, when asked what the majority of Catholics in his care really believed about life after death, said that they believed what the Church teaches them about the immortality of the soul, the resurrection of the body, reward and punishment. He added that they also believed that when a man was dead he was dead like an animal, 'and that's that'.[1]

In any case the 'believer' is more often born than made; he calls himself a Christian or a Muslim because he was born into this or that religious environment. He thinks that he shares the beliefs common to the people around him; with a part of himself he believes, and with another part he disbelieves. But by the same token, those born into a secular, agnostic society, and mouthing the slogans imposed by their education and their conditioning, may none the less be closer to faith than they know; in this case the 'rust' which covers their hearts has come from without rather than from within themselves. A few years before his death in 1934 the great Algerian Sheikh, Ahmad al-'Alawī, became friendly with a Frenchman, Dr. Carret, who had been treating him for various minor ailments. One day Carret tried to explain his agnosticism to the Sheikh, adding, however, that what most surprised him was that people who did claim to be religious 'should be able to go on attaching importance to this earthly life'. After a pause, the Sheikh said to him: 'It is a pity that you will not let your Spirit rise above yourself. But whatever you may say and whatever you may imagine, you are nearer to God than you think'.[2] In this confused age in which we now find ourselves there may be many a believer who is a *kāfir* under the skin, and many a *kāfir* who is closer than he knows to the God in whom he thinks he does not believe.

It is important to be aware of these paradoxes because the distrust of religion – or at least of 'organized religion' – which is so widespread in the Western world, derives less from intellectual doubts than from a critical judgement of the way in which religious people are seen to behave. The agnostic does not concern himself with the supernatural dimensions of religion, let alone with ultimate truth. He sees only that part of the iceberg which is visible above the surface, and he judges this to be misshapen. The whole sad story is summed up in the wise child's prayer: 'Lord, please make good people religious and make religious people good.'

The follower of Islam is called a *Muslim* ('one who submits'), not a *Mu'min* ('one who believes'), and with good reason. 'The Arabs say: We

[1] *The Observer*, London, 22 February 1981.
[2] *A Sufi Saint of the Twentieth Century*, Martin Lings, p. 29.

believe! Say rather: We have submitted! For the faith hath not yet entered your hearts' (Q.49.14). There are three dimensions which may be identified in every religious context. They relate to fear, to love and to knowledge, and it is the first of these that commonly presides over the initial stage of the spiritual journey. 'The fear of God is the beginning of wisdom'; and there are elements in the human personality which respond only to the threat of punishment, just as there are other elements which are drawn into the pattern of unity by love, and yet others which fall into place in the light of knowledge. Some degree of order is imposed upon the city's warring factions by fear, and only then is a place made ready for the kindling fire of love and for *Imān* (Faith), which Islam defines as the state in which the heart accepts the truth and lives by it, the lips and tongue make profession of the truth, and the limbs execute what is required of them by the truth. Beyond this is the knowledge which is equivalent to certainty, that is to say to direct vision. But the first of Muhammad's titles – his 'titles of Glory' – is not 'Messenger' or 'Prophet' but 'slave' (*'abd*), for man must be a slave to the truth before he can be its messenger, and the slave is, by definition, one who submits body and soul to his master, claiming no rights, asking no questions and owning nothing that he can call his own. It is for the master, if he will, to raise him to a higher status.

A great deal of misunderstanding has surrounded these images of submission. Partly from prejudice, but partly also from the genuine difficulty that one culture has in grasping the deepest motivations of another, the West has often pictured the Muslim as cringing before a tyrant Lord and submitting as a beast submits to its incomprehensible fate. Nothing could be further from the truth. The Muslim fears God because he is a realist; he knows that there are things to be feared and that all things – the bitter as well as the sweet – have but one Creator. He submits because he believes that there exists a divine pattern or scheme of things which is both intelligent and beautiful, and he wishes to find his place in this pattern and conform to it; he knows that he cannot do so without instructions – which must be followed meticulously in view of their sacred origin. He does not simply resign himself to the divine Will; he seeks it eagerly and, when he finds it, delights in it.[1]

In an autobiography written in the early 1950s, Muhammad Asad recounts an incident which brings this aspect of the Muslim perspective vividly to life. As a young man travelling through Sinai he came to an area ravaged by fierce winds and was entertained to a meal by the local village headman. 'May God give you life,' says his host; 'This house is your house; eat in the name of God. This is all we have, but the dates are not bad.' The dates proved to be the best Asad has ever tasted, and his host continues:

[1] In order to understand the 'inevitability' of everything that happens to us, it is essential to grasp the fact that 'my' destiny is as much a part of 'me' as the physical and psychological characteristics by which 'I' am identified. Certain mystical philosophers have personified Destiny, and from this point of view each man's personal destiny is his archetype or 'other self' – his 'angel' – with whom he must be reunited if he is to rise above his fragmentary identity as a worldling and become whole, as he is (and always has been) in the mind of God. Segmented by time, we are never truly ourselves in this life. Each being is unrolled, month by month, year by year, like a great carpet which cannot be viewed as a single coherent pattern until the whole is exposed; and to speak of this is, in fact, to speak of the 'Last Judgement'.

'The wind, the wind, it makes our life hard; but that is God's will. The wind destroys our plantations. We must always struggle to keep them from being covered by sand ... But we do not complain. As you know, the Prophet – may God bless him – told us: "God says, *Revile not destiny, for behold – I am destiny*".'

'Never,' says Asad, 'have I seen, even in a happy people, a "Yes" to reality expressed with so much quiet and sureness. With a wide, vague, almost sensual turn of his arm he describes a circle in the air – a circle which encompasses everything that belongs to this life: the poor, dusky room, the wind and its eternal roar, the relentless advance of the sands; longing for happiness and resignation to what cannot be changed; the platter full of dates; the struggling orchards behind their shield of tamarisks; the fire on the hearth; a young woman's laughter somewhere in the courtyard beyond: and in all these things, and in the gesture that has brought them out and together, I seem to hear the song of a strong spirit which knows no barriers of circumstance and is at peace with itself.'[1]

Submission, when it is submission to the truth – and when the truth is known to be both beautiful and merciful – has nothing in common with fatalism or stoicism as these terms are understood in the Western tradition, because its motivation is different. According to Fakhr ad-Dīn ar-Rāzī, one of the great commentators upon the Qurān: 'The worship of the eyes is weeping, the worship of the ears is listening, the worship of the tongue is praise, the worship of the hands is giving, the worship of the body is effort, the worship of the heart is fear and hope, and the worship of the spirit is surrender and satisfaction in Allah.'[2] There is a simple equation here: submission to destiny as it comes upon us out of the unknown equals *al-islām*, self-surrender to God, and this in turn equals worship, which is positive, active and joyful. Through our destiny God speaks to us, and through our worship we speak to Him.

In human experience submission is something that belongs to the realm of darkness, because we can find no simple explanation for the events and circumstances which seize us by the throat and impose themselves upon us – life is 'senseless' in rational terms – but through his submission the Muslim seeks light, assured that it is to be found at the end of the tunnel. Concerning the final reckoning, the Qurān says: 'On that Day thou wilt see the believers, men and women, their light shining before them ... The hypocritical men and the hypocritical women will say unto the believers: Look upon us that we may borrow from your light. It will be said: Go back and seek for light ... !' (Q.57.12–13). To surrender to the light given from beyond ourselves – to which the inner light responds – is to develop a passionate appetite for greater light. 'O Allah, appoint for me light in my heart and light before me and light behind me, light on my right hand and light on my left, light above me and light below me, light in my sight and light in my perception, light in my countenance and light in my flesh, light in my blood and light in my bones; increase for me light and give me light.'[3]

[1]*The Road to Mecca*, Muhammad Asad (Simon & Schuster, 1954), p. 93.
[2]Quoted by Constance Padwick in *Muslim Devotions* (S.P.C.K.)
[3]Padwick op. cit.

The first *Shahādah* – or first part of the confession of faith which identifies a man or woman as Muslim – states a truth which, from the human point of view, would remain an abstraction, though dazzling in its simplicity, if it had no sequel. It is therefore followed by these words: '... and I bear witness that *Muḥammadun rasūlu 'Llāh*, 'Muhammad is the messenger of God.'

The first testimony tells us that God alone truly *is*; the second that all things are related to Him. 'Truly unto Allah we belong and unto Him we return' (Q.2.156). The state of separation in which we live (and but for which we would not 'live' as we understand the term) is due to the veils which hide Him from our sight; but even in apparent separation we are never alone or unobserved; He sees not only our every action but our every thought; He is *al-Khabīr*, the Totally Aware, from whose all-embracing consciousness nothing is hidden. And after a very short time we return whence we came: 'And on the Day when He shall gather them together [it will seem to them] as if they had tarried [on earth] for no more than an hour ...' (Q.10.45). Our period of separation may then seem no more than a dream during a brief sleep (the Prophet is reported to have said: 'Men sleep, and when they die they awaken'), though our dream has been very real to us, since our experience offers us nothing more real that would provide a standard of comparison; it could not be otherwise, for the dream is willed and determined by That which is infinitely more real than we are, and it is shot through with images of what has its being elsewhere.

It could be said that the second *Shahādah* brings the first down to earth, and to deny the second would be to sever all connection with the first. The Prophet is by definition close to God, being His messenger; and 'the Prophet is closer to the believers than their own selves' (Q.35.6). He is therefore the link between Creator and creature.

The name Muhammad means 'the Glorified', and since he is a man and nothing more than a man, this indicates (among other things) the perfection and splendour of creation when it remains true to its Creator's intention – 'and God saw that it was good,' as the Book of Genesis tells us. He represents the human norm and is therefore the model for every Muslim. Without this model we would have no idea of how to conform, in our persons and in our lives, to the truth enunciated by the first *Shahādah*; and if he were a superhuman being, or an angel sent to preach to mankind, we could not attempt to imitate him and would not try to do so. It is because he is *bashar*, flesh and blood – poor mortal clay like us – that he is able to fulfil his exemplary function, though it is said of him that he is 'man, yet not as other men but as a jewel among stones'.

From fear of idolatry, and from fear of distracting the Muslim's attention from the single object of his worship, the Islamic perspective cannot tolerate any notion that implies, even remotely, the possibility of 'incarnation'; God does not become man since He does not 'become' in any sense of the word; He is, and always was and always will be. But He communicates to us something of what He is. The Prophet is reported to have said: 'Whosoever has seen me has seen the Truth.' The significance of this *ḥadīth* is explained by Frithjof Schuon in these terms: 'When the sun is reflected in a lake, one can distinguish firstly the sun, secondly the ray, and thirdly the reflection; it would be possible to discuss interminably whether a creature who saw only the reflection – the sun being hidden from sight by some obstacle – saw only the water or, on the contrary, really saw something of the sun. This much is indisputable: without the sun the water would not even be visible, and it would not carry any reflection what-soever; it is thus impossible to deny that whoever sees the reflected image of the sun thereby also sees "in a certain manner" the sun itself...'[1] No doubt 'interminable discussions' will continue on questions of this kind until the world ends and speech is silenced, but to break heads on account of definitions is an idle pursuit.

Muhammad is usually referred to in Arabic as the *rasūlu 'Llāh*, the 'messenger of God', whereas in Western usage the term 'prophet' (*nabī* in Arabic) is more common, no doubt because it is more familiar to those whose Scripture is the Bible. Islam makes a clear distinction between the two titles. A *rasūl* is one who receives a message from God and is commanded to declare this message publicly, so that it may provide a spiritual framework for a whole sector of humanity. The word *nabī* means 'one who has been informed' (or 'one who has received news'), and the information revealed to him may supplement an established religion with new insights or – as was the case with many of the Jewish prophets – correct distortions which had led to the decadence of an established religion. Every 'messenger' (Moses, Jesus, Muhammad and such others as may have appeared in the course of human history) is also a 'prophet', but not every 'prophet' is a 'messenger'.

The modern mentality, impatient of restraints and rigid frameworks as it is of rules and regulations, prefers the 'prophet' to the 'messenger'. Even in a country such as England, where practising Christians are in a minority, most people – according to recent surveys – claim to 'believe in a God', though they have no use for 'organized religion'. The poetry of prophetic utterance, all fire and ice, has immense attraction compared with 'religion', which is thought to imprison the free spirit and which is, in the last resort, dull; it puts duties in the place of feelings and it requires association with some very unattractive people. Poetry, however, does nothing to build a house in which uninspired men and women can live out their lives in terms of a revealed pattern for living, which may be one reason why the *Qurān* tells us specifically that Muhammad is 'not a poet'. What a 'messenger' brings to us is not only news from heaven but also the blueprint for an earthly structure which keeps us safe from hell.

As was mentioned earlier, Muhammad bears another title which is, as it were, the human basis for his function as messenger. He is *'abdu 'Llāh*, the 'slave of God'. Modern translators usually prefer the word 'servant' because of the ugly and even sinister connotations which the word 'slave' has in the West, due on the one hand to the racialism which was the basis of slavery in the Americas, and on the other to the cruelty and exploitation associated with it. Slavery in the simple society of ancient Arabia had none of these features and was not therefore a term of dishonour. Although the word 'servant' has obvious advantages in this context, it weakens and even

[1]*Dimensions of Islam*, Frithjof Schuon, p. 75.

falsifies the meaning of the Arabic term *'abd*. A servant works for his wages, he may depart if the conditions of his service do not please him, and he may, if he chooses, set his will against that of his employer. But God is not an employer, nor are His messengers employees. The 'slave of God' surrenders his will to that of his Master, exemplifying the quality of spiritual poverty (*faqr*) which lies at the very root of Islam.[1]

This quality of 'slavehood' – of obedient passivity – is a pre-condition of the messenger's activity in the world. The truth of the message itself would be brought into doubt if there were the slightest suspicion that a human will had intervened in the process of revelation. In his recorded sayings Muhammad spoke as the man he was and, except when he was directly inspired, acknowledged his own fallibility, but as the instrument by which the Qurān was conveyed from heaven to earth his aim was to be an attentive and accurate 'scribe'. He said: 'A simple verse of the Book of Allah is worth more than Muhammad and all his family,' and because his conduct in every aspect of daily life exemplified these qualities of receptivity and attentiveness, he was himself an aspect of this message from God to man. Seen from an unprejudiced Christian point of view, 'in its finest form, as exemplified by the Prophet himself and by such successors as 'Umar, this relation of the *'abd* to his Lord means a constant quality of consciousness and will unique to Islam;'[2] and in his translation of the Qurān, Muhammad Asad renders the key word *taqwah*, usually trans- lated as 'fear of God', as 'God-consciousness', thereby emphasizing the qualities of constant awareness, recollectedness and readiness which characterize the Muslim who is true to his faith.

Not only does the messenger who is also a slave subordinate his own will to that of his Lord; there is nothing in his mind or in his memory that could obstruct the free passage of the revelation. Muhammad is *'abd* and *rasūl*; he is also *nabī al-ummi*, the unlettered Prophet; a blank page set before the divine pen. On this page there is no mark made by any other pen, no trace of profane or indirect knowledge. A prophet does not borrow knowledge from the human store, nor is he a man who learns in the slow human way and then transmits his learning. His knowledge derives from a direct intervention of the Divine in the human order, a *tajalli*, or pouring out of the truth upon a being providentially disposed to receive it and strong enough to transmit it. The purity of the stream of revelation remains unsullied in its course from the spring which is its origin to the lake into which it flows; in other words, the Qurān exists in written form exactly as it issued from the divine Presence.

Just as the Catholic Church insists upon the primordial purity of the Virgin Mary, because it is through her that the Word of God was given to this world, so Islam insists that Muhammad was 'unlettered', that is to say uncontaminated by profane knowledge, by the arguments of the philoso- phers, by idolatry or by any worldly influence. This has been an area of constant misunderstanding between the two religions. Christians compare

---

[1]An alternative translation for *'abd* is 'bondsman'; a somewhat archaic term, but one that has the advantage of emphasizing the 'binding to God' which none escape, while avoiding the emotional connotations of slavery.

[2]*Call of the Minaret*, Rev. Kenneth Cragg, p. 46.

Muhammad to Jesus, always to the discredit of the former, because he is found to be unlike Jesus in so many ways, and they also compare the Qurān with the Bible; but, as Schuon and others have pointed out, the only legitimate comparison would be between the Prophet and Mary on the one hand and on the other between the Qurān and Jesus. For Christians the Word was made flesh, whereas for Muslims it took earthly shape in the form of a book, and the recitation of the Qurān in the ritual prayer fulfils the same function as the eucharist in Christianity; at the same time, Mary gave birth to Jesus without passing on to him any taint of earthly sin, and Muhammad acted as a channel for the Word without lending it any taint of merely human wisdom.

It is not as 'Saviour', let alone as divine incarnation, that Muslims love Muhammad and model themselves upon him, yet this love is central in the spiritual life of Islam, lending to an otherwise austere religion something that is at once passionate and gentle. He is loved for his courage and for his tenderness, not only as a warrior and a master of men, but also as the perfect husband, the perfect father and the perfect friend – and the humblest, most wretched man or woman, thinking of him, will dream of having such a friend. Those who were closest to him are known, not as 'disciples' but as 'companions'; almost fourteen centuries after his death, it is in this companionship that the Muslim finds comfort in loneliness and courage in adversity, and this world would be a cold and inhospitable place without him.

'No one', wrote Constance Padwick, a Christian caught in the net of this love, 'can estimate the power of Islam as a religion who does not take into account the love at the heart of it for this figure. It is here that human emotion, repressed at some points by the austerity of the doctrine of God as developed in theology, has its full outlet – a warm human emotion which the peasant can share with the mystic. The love of this figure is perhaps the strongest binding force in a religion which has so marked a binding power.'[1]

Century after century poems have been composed in praise of the Prophet, poems as fit to be chanted beside the cradle as beside the death-bed or in the assemblies of the faithful, expressing a devotion which often astonishes those who know only one side of Islam. They sometimes betray a profound nostalgia for that golden age in which every pious Muslim would have wished to live, not only for the sweet and noble companionship but also because, in retrospect, it is seen as a time when everything was as it should be – and as it has never been since. No detail of the Prophet's life, however trivial it might seem in worldly terms, is found unworthy of praise, and everything with which he came into contact has been, as it were, sanctified by his touch. There is a little Moroccan poem which conveys something of this quality of wonder. 'They sleep in the night of the grave, those women whose luminous hands wove Muhammad's cloak. Where – long whitening – are the bones of the sheep which gave their wool for Muhammad's cloak? Towards what stars have ascended the drops of water which rose as mist when the wool of those

---

[1]*Muslim Devotions*, Constance Padwick (S.P.C.K.), p. 145.

sheep lay drying in the sun? It was supple as smoke. When Muhammad (blessings and peace upon him) let it loose on the breeze you would have thought it a cloud billowing in the wind. It was transparent as air. And those who kissed its hem now drink from the streams which sing in Paradise, and Allah smiles upon them through all eternity.'[1] They are long gone, those women and those sheep and that cloak itself, and the world is bereft.

To love Muhammad is one thing, but to imitate him – to try to be 'like' him – is another. He was the last messenger and the last prophet, so how can we expect to imitate what is by definition unique and unrepeatable? In the first place his virtues are to be imitated, and they were providentially exemplified in the extraordinary variety of human experience through which he passed in his sixty-two years of life. He was an orphan, yet he knew the warmth of parental love through his grandfather's devoted care for him; he was the faithful husband of one wife for many years, and after her death, the tender and considerate husband of many wives; he was the father of children who gave him the greatest joy this world has to offer, and he saw all but one of them die; he had been a shepherd and a merchant when young, and he became a ruler, a statesman, a military commander, and a law-giver; he loved his native city and was driven from it into exile, finally to return home in triumph and set an example of clemency which has no equal in human history. Not only do we know almost everything that he did, we know the exact manner in which he did it.

But what of his function as the Messenger of God? The man who is truly what he should be is described in the Qurān as *al-khalīfatu 'Llāh fi'l-ardh*, the viceregent or representative of God on earth; he is not *rasūl*, since he does not receive the divine message directly from heaven, but he receives it none the less – mediated through Muhammad – and is required to convey it with equal accuracy and with a comparable purity of intention, allowing no personal opinions or feelings to intervene. In this sense, the pious Muslim performs – in a minor key – the task which the Prophet fulfilled on a universal scale.

But there is one of Muhammad's 'titles of Glory' in which every believer shares, the title of *'abd*. Muhammad was the perfect 'slave'. The believer must strive towards this perfection. Just as the Messenger could not have fulfilled his function had he not been the 'slave of God', so the viceregent is effective and true to his vocation only according to the depth and purity of his 'slavehood'.

With the assertion of man's viceregal status we step into dangerous territory. People need little enough encouragement to attribute grandeur to themselves. To tell them that they represent God on earth might seem like an invitation to megalomania. The modern age, sentimental and idealistic despite its superficial cynicism, is even more deeply shocked than were earlier ages by the human capacity for wickedness. This wickedness is indeed the measure of the grandeur of our vocation (no animal is wicked), and like a deep shadow it bears witness to a great light. The monstrous evils of arrogance and oppression are due to men assuming the robes of

---

[1]Quoted in *Maroc: Terre et Ciel* (Lausanne: La Guide du Livre, 1954).

'viceregency' without first submitting as 'slaves' (and knowing themselves to be 'slaves'). Man alone is capable of monstrosity on this scale, because man alone stands above – or is capable of standing above – the tide of time and contingency. It might even be said that if there were no viceregency there could be no hell, for none would merit hell. It is for the betrayal of our vocation – therefore self-betrayal – that we are punished, and it is for living beneath ourselves that we run the risk of being trodden underfoot.

The message which is to be conveyed in its integrity by the viceregent, as it was by the Messenger, has many facets, matched to the multi-faceted human personalities to whom it is addressed, but there is a golden thread which runs through the whole pattern of revelation and binds it together; this is the thread of mercy. Without the link provided by the second *Shahādah* and by the message – the Qurān – to which it relates, this world would be like a frozen planet, too far from the sun to receive its life-giving warmth; this link is therefore itself an aspect of mercy. 'We sent thee not save as a mercy to the worlds' (Q.21.107). One of Muhammad's titles is the 'Key to Mercy', and mercy is the quality which presides over the road leading to God. 'Ā'isha asked him: 'Does one come to Paradise only by the mercy of Allah?' He repeated three times over: 'No one comes to Paradise except by the mercy of Allah!' 'Not even you, Messenger of Allah?' she asked. 'Not even I, unless Allah enfolds me in His mercy.'

He told his companions: 'When Allah completed the creation He wrote the following, which is with Him above His Throne: "My mercy takes precedence over My wrath",' and this *hadith* is decisive for the Muslims; it states categorically that all the 'names' and attributes by which the Qurān indicates various aspects of the divine nature as they relate to humanity are subordinate to this supreme and essential attribute.

A desert Arab, seeing the Prophet kiss his grandson, al-Hasan, said contemptuously: 'What, do you kiss children? We never do so!' to which the Prophet replied: 'I cannot help you, for Allah has withdrawn mercy from your heart.' Speaking in the first person in the Qurān, God says: 'My mercy embraceth all things' (Q.7.156), and this mercy communicates itself to those who are receptive: 'Indeed, those who believe and do good, the Merciful will endow them with loving kindness (*wuddan*)' (Q.19.96); and: 'Who else but those who have lost their way could despair of the mercy of their Lord?' (Q.15.56).[1]

After the two *Shahādahs*, the formula most frequently on the lips of the Muslim is the *Basmillāh*: 'In the name of Allah the Merciful (*ar-Rahmān*), the compassionate (*ar-Rahīm*),' and it is with this formula that every chapter of the Qurān (with one exception) opens. The world itself, we are told by some authorities, was created by 'the Breath (or Exhalation) of *ar-Rahmān*'. It is, according to this view, through the innate expansive and radiating power of mercy, its impulse to give itself and to bestow its

---

[1] According to a *hadith* recorded by both Bukharī and Muslim, some captives were brought to the Prophet, among them a woman whose breasts oozed milk. She ran to and fro, and when she found her child, put him at once to her breast. The Prophet said to his companions, 'Do you think this woman will cast her child into the fire?' When they replied that she would not, he said: 'God is more merciful to His servants than this woman to her child.'

light and its warmth, that creation and all that appears to be outward and separate comes into being; and while, by definition, God has no needs – being totally self-sufficient – yet it might be said, if only as a figure of speech, that He has a need to communicate Himself, because His inmost nature is this radiating mercy, this richness which cries out to be displayed in phenomena more numerous than all the sands of all the oceans. Because the *Basmillāh* has been pronounced over creation as such, the Muslim pronounces it before embarking upon any action, thereby sanctifying the action and re-attaching it to its true Cause – but for which it would be as empty and as futile as the convulsive movements of a corpse.

The Sufis, dazzled by this mercy, have sometimes seen it as all-encompassing not only in principle but also in the most immediate and practical sense. It is related of the Persian Abu'l-Hasan Khurqānī (d. AD 1033) that one night when he was praying he heard a voice from heaven: 'O Abu'l-Hasan! Dost thou wish me to tell the people what I know of thy inward state, so that they may stone thee to death?' 'O Lord God,' he replied, 'dost Thou wish me to tell the people what I know of Thy mercy and what I perceive of Thy grace, so that none of them may ever again bow to Thee in prayer?'[1] 'Keep thy secret,' said the voice, 'and I will keep Mine.'[2] But the more general view is that mercy responds only when repentance invites it to do so, and that the unrepentant – 'covered' as they are, their hearts sealed in rust – are impenetrable.

In Arabic the three consonants RHM, from which the word *rahmah* (mercy) and its derivatives, *ar-Rahmān* (the Merciful) and *ar-Rahīm* (the Compassionate), are formed, have the primary meaning of 'womb', which indicates very clearly the maternal character of mercy, nurturing and protecting the helpless human creature in its gentle embrace. In a related language, Syriac, this same root has the meaning of 'love'.

It is said that *ar-Rahmān* is like the blue sky, serene and full of light, which arches over us and over all things, whereas *ar-Rahīm* is like a warm ray coming from that sky, touching individual lives and events and vivifying the earth. According to the Qurān, 'the Merciful revealed the Qurān, created man, taught him articulate speech,' and it could be said that if God, the One (*al-Ahad*), were not also *ar-Rahmān*, there would be no creation, no outwardness, but only the eternally self-sufficient inwardness of the divine essence; and if He were not also *ar-Rahīm*, the whole creation would turn to ice. Indeed, the man or woman in whom there is no mercy, no compassion, is one whose heart is frozen and can be melted only by fire.

If *ar-Rahmān* is simply what is there – a sky full of light – then it might also be translated as 'joy', and joy by its very nature is expansive and communicates itself; in this case *ar-Rahīm* represents that act of communication. This has an application to all human acts of communication, including art, hence the Quranic reference to 'speech' in the context of

[1] According to a *hadīth* recorded by Bukhari and Muslim, the Prophet said on one occasion that the believer has a right to expect from God that He should not punish anyone who is free from the sin of associating other 'deities' with Him. A man asked: 'Shall I give this good news to the people?' 'No,' said the Prophet, 'do not tell them lest they trust in this alone.'
[2] *Mystics of Islam*, R. A. Nicholson (Routledge & Kegan Paul), p. 136.

'creation by the Merciful'. Between human beings, separated in this world by such barriers – each little ego in its own shell – communication is the mercy which unites, the instrument of love, as is sacred art, and as such it gives a foretaste of Paradise. We speak and, if we are understood, a wall of ice has been melted and from it flow streams like those which water the gardens of Paradise.

But communication between the Infinite and the finite, the Absolute and the contingent, seems logically impossible and therefore qualifies, in the proper sense of the term, as a miracle, which is why the Qurān is called the supreme miracle of Islam. Across unimaginable distances God speaks to man and is heard, and what cannot be described in words, as we describe a tree or a house, is none the less described, not so that we should stop at the surface meaning like animals, which see only what is to be seen, but like a bait to draw us out of this universe of words into a universe of meaning. There is a Muslim invocation which suggests something of this miracle: 'O Thou who art described though no description reaches Thy true being; Thou who art absent from us in mystery yet never lost; Thou Seer who art never seen; Thou who art sought and found; neither the heavens nor the earth nor the space between is void of Thee for the flicker of an eyelid; Thou art the Light of lights, the Lord of lords, encompassing all. Glory to Him whom nothing resembles; the All-Hearer, the All-Seer.'

PART II

The Making of the Faith

Chapter 4

THE WORLD OF
THE BOOK

There is ground to be cleared before we can have any hope of coming close to the Qurān; thorny ground, all the more difficult to negotiate because the thorn trees are not immediately visible. In every religious tradition and in every ancient legend sacred things and sacred places are closely guarded, approachable only through effort and purification. The Qurān is no exception.

So far as the occidental's misunderstanding of Islam is concerned it starts here, at the source of the religion. The non-Muslim who – for whatever reason – wishes to learn something about Islam is encouraged to take in his hands a 'translation' of the Qurān, of which there are said to be at least thirty in English alone. He has been told – and rightly so – that this book is the foundation of the Faith, and that in it he will find all he needs to know about the Muslim, his beliefs, his motivation, his political aspirations and his cultural conditioning. The reader may set off with the best intentions, seeking wisdom as he understands this term and aware that a book which has meant so much to so many cannot be devoid of interest. The outcome is only too often bafflement and disappointment.

There is nothing here that accords with the occidental's sense of order; on the contrary, he finds only a world of words which seems totally incoherent and to which he has no key. We have come yet again to the gulf of incomprehension which divides two religions, two mentalities, two cultures. On the one hand, the simple Muslim cannot understand why anyone who reads the Qurān is not immediately converted to Islam; on the other, the non-Muslim is inclined to feel that, if this is what Muslims regard as a sacred scripture, then they must indeed be simple-minded.

Since many of those who set out to read the Qurān in translation give up before they are half-way through the book, the order in which the *Sūrahs*, the 'chapters', are arranged reinforces this negative impression. The revelation of the text took place over a period of twenty-two or twenty-three years. The earlier and more 'poetic' revelations come towards the end of the book, whereas the later ones, dealing with what are seen as 'mundane' issues, are placed at the beginning. The former approximate more closely to what the occidental expects since they are 'prophetic' in character and in language, dealing with the end of the world, the final destiny of man and so on, whereas in the latter the element 'message' overshadows the element 'prophecy'. Thus the book presents a mirror-image of the process of revelation or 'descent'. The reason for this may be that man, in responding to the revelation and following the way of 'ascent' to which he is called, starts out from the realm of practical affairs and needs to know how to behave in his worldly life before he sets foot on the path which leads beyond this world.

There is, however, a more formidable barrier which faces the reader of a 'translation' of the Qurān, the barrier of language. The power and efficacy of the revealed message reside not only in the literal meaning of the words employed but also in the body in which this meaning is incorporated. It is not only the content but also the container that constitutes the revelation as such, and the two cannot be separated — as they are in translation — without impoverishment.

The Qurān defines itself specifically as an 'Arabic scripture', and the message is shaped to the complex structure of the chosen language, a structure fundamentally different to that of any European tongue. Even if one understands no Arabic – as is the case with the vast majority of Muslims – it is essential to know how meaning and language, essence and form, are married in the text of the Qurān.

Every Arabic word may be traced back to a verbal root consisting of three consonants from which are derived up to twelve different verbal modes, together with a number of nouns and adjectives. This is referred to as the triliteral root, and specific words are formed from it by the insertion of long or short vowels and by the addition of suffixes and prefixes. The root as such is 'dead' – unpronounceable – until brought to life, that is to say vocalized, by the vowels, and it is according to their placing that the basic meaning is developed in a number of different directions. The root has sometimes been described as the 'body' while the vowelling is the 'soul'; or again, it is from the root that a great tree grows. 'In Arabic,' says Titus Burckhardt, 'the "tree" of verbal forms, of derivations from certain roots, is quite inexhaustible; it can always bring forth new leaves, new expressions to represent hitherto dormant variations of the basic idea – or action. This explains why this Bedouin tongue was able to become the linguistic vehicle of an entire civilization intellectually very rich and differentiated.'[1]

A certain ambiguity is inherent in language as such because it is alive and forms a bridge between living and thinking beings. The opposite to the bare precision of mathematics is not vagueness of definition but a wealth of interconnected meanings, sometimes merging into one another, always enriching each other, which cluster around a single basic idea (or, in Arabic, a simple action) – in this case the triliteral root. Such variations upon a single theme may give rise to words which appear, on the surface, unconnected. Awareness of their relationship to their root makes the connection apparent, so that the whole 'extended family' of words is illuminated.

This may be illustrated in terms of a word referred to earlier, *fiṭrah* (primordial nature). The root FTR gives us, in the first place, the verb

[1] *Art of Islam: Language and Meaning*, Titus Burckhardt (World of Islam Festival Publishing Co. Ltd), p. 43.

faṭara, meaning 'he split', 'he broke apart', 'he brought forth' or 'he created'. The connection between 'splitting' and 'creating' is interesting, particularly if we bear in mind the element of continuity so characteristic of Islam; ancient traditions from many different cultures describe the first step in creation as the 'breaking apart' of heaven and earth. God is referred to in the Qurān as *faṭīr as-samāwāti wa'l-ardh*, Creator (or 'Originator') of the heavens and the earth. From the same root we have the *'Īd ul-fiṭr*, the festival which marks the end of the sacred month of Ramadan, and *iftār*, meaning 'breakfast'. Among other derivations there are *faṭr*, a 'crack' or 'fissure', *fiṭrī*, 'natural' or 'instinctive', and *faṭīrah*, 'unleavened bread or pastry', fresh and life-giving.

It is as though each individual word emerged from a matrix which contains, potentially, a variety of meanings that are all subtly interrelated, or as though, when one string is plucked, many others vibrate in the background; and it is precisely through such interrelationships that *tawḥīd* – the 'unity' which is the basic principle of Islam – finds expression in the midst of limitless diversity. Word associations – echoes and reverberations in the ear and in the mind – provide a glimpse of unsuspected depths and extend our perception of the interconnectedness of all things. According to Muhammad, there is no verse in the Qurān which does not have an inner as well as an outer aspect, together with a number of different meanings, and every definition is potentially a source of enlightenment. In other words, the Book is full of 'doors' out of the prison of this world into the 'open'. Islamic art bears witness to this. Writing of the significance of the 'palmettes' (little palm trees) placed in the margins of illuminated copies of the Qur'ān, Martin Lings identifies them as reminders 'that the reading or chanting of the Qurān is the virtual starting-point of a limitless vibration, a wave that ultimately breaks on the shore of eternity; and it is above all *that* shore that is signified by the margin, towards which all the movement of the painting – in palmette, finial, crenellation and flow of arabesque – is directed.'[1]

It is in the nature of a primordial language such as Arabic that a single word should imply all possible modes of an idea, from the concrete to the symbolical and, indeed, the supernatural. The barriers which occidental man places between the spiritual and the mundane are, as it were, pierced by the language itself. An effort of the imagination is required of those accustomed only to English or other hybrid languages, in which a noun indicates a thing in isolation from all others, if they wish to enter the world of the Qurān. Not only were the objects of nature saturated with meaning for the men of earlier times, but language itself reflected this richness, and it is said that the Arabic of the seventh century AD was more ancient in form even than the Hebrew spoken by Moses nearly two thousand years previously;[2] it is imbued with qualities which lie outside all our frames of reference and all our limiting definitions, and it is this above all that made it the appropriate vehicle for the revelation of unity in multiplicity.

It follows that a 'translation', however excellent it may be in its own way

[1] *The Quranic Art of Calligraphy and Illumination*, Martin Lings (World of Islam Festival Trust Publishing Co. Ltd.), p. 74.
[2] See *Ancient Beliefs and Modern Superstitions*, Martin Lings (London, 1964), p. 14.

and however useful as an aid to understanding, is not and cannot be the Qurān, and it is not treated as such. No Muslim will place a copy of the Arabic Qurān under other books or beneath any object on a table or a desk; it must always occupy the highest place. We may do as we please with a translation, and this would still be so even if it conveyed the principles of the Quranic message with impeccable accuracy.

The distinction between revelation and inspiration – even inspiration which has its origin in the divine – is of fundamental importance in Islam, and this can be another cause of confusion for the occidental who has been told that the Qurān is the Muslim 'Bible'. The Old Testament contains material attributable to a number of different authors extending over a very long period of time, sometimes directly inspired and sometimes indirectly, while the New Testament is comparable to the 'traditions' of the Prophet, his acts and sayings, rather than to the Qurān as such. The Bible is a coat of many colours. The Qurān is a single fabric to which nothing can be added and from which nothing can be abstracted.

In the Muslim view, revelation bypasses human intelligence and the limitations of that intelligence, whereas inspiration enlightens intelligence but does not abolish its limitations; an inspired work is still a work of human authorship. The orthodox view in Islam is that the Qurān is 'uncreated', although – as the book we hold in our hands – its mode of expression is necessarily determined by human contingencies. The celestial Qurān, the fullness of wisdom that is with God and remains with Him everlastingly, contains intentions which, in our earthly experience, may be expressed through a variety of created facts and events. It is as though a heavenly substance, itself inarticulate, were crystallized in a language and in modes of thought determined by its predestined milieu.

There is, however, an incalculable disproportion between the truth as such and the slender resources of human language and of the mentalities to which it relates. Even in the most ordinary circumstances we, as human creatures, find it difficult enough to express our deepest feelings in speech with any degree of accuracy, or to convey to other people the precise outlines of ideas which are quite clear in our own minds, even though this speech is a tool fitted to our needs. How much more difficult, then, for God to express the wealth of meaning He wishes to convey in the language of men. It is shredded, it bends and cracks, under this burden; and we find again and again in the Qurān unfinished sentences or the omission of words required to complete the sense of a passage (words usually supplied in brackets by the translators), gaps over which our understanding must make a leap in the dark. 'It is,' says Frithjof Schuon, 'as though the poverty-stricken coagulation which is the language of mortal man were, under the formidable pressure of the heavenly Word, broken into a thousand fragments or as if God, in order to express a thousand truths, had but a dozen words at His command and so was compelled to make use of allusions heavy with meaning, of ellipses, abridgements and symbolical syntheses.'[1]

'And if all the trees on earth were pens, and the sea – with seven seas

[1] *Understanding Islam*, Frithjof Schuon (George Allen & Unwin), pp. 44–45.

added – [were ink] yet the words of Allah could not be exhausted' (Q.31.27). For the Qurān to contain more than a thimbleful of the message it must rely upon images, symbols and parables which open windows on to a vast landscape of meaning, but which are inevitably liable to misinterpretation. The Prophet's wives once asked him which of them would be the first to die. 'The one with the longest arm!' he said. They set about measuring each other's arms with great seriousness, and not until long afterwards did they understand that he meant the one who extended her arm furthest in acts of charity. There have always been Muslims who, like the Prophet's wives, have taken figures of speech literally and others who have maintained that the inner meaning of the text will be revealed to us only on the Last Day, when the secrets of hearts are exposed together with the secrets of the Book; others, again, have regarded the literal meaning as a veil covering the majesty of the content and protecting it from profane eyes. The disputes which have arisen on this subject lead nowhere and are therefore of no consequence. Each man must follow his way according to his nature.

But in whatever sense it may be understood – superficially or in depth – a scripture such as the Qurān provides a rope of salvation for people of every kind, the stupid as well as the intelligent, and limited interpretations do not diminish its efficacy, provided they satisfy the needs of particular souls. No book of human authorship can be 'for everyone', but this is precisely the function of a revealed scripture, and for this reason it cannot be read in the way that works of human origin are read. The sun and the moon are for everyone – the rain too – but their action in relation to each individual is different and, ultimately, to some they bring life and to some death. It could be said that the Qurān is 'like' these natural phenomena, but it would be more exact to say that they are 'like' the Qurān (they have one and the same 'author') and are, as it were, illustrations inserted between the pages of the Book.

It is an article of faith in Islam that the Qurān is 'inimitable'; try as he may, no man can write a paragraph that is comparable with a verse of the revealed Book. This has little to do with the literary merit of the text; in fact a perfect work of literature could never be 'sacred' precisely on account of the adequacy of its language to its content. No conjunction of words, however excellent, could ever be adequate to a revealed content. It is the efficacy of the words – their transforming and saving power – that is inimitable, since no human being can provide others with a rope of salvation made from strands of his own person and his own thoughts. The Qurān, set on a shelf with other books, has a function entirely different to theirs and exists in a different dimension. It moves an illiterate shepherd to tears when recited to him, and it has shaped the lives of millions of simple people over the course of almost fourteen centuries; it has nourished some of the most powerful intellects known to the human record; it has stopped sophisticates in their tracks and made saints of them, and it has been the source of the most subtle philosophy and of an art which expresses its deepest meaning in visual terms; it has brought the wandering tribes of mankind together in communities and civilizations upon which its imprint is apparent even to the most casual observer. The Muslim, regardless of race and national identity, is unlike anyone else because he has undergone the impact of the Qurān and has been formed by it.

Other books are passive, the reader taking the initiative, but revelation is an act, a command from on high – comparable to a lightning flash, which obeys no man's whim. As such, it acts upon those who are responsive to it, reminding them of their true function as viceregents of God on earth, restoring to them the use of faculties which have become atrophied – like unused muscles – and showing them, not least by the example of the Prophet, what they are meant to be. To say this is to say that revelation, within the limits of what is possible in our fallen condition, restores to us the condition of *fiṭrah*. It gives back to the intelligence its lost capacity to perceive and to comprehend supernatural truths, it gives back to the will its lost capacity to command the warring factions in the soul, and it gives back to sentiment its lost capacity to love God and to love everything that reminds us of Him.

It could never be said that the Qurān does not exist to inform, indeed the Book itself asserts that this is one of its functions, but it is very much more than a source of information. It exercises its effect not only upon the mind but on the very substance of the believer, although it can do this only in its integral character, that is to say as the Arabic Qurān. For the listener the sound – and for the reader the script – have a profound transforming effect. The modernist would no doubt suggest that this effect is exercised upon the 'unconscious'. This is to introduce ideas and theories which have no place here, but it could be said that there is an effect upon regions of the personality which are in practice concealed from conscious thought or control. Again, when we refer to the human 'substance' what is meant is not merely the sum total of our faculties, but also the substratum which finds expression in these faculties. Because the Qurān is the divine Word (in which we ourselves originated) it is able to fill every crevice of our being and, in a sense, to replace the debris which previously filled that space with something of heavenly origin.

The Prophet said: 'A believer who recites the Qurān is like a citron whose fragrance is sweet and whose taste is sweet...,' and he said also that 'he who learns it and goes to sleep having it within him is like a bag with musk tied up in it.' When he told his companions that 'hearts become rusty just as iron does when water gets at it' and they asked him how this rust was to be removed, he replied: 'By frequent remembrance of death and frequent recitation of the Qurān.'[1]

The Qurān, says Frithjof Schuon, is like a world of multiplicity which leads directly to the underlying unity. 'The soul, which is accustomed to the flux of phenomena, yields to this flux without resistance; it lives in phenomena and it is by them divided and dispersed ... The revealed Discourse has the virtue that it accepts this tendency while at the same time

---

[1] According to Ibn Mas'ud (a Companion of the Prophet), anyone who has learned the Qurān and holds it lovingly in his heart will 'value his nights when people are asleep, his days when people are given to excess, his grief when people are joyful, his weeping when people laugh, his silence when people chatter and his humility when people are arrogant'. In other words every moment of life will be precious to him, and he should therefore be 'gentle', never harsh nor quarrelsome, 'nor one who makes a clamour in the market nor one who is quick to anger'.

reversing the movement on account of the celestial nature of the content and the language, so that the fishes of the soul swim without distrust and with their habitual rhythm into the divine net ... The Qurān is like a picture of everything the human brain can think and feel, and it is by this means that God exhausts human disquiet, infusing into the believer silence, serenity and peace.'[1]

The faithful Muslim, therefore, lives simultaneously in two worlds: the first is that of common experience and the business of time; the second, which he enters when, as a newborn baby, he hears the words of the *Shahādah* recited in his ear, is the world of the Book. As a child he learns sections of the Qurān, he recites it in his prayers when he is old enough to pray and, if he is fortunate, he dies listening to its recital. At the same time, the world of common experience is vivified by the Quranic formulas constantly introduced into everyday speech.

The Westerner, whether Christian or agnostic, says 'Thank God' or 'Goodbye' – 'God be with you' – or even 'God willing', but these words have for the most part been emptied of meaning. There are many decadent Muslims who use Quranic phrases in an equally thoughtless way, but there is little doubt that the vast majority, when they say *al-ḥamdu li 'Llāh* ('God be praised'), know exactly what they are saying and mean it. This phrase ends and sanctifies every action, just as the *Basmillāh* ('In the name of Allah, the Merciful, the Compassionate') inaugurates action. *Allāhu akbar*, which is like a paraphrase of the first *Shahādah*, indicates not only that 'God is most great' but also that He is incomparably greater than any imaginable greatness. Under all possible circumstances it reminds us of the insignificance of the human before the Divine, the weakness of the mightiest human power before Omnipotence, and the littleness of everything that is other than God. It may also express the awe which the pious man feels when he looks upon the wonders of creation; and without a sense of awe there is no piety.

By the words *in shā'a Allāh*, 'God willing', the Muslim recognizes his total dependence upon the divine Will and acknowledges that he can make no firm plans nor commit himself irrevocably to any course, since he is not the master of his own destiny. We may express an intention or a hope, but no valid predictions can be made regarding future events still hidden in the womb of the unseen and known only to God. This and other such phrases, punctuating every conversation, are like little flags – reminders of transcendence – pinned on a wall-map along the route we take between birth and death, adding an extra dimension to its otherwise flat surface.

The believer is commanded not to approach the Qurān 'in haste', just as he is told not to run to the communal prayers, even if he is late in joining the congregation; for it is said that slowness and deliberation come from God, whereas haste is of satanic origin. In the *Sūrah* called *al-Furqān* the definition of true Muslims includes those who, 'whenever they are reminded of their Lord's messages, do not fling themselves upon them [as if] deaf and blind' (Q.25.73); who, in the words of the commentator

[1]*Understanding Islam*, Frithjof Schuon (George Allen and Unwin), p. 50.

Zamakhsharī, 'listen to it with wide-awake ears and look into it with seeing eyes'. The Qurān holds up a mirror to those who approach it, and if they come to it for the wrong reasons or in the wrong spirit, they will find nothing there. If they are by nature superficial they will find in it only superficialities, and if profound, profundities in corresponding measure. If they come arrogantly they will interpret certain verses as justification for their arrogance – it is true enough that 'the devil can quote Scripture' – and if they seek immediate personal reward they will be rewarded with bitter fruit.

Jalāluddīn Rūmī (d. AD 1273) compared the Book to a bride, unwilling to lift her veil before a rough and importunate lover; and most importunate of all are those who seek to plumb its depths without effort, patience or humility. It is no mere figure of speech to say that those who wish to win the Qurān must indeed woo it, and the illiterate man who wears a verse around his neck as a 'talisman', and who lovingly kisses the Book he cannot read, may be closer to the truth than is the casual reader.

We are told that when Adam and Eve had been expelled from Paradise, 'Adam received from his Lord words [of revelation], and He accepted his repentance, for indeed He alone is the Relenting, the Merciful. We said: Go down together from hence, but certainly there cometh to you guidance from Me; and as for those who follow My guidance, no fear shall come upon them neither shall they grieve' (Q.2.37–38).

The precondition for receiving this guidance, or at least for profiting from it, is awareness of our need, awareness of the fact that we cannot hope to find our way across the landscape of our lives by the use of purely human faculties. For the Muslim – as for the Christian of earlier times – it is axiomatic that reason and logic go to work on material provided, in the first instance, by the Creator. To say this is to expose the triviality of 'modern' thought, philosophy and theorizing, which attempt to operate in a vacuum, dealing only with the facts of the physical environment, if facts they are. Reason is not a source of knowledge but an instrument for dealing with knowledge. It does not contain within itself any substance upon which it could operate (*pace* Descartes' '*cogito ergo sum*'), but works with material supplied from elsewhere – by revelation, intellectual intuition, or the senses. For us to be able to say, '*This* is true, therefore *that* must follow,' '*this*' must be supplied. To insist that reason is true to itself only when it operates on the observed phenomena of this world is to restrict its function inexcusably.

The antithesis between revelation and reason, so frequently debated, is surely a false one. Reason does not become something different simply because it is put to work on information supplied supernaturally rather than by the physical senses; it is still the same faculty, and its function is unchanged. A knife is made for cutting substances. If no substance is provided, it remains unemployed and unemployable. And what is commonly described as 'rationalism' has little to do with reason as such; it indicates no more than the assumption, in itself irrational, that only the objects of the senses are 'real' and that these alone are the proper objects of rational consideration.

What is really at issue, in the context of rationalism, is a deep-seated conviction that only the physical senses provide information that is certain and unquestionable, a conviction which persists in the popular mind in spite of the fact that science, in this century, has in effect demolished the concept of 'solid matter' as it is commonly understood. This attitude of mind has to do with what René Guénon described as the 'solidification' of the world – and of the way in which the world is experienced – in the last days of our cycle of time.[1] Perhaps the first step towards faith in our age is a thoroughgoing scepticism, which pours its corrosive acid upon false certainties and brings awareness that we are like swimmers in an ocean amidst waves which change their shape from moment to moment and offer no hold to our grasping fingers. It is only when we are truly 'at sea' that we learn to distinguish between what is enduring and what is ephemeral.

Sooner or later in the course of considering Islam, not only as it is in itself – unique and self-sufficient – but also in relation to other religions, it becomes necessary to raise a question which admits of no simple answer. 'Who' revealed the Qurān? In other words, do Muslims believe in a 'personal' God as Christians understand this term? To say that the answer depends upon what we mean by 'personal' is true enough but does not take us very far. The Revealer of the Qurān – *Allāh* – is ultimately indefinable within the categories of human thought, let alone those of language. Definitions apply to created things, and He is the Creator. What His hands have made – and even the use of the word 'hands' immediately demonstrates that all talk of God is figurative – cannot grasp Him. The 'most beautiful names' applied to Him in the Qurān indicate aspects of His nature, but they do not tell us what He is in Himself. 'No vision encompasseth Him, yet He encompasseth all vision. He is the Subtle, the Aware' (Q.6.103).

An aspect of the Qurān which the non-Muslim finds particularly confusing is its use of pronouns. The Revealer speaks as 'I', 'We' and 'He', and these pronouns are often closely juxtaposed: '*He* is One God, so of *Me* stand in awe' (Q.16.51). Strictly speaking such pronouns are applicable only to finite creatures. Just when we are ready – in our anxiety to reduce 'Him' to a manageable concept – to settle upon a precise definition of the Divine, 'He' evades us. Having done so, He none the less permits us to approach Him through concepts. According to a *hadīth qudsī*, one of the Prophet's sayings in which God spoke through him: 'I am as My servant thinks I am, and I am with him when He remembers Me' (an alternative translation of this immensely significant saying would be: 'I am with the opinion My servant has of Me, and I am with him when he makes mention of Me'). The Andalusian mystic Ibn 'Arabī, with a daring that has shocked the orthodox ever since, said that what the ordinary believer worships is an image he himself has made – or 'projected' – and that God, in His mercy, accepts to be present in this image. However distasteful this idea may be to many Muslims, it does preserve what might be called the divine 'anonymity' while making God accessible to worship. For the Western unbeliever, who has been persuaded that concepts of the Divine (including

[1]See *The Reign of Quantity and the Signs of the Times*, René Guénon, (Luzac & Co., London).

'God' as such) are 'projections' of the human mind, it may even be enlightening.

In Islam it cannot be said that God is 'not a Person', for this would suggest that He is in some way less than this. Language offers no means of describing what is both personal and infinitely more than personal, which is why anthropomorphism is sometimes called an 'allusion' or 'indication' (*ishārah*); there is a subtle but very important distinction between an 'allusion' on the one hand and, on the other, a definition. The same might be said of the many Quranic references to God as 'seeing' and 'hearing'. Our human faculties of sight and hearing are indications, however remote, of something inherent in the divine nature; and yet they are no more than dim reflections of what is fully itself only in God. He 'sees' everything – even, so we are told, an ant under a rock on a dark night – whereas we see only what is before our eyes, with their very limited range. He 'hears' the rustling of every leaf and the secret thoughts of His creatures; we hear only sounds that are either very loud or very close to us. *We* have the use of these faculties only because *He* has them, but we have them in so limited a form that only by courtesy can we be said to see and to hear. From the same point of view, it could be said that God is supremely a Person, whereas our personal identity trembles on the edge of dissolution and it is only divine courtesy that permits us to say 'I'.

In Christianity, as the Muslim sees it, God has been personalized, even 'humanized', to such a degree that this has become the dominant element in the religion. Profound ideas – and the concept of the divine Person is certainly profound – are eventually simplified to the point of crudity, and Christian personalism has been one of the principal causes of unbelief and agnosticism in the modern age. For many people in the West, 'God loves me' has been take to mean that a person 'just like you and me' – only more powerful – situated in some unimaginable place loves us in the way human beings love; from this it is a very short step to asking how such a person can allow us to suffer as we do and why, if he is omnipotent, he has not created a perfect and pain-free world. There are, of course, no answers to such questions on the level on which they are asked.

The Muslim, when he oversimplifies, tends to see God as a mighty King who does as he pleases for entirely inscrutable reasons and of whom we have no right to ask questions. This image may be no less inadequate than that of the loving and indulgent Father, but in strictly practical terms it seems to protect faith more effectively than does the contemporary Christian concept. The fact remains, however, that all the images we make – serviceable as they may be to human needs – are inadequate and therefore vulnerable to the sceptic's arguments.

Having asked 'who' the Revealer is, we may then ask to whom the revelation is given. 'Had We caused this Qurān to descend upon a mountain, thou wouldst indeed have seen it humbled and cleft asunder from fear of Allah. Such images do We coin for mankind that perhaps they may reflect' (Q.58.21). But it descended upon a man, and he was not cleft asunder, since he was the predestined recipient of this knowledge. Inspiration comes to men diluted or, as it were, softened; but revelation is naked power – an in-break of reality into the world of appearances. Nothing distinguishes man more clearly from the rest of creation than the fact that he alone of all things made is capable of withstanding this shock and absorbing the divine message into himself without being crushed.

Yet this is only one aspect of the burden which the human creature bears – the burden which makes him human – and he bears it, not on account of some arbitrary divine decree, but as something freely accepted. 'We offered the Trust (*amānah*) to the heavens and the earth and the mountains, but they demurred from bearing it and feared to do so. It was man who bore it...' (Q.33.72). The mountains represent firmness and stability and are true to these qualities in which they were created; the earth, with all its variety, obeys the natural laws to which it is subject; and the heavens, whether as celestial space or as the realm of the angelic powers, obey the divine Will and do not deviate from it. There have been many different opinions as to the precise nature of this 'trust', but in general it represents those qualities which distinguish man from the rest of creation: reflexive consciousness, a will that is relatively free, the capacity to choose between good and evil, and an awareness to which no limits are set. The supreme trust was given to the open-eyed creature, capable of choice and, for that very reason, capable of betrayal. As such he receives the revelation, and as such he is shown the law of his being, not as animals receive it (through irresistible instinct) but as a guidance which he may freely accept or reject.

When he betrays this trust he has broken his word. The Qurān speaks of what is known as 'the Day of *Alast*'. 'And when thy Lord brought forth from the children of Adam, from their loins, their descendants, and made them testify concerning themselves [saying]: Am I not your Lord (*Alastu bi rabbikum*)? They said: Yea, truly, we testify!' (Q.7.172); and the passage concludes by explaining that this is 'lest you should claim on the Day of Resurrection that you were unaware of this, or lest you should claim: Our fathers ascribed partners to Allah from ancient times, and we are descended from them.' In other words, we have by our very nature – because we are what we are – committed ourselves even before our conscious life began.

A great part of the Qurān is devoted to the story – or series of stories – of the conflict between faith and infidelity, or between those who were true to this commitment and those who betrayed it. On the one hand we follow the unceasing struggle of Muhammad against the pagans of Mecca; on the other, we are told tales of earlier prophets, both Jewish and Arab, who brought the gift of revelation to their peoples and were rejected and persecuted. The great drama of God's self-revelation to the Semites is unfolded, and beside it all profane history could be said to record little more than the scuttling of mice in a larder.

It has been remarked, as a curiosity, that one of the earliest Muslim historians devoted the major section of his history of the world to the story of Yūsuf (the Biblical Joseph), while dismissing the rise and fall of the Roman Empire in a couple of pages. This order of priorities is entirely understandable, for the real history of humankind has little to do with newspaper headlines, or with the events that would have made headlines. There is an unobserved, almost unrecorded history that is ultimately more significant than the succession of day-to-day events, which are soon scattered like ashes in the wind. Who now cares that such-and-such a great king lived and died long ago? Whereas the story of the prophets is timeless and is presented as such in the Qurān, with an indifference to chronology that has disturbed many Western orientalists.

They have been disturbed also by the apparent contradiction between the claim that Muhammad was 'unlettered' and the inclusion in the Qurān of stories and 'legends' – sometimes of Biblical origin – which were part of the cultural heritage of the Arabs. A false alternative is put forward: either he received his knowledge directly from God or else he absorbed it from the milieu in which he lived. The Qurān states explicitly that 'never did We send any messenger save with the language of his people, that he might make [the message] clear to them' (Q.14.4), and in this case the term 'language' has a wide significance and means a great deal more than the collection of words used by the people concerned; it includes the images and thought-forms – indeed the whole culture – familiar to them, for only in this way can the message be clearly understood. The Biblical stories in question, together with certain traditional Arab materials, such as the stories of Hūd and Salih, were part of the milieu in which the Quranic message was embodied. Just as the revelation clothes itself in words that are in common use rather than in an incomprehensible tongue new-minted for its purpose, so it makes use of illustrative stories found in the store of common knowledge. It is axiomatic in every religious context that God works with the materials available to Him in a given milieu, materials which are, in any case, His own creations. The Qurān as it exists in this world – though in its essence 'uncreated' – is composed out of elements of the environment into which it was projected, just as the spirit, humanized, clothes itself in the physical and psychic material of the world into which it has entered.

The divine intention, however, is to 'save' and 'remind' mankind, not to provide us with historical information. 'All that We relate to thee concerning the messengers is to strengthen thy heart thereby; and in this has come to thee the truth and a reminder for believers' (Q.11.120). In other words, their purpose is to confirm the message given to Muhammad in terms of continuity – demonstrating that there is nothing strange or outlandish in it – while at the same time calling to mind the persecution of earlier messengers and the unwillingness of mankind throughout history to face the truth and fulfil the 'Trust'.

'It cannot be stressed too often,' says Muhammad Asad, 'that "narrative" as such is never the purpose of the Qurān; whenever it relates the stories of earlier prophets, or alludes to ancient legends or to historical events that took place before the advent of Islam or during the lifetime of the Prophet, the aim is invariably a moral lesson; and since one and the same event, or even legend, usually has many facets revealing as many moral implications, the Qurān reverts again and again to the same stories, but every time with a slight variation of stress on this or that aspect of the fundamental truths underlying the Quranic revelation as a whole.'[1] Elsewhere he adds that the 'many-sided, many-layered truth' underlying

---

[1] *The Message of the Quran*, Muhammad Asad, p. 321.

these stories invariably has a bearing 'on some of the hidden depths and conflicts within our own human psyche'.[1]

The Qurān is not a book of philosophy, but it is the source-book of philosophy; not a treatise on psychology, but the key to a psychology. Writing from an entirely different point of view, yet in perfect agreement with Asad, Seyyed Hossein Nasr remarks that the message couched in historical terms is 'addressed to the human soul'. 'The hypocrite (*munāfiq*) who divides people and spreads falsehood in matters concerning religion also exists within the soul of every man, as does the person who has gone astray, or he who follows the "Straight Path" . . . All the actors on the stage of sacred history as recounted in the Qurān are also symbols of forces existing within the soul of man. The Qurān is, therefore, a vast commentary on man's terrestrial existence.'[2]

It might well be asked what relevance to his own life the Muslim of the Middle Ages would have seen in the constant Quranic references to the *kāfirūn* – the 'unbelievers' or 'deniers' – if he was unaware of this psychology, for he was unlikely ever to have met such creatures, and unless he was a learned man, might well have supposed them to be extinct. Even in our time a traveller in Arabia noted recently that some Bedouin with whom he talked in a remote part of the country thought that everyone in the world was Muslim; it had not occurred to them that there might still be Christians, let alone unbelievers, surviving in odd corners of the globe.

The Muslim who follows the Quranic injunctions to 'think' and to 'meditate' knows that he harbours a variety of *kāfirūn* within his own soul and that he must wage war on them if he is to survive as a man of faith. The Christian talks of 'doubts' and sometimes treats them with respect – are not all opinions worthy of respect? – whereas the Muslim is more likely to identify them as whisperings of the devil, whose habit it is, according to the last *Sūrah* of the Qurān, to 'whisper in the breasts of men'. 'A'isha recounted how one night the Prophet left her bed for a while and she was troubled. When he returned he asked what was the matter with her and whether she was jealous. 'Why should someone like me not be jealous concerning someone like you?' she asked. 'Your devil has come to you!' he said. 'Messenger of Allah, have I a devil?' He told her that she had, so she asked if he had one too. 'Yes,' he said, 'but Allah has helped me against him . . .'

This strikes a note which the occidental, with his Christian background, finds strange and somehow out of place in the traditions of the Prophet; when he meets with something similar in the text of the Qurān he is usually either astonished or shocked. He asks how it is possible to believe that the Creator of the heavens and the earth could concern Himself – in a revelation destined to transform a great sector of humanity – with instructing the Prophet's wives in their duty, warning Muhammad's dinner guests not to outstay their welcome, or clearing a young girl of unjust suspicions. It is the last of these examples, the case of 'A'isha's necklace, which has been the focus of the most derisory comments.

According to traditional accounts of the incident, the Prophet was

[1]Ibid., p. 576.
[2]*Ideals and Realities of Islam*, Seyyed Hossein Nasr (George Allen & Unwin), p. 51.

returning with his troops from a campaign in the sixth year after the Emigration to Medina; they halted briefly in the desert on the final stage of their journey. 'A'isha left her litter to answer a call of nature. Returning to the encampment she realized that she had lost her necklace of Yemenite agates and went back to look for it. The time had come to break camp, and the people who lifted her litter on to a camel did not realize that she was no longer in it. The army continued on its way, leaving her behind. Finding herself abandoned, she sat down in the sand and fell asleep, and it was here that a young man following in the rearguard discovered her. Mounting her on his camel, he hurried on and caught up with the main body of the army.

Tongues wagged, as they were bound to do, and those who resented her influence or, more probably, that of her father were quick to voice their suspicions. Hostilities and rivalries previously unvoiced came to the surface, and the Prophet himself was assailed with contradictory advice. His son-in-law, 'Alī, pointed out that troubles of this kind afflicted many husbands and that there were, after all, plenty of other women in the world, a remark for which 'A'isha never forgave him, with far-reaching historical consequences; she herself, between fits of weeping, remained defiant. When Muhammad came to her, sad and deeply troubled, she told him: 'I know what they are saying about me. You seem to believe it. I am like Jacob when he said: "Patience is most becoming, and Allah it is whose help is to be sought".'

A month passed, a month during which the Prophet received no further revelations. Then 'A'isha's patience was rewarded, not through a dream – which was the most for which she had dared to hope – but in the verses contained in the *Sūrah* called 'Light', a revelation which exonerated her and condemned her detractors, who were told: 'When you took it up with your tongues, uttering with your mouths something of which you had no knowledge, you thought it a trifle. In the sight of Allah it is something immense' (Q.24.15). With this came verses of legislation concerning accusations of adultery which have remained valid for ever after.

An affair that might have seemed a mere trifle – and might seem so still under different circumstances – was shown to be 'something immense in the sight of God'. 'A'isha could not have understood the vast dimensions of the stage upon which she had been summoned to play her part, but everything that happened upon this stage took place in so brilliant a light – and had such tremendous consequences – that we should not think it strange if God chose to intervene in the matter; nor is it difficult with hindsight, aware of the significance of this incident in the development of Islam, to realize that the loss of a necklace by a fifteen-year-old girl travelling through an earthly desert might be of greater significance than galactic catastrophes or the death of stars.

Among the comedies of misunderstanding which can arise between men of different cultures none is more frustrating than the situation in which two people say the same thing in almost the same words and mean quite different things by what they say. The occidental, looking up at the night sky and reflecting on astronomical space will confess, sometimes with a shiver, how insignificant he feels in the midst of such distances. The

Muslim readily acknowledges his insignificance before God – *Lā ilāha illa 'Llāh!* – but he never feels alone in an alien universe. The Muslim will also say that the natural world was created for man; the occidental agrees with enthusiasm and proceeds to tear up the earth with his bulldozers.

The Muslim does not feel dwarfed by the immensities of nature because he knows himself to be the viceregent of God standing upright in the midst of these immensities. We, though small in stature, see the stars; they do not see us. We hold them within our consciousness and measure them in accordance with our knowledge; they know us not. We master them in their courses. Immensity cannot know itself; only in human consciousness can such a concept exist. In this sense man is the eye of God and is therefore the measure of all things, and they, far from being alien (and therefore menacing), have existence within our awareness of them and are therefore like extensions of our being.

As to the world being made for man, the Muslim means by this that it is like a vast picture-book through which God communicates with His viceregent – the observer of the universe – and with him alone. He has no inclination to tear this picture-book to pieces like an unruly child.

The Qurān and the great phenomena of nature are twin manifestations of the divine act of Self-revelation. For Islam, the natural world in its totality is a vast fabric into which the 'signs' of the Creator are woven. It is significant that the word meaning 'signs' or 'symbols', *ayāt*, is the same word that is used for the 'verses' of the Qurān. Earth and sky, mountains and stars, oceans and forests and the creatures they contain are, as it were, 'verses' of a sacred book. 'Indeed Allah disdaineth not to coin the similitude of a gnat or of something even smaller than that' (Q.2.26). Creation is one, and He who created the Qurān is also He who created all the visible phenomena of nature. Both are a communication from God to man.

'In your creation and in all the beasts scattered on the earth there are signs for people of sure faith. In the alternation of night and day and in the provision Allah sendeth down from the heavens whereby He quickeneth the earth after its death, and in the distribution of the winds, are signs for people who are intelligent' (Q.45.4–6). And: 'Truly in the creation of the heavens and of the earth, and the succession of night and day, and in the ships which speed through the sea with what is useful to man, and in the waters which Allāh sendeth down from the heavens . . . and in the order of the winds, and the clouds that run their appointed courses between heaven and earth, are signs indeed for people who are intelligent' (Q.2.164). Because: 'He it is who hath spread the earth wide and placed in it firm mountains and running waters, and created therein two sexes of [many kinds of] plant, and causeth the night to cover the day. Truly in all this are signs for people who reflect.' Whether we scan great distances or look within ourselves, the message is the same: 'We shall show them Our signs on the horizons and within themselves until they are assured that *this* is the truth. Doth not thy Lord suffice thee, since He is over all things the Witness?' (Q.41.53).

The view of the natural world as a 'book'[1] is familiar in occidental

---

[1]'That universal and public manuscript,' as Sir Thomas Browne called it.

poetry, but this image is usually figurative if not fanciful or sentimental. For the Muslim it is fact, as sure as the fact that a man has two eyes and a nose. Whether we can read these signs or not, their presence all around us is something concrete, like writing on a page. Another way of putting this would be to say that, for Islam, there is nothing that does not have a meaning, and these meanings are not isolated words on the page; they are coherent and interconnected, and it may be mentioned in passing that the ancient science of astrology is founded, not on the improbable notion that the stars and the planets 'influence' human lives, but upon the belief that we and they are part of a single pattern, and that a relationship necessarily exists between the different elements which make up the pattern.

This leads directly to the key concept of *taWHīD*, sometimes translated as 'monotheism' and occasionally treated as an alternative designation for the religion of Islam. The root WHD has the meaning of both unity and the act of unification. *Waḥada* means 'he was unique'; when the 'h' is doubled the verb means 'he united' or 'he made into one', and *waḥīd* is 'one'; *waḥdānīyah* is 'solitude', a *muwaḥḥid* is a 'monotheist', and a *mūtawaḥ-ḥid* is a 'solitary'. Since the basic theme of Islam is the oneness of God and the unity of His creation, it is obvious that the terms derived from this root are at the heart of the religion.

The principle of *tawhīd* is demonstrated by the unity of the very substance of the universe, from the farthest galaxies to our own bodies and everything we handle, as it is by the physical laws which govern them. Whatever may be perceived or surmised about the inner structure of 'matter', its ultimate nature is a mystery known only to 'the Knower of the unseen and the apparent'. What can be clearly seen is that the entire natural world is a single fabric of innumerable threads, and that the lives of all the creatures in it depend, directly or indirectly, upon the light of the sun and the outpouring of water, just as all depend, from one moment to the next, upon the divine Light and the outpouring of vivifying grace. Being is one, and all that has being participates in this oneness. There is no way in which Being could be divided into separate and sealed compartments, for such a compartment would at once fall back into nothingness. Modern man has taken the road to death precisely because, in his study and his treatment of the natural world, he has acted as though such divisions existed.

In all living things, as also in the very substance of rocks and soil, we see the unfolding of chemical cycles depending upon interaction between the sun's heat, the atmosphere and the oceans; in all of them the role of water is crucial, and this is the substance most frequently mentioned in the Qurān. 'Allah created out of water every creature . . . Allah createth what He will. Behold, Allah is over all things all-determining' (Q.24.45). Water is shown as the life-giving symbol of blessing, mercy, fecundity and purity, and in the cycle of its movements – ascending to form clouds and descending as rain – it is the supreme intermediary between what is above and what is beneath.[1] The Prophet's close companion Anas reported: 'A

[1]For these, and other observations in this chapter regarding the relationship between the phenomena of the natural world and the Quranic revelation, the author is indebted to an as yet unpublished work by Mr J. Peter Hobson.

shower of rain fell when we were with the messenger of Allah and he removed his garment until some of the rain fell upon him. We asked him why he did this and he replied: "Because it has so recently been with its Lord".'

The transformations of water – the only substance we find in its natural state in the three forms of solid, liquid and vapour – in themselves constitute a 'message'. We think of it as cool, yet it is unique in its capacity to store heat; the placid surface of a lake is a common symbol of peace and quietude, yet water is transformed into lashing rain, tempestuous seas and flood-swollen rivers. In the Far East it is the symbol of humility, yet it is not inert, and without it the chemistry of life would be impossible. For the Muslim it is the great purifying agent which washes away even the most deeply rooted sins, and it has been chosen by God to be intimately associated with our prayers through the ablution which precedes them. 'Do not the unbelievers see that the heavens and the earth were of one piece before We clove them asunder, and We made from water every living thing. Will they not then believe?' (Q.21.30).

If the term 'science' has any precise meaning – relating it to knowledge of the real – then it is the science of *tawḥīd*. It could be said, and with good reason, that the *kāfir* should never be permitted to approach the physical sciences or to involve himself in them. He does not possess the key to them, and he is therefore bound to go astray and to lead others astray. He divides when he should unite, and his fragmented mind deals only with fragments: it is little wonder that he splits the atom, with devastating results. Those who know nothing of the Principle are incompetent to study its manifestations. 'Pursue not that of which thou hast no knowledge. Surely hearing and sight and heart – all these – shall be called to account' (Q.17.36).

Although signs may be found in everything that comes to us, as though a river at our doorstep carried these messages on its surface, the Qurān (like other sacred books) speaks in terms of empirical experience, since it is intended to endure through the ages and cannot bind itself to the 'scientific' theories of any particular time. Its images are the phenomena of nature as they appear to us in our experience – the rising and setting of the sun, the domed sky above and the mountains, which are like weights set upon the earth. Scientific observations change according to the preconceptions of the observer and the instruments at his disposal, and the speculations which blinkered human minds construct on the basis of these observations change no less swiftly. But man's experience of the visual universe does not change. The sun 'rises' for me today as it 'rose' for the man of ten thousand years ago.

Symbolism resides also in the incidents and patterns of our experience, but it is less easily found in the underside of things – the mechanism by which they are brought about. A clock is a clock. The hands moving on its face convey information. Its inner works do not tell us the time.

To be fully aware of this flood of messages requires a closeness to the natural world that is uncommon in our time, and the man who is wholly indifferent to nature is much like the man who is deaf to the Qurān; not only is he separated from the world about him, but he is inevitably divided within himself. The French writer Jacques Ellul, whose book *La Tech-*

nique is among the most profound and perceptive critiques of the modern world published in this century, has remarked (as have many others) that the sacred has always been an experience related to nature, to the phenomena of birth, death, generation, the lunar cycles and so on. 'Man who leaves that milieu is still imbued with the feeling and imagery derived from the sacred, but these are no longer revived and rejuvenated by experience. The city person is separated from the natural environment and, as a consequence, the sacred significations no longer have any point of contact with experience. They soon dry up for lack of support in man's new experience with the artificial world of urban technology. The artificial, the systematized, and the rational seem incapable of giving birth to an experience of the same order...'[1]

He adds that it was 'in relation to the forest, the moon, the ocean the desert, the storm, the sun, the rain, the tree ... that the sacred was ordered', and elsewhere he defines the sacred (in relation to man) as 'the guarantee that he is not thrust out into an illogical space and a limitless time'. The novelty of our era, he says, 'is that man's deepest experience is no longer with nature ... Man in the presence and at the heart of the technical milieu feels the urgent need to get his bearings, to discover meaning and an origin, an authenticity in this inauthentic world.'[2] The outcome, he says, is 'a sacralization of society', as also of the 'masters of desacralization in our modern era (Marx, Nietzsche, Freud)', while political manifestos replaced sacred scriptures. Then blood begins to flow and the broken bodies pile up, and a new idolatry, more deadly than the old, demands human sacrifice. To save him from falling into this trap the Muslim needs the Qurān, but he also needs its complement, the revelation written in natural phenomena; without this, much of the Qurān is incomprehensible.

The sacred rites of Islam, in particular the five daily prayers and the month of fasting, are intimately related to the natural cycles rather than to mechanical time. The times of prayer are determined by the breaking of dawn, the rising of the sun, its coming to the zenith, its mid-decline, sunset and the close of day. And although the calendar tells us when the month of Ramadan begins and ends, it is considered essential that the dates should be established by the physical sighting of the new moon, so that the lived experience takes precedence over all scientific calculations. A computer can establish not only the minute but the exact second at which the new moon will become visible in a given locality; this counts for nothing beside the actual sighting of that slim luminous crescent on the horizon. By clinging stubbornly to the principle of 'sighting', the Muslims – not least those living in the West – demonstrate their awareness that the 'signs' of God are to be found in our experience of nature rather than in our thought processes.

The natural world was compared earlier to a 'picture-book'; it must now be added that this is a book filled with life and activity, and that these pictures leap out from the page. Their activity is praise, and their life is nourished and sustained by the divine mercy. 'Seest thou not that it is Allah whom all things in the heavens and the earth praise – and the birds in flight

[1]*The New Demons*, Jacques Ellul (Mowbray), p. 62.
[2]*Ibid.*, pp. 65–67.

outstretched? Each knoweth its [mode of] prayer and praise to Him, and Allāh is aware of all that they do' (Q.24.41). And again: 'The seven heavens and the earth and all that they contain praise Him, nor is there anything that does not celebrate His praise, though ye understand not their praise. Behold, He is clement, forgiving' (Q.17.44). And: 'Hast thou not seen that unto Allah prostrate themselves whatsoever is in the heavens and whatsoever is in the earth – the sun and the moon and the stars and the hills and the trees and the beasts and many of mankind ...?' (Q.22.18).

According to a *ḥadīth*, Muhammad told his people that there was once a prophet who was stung by an ant and therefore ordered that a colony of ants should be burned, and God reproached him: 'Because an ant stung thee, thou hast burned a community which glorified Me.' All creatures and all phenomena are instructed in their courses and guided towards the fulfilment of their destiny (which is their place in the universal pattern): 'And thy Lord inspired the bee: Choose for thyself dwellings in the mountains and in the trees and in what [men] build; then eat of all fruits and follow humbly the paths of thy Lord made smooth ...' (Q.16.68–69).

The praise which ascends from all creation reflects, as though in mirrors beyond number, the mercy which descends from heaven and which brought everything into being. Natural beauty and the nourishment which keeps all living creatures in existence, together with the rain which revives the dry earth, are the most frequently quoted examples of the operation of this mercy. 'The earth, He set it down for living creatures; in it are fruit and date-palms with their sheaths, the grain with its fodder-leaf, and the fragrant herbs. Which then of thy Lord's benefactions will ye both gainsay?' (Q.55.10–13). And so: 'Let man look upon his nourishment: how We pour out the pouring rain and split the furrowed earth, and therein grow grain and grapes and clover, olives and palms, orchards rich with trees, and fruit and provender, a ministration for you and your flocks' (Q.80.24–32).

Here again the principle of *tawḥīd* is but thinly veiled by multiplicity, for all creatures are sustained by food exchanged between them in a vast web of mutual dependence, in which both competition and co-operation play their part, the death of one being the life of another, the gift of one being the sustaining of another or of many. This fragile web of mutual dependence within which all creatures exist, protected from lethal radiation only by the thin coverlet of the atmosphere, is situated in a precarious confine between the unknowable extent of the cosmos and the impenetrable depths of the earth with its fiery interior. Both above and within these physical realms of the unknown is the greater 'Unknown' (*al-ghayb*), beyond the firmament and beneath the deepest layers of our existence.

Within this narrow confine – vulnerable as we are – we must tread carefully upon the earth, treating it with the same respect that we show to the Book of Allah, for although 'He hath made the earth humbled to you', and although we are free 'to walk in its tracts and eat of His providing', yet: 'Are ye assured of Him that is in heaven that He might not cause the earth to swallow you? For behold! The earth is quaking' (Q.67.15–16).

Again and again the Qurān reminds us of the fragility of all that exists. The vegetation which springs into life under the blessing of rain is soon cut

down and becomes 'as straw'. Even the mountains – images of stability –
are precarious: 'And thou seest the mountains, which thou deemest so
firm, pass away as clouds pass away . . .' (Q.27.88). The alternations of life
and death, like those of day and night, are as a shadow-play in which
nothing endures under the moon – that inexorable time-keeper – which,
after waxing, 'returns like an aged sickle-branch of a palm' (Q.36.39). Yet
the transience of all things – nothing enduring, nothing exempt from death
– has a positive aspect, for it is precisely this fragility which makes the thin
screen of existence transparent to what lies beyond it; were it solid, it
would be opaque. Even on the simplest human level, no man would think
of God if he did not know that he has to die.

Beyond the multiplicity of created phenomena and the apparent endless-
ness of space and time stands *Allāh*, the One, after the mention of whose
name the pious Muslim adds, 'Glorified be He and far above all association,' veiled – so it is sometimes said – by seventy thousand veils of light
and of darkness; for were He to show Himself plain, unveiling His majesty
over the world, everything would dissolve in the instant, as would this
earth if brought close to the sun. For a little while, then, we are free to
wander in a kind of twilight and even with an illusion of safety, obedient to
the revealed Law or disobedient as the case may be, blind and deaf to the
truth if we choose to be so. In this way we commit ourselves, identify
ourselves, demonstrating openly who and what we are; and very soon our
'little while' is over, and we come to judgement.

One of the subsidiary names sometimes given to the Qurān is *al-Furqān*,
derived from a verbal root meaning 'he separated' and usually translated
as 'The Discrimination' or 'The Criterion'. This identifies the Book as a
'Sword of Discrimination' which cuts through the confusion in human
experience between truth and falsehood, as also between good and evil. In
a chaotic environment people live out their lives in a kind of 'grey zone' in
which all distinctions are blurred. The Qurān warns repeatedly that the
coming of a messenger with a revelation from heaven is like a foretaste of
the Last Judgement, after which there can be no excuse for remaining in a
state of uncertainty. Revelation casts upon the whole scene a brilliant light
in which everything can be seen as it is and assigned its proper place.

'There is no coercion in religion. The right way is henceforth distinct
from error. He who rejecteth the powers of evil and believeth in Allah hath
indeed grasped a firm handhold . . .' (Q.2.156). We are told that 'thy Lord
would never destroy a community for their wrongdoing so long as they
were unaware' (Q.6.131), but 'for every people there is a messenger and,
when their messenger hath come, it will be judged between them fairly and
they will not be wronged' (Q.10.47).

However neutral an individual may appear to be so long as he is in an
undifferentiated milieu, and however obscure his fundamental tendencies
while he is in this milieu, these tendencies are actualized on contact with
the light of revelation. Just as the brightness of physical light brings out all
potential contrasts, so spiritual light gives each thing the primary qualities
of positive or negative value. The messenger says in effect: 'I have been sent
to warn you. Now choose, and live for ever with the consequences of your

choice'; which is no doubt why it is said that when the gates of Paradise are opened; the gates of hell open likewise. In the words of a popular American phrase, we are invited 'to hear the truth before it bites you'.

One of the fundamental themes of the Qurān is man's flight from reality. Given the basic premise that God *is*, and that His being both transcends and encompasses all existence, then unbelief is precisely such a flight. Men and women throughout the centuries have tried at every opportunity to evade total Reality and to take refuge in little corners of private darkness. Even at the simplest everyday level there is constant avoidance of the thought of death; there is evasion of our inward solitariness, which no amount of conviviality can entirely overcome, and there is a refusal to acknowledge our limitations and our sins. Not only is it the innate tendency of fallen man to 'forget' God, but there comes about a luxuriant growth of forgetfulness in every sphere.

The sword of the Qurān cuts also through the dreams which hold men and women in their net even when outward circumstances – like a shower of ice-cold water – might persuade them to open their eyes to reality; dreams, the last refuge of the would-be escaper, still cling when all other temptations have lost their grip on the soul. In the words of the Christian author Gustave Thibon: 'It is not against sleep but against the dream that we must fortify ourselves. One who dreams is more difficult to awaken than one who sleeps ... Sleep is the absence of God, but the dream is His phantom image; and God is doubly absent in the dream, first because His place is empty, secondly because it is occupied by something that is not He. The Day of the Lord will come like a thief in the night less for those who sleep than for those who dream.'[1]

There are, moreover, a number of passages in the Qurān which expose what might be considered a typically modern illusion, the belief that we can, as it were, slip quietly away and not be noticed, so long as we do not draw attention to ourselves and so long as we live – according to our own opinion – a decent and harmless life. It is the tearing-away of all such illusions of security that characterizes both the Last Judgement and its anticipation in the Qurān; and this is the background against which life is seen as a brief but immensely precious opportunity, offering a once-and-for-all choice.

Hence the sense of urgency which informs the whole Qurān, making the very thought of 'passtimes' an outrage against common sense; for to waste the little time we have seems to the Muslim like insane profligacy. The common plea of those described in the Qurān as 'the losers' (*al-khāsirūn*) – those who face damnation – is to be sent back, if only for a short while, to human life; and one understands that even a single day in which to make good use of time would be, for them, a treasure beyond anything they desired while living. 'So warn mankind of the Day when the punishment comes to them and the wrongdoers exclaim: Our Lord! Grant us respite for a short while – we will obey Thy call and follow the messenger!' (Q.14.44).

Both Qurān and *hadīth* emphasize the helplessness of those who have

---

[1] *L'Échelle de Jacob*, Gustave Thibon (Paris: Lardanchet), p. 108.

died and who are going through the period of trial or questioning which culminates in the Judgement, and it is in contrast to this that the supreme privilege of the living is seen as that of free movement and opportunity. This freedom is a mercy from heaven and an aspect of the 'Trust' accorded to man, for 'Had We so willed We could indeed have fixed them in their place, leaving them powerless to go forward or to turn back' (Q.36.67). Just as the paraplegic will remember the days when he could put one foot in front of the other as a time of unappreciated happiness, so do the dead look back upon their former agility, which is why it is often said in Islam that 'only the dead know the value of life'. And once judgement is pronounced, regret and repentance have no further function: 'Whether we rage or patiently endure is now all one to us; we have no refuge' (Q.14.21). This aspect of the matter is already familiar to the Christian, who reads in St Luke's Gospel of the day 'when they begin to say to the mountains, fall upon us, and to the hills, cover us', and who learns from the Book of Revelations that 'in those days shall men seek death and shall not find it, and shall desire to die and death shall flee from them'.

When the warnings have been given, the rules laid down, the stories told and all the images coined, then the Qurān turns to the moment 'when the sun is folded up, and when the stars are darkened, and when the mountains pass away ... and when the seas boil over ... and when the scrolls are laid open, and when the sky is torn away, and when hell is kindled, and when the Garden is brought close – then shall every soul know what it has prepared [for itself]' (Q.81.1–14). When that moment comes, 'mankind will be as thickly scattered moths, and the mountains as carded wool' (Q.101.4–5), and all that was hidden, deeply buried in the patient earth, from the beginning of time to the end of time, will be made apparent, 'when the earth is shaken with her convulsion and the earth casts up her burdens ... on that Day will she declare her tidings for her Lord will have enlightened her' (Q.99.1–5). This is the inbreak of the Real and the destruction of the entire fabric of the dream in which we lived: 'That will be the Day of Reality; therefore let whoso will take a [straight] return to his Lord. We have indeed warned you of a penalty that is close – the Day when man will see what his hands have wrought, and the unbeliever will say: Woe unto me – would that I were dust!'

That moment, although chronologically at the end of time, over-shadows the present almost as though it were in sight, because the Real necessarily overshadows what is less real and because the timeless is always, in a certain sense, here and now; moreover, each individual death is – for the individual concerned – a prefiguration of the end of all things under the sun.

'Even believers themselves,' says Frithjof Schuon, 'are for the most part too indifferent to feel concretely that God is not only "above", in "Heaven", but also "ahead" of us at the end of the world, or even simply at the end of our own lives; that we are drawn through life by an inexorable force and at the end of the course God awaits us; the world will be submerged and swallowed up one day by an unimaginable irruption of the purely miraculous – unimaginable because surpassing all human experience and standards of measurement. Man cannot possibly draw on his past to bear witness to anything of the kind, any more than a mayfly can expatiate on the alternation of the seasons; the rising of the sun can in no way enter into the habitual sensations of a creature born at midnight whose life will last but a day . . . And it is thus that God will come. There will be nothing but this one advent, this one presence, and by it the world of experiences will be shattered.'[1]

Each of us in his little corner is a participant in a drama — both cosmic and metacosmic — beside which the greatest earthly convulsions of storm and hurricane, of earthquake and volcanic eruption, are little more than the shifting of theatre scenery. But the dominant theme which runs through the Qurān from beginning to end is the mercy of God, in whose hands even such a drama as this is but a small thing, and we are assured that those who have grasped the 'firm handhold' offered to them have nothing to fear.

At journey's end is the greeting: 'O thou soul at peace — Return unto thy Lord, content in His contentment' (Q.89.27–28): 'As for such, He hath inscribed faith upon their hearts and strengthened them with a Spirit from Himself, and He will bring them into Gardens beneath which flow rivers [of grace], therein to abide. Allah is content with them, and they are content with Him' (Q.58.22).

[1]*Light on the Ancient Worlds*, Frithjof Schuon (London: Perennial Books), p. 49.

Chapter 5

THE MESSENGER OF GOD

The encounter with the story of Muhammad's life, like the encounter with the Qurān, requires a shift in perspective both on the part of the Christian and of the secularist, as also on the part of all those (including contemporary Muslims) whose minds have been shaped by a 'modern' education.

The Christian, if he wishes to understand Islam, must resist the temptation to compare Muhammad with Jesus, for these two had entirely different roles in the scheme of things; and the secularist is invited to taste – if only as a hypothesis – the flavour of the sacred and of a human life totally determined by a divine intention. The contemporary mind seeks for causes to 'explain' phenomena and, having discovered *how* this or that came to exist, forgets to ask *why* it came to exist. For the traditional Muslim, on the other hand, a person, a thing, or an event is what it is because God has looked upon this possibility hidden in His treasury – as yet unmanifested, unexpressed – and has thereby brought it out into the light of existence: 'His command when He intendeth a thing [to come into being] is only that He saith unto it: Be! and it is' (Q.36.82). What we see as a causal sequence of events is then seen as a pattern already complete in the mind of God. Causal factors can be discovered for every event, since they exist in the network of relationships which make up the total pattern, and the human mind functions in the context of causality – like a blind man feeling his way from one object to the next – but they do not explain why such an event was necessary.

Modern biographers of Muhammad say, in effect, that because such and such chance events came his way, therefore he was the man he was, acted as he did and said what he said. This approach makes no sense to the traditional Muslim, for whom this man was what he had to be, did what he had to do and said what he had to say in accordance with the divine intention. 'We have not created heaven and earth and all that is between them without meaning and purpose – as is the surmise of those who are bent on denying the truth' (Q.38.27 in M. Asad's translation). Orientalists – in particular von Grunebaum – speak of Muhammad's 'luck', as though the world were so lacking in direction and so empty that a religion must depend upon luck to establish itself; or as though, having decided to transform a great part of humanity by means of a divine revelation, God turned His back and left the whole matter to blind chance.

It follows that, from the Muslim point of view, the world into which Muhammad was born – Arabia in the seventh century of the Christian era – was a world providentially designed to receive him and to give both the message of the Qurān and the message contained in the story of his life the precise shape and colouring they have. The gem-stone was matched to its setting, as was the setting to the gem; and to suppose that either could have been other than they were is to introduce a concept of 'chance' which has no place in this context.

Arabia in that period was divided into three zones. The north lived under the shadow of two great empires, Christian Byzantium (known to the Arabs as 'Rome') and Zoroastrian Persia, empires in perpetual conflict and so evenly matched that neither could achieve definitive victory over the other. These great powers occupied the stage, while in the shadows – in the wings – the Arabs of the northern region allied themselves now with one, now with the other, according to where their advantage lay.

In the south lived the people of Ma'īn, Saba', Qatabān and Hadramawt, no strangers to history, for this was the land of frankincense and myrrh and 'all the perfumes of Arabia', the happy land called by the Romans *Arabia Felix*. Unfortunately, the south was desirable property. The conversion of the Ethiopian ruler, the Negus, to Christianity had brought his country into alliance with Byzantium, and it was with Byzantine approval that the Ethiopians crossed the narrow straits early in the sixth century and took possession of this fertile territory, proving – as has been proved so often before and since – that to be fortunate is not always good fortune.[1] Before their ruin at the hands of a ruthless conqueror, however, the southerners had opened up the deserts of central Arabia to trade, introducing a measure of organization into the life of the Bedouin (who served as guides for their caravans) and establishing trading-posts in the oases.

If the symbol of these sedentary people was the frankincense tree, that of the arid zone was the date-palm; on the one hand the luxury of perfume, on the other necessary food. No one could have regarded the Hejaz – 'where no bird sings and no grass grows', according to a southern poet – as desirable property. There was nothing in that region to attract the predators. The subordination of man to man and of one people to another has been the common and formative human experience throughout the ages, but the tribes of the Hejaz had never experienced either conquest or oppression; they had never been obliged to say 'Sir' to any man. In this they must have been almost unique; the only possible comparisons might be with the Mongols of the Siberian steppes and the Indians of North America before the coming of the white man.

Poverty was their protection, but it is doubtful whether they felt poor. To feel poor one must envy the rich, and they envied no one. Their wealth was in their freedom, in their honour, in their noble ancestry and in their incomparable language, the pliant instrument of the only art they knew,

---

[1]'Thus more than one thousand years of developed civilization came to an end. The very settlements were abandoned as the people drifted off either into a primitive nomadic existence or trekked into the mountains to carve small fields out of the slopes ... The glory that was Ma'in, Qataban, Ausan, and Hadramaut, and above all Sabā and Himyar, faded in the collective memory. The incense route was forgotten ... Even the Himyaritic inscriptions had become meaningless within a hundred years. The incense tree became a rarity, due to neglect of organized cultivation. The irrigation schemes fell into disuse and the fields returned to desert sand.' *Yemen Rediscovered*, Michael Jenner (Longman, 1983). The early Muslims had, close at hand, a striking example of the dissolution of a civilization.

the art of poetry. All that we would now call 'culture' was concentrated in this one medium, which required no heavy baggage such as would have encumbered them on their journeying. Language was something they could shape and model to glorify courage and freedom, to praise the friend and mock the enemy, to extol the bravery of the men of the tribe and the beauty of its women, in poems chanted at the fireside or in the vastness of the desert under the vast bowl of the sky, bearing witness to the grandeur of this little human creature for ever travelling across the barren spaces of the earth.

For the Bedouin the word was as powerful as the sword. When hostile tribes met for trial in battle it was usual for each side to put up its finest poet to praise the courage and nobility of his own people and heap contempt upon the ignoble foe. It is said that there were occasions when a poet's tongue was so eloquent and his words so compelling that the opposing tribe would slink away, defeated, before a blow had been struck.[1]

Such battles, in which combat between rival champions was a major feature, were more sport than warfare as we now understand the term; affairs of tumult, boasting and display, with few casualties. They served a clear economic purpose through the distribution of booty, and for the victor to press his advantage too far would have been contrary to the concept of honour. When one side or the other acknowledged defeat the dead on both sides were counted and the victors would pay blood-money – in effect reparations – to the vanquished, so that the relative strength of the tribes was maintained in healthy balance. The contrast between this and the practices of civilized warfare is striking.

Whether in conflict or in desert wandering, survival depended upon qualities of courage and endurance, loyalty to the tribe and a cult of excellence, which carried with it all the obligation to protect the weak, in particular women – the bearers and nurturers of life – and children, in whose frail existence the future of the tribe was enshrined. The hero of pre-Islamic Arab poetry was always the Bedouin 'knight', standing upright, true to himself, in a world reduced, as it were, to the bare bones of sun, sky, sand and rock, proud even in poverty and seeking joy in self-mastery, scornful of security and all the ambiguities of wealth, and ready to look death in the face without flinching. Among such people one finds neither the dregs of humanity nor the scum, which is one way of saying that the principles by which they lived and died were those which the Western tradition associates with aristocracy in the true sense of the term.

These are not the principles which govern the lives of townsfolk, and by the sixth century of the Christian era the Arabs of the Hejaz had discovered the pleasures and temptations of city life. The ancient Ka'ba had long been the centre of this little world, with the tents of the nomads pitched around it, but late in the previous century a certain Qusayy, chieftain of the

---

[1]Perhaps we may detect a vestige of this even today when some Arab leader makes a violent speech, full of blood and thunder, and returns home convinced that he has won a war and destroyed his enemies. He is genuinely puzzled when these same enemies refuse to lie down and play dead. Had he not cut them to pieces with his tongue?

powerful tribe of Quraysh, had established a permanent settlement. This was the city of Mecca (or 'Bakka', a word derived from a Sabaean term meaning 'sanctuary'). The circumstances of the time favoured its development as a major commercial centre. The wars between Persia and Byzantium had closed the more northerly trading routes between east and west, while the influence and prosperity of southern Arabia had been destroyed by the Ethiopians. Moreover, the city's prestige was enhanced by its role as a centre of pilgrimage, as was that of Quraysh as custodians of the Ka'ba, enjoying the best of both worlds. The combination of nobility – were they not descended from Abraham through Ishmael? – with wealth and spiritual authority gave them grounds for believing that their splendour, compared with that of any other people on earth, was as the splendour of the sun compared with the glitter of the stars.

The trade routes fanned out from the city. Wealthy merchants dispatched their private caravans throughout the year, but there were also two great annual caravans, to Yemen in the summer and to Syria in the winter, in which the entire population was involved. A sophisticated system of credit enabled even the poorest citizens to subscribe, and vast armies of two or three thousand camels carrying gold, silver, leather and precious goods, and supported by up to 300 men, brought profit to all concerned. The city was never still. The camel trains passed through the narrow streets in file, their bells tinkling, amidst a crowd which included Christians, Jews and Africans, wizards, conjurors and prostitutes, while the great merchants walked in finery, dressed in silk with amber in their hair and perfumed beards, and the busy money-changers cried their rates for Persian and Byzantine currency. The Bedouin, so often cheated when they came to sell their poor wares, said that the name Quraysh was derived from a word meaning 'shark'.

Every spiritual centre is a symbol of the Heart, the centre of man's being, but Mecca was so in more than one dimension, since the trade routes were like veins and arteries supplying sustenance to the outlying lands and bearing wealth which ultimately clogs the heart. Corruption had set in on two levels. In the first place, the Ka'ba was no longer the temple of the One God. The Arabs, like others before and since, had followed the downward slope which leads from monotheism to idolatry. They had not lost all awareness of Allah, but thought of Him as a supreme deity too remote and too impersonal to concern them in their daily lives. Practical help was to be expected from lesser gods and from the unseen spirits, the *jinn*, and some 360 idols surrounded the Ka'ba in a forest of false deities, catering for every taste among the pilgrims who came each year to worship whomsoever they chose and who brought with them further profit for Quraysh. The heart was cluttered with debris.

At the same time the Spartan virtues of the desert Arabs found no place in so wealthy a city. The connection between idolatry and worldliness is obvious, and the oligarchy of tribal elders, successful merchants and outstanding orators (the power of the word was still respected) which controlled the affairs of Mecca, regulating trade and adjudicating in disputes, had developed a taste for the good life which their forefathers would have considered despicable. Drunkenness and gambling were rife, and the Meccans speculated on rates of exchange, the price of commodities, the arrival or loss of caravans and the spoils of war. Honour had degenerated into false pride, and the obligation to protect the weak, although still observed within the great families, was not applied to the 'foreigners' who had flocked into the city and who had no place in what was still essentially a tribal social structure.

Such a city was necessarily vulnerable, a tempting prize, and in the year 570 of the Christian era Abraha, the Ethiopian Viceroy of Yemen, mounted a great expedition against Mecca. He had built a splendid cathedral in Sana'a, and Quraysh, seeing in this a rival centre of pilgrimage to the Ka'ba, had sent one of their people to pollute it. Abraha needed no further excuse. Vowing to raze the Ka'ba to the ground, he set out with a large army, placing in the forefront an elephant, a beast never before seen in those parts; and there was no serious opposition to his advance. He was within striking distance of Mecca – and Quraysh had already evacuated the city – when the elephant halted, refusing to go further. Some say that the Arab guide who accompanied the army, having by now learned the words of command to which the beast was accustomed, had whispered in its ear; whatever the reason, the elephant made its decision and the army stopped in its tracks. At this point there occurred a miracle which is recorded in the Qurān, although its exact nature remains obscure: 'Hast thou not seen how thy Lord dealt with the owners of the elephant? Did He not bring their plans to naught and send against them swarms of flying creatures...?' (Q.105). Abraha turned back, his army in disarray, and the Ka'ba remained inviolate, as it had been from the beginning of time.

It was in this year, known as the Year of the Elephant, that Muhammad was born, probably – so far as can be established – on 20 August. His father, Abdullah, was a great-great-grandson of Qusayy, the founder of the city, and belonged to the Hashimite branch of Quraysh, and his mother, Āmina, was descended from Qusayy's brother, Zuhrah. Returning with a caravan from Syria and Palestine, Abdullah stopped to visit relatives in Yathrib, an oasis to the north of Mecca, fell ill there and died several months before his son's birth.

It was customary to send the sons of Quraysh into the desert to be suckled by a wet-nurse and spend their early childhood with a Bedouin tribe. Apart from considerations of health, this represented a return to their roots, an opportunity to experience the freedom of the nomad and to learn, in a formative period of their lives, what it meant to be a Lord of Space, moving with the flocks and experiencing the impact of the changing seasons. Thus the bond with the desert was renewed in each generation, and the alliances formed in this way between Bedouin and townsmen were useful to both. A fatherless boy, however, was an unattractive investment. Muhammad was accepted by Halīma, the wife of a shepherd of the Banu Sa'd, only because she was among the poorest of those who came that year to seek sucklings and could find no other. He spent four or five years with this Bedouin family, tending the sheep as soon as he was old enough to walk, learning the ways of the desert and, according to the traditional stories, bringing great good fortune to his foster parents.

When he was six, not long after he had rejoined his mother, she took him on a visit to Yathrib, where his father had died, and herself fell ill with one of the fevers prevalent in the oasis, dying on the return journey. The Arabs' fondness for children and the nature of the extended family assured the security of an orphan, and Muhammad now came under the guardianship of his grandfather, 'Abdu'l-Muttalib, chief of the Hashimite clan. The old man (he was in his eightieth year), although he had many children of his own — including a son, Hamzah, who was the same age as Muhammad — had developed a particular affection for his little grandson and made a point of keeping the boy with him when, as was his custom, he rested in the evenings on a carpet set down for him in the shadow of the Ka'ba. Here the two of them could watch the world go by, one too old to participate and the other too young, while the great men of Quraysh strolled past in the cool of evening discussing the affairs of the city.

When the boy was eight years old 'Abdu'l-Muttalib died and he became the ward of the new Hashimite chieftain, his uncle Abu Tālib who, as soon as he was old enough, took him on the caravan journey to Syria so that he could 'learn the trade'. In the formative years of childhood and adolescence he had experienced double bereavement, the joys and rigours of desert life, intimate association with the sacred sanctuary of the Ka'ba, travel in the 'civilized' world and, according to legend, a fateful meeting with a Christian monk, who recognized in him one of God's chosen. He had grown up in the midst of life's ambiguity. Death had struck down those he loved most, yet he had been surrounded with affection and kindness; impressed upon his heart was an intense awareness both of human fragility and of the only thing that makes this fragility bearable, human affection.

When he was twenty he was invited to take charge of the goods of a merchant who was himself unable to travel, and success in this enterprise led to further similar commissions. The penniless orphan was making a reputation for himself.

Among the substantial fortunes of Mecca was that of the twice-widowed Khadīja. Impressed by what she heard of Muhammad, who was now commonly known as *al-Amīn*, 'the trustworthy', she employed him to take her merchandise to Syria. Even more impressed by his competence, when this task was completed, as also by his appearance and personal charm, she sent a woman friend to ask him how it was that he had not married. He explained that he did not yet have the means. 'Supposing,' asked the go-between, 'that you were offered the hand of a noble lady who combines beauty with wealth?' He asked who she had in mind, and she answered that it was his employer, Khadīja. 'How could such a match be mine?' 'Leave that to me,' she told him. 'For my part,' he said, 'I am willing.'

At this time Muhammad was twenty-five and Khadīja forty, though still a remarkably handsome woman. It was inevitable that her family should disapprove of such an alliance, but her father was prevailed upon to give his consent; while Abu Tālib, with a generosity he could ill afford, paid a bride-price of twenty camels, and at the betrothal party made a speech extolling his nephew's virtues which was a marvel of Arab eloquence. Khadīja presented her husband with a young slave, Zayd, who was freed by Muhammad; but when his relatives came to ransom him, he chose to remain with the family. The household was further increased by the adoption of 'Alī, one of Abu Tālib's sons, and Khadīja bore Muhammad six children, including at least one boy, al-Qāsim, who died before his second birthday. A pattern of personalities which would only become clear many years later was forming, a pattern which the finger of history probes with an uncertain and anxious touch.

In the year 605 the governing council of Quraysh, the *malā*, decided that the Ka'ba should be rebuilt. Although this temple of Abraham is, in essence, timeless, its earthly form – being perishable – has been reconstructed a number of times. In that year a Byzantine ship had been wrecked on the coast, providing excellent timber for the purpose, and there was a Christian carpenter living in Mecca who was competent to erect the scaffolding. The main work of construction was divided between the clans, but when it was done, disagreement arose as to who should have the honour of replacing the sacred Black Stone in its niche. It was decided that the first man to enter the square by a particular gate should be asked to act as arbitrator, and the first comer was Muhammad. He told the people to bring a large cloak, placed the stone on it and called upon representatives of each of the clans to join together in raising it into position; he himself then fixed the stone in its niche.

He was by now a man of substance, respected in the community, admired both for his generosity and his good sense. His future seemed assured. In due course, having re-established the prosperity of his clan, he would become one of the more influential elders of the city and end his life, perhaps, as his grandfather had done, reclining in the shade of the Ka'ba and recollecting long years well spent in terms of the world's accounting. Yet his spirit was uneasy and became increasingly so as he approached middle age.

A need for solitude possessed him and drove him out of the busy city into the rocky hills and wastelands which surround Mecca. There he was seized by certain premonitions and visions, sometimes frightening and sometimes 'like the coming of dawn'. Little is known concerning the exact nature of these experiences, but the accounts that have come down to us suggest that a great force – a light, a splendour – was approaching ever closer, and, like a bird beating with its wings against a window-pane, trying to reach him through the membrane which isolates us in our little world of experience. Such an approach must have its repercussions in nature, which trembles before the power of unseen dimensions. We are told that the world of stones and rocks and barren valleys seemed to Muhammad to have come to life; he heard strange voices calling, and he covered himself in his cloak, fearing death or madness in the embrace of some dark power. It seemed as though the demons which cluster in such desert places and buzz about the traveller's ears pursued him even to the cave in which he took refuge on Mount Hira.

His family and friends observed the change in him with increasing anxiety, but there was nothing he could explain to them; there was no way in whch he could have understood that his deepest nature was being, as it were, forged anew – its receptivity laid bare – during these solitary vigils, full of terror and expectation. In the blaze of day and during the clear desert nights, when the stars seem sharp enough to penetrate the retina of the eye, his very substance was becoming saturated with the 'signs' in the heavens, so that he might serve as an entirely adequate instrument for a revelation already inherent in these 'signs'. It would come when he had been made entirely ready.

It came on a night late in the sacred month of Ramadan, the night known to us as *Laylatu'l-Qadr*, the 'Night of Power'. It is said that on that night nature falls asleep: 'The streams cease to flow, the winds are still and the evil spirits forget to watch over the wonders of the earth. In the night of *al-Qadr* one can hear the grass grow and the trees speak . . . the sands of the desert lie in deep slumber. Those who experience the night of *al-Qadr* become saints or sages, for in this night man may see through the fingers of God.'[1] Since no one can be sure which night this is, the believer is invited to prepare himself, to open the gates of awareness, sharpen his gaze and tune his hearing to receive what comes when it comes.

Muhammad was asleep in the cave on Mount Hira. He was awakened by the Angel of Revelation, the same who had come to Mary the mother of Jesus, Gabriel (called by the Arabs Jibrā'il), who was clothed in light and who seized him in a close embrace. A single word of command burst upon him: '*Iqra*' – 'Recite!' He said: 'I am not a reciter!' but the command was repeated. 'What am I to recite?' he asked. He was grasped with overwhelming force and thrown down, and now the first 'recitation' of the Qurān came upon him: 'Recite in the name of thy Lord who created – created man from a clot. Recite: for thy Lord is Most Bountiful, who teacheth by the pen,[2] teacheth man that which he knew not' (Q.96.1–5).

The story of this first revelation has been told as often as any story in the world, yet to gain some personal inkling of what it was like we are obliged to make an imaginative leap through the screen which keeps us locked into our habitual everyday experience. There is no simple way of provoking this act of release, since each individual is different, his nature unlockable only by a particular key. Those who have come face to face with the most powerful among the manifestations of the natural world – great storms at sea, hurricanes, volcanic eruptions – may find in their experience a clue to what is meant by an encounter with a power from another dimension of being, but the people of our time find it difficult to imagine the shattering of the habitual personality which takes place in the presence of the *mysterium tremendum*, in the presence of the Sublime. No doubt the

[1]Quoted from *Mohammed* by Essad Bey (London: Cobden-Sanderson, 1938).

[2]The significance of the pen has been richly elaborated in the traditions. It is said that the first of all things to be created was the 'preserved tablet' upon which was entered all that is to be throughout time. Then Allah created, from a single jewel, a mighty pen, 'the point of which is split and from which light flows as ink flows from the pens of this world. Then a command came to the Pen, "Write!" whereupon the Pen trembled and shook from terror at this summoning, so that there was a quivering in its *tasbīh* (glorification) like the rumbling of thunder. Then it entered on the Tablet all that Allah bade it enter of all that is to be till the Day of Resurrection' (from the *Qiṣaṣ all-Anbiyā'* of al-Kisā'i). The phallic symbolism of the pen is well known, but this is merely one aspect of its role as the supreme instrument of creation. The implied connection between 'knowledge' and 'creation' as such is particularly significant in the Islamic context.

appropriate word is 'awe', yet this word has become so devalued in the English language that it will no longer serve unless we can cleanse it from trivial associations. Even in our time, however, one occasionally meets a pious man who has been accorded the rare privilege of entering the Prophet's tomb in Medina, and who has been so transformed by wonder and by awe that the experience can only be described in terms of 'terror' in the full and majestice sense of this term. If the human substance is so shaken in the place where this man's body was buried long ago, we may judge from this what was his own experience when the angel approached him.

At the same time – since past events are seen in the light of their consequences – we have to bear in mind that this encounter of an Arab, fourteen centuries ago, with a being from beyond the screen was an event of momentous significance which would move whole peoples across the earth and affect the lives of hundreds of millions of men and women, building great cities and great civilizations, provoking the clash of mighty armies and raising from the dust much beauty and much splendour; it would also bring teeming multitudes to the Gates of Paradise and, beyond, to the beatific vision. The word *Iqrā'*, echoing around the valleys of the Hejaz, broke the mould in which the known world was fixed; and this man, alone among the rocks, took upon his shoulders and into his heart a burden which would have crushed the mountains had it descended upon them.

Muhammad was forty years old and he had grown to maturity in the world. The impact of this tremendous encounter may be said to have melted his substance. The person he had been was like a skin scorched by light and burned away, and the man who came down from the mountain and sought refuge between Khadīja's breasts was not the same man who had climbed it.

For the moment, however, he was like a man pursued. As he descended the slope he heard a great voice crying: 'Muhammad, thou art the Messenger of Allah and I am Jibrā'il.' He looked upwards, and the angel filled the horizon. Whichever way he turned his head, the figure was still there, inescapably present. He hastened home and called to Khadīja: 'Cover me! Cover me!' She laid him down, placing a cloak over him, and as soon as he had recovered himself a little he told her what had happened. She held him against her body, giving him, as it were, the earthly contact which saves a man's sanity after such an encounter. She reassured him with human reassurance and believed in the truth of his vision. When she had settled him and he had fallen into a deep sleep, she went at once to see her cousin Waraqa, one of the *ḥunafā'* (these were isolated individuals who rejected idolatry, seeking knowledge of the One God either in the tradition of Abraham or through Christianity).

After listening to her account of her husband's experience, Waraqa told her: 'By Him in whose hand is the soul of Waraqa, if what you say is true there has come to Muhammad the great *Nāmūs*, even he who came to Moses. Truly Muhammad is the Prophet of this people. Calm your husband's fears and banish your own!'

Some further revelations came to Muhammad – it is not known

precisely which or how many – and then the heavens were silent for some weeks, perhaps for many months. Darkness descended upon his spirit. However terrifying the great vision might have been, the angel's absence was even more disturbing, for he was now left alone with his human weakness. It was as though a crack had opened in the carapace which encloses this world, so that he had seen and heard things which make the ordinary life of mankind appear unbearably narrow and suffocating; now it had closed. Having been taken out of this world and made a stranger to his own people, he found himself abandoned in a kind of no man's land between heaven and earth. He had asked Khadīja: 'Who will believe me?' and she had answered, 'I believe you!' But this was love speaking. How could he expect others to believe when he himself was in doubt as to the nature of his vision?

The fear of insanity, which had been with him for some time, now became acute. He had seen such people often enough: lunatics raving about the 'unseen', aliens in the community and objects of scorn to the sensible, hard-headed townsmen. He himself had always been a practical man, a man of business, and he belonged to a race which tends to take a down-to-earth view of things and to regard spiritual extravagance with suspicion (a dreamer would not survive for long in the desert). Walking alone in the hills, hoping for some relief, he came to a steep precipice and his foot dislodged a stone, which tumbled into the abyss. He was seized by the impulse to follow it. 'I wanted,' he said long afterwards, 'to find lasting repose and to rid my soul of its pain.' It is said that he was about to throw himself over the cliff when the angel's voice intervened, saying: 'Muhammad, you are the true Prophet of Allah!' He returned home, and soon after this a fresh revelation came to him: the *Sūrah* called *ad-Ḍuḥa*, 'The Morning Hours'.

'By the morning hours and by the night when it is most still, thy Lord hath not forsaken thee nor doth He hate thee. Truly that which is to come shall be better for thee than that which came before, and truly thy Lord shall give unto thee and thou shalt be well pleased. Did He not find thee an orphan and shelter thee? Did He not find thee wandering and direct thee? Did He not find thee needy and enrich thee? Therefore oppress not the orphan, neither repulse the beggar, but declare the goodness of thy Lord' (Q.93).

From this time on the revelations continued for the rest of his life, memorized and written down by his companions on pieces of sheepskin or whatever else was at hand. 'Sometimes,' he said, 'they come to me like the reverberations of a bell, and that is the hardest upon me; the reverberations abate when I am aware of their message. And sometimes the angel takes the form of a man and speaks to me, and I understand what he says.' Khadīja had been the first to believe. The question as to who was the second is a matter of dispute between Sunnis and the Shī'a sector of Islam. The former say that it was the merchant Abu Bakr, Muhammad's close friend, a quiet, sensitive man of humble origin who was much respected as a conciliator. Many years later the Prophet said of him: 'I have never called anyone to Islam who was not at first filled with doubt, questions and contradictions, with the exception of Abu Bakr.' The Shī'a believe that it was 'Ali, who would have been about ten years old at the time, and certainly the other member of the household, Zayd, followed soon after. It is unlikely that there were more than twenty 'converts' in the first two or three years, and when Muhammad invited all the senior members of his clan to a grand dinner, and preached the message to them, the occasion ended in disaster. One of his uncles, Abū Lahab, was openly abusive and soon became the most implacable enemy of the new religion.

The situation changed when the command came to him to preach openly and to speak out against idolatry. At first the elders of Quraysh had been able to ignore this strange little group, treating Muhammad as a sad case of self-deception, but now they began to realize that his preaching, which was attracting adherents among the poor and the dispossessed (and could therefore be seen as subversive), represented a threat both to the religion and the prosperity of Mecca. Open conflict, however, would have been against their interests. Their power depended upon their unity, and with the example of Yathrib – torn asunder by factional conflict – as a grim warning of what could happen in their own city, they were obliged to bide their time; moreover, the clan Hashim, whatever it might think privately of its rogue member, was bound by custom to defend him if he was attacked. They confined themselves for the time being to mockery, perhaps the most effective weapon in the common man's defence against the inbreak of truth, since it does not involve the degree of commitment inherent in violence. His former guardian Abū Tālib, begged him to go slowly and not to rock the boat. 'O my uncle,' he said, 'even if they set against me the sun on my right and the moon on my left, I will not abandon my purpose until Allah grants me success or until I die.' Abū Tālib answered with a sigh: 'O my brother's son, I will not forsake you.'

Tension in the city increased gradually, month by month, as Muhammad's spiritual influence spread, undermining the hegemony of the elders of Quraysh and bringing division into their families; and this influence became even more dangerous to the established order when the content of the successive revelations was broadened to include denunciation of the callousness of the Meccan plutocracy, their greed for 'more and more' and their avarice. The opposition was now led by a certain Abū Jahl, together with Abū Lahab and the latter's brother-in-law, a younger man who was more subtle and more talented than either of them, Abū Sufyān. Returning one day from the hunt, Muhammad's boyhood friend Hamzah, who had so far remained neutral, was so angered on being told of the insults heaped upon his friend that he sought out Abū Jahl, struck him on the head with his bow and announced there and then his conversion to Islam.

More important still was the conversion of one of the most formidable young men in the city, 'Umar ibn al-Khattāb. Infuriated by the increasing success of the new religion – so contrary to all that he had been brought up to believe – he swore to kill Muhammad regardless of the consequences. He was told that before doing so he should look into the affairs of his own family, for his sister and her husband had become Muslims. Bursting into their home he found them reading the *Sūrah* called 'Tā-Hā', and when his sister acknowledged that they were indeed converts, he struck her a harsh blow. More than a little ashamed of himself, he then asked to see what they had been reading. She handed him the text, and as he read these verses of the Qurān, his nature underwent a transformation so sudden and so total that this incident has sometimes been compared to the conversion of Paul on the road to Damascus. He went directly to Muhammad and accepted Islam.

Men such as these were too important in the social hierarchy to be attacked, but most of the new Muslims were either poor or in slavery. The poor were beaten and the slaves tortured to make them deny their faith, and there was little Muhammad could do to protect them.

A black slave named Bilāl was pegged down naked under the devouring sun with a heavy stone on his breast and left to die of thirst. In his torment he cried out repeatedly *Aḥad! Aḥad!* ('One! One! God is One!') and it was in this state, on the point of death, that Abu Bakr found him and ransomed him for an exorbitant fee. He was nursed back to health in Muhammad's home and became one of the closest and best-loved of the companions. When, much later, the question arose as to how the faithful should be summoned to prayer, 'Umar suggested the human voice as the best of all instruments, and Bilāl became the first *mū'ezzin* of Islam: a tall, thin black man with a magnificent voice and, so it is said, the face of a crow under a thatch of grey hair; a man from whom the sun had burned out, during his torment, everything but love of the One and of the messenger of the One.

The persecution became so severe that Muhammad advised the more defenceless of the new Muslims to emigrate, at least temporarily, to Ethiopia, where they would be well received by the Christian Negus, 'an upright King'. About eighty converts fled there in AD 614 and with them went the future Caliph, 'Uthmān ibn 'Affān. He had long been in love with Muhammad's daughter Ruqayya, who had been previously married to her cousin, one of Abū Lahab's sons. The choleric 'Father of Flame' (as he was called on account of his red face) had compelled his son to divorce her, and as soon as she was free, 'Uthmān had entered Islam and married her.

This apparent alliance with a foreign power further infuriated the Meccans and they sent envoys to the Negus demanding the Muslims' extradition. A great debate was held at Court and the Muslims won the day, first by demonstrating that they worshipped the same God as the Christians and then by reciting one of the Quranic passages concerning the Virgin Mary, whereupon the Negus wept and said: 'Truly this has come from the same source as that which Jesus brought ...'

Frustrated on every side the Meccan oligarchy, under the leadership of Abū Jahl, now drew up a formal document declaring a ban or boycott against the clan Hāshim as a whole; there were to be no commercial dealings with them until they outlawed Muhammad, and no one was to marry a woman of Hāshim or give his daughter to a man of the clan. The ban lasted for two years but, like sanctions in later times, proved ineffectual. The structure of Quraysh was too well integrated, particularly by intermarriage between the clans, for such an act of exclusion to be workable. In any case, it was bad for trade. The proclamation of the ban, so it is said, was eaten by insects leaving only the words 'In thy name, O Allah' as a sign for those who were prepared to understand it.

The year 620 of the Christian era, however, is known to history as 'The Year of Mourning'. Now over eighty years old, Abū Tālib died. Henceforth Muhammad could no longer rely with any certainty upon the protection of his clan. His enemies now encircled him, warily but with growing determination, convinced that if they could destroy him no more would be heard of the religion of Islam. Then Khadīja died. The two pillars upon which his personal and emotional security had rested were gone, and the world was a colder place than it had been before. If ever there was a time for a miracle – a divine intervention to supplement the Quranic revelations – this was it. Towards the end of that year the miracle came.

The relevant verses of the Qurān are, to say the least, succinct; first: 'Glorified be He (Allah) who carried His slave by night from the sacred Mosque to the far-distant Mosque, whose precincts We have blessed, in order that We might show him some of our signs. He (Allah) is the Hearer, the Seer' (Q.17.1). Secondly: 'When there veiled the Lote Tree that which veils, the eye wavered not nor did it transgress. Truly he beheld – of all the signs of his Lord – the greatest' (Q.53.16–18).

These verses refer to two successive events: the *Isrā*' ('Night Journey') and the *Mi'rāj* ('Ascension'). They have been illuminated by the authentic sayings of the Prophet, elaborated by tradition and embroidered in legend. The religious imagination has gone to work on the available material and given birth to a vast literature, so that it is often difficult to locate the dividing-line between fact and fantasy; perhaps this does not really matter, because the Creator of all facts is also the Creator of those products of the inspired imagination which reveal the underlying significance of the factual.

Gabriel, the angelic messenger, came to Muhammad when he was sleeping in a room close to the Ka'ba and touched him with his foot; the sleeper awoke but, seeing nothing, lay down again. 'A second time he came; and a third time, and then he took me by the arm and I rose and stood beside him, and he led me out to the gate of the Mosque, and there was a white beast, between a mule and an ass [in appearance] with wings at his sides wherewith he moved his legs, and his every stride was as far as his eye could see.'[1]

He mounted this strange beast, whose name was Burāq (meaning 'Lightning'), and was carried at a speed beyond all conceivable speeds across the mountains and the deserts, halting briefly at Mount Sinai, where Moses had received the tablets of the Law, and at the birthplace of Jesus in Bethlehem, before alighting in Jerusalem, the city already sacred to the two other monotheistic faiths and thenceforth sacred also to Islam. The threads which might seem so widely separated were knit together, and in Jerusalem Muhammad led a host of prophets – with Abraham, Moses and Jesus at their head – in prayer to the One God.

Here, where the Temple of Solomon had once stood and where the Dome of the Rock would one day be built, a great ladder was placed before him – 'the like of which for beauty I had never seen before'. This, it is said,

---

[1]Quoted from the life of the Prophet by Ibn Ishāq.

is the ladder which the dead yearn to see brought forth, for it leads to all that humankind could ever desire, and onwards, beyond desire, to the realms of 'light upon light'. Guided by the angel, he mounted through the heavenly spheres, meeting again those prophets with whom he had prayed in Jerusalem. There they had appeared to him in their human forms, but now he saw them in their celestial reality – transfigured – even as they now saw him. Of the gardens which adorn each heavenly sphere he was to say later: 'A fragment of Paradise the size of a bow is better than all beneath the sun ... and if a woman of the people of Paradise appeared unto the people of earth she would fill the space between the heavens and here below with light and with fragrance.'

In each heaven he met the angel of angels presiding over it, each of them commanding a host of thousands, each of whom has under his command many thousands more. Accounts of the Mi'rāj and commentaries upon it are filled with images of astonishing richness and profusion, as aspect is piled upon aspect and numbers are multiplied by ever greater factors, images that dazzle and confuse because, if we are not sometimes dazzled and confused, we may think that we have grasped in an earthly manner what can never be grasped in this way. The same technique, whereby it is partially possible to describe the indescribable and to imagine the unimaginable, was employed by the early Christian Fathers in writing of the Cherubim and Seraphim and other ranks of the angelic hosts.

Here, for example, is Gabriel seen through Muslim eyes: 'He has six thousand wings and between each pair is a distance of a journey of five hundred years, and he has plumage which goes from his head to his feet and which is of the colour of saffron, and each plume looks like the light of the sun. He plunges each day six hundred and sixty times into the ocean of Light. When he comes forth drops of light fall from him and Allah creates from these drops angels in the image of Jibrā'il who glorify Allah until the Day of Resurrection.'

But even such a creature as this, in all his splendour, is still a slave of God, hardly more than a speck of dust in the radiance of the divine majesty; and having guided Muhammad to the Lote Tree of the Uttermost Boundary, he could go no further. This is the limit of creation, both natural and supernatural, human and angelic, and here Gabriel spread his wings saying: 'O Muhammad, approach as close as you may and prostrate yourself.' Alone, exalted above time and space and even above the angelic spheres, Muhammad went forward and bowed down before the Throne of God. With the Eye of his Heart he contemplated his Lord, and with the voice of his spirit held converse with Him, while in the depths beneath the angel hosts cried out: 'We bear witness that the Most High is One and Living and there is no other god but He, and we bear witness that Muhammad is His slave and His messenger.'

When, in his earthly identity, he was asked: 'Did you see your Lord?', he replied: 'I saw Light.'

Here we leave behind us every possibility of comment or explanation, and it may be for this very reason that the record now turns to practical matters. Muhammad was commanded that he and his community should pray fifty times each day; this number was reduced first to forty, then thirty and finally to five. This easing of the burden was accompanied by the promise that whoever recites these five prayers daily, believing sincerely in their efficacy, will receive the reward due for fifty. The connection between these instructions and the vision of God is not far to seek. In relation to such a vision it must surely be axiomatic that a constant state of prayer is the only reasonable condition in which a man or woman can exist; reasonable, that is to say, in terms of Reality, now known at first hand. In recognitition, however, of human weakness and of the fact that we seldom if ever use our spiritual faculties – or even our mental faculties – to their full potential, five daily prayers are as much as can be expected of us; not that this diminishes the absurdity of the life lived between these prayer-sessions unless we retain, in the midst of worldly activity, an awareness of the connection established in prayer and something of its flavour.

Returning from the supreme station, Muhammad was again met by Gabriel, who showed him the boundless vistas of Paradise and the suffocating corridors of hell; delight and misery, beauty and ugliness, harmony and uproar, the open and the closed. What was said earlier regarding the utter incommensurability between human language on the one hand and celestial – or infernal – realities on the other applies with particular force here; but since all things are linked a link must exist and must be discoverable in our human experience, provided we are able to extend our awareness beyond the local causes of such experience and seek its essence. Real joy – the joy of Paradise – may to some extent be tasted through images of earthly joy; and the ultimate pain may be glimpsed through the pain we suffer here.

Muhammad said once: 'Paradise is closer to you than the thong of your sandal, and the same applies to hell;' it might even be said that this follows logically from the Quranic statement that God is closer to man than his jugular vein (Q.50.16). The whole mystery of human existence turns upon the fact that God – and all that lies beyond our sphere – is so very close to man, while man, at least in his everyday experience, is so very far from God and from other dimensions of Reality. Imagery such as that employed in traditional accounts of the Prophet's vision of heaven and hell,[1] however exaggerated and even fantastic it may sometimes appear, is there to serve as a bridge over this gulf, but it can do so only if it is used as a key to intuitive understanding rather than taken literally.

There is, however, one question which has been hotly debated in the Islamic world from that day to this. Did the Prophet travel and ascend only in spirit or did he do so bodily? What both sides in the argument seem to forget is that the world we experience through our senses is not a lump of inert matter, isolated from other dimensions; they forget that what we see here is, as it were, bathed in the unseen, penetrated by it in every atom. The body comes, the body goes, changing as the clouds change form, finally to be resurrected, transmuted; and the Muslim knows that what God has created He can – if He will – re-create, here, there, or anywhere, now or at

---

[1] A Spanish priest, Fr Asin Palacios, devoted twenty-five years of his life to tracing the Florentine poet Dante's indebtedness to these Islamic sources for the imagery of the *Divine Comedy*. See *Islam and the Divine Comedy*, Miguel Asin Palacios, trans. Harold Sutherland (Frank Cass & Co., 1926).

any time in the future. Did the Prophet ascend bodily or spiritually? *He* ascended. Was his experience 'subjective' or 'objective'? It was *real*; which is all that matters.

His companions, certainly raised this question when the traveller returned to time and space and met with them in the earthly day, for they were practical men concerned with practical matters. Only a few intimates were told the full story, but even so the idea that he could have travelled in the twinkling of an eye from Mecca to Jerusalem and back again was hard for some to accept. It is one thing to know in principle that God, who made the laws of nature, can override them if He wishes to do so, quite another to accept that this has actually happened. Some of the doubters consulted Abū Bakr. 'Did the Messenger of God himself tell you this?' he asked them. 'Yes,' they said. 'Then it is true!' From that day on Abū Bakr was known as *as-Ṣiddīq*, 'the Truthful' or 'the Witness to truth'.

Not for the first time – or the last – the people were being tested. They held firm. Very soon they would emigrate with the Prophet to the city in which Islam was to become a world religion. They were the nucleus, and it was upon their faith that everything depended.

Chapter 6

THE CITY OF THE PROPHET

Particularly galling to Quraysh was Muhammad's practice of going among the pilgrims in the annual season of pilgrimage and preaching his message. It was easy to guess what he must be saying about their gods to these 'foreigners' who had come to worship at the shrines, come – moreover – with money in their baggage; nor did they welcome the idea of a domestic dispute being noised abroad throughout the length and breadth of the Arabian peninsula. Quraysh were nothing if not proud of their city and its reputation.

It was probably in the Year of Mourning that he made his first converts among the pilgrims from Yathrib. This town, 270 miles to the north, was fortunate in its location in a pleasant oasis, famous even to this day for the excellence of its dates, but unfortunate in every other way. It seems originally to have been a Jewish settlement (although these Jews were probably Arabs converted to Judaism), but at some time in the past two tribes from the Yemen, Khazraj and Aws, had arrived there, liked what they found and stayed on. The oasis had been the scene of almost unceasing factional strife. Jews fought Jews and Arabs fought Arabs; Arabs allied themselves with Jews and fought other Arabs allied with a different Jewish community. While Mecca prospered, Yathrib lived in wretchedness. What was needed – as any sensible person could see – was a leader capable of uniting the people, but no leader chosen from one faction or another would be acceptable to all. There was much to be said for seeking an outsider to fill this role, and it seems likely that some of the pilgrims, deeply impressed by Muhammad's personality and force of character, began to discuss among themselves a startling possibility. Since this man was in trouble in his own city, should they invite him to emigrate to Yathrib? Apart from all other considerations, this would be a nicely calculated insult to Quraysh, whose arrogance must have been very trying to them and whose prosperity could only arouse envy.

In the summer of AD 621 about a dozen men from Yathrib, representing both Khazraj and Aws, met secretly with Muhammad at 'Aqaba in the valley of Mina on the outskirts of Mecca and pledged themselves to him, in their own names and in those of their wives, undertaking to associate no other creature with God, neither to steal nor to commit adultery nor to kill their infants, even in dire poverty; and they undertook to obey this man in all things just. This is known as the First Pledge of 'Aqaba, or the Women's Pledge, not because any woman was present but because it contained no provision for fighting. When they returned to Yathrib they took with them one of the Prophet's companions, Mus'ab, a man known for his diplomatic skills who, in addition to teaching new converts the rudiments of the faith, was competent to negotiate with the clan chieftains in the oasis.

In June the following year, as soon as the pilgrimage was ended, seventy-two men and three women slipped quietly into the valley of Mina and sat waiting together on the rocks at 'Aqaba.[1] At midnight a small group of white-cloaked figures came to them out of the darkness, Muhammad and some of his companions, together with his uncle, al-'Abbās (another of Abdu'l-Muttalib's numerous progeny), not himself a Muslim but present as the official representative of the clan Hāshim. The proceedings opened with a speech from al-'Abbās and, as one would expect of an elder of Quraysh, he spoke eloquently and with authority. He made a modest but pointed reference to his own role in protecting his nephew against the latter's many enemies and continued in a tone slightly reminiscent of a Victorian father interrogating a suitor for his daughter's hand. 'He,' he said (referring to Muhammad), 'has resolved to turn to you and join himself with you. If you can be sure that you will keep to what you promise him and that you will protect him against all who oppose him, yours shall be the burden you have taken upon yourselves. But if you think you will fail him and betray him after he has gone out to you, then leave him now.'

A spokesman for the people of Yathrib then made the pledge of allegiance, but a man of Aws interrupted and said: 'O Messenger of Allah, there are ties between us and other men' – he meant the Jews – 'and we are willing to sever them. But might it not be that, if we do this and if thereafter Allah gives you victory, you will then return to your people and leave us?' Muhammad smiled and said: 'I am yours and you are mine. Him you war against, him shall I war against. With whomsoever you make peace, with him I shall make peace.' Before the matter was concluded, a man of Khazraj reminded his companions of what al-'Abbās had said adding: 'If you think that when you suffer the loss of possessions and some of your nobles are slain, you will forsake him, then forsake him now ... But if you think you will fulfil your pledge, then take him, for in this – by Allah! – is the best of this world and of the next.' The people then pledged themselves, one by one, undertaking to defend the Prophet as they would their own wives and children.

This is known as the Pledge of War, because it involved protecting the person of the Prophet, by arms if necessary; but some doubt exists as to when the Quranic verses permitting holy war in defence of the religion were revealed. These verses are crucial in the history of Islam: 'Permission is given unto those who fight because they have been wronged, and Allah is indeed able to give them victory; those who have been driven from their homes unjustly only because they said – Our Lord is Allah! For were it not

[1]Considering how misty are the outlines of European history in the seventh century, it is remarkable how detailed are the records of events in the Prophet's life, particularly from this point on. Ibn Kathir actually records the names of every one of the pilgrims present at 'Aqaba.

that Allah repels some people by means of others, monasteries and churches and synagogues and mosques in which the name of Allah is extolled would surely have been destroyed ...' (Q.22.39–40). According to the earliest of the Prophet's biographers, Ibn Isḥāq, this revelation came before the Second Pledge of 'Aqaba, whereas all other authorities date it soon after the emigration to Yathrib.

Be that as it may, a turning-point had come for Muhammad, for the Muslims and for the world. It was Muhammad's destiny – and an aspect of his prophetic function – that he should demonstrate the alternatives open to the persecuted and the oppressed; on the one hand, forbearance and the 'turning of the other cheek'; on the other, what is called by Christians the 'just war', but for which – in the words of a later Quranic revelation – 'corruption would surely overwhelm the earth' (Q.2.251). For almost thirteen years he and his people had suffered persecution, threats and insults without raising a hand in self-defence. They had proved that this was humanly possible. Circumstances were now changing and called for a very different response if the religion of Islam was to survive in the world. Peace has its seasons, but so has war, and the Muslim never forgets that every man born is born to war in one form or another, at one level or another; if not physical, then spiritual. Those who try to ignore this fact are, sooner or later, enslaved.

In twos and threes the Muslims slipped out of Mecca and took the road to Yathrib. The *Hijra* had begun. This word has been quite wrongly translated as 'flight', or else, quite acceptably, as 'emigration', but the precise meaning relates to the severing of all past relationships in preparation for forming new ones; a break with the past, a fresh start. Houses once full of people and noisy with life now stood empty and silent. Everything in this prosperous and united city had changed in ten years, as it does in the human personality when spiritual lightning strikes.

For Quraysh the limits of what was bearable had been passed. Enemies within the city were bad enough, but now these enemies were setting up a rival centre to the north. Restrained hitherto by principles inherited from their Bedouin forefathers and by the fear of causing a troublesome blood-feud, the leaders decided that Muhammad must die. Abū Jahl proposed a simple plan. Young men should be chosen from different clans, each one to strike a mortal blow, so that Muhammad's blood would be upon all of them. Hāshim could not seek retribution from all the other clans.

Meanwhile, the Prophet, with a few intimates, had been awaiting the divine command to join the other Muslims in Yathrib. He did not feel free to emigrate until this command came to him, but over the course of several weeks Abū Bakr had been preparing two fast she-camels for the journey, feeding them on gum-acacia leaves to enhance their powers of endurance. At last the command came. The assassins were already surrounding his house when Muhammad slipped out unseen. They could not enter the house, since this would have involved violating the privacy of the women (no one could say that the young men of Quraysh were not gentlemen), but one of them peered through a window and saw a figure curled up on the Prophet's sleeping-mat. Unaware that this was in fact 'Alī, acting as a decoy, they settled down to wait for morning.

To confuse pursuit, Muhammad and Abū Bakr headed south, a friendly shepherd using his sheep to cover their tracks, and took refuge in a cave on Mount Thawr on the road to Yemen. Here Abū Bakr's son Abdullah came to them, bringing news that Quraysh had offered a reward of a hundred camels for their capture, while his daughter Asma' brought provisions and was known ever after as 'She-of-the-two-girdles', because when they needed a rope she cut her girdle in two and gave them half of it. Meanwhile, finding no trace of the fugitives to the north, the hunters extended their search, and one evening the sound of strange voices was heard close to the mouth of the cave. Five or six men had gathered there and were debating whether to search the interior. Abū Bakr feared that the end had come, but Muhammad asked him: 'What think you of two when Allah makes a third?' After a little while the voices faded into the distance, and when Muhammad was able safely to emerge, he saw the reason for their failure to search further. A shrub, which had not been there previously, had grown in a matter of hours, partially covering the cave entrance, a spider had woven its web between this plant and the rock wall, and a pair of doves had built their nest close by. Nature, reconciled to Spirit, had protected God's messenger. 'These three things,' remarks Dermenghem, 'are the only miracles recorded in authentic Muslim history: the web of a spider, the love of a dove, the sprouting of a flower – three miracles accomplished daily on God's earth.'[1]

The specially prepared camels were now brought to them and, skirting round Mecca to the West, they made their way towards Yathrib, sighting the oasis after twelve days. They rested in a village on the outskirts, where 'Alī, who had made the journey on foot, now joined them. The *Hijra* had been completed. It was 24 September 622 by Christian reckoning, and the Islamic era – the Muslim calendar – begins on the first day of the Arabic year in which this event took place: 16 July. And from this day on Yathrib had a new name, a name of glory: *Madīnat-an-Nabi*, the City of the Prophet; in brief, Medina.

Dressed in festive garments Muhammad entered the town accompanied by seventy riders, one of whom carried before him a green turban fixed to the end of a lance. The persecuted visionary was now a ruler with the authority to impose a revealed pattern of harmony and order upon human chaos. Even as he crossed the boundary, however, he faced an immediate political problem. Where should he stop? In the territory of which faction? One after another the people grasped the halter of his camel, Qaswa. 'Let her go her way,' he said, 'for she is under the command of Allah.' After wandering for some distance, seeming ready to settle (amidst growing excitement), then ambling forward again, taking her time and fulfilling her destiny, Qaswa at last halted and sank to the ground, with all the groaning and grumbling of which a noble and self-important camel is capable. Here was built, in due course, the first mosque of Islam, together with the Prophet's house and the apartments of his wives.

[1] *Life of Mahomet*, Emile Dermenghem, p. 149.

Mecca had its famous sanctuary, but Medina now had a living Prophet, and that was better still.

The people of the oasis did not achieve unanimity overnight, but the outlines of an ordered society were established with surprising speed. Muhammad made a covenant of mutual obligation between his people and the Jews of Medina in which it was agreed that they would have equal status and fight as one if attacked. Those among the Arab inhabitants who resented the newcomers held their peace for the time being. The most powerful man of Khazraj, Ibn Ubayy, accepted Islam as a matter of form, though he would later show his true colours as the leader of the 'hypocrites', the *munāfiqūn*. Things fell into place, and the eddies which had previously swirled in opposite directions now formed a pattern around the Prophet. By sheer force of character, combined with extraordinary diplomatic skill, he began to reconcile the factions.

To unite the 'emigrants' (*muhājjirīn*) with the local Muslims, the 'helpers' (*anṣār*), he established a system of personal relationships: each 'helper' took an 'emigrant' as his brother, to be treated as such under all circumstances and to stand in order of inheritance before members of the natural family. With a few exceptions – in particular 'Uthmań ibn 'Affān, who placed his wealth at the service of the community – the 'emigrants' had lost everything they possessed and were completely dependent upon their new brothers. In view of the clannishness of the Arabs, one is tempted to describe as a 'miracle' the fact that this situation seems to have caused no resentment whatever among those who were so suddenly obliged to take complete strangers into their families. Seldom has the power of religious faith to change men been more clearly demonstrated.

The Meccan Muslims, however, had not forgotten their old skills. The tale is told of an 'emigrant' who, when his new brother said to him, 'O poorest of the poor, how can I help you? My house and my funds are at your disposal!' replied: 'O kindest of kind friends, just show me the way to the local market. The rest will take care of itself.' This man, it is said, started by selling butter and cheese, soon became rich enough to pay the bride-price of a local girl and, in due course, was able to equip a caravan of 700 camels. Of another, Muhammad said: 'He could make a fortune selling sand.'

Such enterprise was encouraged, but there were also those of a more contemplative temperament who had neither the skills nor the inclination to earn their own living, and they – as though to prove that the Muslim does not have to be an 'activist' – were given an honoured place in the community. A space was found for them to sleep in the covered section of the new mosque and they came to be known as 'the People of the Bench'. They were fed with food from the Prophet's own table, when there was any to spare, and with roasted barley from the community chest; and of all these the most famous was Abū Huraira, which means 'Father of the little cat', who followed Muhammad everywhere – just as his little cat followed him – and to whose prodigious powers of memory we owe a great number of the recorded *ḥadīths*. Perhaps he might be regarded as the first of those of whom Muhammad was to say: 'The ink of the scholars is more valuable than the blood of the martyrs.'

Muhammad himself had no wish to live in any less Spartan fashion than did his people. His main meal was usually a boiled gruel called *sawīq*, with dates and milk, his only other meal of the day being dates and water; but he frequently went hungry and developed the practice of binding a flat stone against his belly to assuage his discomfort. It was only too well known that 'he could refuse nothing'. One day a woman gave him a cloak – something he badly needed – but the same evening someone asked him for it, to make a shroud, and he promptly gave it up. He was brought food by those who had a small surplus, but he never seemed to keep it long enough to taste it. There was always someone in greater need. With diminished physical strength – now fifty-two years old – he struggled to build a nation based upon religion out of the varied assortment of people God had given him as his raw material.

It was obvious, however, that the emigrants, whose property in Mecca had been confiscated, could not continue indefinitely as the impoverished guests of the *anṣar*, who were themselves living at subsistence level. At this rate Quraysh needed only to wait until Islam died of hunger. Arab tradition, which permitted tribes that had been impoverished by misfortune to raid those more fortunate than themselves – but for which the desert Arabs might not have survived through the centuries – together with the revelation concerning the right of those who had been 'driven unjustly from their homes' to take up arms, offered the only solution. Early raids on the Meccan caravans, however, had little success. The decision was then made to attack the great annual caravan from Syria, which was under the personal command of Abū Sufyān. Scouts reported that it would be halting at the wells of Badr, and the Muslims now prepared themselves for war.

News of these preparations reached Abū Sufyān on his southward journey, and he himself led a scouting party to Badr, where the stones of Medina dates were identified in camel dung close to the wells. Reading the signs correctly, he sent an urgent message to Mecca that an army should be dispatched to deal with the Muslims; soon afterwards he diverted his caravan – valued, it is said, at approximately three million dollars in modern currency – to an alternative route along the seashore.

A Meccan army numbering about a thousand men marched northwards, while the 'emigrants' and the 'helpers', numbering in all 305, made their way as best they could to Badr; they had only seventy camels and three horses between them, so the men rode by turns – or several on one beast. They were already on their way when news came of Abū Sufyān's change of plan. The Prophet held an immediate council. Should they pursue the caravan or face the army? The decision was not really in doubt. They went forward to what is known in history as *al yawm al-furcān*, the Day of Discrimination; discrimination between light and darkness, good and evil, right and wrong.

The battle was fought on 17 Ramadan in the second year of the Hijra; Friday 17 March AD 624. It began in the customary manner with single combat between opposing champions, three from each side, and in this 'Alī, Hamzah and a third Muslim were victorious. This was followed by general fighting, in which the Meccans proved rather less than enthusiastic whereas the Muslims – lean and hungry – rejoiced in the opportunity to avenge their wrongs. Muhammad had devised a tactic unfamiliar in Arab warfare, keeping his people close together under strict discipline and allowing their opponents to exhaust themselves in repeated charges. When the time was ripe he signalled the advance by taking up a handful of sand and casting it towards the enemy. As they charged forward, there were some among the Muslims who heard, above the din of battle, the rustling of angel wings, and thereafter never doubted that unseen hosts had come closer to earth that day than ever before. The great army of Quraysh was put to flight, leaving the Muslims alone on the field, quiet in their hour of triumph, perhaps overawed by the magnitude of their victory. In this, one of the few really decisive battles in human history, the total casualties were between seventy and eighty dead.

'How do you know,' the Prophet asked his companions some time later, 'that Allah has not looked upon the men of Badr and said to them: Do what you will, for I have forgiven you!' So long as any of them lived these were the most respected among the Muslims, and of their number none was more esteemed for his courage than 'Alī who was now given the hand of Fātima, the Prophet's daughter, in marriage.

Mecca reeled under the shock. Abū Jahl had been slain at Badr, and Abū Lahab – 'the Father of Flame' – died soon after, some say from anger when the news reached him, others say from shame, after a woman beat him around the head because he had flogged a slave; in either case, this fulfilled a Quranic prophecy: 'The power of Abū Lahab will perish, and he will perish. His wealth and gains will not exempt him. He will be made to endure a fire fiercely glowing ...' (Q.111). This left Abū Sufyān as the dominant figure in the city, and he knew better than anyone that the matter could not be allowed to rest there. Success breeds success, and the Bedouin tribes – never slow to assess the balance of power – were increasingly inclined towards alliance with the Muslims. He swore a mighty oath never again to perfume his beard until Badr had been avenged.

Al-'Abbās, still acting as mediator, sent word to the Prophet that a Meccan army numbering 3,000, with 700 armoured men and a troop of horse 200 strong, was preparing to march on Medina under the command of Abū Sufyān; moreover, they were planning to bring their womenfolk with them. This was a grave matter. The Arab warrior was well aware that there are many occasions when discretion is the better part of valour or when – to use a Jamaican phrase – 'absence of body is better than presence of mind'. When women were present, however, he was bound to live up to his boasts, however mistaken he might be in supposing that women believe men's boasting. Abū Sufyān was taking with him his wife Hind, one of the most notorious women in history, who, as the army prepared for battle, led the rest in a chant promising the warriors that if they fought bravely, their wives would embrace them, but if they fled from the field they must expect to be cast from the marriage-bed.

The Meccans were camped on a strip of cultivated land beneath Mount Uhud, which overlooks Medina from the north. The Prophet held a council of war; his own inclination was to remain in the town and allow a siege, but he submitted to the majority opinion in favour of going out to battle. 'Messenger of Allah,' said one of his counsellors, 'we have before us one of two good things. Either Allah will grant us mastery over them, which is what we would like; or else Allah will grant us martyrdom. I care not which it be, for truly there is good in both.'

The Meccans had by now taken up their positions, with Abū Sufyān commanding the centre and Khālid ibn al-Walīd commanding the cavalry on the right wing. A strange pattern is apparent to hindsight, for this man and others among the pagan leaders would live to become, in the course of time, the supreme champions of Islam, the world-conquerors. This pattern appears less strange if we bear in mind the symbolism of these wars of religion, which is rooted in the nobility of Quraysh hidden beneath the layers of corruption. Inwardly and in terms of spiritual conflict they represent the noble impulses of the soul, positive in their essence but gone astray, awaiting rectification. In sacred history – and these events would be mere trivialities were they not a part of sacred history – fact and vision merge, and what happens in the dust of battle is but an outward sign, and a 'reminder', of the inward dramas through which the human creature passes on the journey to God.

In Islam there is a wall set between the realm of Mercy and the realm of Wrath – though even this wall is pierced by an opening – but there are no hermetically sealed compartments such as the Western mind finds conceptually convenient. What happens on one level – earthly, psychic or spiritual – may always be transposed, as it were, to another key, another dimension. Nothing occurs only at one level, in isolation; what happens *here* is also happening *there*, and vice versa. Behind the shadow-dance of sacred history are real figures locked in universal combat.

And now the Muslims came out to battle, seven hundred strong – the odds even less favourable than at Badr – and charged the enemy in the name of Allah, caring little whether they lived or died. The Meccan line broke under the impact, and in the ensuing chaos of one-to-one combat, the way to their camp was laid open. Muhammad had placed fifty chosen archers on high ground to his left, with strict orders not to leave their position under any circumstances. Seeing, as they thought, the battle ended and the enemy in flight, and fearing that they might be left out in the distribution of booty, they came down the hillside in thoughtless haste. Khālid, who had held his cavalry in reserve waiting for just such an opportunity, at once seized the heights and attacked the Muslims from their rear.

Many that day were cast from the field of battle into Paradise – Muhammad said of one, 'Truly he passes through the gardens of Paradise as freely as a swimmer passes through water!' – for we are told that martyrdom wipes out all sins and the soul comes from the body as pure as when it was created. Self-transcendence is the universal key to spiritual life and such a sacrifice is the clearest possible assertion of self-transcendence; what may have been done physically or by the psychic substance has perished on the battlefield and what lives on is freed of all encumbrances. 'Paradise,' said Muhammad, 'is under the shadow of the swords,' but because Islam is always careful to maintain a balance between rigour and mercy, he said also: 'Paradise is at the feet of the mothers.'

A number of close companions surrounded the Prophet at the foot of Mount Uhud. The tide of battle swirled towards them and several attacks by small groups of the enemy were repulsed. A sword blow, only partially diverted by one of his companions, stunned the Prophet, driving two of his helmet-rings into his cheek. Shammās of Makhzūm placed himself in front of the body as a living shield, and when he was cut down, another took his place, and then another. As soon as the fighting shifted to a different quarter, one of the companions drew out the metal rings with his teeth, losing two of them in the process so that his mouth bled profusely. 'He whose blood has touched my blood,' said Muhammad, 'him the Fire cannot reach.'

The cry went up amongst the people that the Prophet had been killed. Some lost heart, but others fought even more fiercely, seeing no further point in living. 'What will you do with life after this?' one of the men asked another. 'Rise and die even as he died!' was the answer. The Meccans believed that they had achieved their object, and in any case, they had no stomach for continuing the fight against men who seemed prepared to welcome death, even to seek it out. The field was theirs, and now the women of Quraysh moved among the corpses, lamenting the slain amongst their own people and mutilating the Muslim dead. Hamzah, the Prophet's boyhood friend, was among the latter, and the abominable Hind – Abū Sufyān's wife – who bore Hamzah a particular grudge and had offered a reward to the man who killed him attempted to eat his liver, which had been plucked from the still warm body.

Abū Sufyān, although by now he knew that the Prophet was still alive, withdrew his forces, and as he passed the foot of Mount Uhud, shouted to the Muslims grouped higher up on the slope: 'War goes by turns. This is a day for a day.' Knowing that his victory had been far from complete, he challenged them to meet him again the following year at the wells of Badr. But the day had not yet ended. Though weakened by his wound and by loss of blood, Muhammad led his people in pursuit of the victors, camping for several days in a village close to Mecca; there the weary men were ordered to gather kindling, and each night more than 500 beacons were lit as a gesture of defiance (the Meccans feared that the entire population of Medina must have turned out to deal an immediate counter-blow). He understood the psychology of his people, and in this way he rid them of the taste of defeat while undermining his enemies' sense of triumph.

In Medina itself opponents of Islam now raised their voices as they had not dared to do before and the 'hypocrites' rejoiced. If Badr had been proof of Muhammad's mission, then Uhud must surely disprove it. The Bedouin became troublesome, and Muhammad went into Najd by forced marches in stifling heat, his men binding their feet with rags to prevent them from being burned by the scorching sands. No one turned back. 'They rendered homage to him,' says Dermenghem, 'with death threatening them, so transfigured were they by the faith of their leader, who was so ardent that even in this small deserted corner of the world, between two ridiculous skirmishes, between two exhausting marches and two raids, he was preparing to change the face of the world.'[1]

It is almost impossible to grasp the extent of the Prophet's activity in this period. During the ten years in Medina he organized seventy-four campaigns, leading twenty-four of them in person, campaigns which finally placed the whole of Arabia in his hands. Yet this was only one aspect of his life – a minor aspect, one might think, when reading the *hadīth* literature. Far more important was his function as a teacher, and while counselling all who came to him and acting as judge in every dispute – constantly interrupted by the overwhelming experience of repeated revelations – he still found time for his family and his friends.[2]

He taught his people that the ideal at which they must aim was to perpetuate their consciousness of spiritual realities in the midst of their daily lives and ordinary business. 'By Him in whose hand is my soul,' he said 'if you were to remain perpetually as you are in my presence or in your times of remembrance (*dhikr*) of Allah, then would the angels come to take you by the hand as you lie in your beds or as you go on your ways ...'

For simple people he had simple answers, which were none the less entirely adequate. A man who asked what were the essentials of Islam was told: 'Say, I believe in Allah; then keep to the straight path.' Another asked what are the essentials of the pious life. 'Speak no evil of anyone!' was the answer. Asked about the nature of evil the Prophet replied: 'Do not ask me about evil, but ask me about good;' and when he was asked what actions were most pleasing to God he said: 'Prayer at its proper time ... kindness to parents ... and holy combat in God's path.' A man asked how he could honour his dead mother and was advised: 'Through water. Dig a well in her name and give water to the thirsty.' To others he said: 'You will not enter Paradise until you believe, and you will not believe until you love one another ...,' and he warned a man, 'Do not consider any act of kindness insignificant,' adding, 'even meeting your brother Muslim with a cheerful face!' In the same vein he said: 'If anyone removes one of the anxieties of this world from a believer, Allah will remove one of the anxieties of the Day of Resurrection from him ...'

For certain intimate companions his teaching was of a deeper and more far-reaching nature, but he did not lightly disclose the mysteries to those unready to receive them. 'I have kept in my memory,' said Abū Huraira, 'two great vessels of learning from the Messenger of Allah, one of which I have disclosed to you; but were I to disclose the other, my throat would be cut.' In this the 'Father of the little cat' was following the example of spiritual discretion set by the Prophet.

The household – the sacred family upon which Muslims call down blessings today and every day – had grown gradually. Following upon a visionary dream in which he had seen Abū Bakr's daughter, 'Ā'isha (still,

---

[1] *Life of Mahomet*, Dermenghem, p. 235.

[2] Among the people of Medina there was a particularly ugly little man called Zāhir. The Prophet was fond of him, and seeing him one day in the market, came up behind him and slipped his arms round his waist. Turning in surprise, Zāhir shouted, 'Who's this?' and then, seeing who it was, leaned back against the Prophet's chest. The Prophet called out: 'Who will buy this slave from me?' 'Alas,' said Zāhir, 'you will find me worthless goods, I swear by Allah.' 'But in the sight of Allah you are by no means worthless,' said the Prophet.

at that time, a child), brought to him by an angel, he was betrothed to her while still in Mecca, and he married her in Medina when she came of age. He had already, after Khadīja's death, married the widow Sawda and, soon afterwards, 'Umar's beautiful daughter Hafsa (also widowed). The widow of one of the emigrants to Ethiopia, Umm Salma, who had already refused both Abū Bakr and 'Umar, agreed to join the harem, while warning him that she was of a jealous disposition ('I will pray to Allah to uproot it from your heart,' he said). Like the others, she received her marriage-portion of a small sum of money, a sack of barley, a hand-mill, a cooking-pot and a mattress of palm-fibre. Later came Zaynab bint Jash, the former wife of Zayd and the most beautiful girl of her tribe, and there were still others in due course.

Occidentals usually find polygamy, not least in this particular case, either shocking or slightly comic. That is their business and need not concern the Muslim unless, in a moment of weakness or of imbecility, he thinks himself under an obligation to justify the Prophet in accordance with the criteria of a different religious dispensation and a different culture. There are strengths and virtues in a polygamous marriage as there are in a monogamous one, and it was Muhammad's destiny to demonstrate both in their perfection; but there is one aspect of the matter which cannot be passed over.

The fact that divine revelation – the Qurān itself – came, as it were, to Muhammad's assistance in certain difficulties connected with his marriages has been taken by some orientalists to cast doubt upon the authenticity of the revelation as such (assuming that they were ever prepared to consider the possibility of its authenticity). How could God have intervened to satisfy his desire to marry Zaynab? Here one immediately detects a bias rooted in the Christian doctrine of original sin and in the Christian tendency to see an absolute opposition between the spiritual and the natural. This may be appropriate in the context of Christianity, but it has nothing to do with Islam, the religion of *tawḥīd*. The Muslim sees no necessary contradiction between the wishes of heaven and the needs of earth; on the contrary, he believes that they are well matched. The Prophet's needs as a man were willed by heaven and their satisfaction was therefore in accordance with a certain primordial harmony which, in spite of appearances, is never irrevocably breached. It should hardly be necessary to add that what applies to a being at the summit of humankind does not always apply to lesser mortals.

Having said that there is nothing 'comic' about polygamy, it must be allowed that every family has its comedies and that Muhammad's household was no exception. In accordance with the Quranic injunction, he treated his wives equally in all material matters and in matters of justice, he divided his nights fairly between them and he drew lots to determine who should accompany him on his campaigns; but, as he himself said, a man's affections are outside his control, and his particular fondness for 'Ā'isha was common knowledge. Jealousy was inevitable, and he tended to make light of it. Once he came into a room where his wives and other members of the family were assembled bearing in his hand an onyx necklace, which had just been presented to him. Holding it up, he said: 'I shall give this to her whom I love best of all!' He allowed a pause while they whispered together, sure that he would give it to 'the daughter of Abū Bakr'. When he had left them long enough in suspense, he called his little granddaughter to him and clasped it round her neck.

'If the revelation comes to me when I am under the coverlet of a woman,' he said once, 'it is only when I am with 'Ā'isha.' She herself, as was mentioned previously, was not without a streak of jealousy. He asked her once, half-teasing, if she would not like to die before him so that he could bury her and pray at her funeral. 'I should like that well enough,' she said, 'if I did not think that on returning from my funeral you would console yourself with another woman.' His companions were often astonished by the freedom of speech in the household. 'Umar on a certain occasion reproached his wife for daring to answer him back. 'You astonish me!' she said; 'You do not want me to say a word to you, yet your daughter does not hesitate to reply to the Messenger of Allah.' 'She shall be well punished,' said 'Umar, and he hastened to Hafsa's apartment. 'By Allah, yes,' she said, 'We answer him back!' Nonplussed, 'Umar could only growl, 'I warn you against the punishment of Allah and the wrath of His Prophet.'[1]

The tense and delicate balance between the glory of Muhammad's prophethood, his closeness to God and his visionary gifts, the Herculean tasks he undertook and accomplished in the world, and the warmth and liveliness of his household is at the heart of the Muslim view of life; if this is understood, Islam is understood.

Problems in Mecca prevented Abū Sufyān from keeping his appointment at the wells of Badr in the year following Uhud, but he was not idle. By now he must have understood very well that the old game of tit for tat was no longer valid. Either the Muslims must be destroyed or the game was lost for ever. With great diplomatic skill he set about forming a confederacy of Bedouin tribes, some no doubt opposed to the Muslims and others merely eager for plunder, and at the same time he began quietly to sound out the Jews in Medina regarding a possible alliance. In the fifth year of the Hijra (early in AD 627) he set out with 10,000 men, the greatest army ever seen in the Hejaz. Medina could raise at most 3,000 to oppose him.

The Prophet presided over a council of war, and this time no one suggested going out to meet the enemy. The only question was how the town could best be defended. At this point Salmān the Persian, a former slave who had become one of the closest of the companions, suggested the digging of a deep ditch to join the defensive strongpoints formed by the lava fields and by fortified buildings. This was something unheard-of in Arab warfare, but the Prophet immediately appreciated the merits of the plan and work began at once, he himself carrying rubble from the diggings

---

[1] Even the closest among the companions seem to have had difficulty in adjusting to the freedom and ease of the Prophet's household. Coming to the house one day Abū Bakr heard his daughter 'Ā'isha's voice raised in argument. Upon entering he caught hold of her saying: 'Never again let me catch you raising your voice to the Messenger of Allah!' Muhammad prevented him from slapping her and he left the house, shaking his head over such behaviour. Returning next day he found husband and wife together in perfect amity. 'Will you bring me into your peace as you brought me into your war?' he asked. 'We have done so,' said Muhammad; 'indeed we have done so!'

on his bare back. In spite of approaching danger, the diggers seem to have been in festive mood, singing and joking together.

The work was barely finished when the confederate army appeared on the horizon. The Prophet brought every available man to the ditch, leaving the town itself under the command of a blind companion, and the enemy was met with a hail of arrows as they came up to the unexpected obstacle. They never crossed it, but remained in position for three or four weeks, exchanging arrows and insults with the defenders. The weather turned severe, with icy winds and a tremendous downpour, and this proved too much for the Bedouin confederates. They had come in the expectation of easy plunder and saw nothing to be gained from squatting beside a muddy ditch in appalling weather and watching their beasts die for lack of fodder. They faded away without so much as a farewell to Abū Sufyān. He, however, was busy with what must have seemed a more promising plan. The Jewish tribe of Bani Qurayzah showed definite interest in betraying the city from within, and this offered him his only hope of victory. Negotiations dragged on, however, and the army was disintegrating as he waited. He withdrew. The game was over, and he had lost.

Nothing is worse, in Arab eyes, than betrayal of trust and the breaking of a solemn pledge. It was time now to deal with Bani Qurayzah, and they were told to choose an arbitrator who would decide their punishment. They chose the head of the clan with which they had long been in alliance, Sa'd ibn Mu'ādh of Aws, who was dying from wounds received at Uhud and had to be propped up to give judgement. Without hesitation, he condemned the men of the tribe to death, and the sentence was carried out.

It is doubtful whether any incident in the Prophet's life shocks the Westerner more deeply than this; he may succeed in accepting much else that is contrary to his own traditions, but here he comes to the sticking-point. Perhaps this tells us more about the contradictions inherent in contemporary Western sensibility than it does about Islam. Ours is a century in which there has been greater slaughter than in all the preceding centuries of recorded history put together, and we find it acceptable to kill any number of people, including women and children, provided this is done at a distance and never on a one-to-one basis. Yet these same slaughterers of the innocent shrink from executing a traitor who is undermining the very structure of their society, or a criminal whose crimes are so hideous that his continued existence is an offence to humanity. One may be allowed to speculate as to how our behaviour and our 'principles' would appear to an Arab of the seventh century.

In any case, the Prophet's acts of rigour (but for which the religion of Islam could scarcely have survived) were no different in substance to the rigour of the Hebrew prophets or of the leaders of Christendom in its period of greatness. As Schuon has remarked, when Westerners reproach Muhammad for this, 'they start either from the assumption that the victims were necessarily innocent or else from the error that there are none so guilty as to merit such treatment. The Muslim's rejoinder is that this treatment was proportionate to the degree of moral or physical guilt, which is irrefutable once one admits that the guilt was real ...'[1]

Mecca was now so weakened that, following upon a visionary dream in which he entered the Ka'ba, the Prophet decided to perform the Lesser Pilgrimage. He set off with about a thousand of his people, mounted on his camel Qaswa, the one that had chosen the site of the first mosque. They halted at a place called Hudaybiyyah. After they had rested Qaswa refused to go a step further, so there they stayed while envoys negotiated with the leaders of Quraysh. While they were waiting, the Prophet received a revelation instructing him to call for an act of allegiance from his people. They came to him one by one as he sat under an acacia tree with its spring foliage breaking into leaf, and one by one they pledged themselves to him. Of this pledge the Qurān says: 'They that swear allegiance unto thee swear it unto none but Allah. The hand of Allah is over their hands. So whosoever breaketh his oath breaketh it only unto his soul's hurt and whosoever keepeth his covenant with Allah, truly unto the same He will give immense reward' (Q.48.10).

As so often in Islam, the spiritual and the practical come together in a single act. These same words are used to this day when an initiate into a Sufi brotherhood takes the hand of his Spiritual master and pledges allegiance to him. It is no small thing to feel 'the hand of God', so close and so compelling, over a human hand. At the same time, the pledge of Hudaybiyyah ensured that the Muslims would stand up to their most severe test and accept what is most unacceptable – particularly to an Arab – a far-sighted compromise in which present advantage is sacrificed for future gain.

An agreement was drawn up with the representatives of Quraysh, and, to the horror of his companions, the Prophet allowed them to strike out from the heading the words 'In the name of Allah, the merciful, the compassionate'. He agreed to withdraw on this occasion, on the understanding that in the following year Quraysh would evacuate Mecca and permit the Muslims to perform the Lesser Pilgrimage. It was also agreed that any fugitives from Mecca who came to Medina would be returned. At the time this must have seemed a major concession; in the event, the Meccans themselves had to request its cancellation soon afterwards, since all that happened was that men who would otherwise have made their way peacefully to Medina now fled westwards to the coast and became freebooters, preying on the caravans of Quraysh.

Negotiating with Quraysh on terms of equality, Muhammad knew that this was the turning-point, and if his people did not entirely understand the necessity for the truce, it was sufficient that they trusted his judgement totally. Long afterwards, when a mighty empire had grown from the seeds planted in these years of struggle, those who had taken the oath of loyalty at Hudaybiyyah were shown a respect second only to that shown to the survivors of Badr.

Soon after this Muhammad married Umm Habība, a daughter of Abū Sufyān (she had been a Muslim for some years), forging an important

[1] *Islam and the Perennial Philosophy*, Frithjof Schuon (World of Islam Festival Publishing Co., 1976), p. 28.

blood-tie with 'the enemy', and at about this time he received a revelation to the effect that: 'It may be Allah will establish love between you and those with whom you are at enmity'. The truce now enabled him to deal with the long-standing problem of Khaybar, a fortress occupied by Jews hostile to Islam. They were offered their lives if they departed from the fortress, leaving their property behind. They at once pointed out that no one was better equipped to look after this property on behalf of the Muslims than themselves; they stayed as they were, simply paying rent to Medina. One of their women roasted a lamb and poisoned the shoulder, which was known to be Muhammad's favourite joint; as soon as he tasted a mouthful he spat it out (a small amount of the poison may, however, have been ingested), whereupon the poisoner explained that she had only been testing his claim to be a prophet. A beautiful woman of Khaybar, Safiyyah by name, converted to Islam and married the Prophet at the first halt on the homeward march.

In the following year Quraysh withdrew to the hills, in accordance with their undertaking, and some two thousand Muslims performed the rites of the Lesser Pilgrimage. Bilāl, the former slave who had been tortured for his faith, made the Call to Prayer from the roof of the Ka'ba, so that his resonant voice filled the valley. Another major step had been taken towards the great reconciliation, the 'Day of Mercy', and even while Quraysh waited among the rocks to be allowed to return to their city, more Bedouin tribes were coming over to the Muslims; the process had now taken on its own momentum.

Soon afterwards an emissary sent by Muhammad to the Governor of Basra was killed by a northern tribe allied to the Byzantines, and Zayd – the former slave who had entered Muhammad's household at the time of his marriage to Khadīja – set off in command of a large force to deal with the situation. He was killed in a skirmish and the day was saved by Khālid ibn al-Walīd (recently converted to Islam), who had nine sabres snap off in his hand before the enemy was driven back. Zayd's death was a profound personal blow to Muhammad and he wept unashamedly when the dead man's little daughter met him in the street and threw herself into his arms. 'What is this, O Messenger of Allah?' asked a passer-by (rather unnecessarily). 'I shed the tears of friendship for the loss of a friend,' he said.

An unintentional infringement of the truce, when a Muslim was killed in a scuffle, threw Mecca into a state close to panic. Abū Sufyān was at once dispatched to Medina to see what could be salvaged from the disaster. Having failed to persuade either Abū Bakr or 'Umar to intercede for him with the Prophet, he went to his daughter Umm Habībah. He was about to sit down on a rug when she snatched it from under him; the great chieftain of Quraysh, the proudest man in Arabia, was not good enough to sit where the Prophet had sat. In despair he paid a visit to Fātima, who had her little son Hasan with her. Attempting to combine diplomacy with flattery, he told her: 'You may instruct this son of yours to give me protection – in this way he will achieve renown among the Arabs'. Fātima, always sparing of words, answered simply: 'He is too young.' Accounts vary as to whether he actually obtained an audience with the Prophet, but it seems clear that he now had it in mind to seek terms for the surrender of Mecca.

Late in the eighth year of the Hijra (at the end of AD 629), 10,000 Muslims set out for Mecca under the personal command of the Prophet and pitched camp on the heights overlooking the city. Here he received his uncle, al-'Abbās, who had decided that the moment had finally come to accept Islam. 'You are the last of the "emigrants" just as I am the last of the Prophets,' he said, with an irony that was probably lost on this subtle man. The final act of the great drama was certainly not without humour. Having persuaded Abū Sufyān that he alone could save him from having his head chopped off, al-'Abbās brought the Meccan leader into camp riding behind him on his mule. The powers of this world, when they finally come to God, do not always preserve their dignity.

'Umar drew his sword as they approached and was promptly ordered to sheathe it. The Prophet said: 'Is it not time, O Abū Sufyān, that you realized there is no God but Allah?' 'I already know it,' he replied, 'for had there been another, He would have helped me.' He was prepared to pronounce the first *shahādah*, but – presumably to preserve some shred of dignity – hesitated over the second (recognizing Muhammad as the Messenger of Allah) and asked to be allowed to sleep on the matter. Next morning he made the full profession of faith. It is too easy in this context to speak of insincerity, and a good Muslim is not permitted to do so, since he cannot read the secrets of hearts, but Abū Sufyān was a man of power who could only recognize truth when it manifested itself as power. He said quietly to a friend: 'I have never before seen such sovereignty as this!' A natural survivor, he lived on to the age of ninety-two, having lost his sight fighting under the banner of Islam; an old man who had seen the world transformed and earned his niche in the history of great events.

His wife Hind also submitted, but when told she must not steal, asked incredulously whether this meant that she could not steal from her husband, who was notoriously stingy. 'That,' said the Prophet with a smile, 'is not stealing.' Her vindictive nature does not seem to have been changed by her conversion. Abū Sufyān divorced her and when, many years later, their son Mu'āwiyah became Caliph of Islam, she forbad him ever to see his father or to help him in any way.

The Prophet's powers of command were now put to their greatest test, for the Muslims had much to avenge; fighting almost broke out when Khālid's cavalry was attacked, but he controlled the situation. In the words of Dermenghem, 'Dawn brought a new day of which humanity might well have been proud.' Mounted on Qaswa, Muhammad rode into his birthplace unopposed and immediately proclaimed a general amnesty. 'This,' he said, 'is the Day of Mercy, the day upon which Allah hath exalted Quraysh.' He had come, not to destroy, but to rectify, and a noble people had been reborn. The historical consequences of this act of clemency were incalculable. Over the succeeding centuries no conquering Muslim general could enter a territory or city without knowing himself subject – on pain of damnation – to the obligation of mercy and the necessity to follow the example set that day; and this in turn led to countless conversions among people who learned forebearance from this example.

To complete the reconciliation Quraysh were treated with the utmost generosity over the following months; Abū Sufyān, instead of losing his head, received a gift of two hundred camels. Understandably, the *anṣār* began to feel resentful. 'O Helpers!' the Prophet said to them; 'Are you stirred in your souls concerning the things of this world by which I have reconciled men's hearts, that they may submit to Allah, while you I have entrusted to your *islām*? Are you not well content, O Helpers, that these people take with them their sheep and their camels, while you take with you the Messenger of Allah in your homes?' They were content; but already one senses a division – which would grow more pronounced as time went by – between the people of this world and the people of Paradise.

But the time for rest had not yet come. In spite of infirmity the Prophet led an army against the Syrian frontier in midsummer of the following year. The crossing of the desert was harsh and a tempest of sand overtook them. They camped that night without food or drink, sheltering behind their camels; and so they reached the oasis of Tabūk, finally returning to Mecca after converting several tribes. It was a hard road to Tabūk and the expedition probably shortened the Prophet's life, but this was his way, and no earthly heat or tempest could now afflict one whose awareness of what lies beyond this life was more acute and more concrete than any sensation experienced here.

The end, however, was drawing closer, and in the tenth year of the Hijra he set off from Medina with some 90,000 Muslims from every part of Arabia to perform the Great Pilgrimage, accompanied by his nine wives borne in litters upon garlanded camels. This triumphal journey of the aging man, worn by years of persecution and then by unceasing struggle, is surrounded by a kind of twilight splendour, as though a great ring of light had finally closed, encompassing the mortal world in its calm radiance.

After the principal rites had been completed the Prophet climbed to the summit of Mount 'Arafā and preached from his camel to the multitude. After praising God, he said: 'Hear me, O people, for I do not know if I shall ever meet with you in this place again.' He exhorted them to treat one another well and reminded them of what was permitted and what was forbidden. Finally he said: 'I have left amongst you that which, if you hold fast to it, shall preserve you from all error, a clear indication, the Book of Allah and the word of His Prophet. O people, hear my words and understand!' He then imparted to them a revelation which had just come to him, the final revelation of the Qurān: 'This day have I perfected for you your religion and fulfilled My favour unto you and chosen for you as your religion *al-Islām*' (Q.5.3). He ended by asking twice: 'O people, have I fulfilled my mission?' A great cry of assent arose from the many thousands assembled on the lower slopes and at the foot of the hill. As he came down the hillside the last rays of the setting sun caught his head and shoulders; then darkness fell. Islam had been established and would grow into a great tree sheltering far greater multitudes. His work was done and he was ready, perhaps eager, to lay down his burden and depart.

He returned to Medina. Had he not promised that he would never forsake the *anṣār*? There was still work to be done; but one day, just as the army was setting out for Syria under Zayd's son Usāmah, he was seized by a painful illness due, some suppose, to the delayed effect of the poison consumed at Khaybar. He came to the mosque wrapped in a blanket and there were those who saw the signs of death in his face. 'If there is anyone among you,' he said, 'whom I have caused to be flogged unjustly, here is my back. Strike in your turn. If I have damaged the reputation of any among you, may he do likewise to mine. To any I have injured, here is my purse ... It is better to blush in this world than in the hereafter.' A man claimed a debt of three dinars and was paid.

When he returned to the wife whose day it was – for he was meticulous in apportioning his time – he asked her, 'Where am I tomorrow?' She told him which wife he was due to visit. 'And the day after tomorrow?' Struck by his insistence, she realized that he was impatient to be with 'Ā'isha and went at once to speak to the others. They came to him together and said: 'O Messenger of Allah, we have given our days with you to our sister 'Ā'isha,' and he accepted their gift. But 'Ā'isha was suffering from a headache, groaning: 'Oh my head!' 'No,' he said, with a last glint of humour, 'No, 'Ā'isha – *my* head!'

He had said once: 'What have I to do with this world? I and this world are as a rider and a tree beneath which he shelters. Then he goes on his way and leaves it behind him.' And now he said: 'There is a slave among the slaves of Allah who has been offered the choice between this world and that which is with Him, and the slave has chosen that which is with Allah.'

On 12 Rabī'u'l-awwal in the eleventh year of the Hijra, which in the Christian calendar is 8 June 632, he entered the mosque for the last time. Abū Bakr was leading the prayer, and he motioned to him to continue. He watched the people, his face radiant. 'I never saw the Prophet's face more beautiful than it was at that hour,' said his friend Anas. Returning to 'Ā'isha's apartment he laid his head on her breast. He had used the last of his strength and soon afterwards he lost consciousness.

She thought this was the end, but after an hour or so he opened his eyes and she heard him murmur: 'With the supreme communion in Paradise ...'; or perhaps he had said: 'With the companions ...' These were his last words. His head grew heavy on the girl's breast, and when she was sure that he had gone, she laid him gently down and rose to express her sorrow and the people's sorrow in the accustomed ways, breaking death's silence with the cries which expose all human grief to the earth and the sky and the four corners of the world.

A woman, weeping as she came from the chamber, said: 'Not for him do I weep. Do I not know that he is gone to that which is better for him than this world? But I weep for the news of heaven that has been cut off from us.'

Chapter 7

THE SUCCESSORS

It is said that the Arabs will follow a man they love and admire to the ends of the earth; they will not stir for a lesser man, and their interest in abstract ideas is limited. The history of the Arabs is therefore a story of individuals – one might perhaps describe it as a 'Shakespearean' history – with high peaks and deep troughs. The same might be said of the inward history of Islam, with its vertiginous ups and downs, its great 'renewers of the religion', great saints, great scholars and great 'warriors in the path of Allah', but also with its bigots and hypocrites.

Muhammad had brought the religion of Islam, but for at least some of his people he *was* Islam. Now he was dead, and they were stunned. 'Umar, losing his head for the first and only time in his life, refused to believe it and threatened anyone who dared speak of death. Meanwhile 'Ā'isha summoned her father, Abū Bakr, who had gone to his home under the impression that the Prophet's condition was improving. He hastened to the chamber, kissed his friend's still face, and then came out to the people. 'If it is Muhammad that you worship,' he said, 'then know that Muhammad is dead. If it is Allah that you worship, then know that Allah lives and cannot die.' He quoted to them a verse of the Qurān: 'And Muhammad is only a messenger; [other] messengers have passed away before him. If then he dies or is slain, will you turn about on your heels?' (Q.3.144).

While some of the relatives, including 'Alī, kept vigil by the body, a group of the companions met in a roofed enclosure nearby and there was fierce argument as to what should be done. Taking advantage of a pause in the discussion, 'Umar pledged himself to Abū Bakr by grasping his hand, as was the custom when a pact was made. The strong man pledged himself to the gentle one, and the profound friendship which existed between these two utterly different men saved the situation. The other companions followed suit, understanding that they must now go forward as best they could in this grey world without their guide and anchor. Abū Bakr, who had known the Prophet for longer than any of them and had certainly loved him no less, seems to have been alone in comprehending at once that it was not the man who mattered but the message, so that 'Alī said to him: 'You do not seem greatly troubled by the death of the Messenger!'

What troubled him was the threat to Islam at that moment. It was a moment for daring, though he was not by nature a man to take risks. He ordered Usāmah to proceed against the Syrian frontier in accordance with the instructions given by the Prophet before his death, thus leaving the city defenceless against likely revolt by the tribes. 'Were the city swarming around with packs of ravening wolves,' he told Usāmah, 'and I left solitary and alone, the army should still go.... !' He went some way with them, barefoot, and Usāmah begged him to ride. 'No,' he said, 'I will not mount. I will walk and soil my feet a little moment in the Way of Allah.' His parting instructions were to avoid any act of treachery or deceit, not to kill any woman, child or old person, or to injure date-palms or cut down any tree that provided food for man or beast, to slay no flocks except for minimum sustenance and under no circumstances to molest monks.

As news of the Prophet's death spread through the peninsula many of the tribes renounced Islam, refusing any longer to pay the poor-due. They were brought to order in what are known as the Wars of the Apostasy, although 'wars' seems a somewhat excessive term for a number of small skirmishes which soon taught the desert Arabs that authority still resided in Medina. Within a year order had been re-established.

But Abū Bakr's principal concern was with the people in his charge. 'I wish,' he said once, 'that I were that palm-tree, to yield food and then, when that was over, to be felled.' On the first morning of his caliphate he was only prevented by 'Umar from going to the market to trade. 'But how will my household eat?' he asked. Power was meaningless to him except as a means of perpetuating the example of the Prophet. He himself set an example which was to be followed throughout the history of Islam when any question of legal judgement arose. First he would seek guidance from the Qurān. If he found no decisive text there, he would seek a prophetic tradition relating to such a case and, if necessary, go out into the town to ask other companions if they knew of any relevant tradition; if he still had no sure answer to the problem he would summon a council and seek consensus.

Worldly duties weighed heavily upon him. Some simple people from Yemen came to Medina, and when they listened to the reader in the mosque chanting the Qurān, tears fell from their eyes. 'We were like that once,' he said, 'but our hearts have grown harder since.' But not his heart. At night he would go into the city to seek the destitute and the oppressed, listening with untiring patience to their troubles. On one occasion, in the hut of a poor blind widow, he met with 'Umar, who had come independently on the same errand. The two great men, moulders of a new world of openness to the Divine and of human order, one of them soon to be engaged in world-conquest, squatted side by side in the widow's hut. They thought that this was what rulership meant in Islam. What else could it possibly mean?

Like the palm-tree, Abū Bakr was soon cut down. After bathing incautiously on a cold morning, he developed a fever and became gravely ill. The people wanted to send for a physician, but he knew his time had come: 'He has already visited me,' he said, meaning the divine Physician. On his deathbed he received a message from Khālid ibnu'l-Walīd, commander on the Persian frontier, asking for reinforcements. 'Do not delay,' he told 'Umar; 'If I die – as I think – this day, do not wait till evening; if I linger till night, do not wait till morning. Do not let sorrow for me divert you from the service of Islam and the business of your Lord.'

He died soon after, in August AD 634, aged sixty-three, and 'Umar was chosen to succeed him. The institution of the caliphate was by now acceptable to the majority of Muslims, since few doubted that the community – indeed any community – must have a leader, just as a tribe must have a chieftain, although it would be many years before the political philosophers of Islam worked out an appropriate theory of leadership. The prophetic function had ended with the death of the Prophet; his successors inherited only the political function and the duty of administering the laws set out in the Qurān and in the Prophet's recorded sayings. The caliph, then as later, had three principal functions. In the first place, he was the viceregent of Muhammad as temporal head of the *Ummah*, the community, with the duty of 'judging righteously between men'; secondly, he was the *Imām* of the community and the upholder of the Law; and thirdly, he was the Commander of the Faithful (*Amīr al-Mu'minīn*), responsible for their protection from every danger, moral as well as physical. Since there could be no legislation to supersede the revealed Law, the instruments of government existed only to enforce this Law within the community and to organize defence against external dangers. In all that he did the caliph was bound by the obligation of *Shūrā*, 'mutual consultation', laid down in the Qurān; but, having consulted with the people and sought consensus among them, the final decision and the final responsibility were his.

'Umar inherited from Abū Bakr a land at peace. The Arabs were united as they had been in the closing years of the Prophet's life. Whether he immediately envisaged the expansion of the 'House of Islam' beyond the peninsula is impossible to say, but it seems likely that he would have been amazed to know that historians call him ' 'Umar the Conqueror'. Just as it had been impossible, in practical terms, for the Muslims in Medina to co-exist with the pagan Meccans, so now it was impossible for Islam in Arabia to co-exist with the great empires of Persia and Byzantium. Moreover, the new community, still so close to the source of revelation, found itself in the midst of a decadent and disordered world; Islam went through it like a knife through butter, not so much to make converts (this came later) but to establish order, equilibrium and justice on earth; and in the words of Laura Vaglieri, 'If an isolated episode in Arab history, such as Islam was before the death of the Prophet, was transformed into an event of world-wide importance and the foundations were laid of a Muslim Empire which civil wars, lack of unity and attacks from abroad might shake but could not destroy, the chief credit for these things must be attributed to the political gifts of 'Umar.'[1]

He showed a particular genius for co-ordination and for correcting errors due to the rashness of commanders, together with remarkable diplomatic talents, taking the edge off disputes and controlling the ambitions of the less tractable among the companions. Although he is known as 'the Conqueror', he has some claim also to be known as 'the Peacemaker'. If we think of the wild young man who had sworn to murder the Prophet, and whose conversion had been so sudden and so dramatic, it becomes possible to observe how Muhammad had moulded this rough

[1]*Cambridge History of Islam*, Vol. 1, p. 64.

substance into greatness, a flowering of what was already latent within it; 'Umar's essential characteristics had not been annihilated – God and His messenger do not 'annihilate' – but had been purified, channelled and then integrated into an excellence both spiritual and human.

On a lesser scale, the same might be said of Khālid ibnu'l Walīd and 'Amr ibn al-'Ās, once the champions of pagan Mecca, then warriors of the Prophet and now the commanders of Muslim armies. The battle for the world began, however, with what would now be called guerilla warfare. The Arabs came out of the desert to strike swiftly here or there on the frontiers; by the time the cumbersome armies of the great powers had got to their feet, the Arabs had disappeared again into the vast spaces where no Persian or Byzantine forces could pursue them. Just so does the Muslim mystic come out into the world with the Void – an infinite space – at his back.

The fatal weakness of the Byzantine Empire in Syria, Palestine and Egypt lay in the religious domain. The Greek Orthodox regime in Byzantium regarded most of the Christians in these territories as heretics and treated them accordingly; far from uniting the Empire, Christianity divided it. When Khālid appeared with a small force outside Damascus and laid siege to the city, it was the bishop, a Monophysite Christian, who supplied him secretly with scaling ladders. A number of Muslims crossed the walls by night and opened the city gates, whereupon the Byzantine Governor surrendered without a fight. There was no killing or looting whatsoever (until early in the last century cities in Europe were automatically sacked when taken), and the cathedral was divided into two by a partition, so that Muslims could pray on one side and Christians on the other. Khālid moved northwards, but suffered a temporary reverse; before making a strategic withdrawal, he returned to the people of the towns the taxes they had paid for a protection he could no longer guarantee, then drove his troops against the enemy (commanded by the Emperor Heraclius himself) through a dust storm, crying: 'Paradise is before you – the devil and hell behind!' The Emperor was put to flight. The thousand-year-old Graeco-Roman domination of Syria had ended.

Meanwhile, Khālid's fellow general, 'Amr, was busy in Palestine, and here too gates were thrown open. Jerusalem surrendered in AD 637. The Patriarch, however, insisted that he would hand the keys only to 'Umar in person, and, on account of the sacredness of the city, the Caliph came. The Christian commanders and bishops in their magnificent robes awaited him at the city gates. In his patched cloak, seated on a donkey, he received their surrender, giving them a solemn guarantee of security for their lives, their homes, their churches and their crucifixes. He then visited the Basilica of Constantine, but out of courtesy prayed on the steps leading to the entrance, lest the Christians should think that he intended to take the church over as a mosque.[1]

Byzantium was in retreat and the people of Syria and Palestine –

[1]By way of contrast, Christian as well as Muslim writers always remind us that when the Crusaders captured Jerusalem in 1099 they slaughtered every man, woman and child they could catch, riding in blood, so it is said, 'up to their bridle reins'. But this – or so they supposed – was required by Christian doctrine concerning heretics and 'pagans'.

numbering about five million, almost all of them Christians – were at peace. The Muslims showed no interest either in imposing Islam or in creating a uniform legal and political system; Christians and Jews were left to govern themselves by their own laws, and the conquerors kept to their military encampments, guardians of the peace. But the proud and ancient empire of the Persians remained impregnable, or so it seemed. A group of young Muslims came to Court and called upon the Great King, Yazdagird, to embrace Islam; amused by their effrontery he sent them home with gifts of Persian earth to carry on their heads – that was as much of his territory as he was prepared to surrender to these upstarts.

Arab raids on the frontiers were, however, becoming a nuisance. They were unlikely to become anything more than a nuisance since 'Umar, always fearful of over-extension, had forbidden the army to cross the Zagros mountains into the Persian heartland; but Yazdagird was young and rash, though not without some justification for his rashness. It must have seemed absurd to suppose that a handful of Arabs would attempt to take on the two superpowers simultaneously. He ordered his commander, Rustam, to cross the Euphrates and drive these 'desert rats' back into the barren wastes where they belonged.

Envoys went to and fro between Rustam and the Muslim commander, Sa'd; an encounter of two different worlds, almost of two different planets. The Arab, clothed as he might be clothed when tending his flocks, would ride his horse as near as he could to where Rustam sat in state, surrounded by the nobles in their diadems and finery, then stride up to confront the Persian general. Pointing to the slender spear of one such envoy, Rustam asked: 'What toy is that in your hand?' 'A burning coal,' said the Arab, 'is no cooler for being small!' To another Rustam remarked upon the shabbiness of his weapon. 'Shabby sheath, sharp edge!' was the reply.

Battle was joined in the summer of AD 637 and lasted three days, in the midst of a blinding sandstorm; and on the third day Rustam was slain. The Persians fled in panic leaving most of Mesopotamia – or what is now Iraq – in the hands of the Muslims. The spoils of war were beyond anything the Arabs could have imagined even in their dreams. One of the soldiers was mocked when he sold his share for a thousand dinars, though it was worth far more. 'I never knew,' he said, 'that there was a number above ten hundred!' But this was as nothing compared with the treasures of Ctesiphon, the capital of the Empire, which fell soon afterwards. Amazed beyond amazement, the conquerors wandered amongst the gardens and pavilions of the most luxurious Court on earth, taking in their hands vessels of gold and silver, magnificent vestments heavy with jewels, together with the crown and robes of the Great King himself. There was a life-size camel made of silver, with a rider all of gold, and a golden horse with emeralds for teeth, its neck set with rubies. But the greatest treasure of all was the royal carpet, representing a garden set against a background of wrought gold, its walks of silver and its lawns of clustered emeralds, with rivulets of pearls to water them and trees, flowers and fruit of diamonds and other precious stones.

'Umar was in favour of keeping the carpet whole, as a trophy, but 'Ali reminded him of the instability of all earthly things, and so it was cut into pieces and the pieces distributed among the people. Surveying the spoils of Persia 'Umar wept. 'I see,' he said, 'that the riches which Allah has bestowed upon us will become a spring of worldliness and envy and, in the end, a calamity for the people.' His sensitive nostrils had, as it were, caught the stench of corruption borne on a wind out of the future.

Late in 639 'Amr ibn al-'Ās, who had halted close to the border between Palestine and Sinai, received a letter from the Caliph. Aware of the doubts in 'Umar's mind about this further expedition into the unknown, he immediately led his men across the frontier, and only when this was done did he open the sealed orders: 'If, when you read this letter, you are still in Palestine you must abandon the undertaking; if, however, you have already crossed into Egypt you may proceed.' 'Amr then enquired innocently of those around him whether he was now in Palestine or Egypt.

In the following year he defeated the Byzantine army and, in 641, crossed the Nile; soon afterwards he was able to report: 'I have captured a city from the description of which I shall refrain. Suffice it to say that I have taken therein 4,000 villas, 4,000 baths, 40,000 Jews liable to poll-tax, and 400 pleasure palaces fit for kings.' This was Alexandria, the greatest city of the time, with over a million inhabitants. But the Caliph had a profound dislike for boastful generals who attributed victories to their own skill or daring: in the sight of God no man's skill amounted to anything, nor any man's daring. Instead of congratulations 'Amr received an angry letter accusing him of having grown rich, and soon afterwards a special envoy arrived to confiscate half his property. He complained of the 'evil age' in which an honourable man could be so ill treated. 'Were it not for this age which you hate,' replied the envoy, 'you would now be kneeling in the courtyard of your house at the feet of a goat whose abundance of milk would please you or its scarcity dismay you.' There was really no answer to that; but some time later, when he was military Governor of Egypt, but without control of the finances of the province, 'Amr grumbled that he was like a man who holds a cow's horns while someone else enjoys her milk.

This same envoy visited Sa'd, the conqueror of Iraq, at his base in Kufa and handed him a letter from 'Umar: 'I hear that you have built yourself a mansion and erected a door between yourself and the people ... Come out of it! And never erect a door to keep people out and banish them from their rights, so that they have to wait until you are ready to receive them.' Such was the influence of the early caliphs upon the subsequent history of Islam that, to this day, a senior official in the Arab world may face grave criticism if he tries to keep people out of his office and expects them to wait until he is 'ready to receive them'. Khālid, of whom the nineteenth-century orientalist Sir William Muir wrote that 'his conduct on the battlefields. ... must rank him as one of the greatest generals of the world',[1] was even more harshly treated. He was honourably – but compulsorily – retired from his command and died in poverty.

What one senses in 'Umar's conduct of affairs throughout his caliphate

[1] *Annals of the Early Caliphate*, Sir W. Muir (London: Smith, Elder & Co., 1883), p. 21.

is a desperate struggle to prevent the forces of this world – pride, power and wealth – from infiltrating the sacred community; yet still they seeped in. He may well have known that this was one battle he could not hope to win, but it had to be fought none the less; and if the great men of the time – such military geniuses as Khālid, 'Amr and Sa'd – had to be brought low, this was of little consequence and was, in any case, for their souls' good. In his own life 'Umar observed the most rigid discipline and self-denial. 'Nothing of the Lord's goods is allowed me,' he said, 'except a garment for winter and one for summer, and enough for the Pilgrimage and the rites, and food for me and my household at the middle rate allowed one of my people; beyond that I have no more right than any other Muslim.'[1]

In fact he did not even observe the middle way, but was so frugal in his habits that his daughter Hafsah begged him to take better care of himself, if only for the Muslims' sake. 'I take your meaning,' he replied, 'but it was in a certain path that I said farewell to two companions of mine' – he meant the Prophet and Abū Bakr – 'and if I turned away from the path in which I walked with them I should never find them again at journey's end.' So tall that he towered above the people 'as though on horseback', grey and prematurely aged, he went about the town barefoot, drawing his patched cloak about him, never satisfied that he was doing his duty as he should. He planned to spend a year travelling among the Muslims, for he knew not – he said – what demands might have been cut short before they came to his attention. 'By God,' he said once, 'I do not know whether I am a caliph or a king; and if I am a king, that is a fearful thing'; this was said in connection with the necessity for taxation, which suggests that he was aware – as are few earthly rulers – of the profound moral problems involved in the seizure of the people's goods or earnings for the purposes of the state.

Distinguished prisoners of war, when they were brought to Medina, expected to see palaces, splendour and pomp such as they might have seen in Byzantium or Ctesiphon. In the dusty square of a little mud-brick town they met, instead, with a circle of Arabs seated on the ground, one of them – treated by the others as an equal – taller than the rest; it was little wonder that they had some difficulty in grasping that this was the ruler of an empire which was expanding week by week. An ally, a prince of the Ghassanids, who had been allied previously with Byzantium but had turned to Islam after the Emperor fled from the field of battle, arrived in Medina splendidly clad and with an entourage of grandees. A Bedouin chanced to step on his robe, causing him to stumble, and he struck the man in the face. He was hauled before 'Umar and the Bedouin was given the right to return the blow. The prince reverted to the Christian faith, in which due respect was paid to his rank.

Riches were now pouring into the treasury, but 'Umar had an intense distaste for keeping wealth locked up and insisted upon immediate distribution. A register of 'pensioners' was instituted, headed by 'Ā'isha, followed by the other surviving 'Mothers of the Faithful', then by relatives of the Prophet, men who deserved well of Islam (such as the survivors of

---

[1]Quoted from an anthology of original texts: *Muhammad's People* by Eric Schroeder (Portland, USA: Bond Wheelright Co.), p. 167.

Badr), men who had learned the Qurān by heart, and soldiers who had fought bravely in the wars. An administration was being built up, but since the Arabs had little experience of such matters, it was a question of devising appropriate institutions as they went along. Yet, for all his labours in Medina, the Caliph found time to travel, and in doing so lost no opportunity to set an example for future generations of Muslims. On one of his journeys, in a year of famine, he came upon a poor woman seated at the roadside with her children beside a fire upon which was an empty pot; he hastened to the nearest village, procured bread and meat, and returned to cook her a meal.

He made a tour of Syria, and before he left the province, an event occurred which stirred the hearts of the faithful. Bilāl, the first *mu'ezzin* of Islam, had retired there, having refused after the Prophet's death ever again to make the public Call to Prayer. The leaders now came to him and begged him to make the Call on this very special occasion. The old African consented, and as the familiar voice rose over the multitude, still loud and clear, the people remembered so vividly the radiant time when the Prophet used to lead the prayers after Bilāl's Call that the whole assembly was moved to tears and 'Umar sobbed aloud.

'Umar had been caliph for ten years when, in November 644, a young man, who thought himself badly treated in the matter of his salary, stabbed him three times as he came out of the mosque in Medina and then killed himself. Knowing that he was mortally wounded, 'Umar appointed a committee of six Qurayshites to choose one of their number to succeed him. 'To him who shall follow me,' he said, 'I give it as my wish that he be kind to this city which gave a home to us and to the Faith, that he make much of their virtues and pass lightly over their faults. And bid him treat well the Arab tribes, for they are the strength of Islam ... O my Lord, I have finished my course.' They carried the body to 'Ā'isha's chamber, where the Prophet and Abū Bakr were buried. The dead man's son saluted her and said: ''Umar requests permission to enter.' 'Bring him in,' she said.

Violent death seems inherently 'wrong' to the contemporary Westerner, who would prefer to drain the last drop from his cup – however bitter – and die rotting on a bed, the dulled mind imprisoned in a stricken body, rather than face the dagger or the flashing sword, and in a final gasping thought of God, to fall. 'Umar would not have seen the matter in this way. Up to the time of the Prophet's death – which obliged him to change his views – he had thought it despicable to die of 'natural causes'. A noble life, he assumed, should be crowned by a noble death, which in practice meant death in battle or in defence of one's honour. As it was, his end had come at the hands of a deranged young man with an imagined grievance, but this too might have been acceptable to him. The insane are as much God's instruments as the sane and have their part to play in the divine economy. Nothing is out of place – so the Muslim believes – whatever appearances might suggest, and each man's destiny is hung like a medallion around his neck. 'Umar had finished his course.

The committee met to choose a caliph, and 'Alī was not of their number. One can only guess at the reasons for his exclusion. Shi'a Muslims would ascribe it to malice and the subtle work of Satan, and there are those among them who, to this day, curse the memory of 'Umar. The fact remains that a man may have great qualities and noble virtues and yet be unfitted by temperament and vocation for rulership, and it may well have been 'Umar's belief that this was the case with 'Alī.

The choice fell upon 'Uthmān ibn 'Affān. He was now a man of seventy, still strikingly handsome and, in temperament, genial and easy-going. The Prophet's daughter Ruqayya, for love of whom he had first come to Islam, had died long since – before her father, in fact – and it was a quarter of a century since the Prophet had said, to an envoy who returned later than anticipated from visiting the Muslim exiles in Ethiopia: 'I know what delayed you. You must have stopped to marvel at the beauty of 'Uthmān and Ruqayya!' He had been one of the few wealthy men to embrace Islam in the early days and the only one to retain his wealth after the emigration to Medina; noble and pious, he had many of the characteristics of a traditional Arab aristocrat, but there were those among the companions who soon began to doubt whether he possessed the qualities required by his great office.

The Empire continued to expand by its own momentum or through the ambition of high officials. Abū Sufyān's son, Mu'āwiyah, who was now Governor of Syria, had for some time been anxious to mount an expedition against Cyprus (he complained humorously that the barking of Cypriot dogs kept him awake at night), but 'Umar had forbidden this after 'Amr warned him of the dangers of the sea: 'Trust it little, fear it much! Man at sea is an insect floating on a splinter.' Now, for the first time, Muslim ships sailed out against the Byzantine navy. Cyprus surrendered, and soon afterwards the island of Rhodes. In the east, Afghanistan, Turkestan and Khurasan were conquered, and Muslim soldiers walked beside the Black Sea, while in North Africa the tide still moved forward and the Berber tribes were brought into the fold.

But in Medina all was not well. As 'Uthmān grew older he increasingly favoured worthless relatives over men of substance, and these relatives were usually of the Umayyad clan – Abū Sufyān's clan – including some who had been among the Prophet's most bitter enemies. At Kufa the son of the man who had shielded the Prophet on the day of Uhod was replaced as Governor by a drunken sot who, when he disgraced himself, was in his turn replaced by an inexperienced youth who lost control of the town. 'Amr, the conqueror of Egypt, was deposed and replaced by the Caliph's foster-brother, and it was not long before the Umayyads were in control of all the main organs of the state, including the treasury. A time came when the old companions would no longer set foot in the Caliph's house. 'Alī came to remonstrate with him, saying: 'The way lies plain and wide before you, but your eyes are blinded so that they cannot see it. If blood is once shed it will not cease to flow until the Day of Judgement; right will be blotted out and treason rage like the turbulent waves of the sea.' Stubborn and set in his ways, 'Uthmān replied: 'For my part, I have done my best.'

The problem was simple yet insoluble. Traditionally, the Arab tribes had always forced the resignation of a chieftain who did not fulfil his duties to their satisfaction, but the removal of a caliph was a different matter and no one knew how it could be done, except with a sharp blade. Seeing the way matters were shaping, Mu'āwiyah begged 'Uthmān to come to Syria for his own safety; finding him immovable, he said to the companions: 'I leave this old man in your hands. Have a care of him!' He waited for some response but received none. Before returning to his base in Damascus he suggested to 'Uthmān that he should send trustworthy troops of his own to protect him. 'No!' said the Caliph; 'I will never put force on those who dwell around the Prophet's home.'

The tribes feared tyranny. Their traditions were democratic – some would say anarchistic – and the idea of a centralized state was hard enough to accept even when headed by an Abū Bakr or an 'Umar; it was now becoming increasingly unacceptable. The people of Medina kept to their houses and could only watch as the storm clouds gathered with a kind of dreadful inevitability. 'Uthmān might have forfeited their loyalty, but they could not bring themselves to turn against him, knowing him to be a good old man for all his faults. Many looked to 'Alī for leadership, but he maintained an unhappy, indecisive neutrality. A man more skilled in the ambiguous arts of politics and in the management of affairs might perhaps have taken over power without actually removing the Caliph, but 'Alī was not the man for this. 'Uthmān himself waited calmly for what might come. He was now eighty-two and incapable of dealing with the situation even if he had really wished to do so. Such few friends as he had left urged him to take firm action against his enemies, but he would not use violence to save himself.

While conspirators in Iraq planned revolt, Muhammad ibn Abū Bakr (son of the first caliph) set out from Egypt at the head of five hundred men, pretending to be taking part in the Pilgrimage. Arriving in Medina they demanded 'Uthmān's resignation. 'How can I cast off the mantle which Allah has placed on my shoulders?' he asked. They stoned him in the mosque and he was carried unconscious to his home. Here he was besieged until, in June 656, some of the rebels broke in and came to him in the room where he sat reading the Qurān, his wife Naila beside him. They were so awed by his calm and majestic demeanour that they withdrew in confusion. He continued reading. Then the leaders of the rebellion burst in, seized him by the beard and killed him, while his wife – attempting to shield his body with her own – lost the fingers of one hand. Blood soaked the leaves of the Qurān. While the body was still warm a man slipped into the chamber, removed 'Uthmān's bloody shirt and set off with it post-haste on the road to Damascus.

The people of Medina went to 'Alī, seeing in him the only hope for Islam, and tried to swear allegiance to him, but he said: 'This does not lie with me. It lies with the men of Badr! Whomsoever they choose, he shall be Caliph.' He was not a man to welcome power, least of all at that moment of bitter crisis, and for some while he resisted all pressure; but he was finally persuaded that strife would never cease unless he consented. Meanwhile, in Damascus, 'Uthmān's blood-soaked shirt was publicly displayed, and it is said that no less than 60,000 of the people there wept at this sight, cursing the murderers and crying out for vengeance.

The figures of Abū Bakr, 'Umar and 'Uthmān are clearly defined in the mirror of history, but 'Alī was a more complex man, and it is all the more difficult to assess him because of the passions which still surround his name, dividing Shī'a Islam from Sunni Islam for the past thirteen centuries. In many ways he was the exemplary Muslim: a warrior, courageous and honourable, yet at the same time a contemplative and – so far as the people of this world are concerned – an 'outsider'. One senses that even in his own day people were not at ease with him; there was something about him that escaped them and therefore made them uneasy. More important, however, he lacked a quality which is also 'typically' Muslim (since it derives from the example of the Prophet): he was not a man of sound judgement in the affairs of the world, and his sense of timing – when to advance and when to draw back – was disastrously deficient.

Even in the Prophet's household and among those closest to him there had been an incipient division. On the one hand Abū Bakr and 'Umar, together with their respective daughters, 'Ā'isha and Hafsah (close friends as well as sister-wives), within the household: this might perhaps be called the party of common sense, of practicality – even of expediency – and of meticulous legalism. On the other hand there was the Prophet's daughter, Fātima, a somewhat mysterious (and undoubtedly saintly) figure, withdrawn, undemonstrative and long-suffering; a woman saddened by experience, loving God and loving her father, God's Messenger, possible more deeply than anyone else; and with her was her husband 'Alī, who had been taken into Muhammad and Khadīja's home because his father, Abū Tālib, had too many mouths to feed, and who had seen the transformation of the household under the impact of the revelation. He had been still a boy when the worst persecutions took place, and they must have left their mark upon him.

There seems little doubt that, in her quiet way, Fātima had often resented the power of 'Ā'isha – this young girl who had taken her dead mother's place in the Prophet's affections – and this may be one reason why 'Alī had done nothing to defend 'Ā'isha's reputation after the incident of the lost necklace (thereby making a dangerous enemy). Since those distant days he had always been a central figure in the developing history of Islam, and he had held many high offices and many titles, but he still preferred the nickname given him by the Prophet, when he found him one day stretched out on the dusty floor of the mosque: 'Abū Turab', meaning 'Father of Dust'. It was strangely appropriate, for this world appeared to him a dusty place, and he said once (in his later years): 'The world is a carcase; whosoever wishes for a part of it should accustom himself to the company of dogs.' It was because he had little taste for the company of dogs that he shunned power, though it was thrust upon him.

He had accepted the caliphate as an unwelcome duty, but in so doing he had stepped into the shoes of a murdered man. 'He was still a living legend, but he was a legend fighting against a ghost – the ghost of 'Uthmān, whose bloody shirt hung in the mosque at Damascus with the three severed fingers of his wife pinned to it and the bloody page of the Qurān below it.

Because he refused to punish the murderers, or was unable to punish them, the ghost of 'Uthmān haunted him to the end of his life.'[1]

This was a question which could not be evaded, yet he took no action. Mu'āwiyah, from his seat of power in Damascus, refused to acknowledge him as Caliph until the murderers were punished; but he said only: 'Let us wait, and the Lord will guide us!' He was not prepared to base his leadership of the community upon the killing even of those who might be considered to deserve death, considering that no true and faithful Islamic leadership could rest upon such a basis. He believed in reconciliation and sought reconciliation, but to many this looked like complicity in the crime. Now fifty-six years old, a stout, bald man of middle height, with a beard white as cotton which spread from shoulder to shoulder, he had put the years of battle behind him and longed only for peace.

Meanwhile, in Mecca, the lady 'Ā'isha was plotting revolt. She was joined there by two of the most senior among the companions, both of whom would have been candidates for the caliphate had 'Alī not consented to assume it: Talha and Zubayr. Whether it was they who persuaded her into rash action or whether – as has been suggested – it was her spell that worked upon them is known to God alone, but the outcome of their meeting was that the three of them set out with a considerable force to make war on the Caliph, proclaiming that they would have vengeance for 'Uthmān's blood. It was a strange journey. They came, on their way, to a place called the Valley of *Hawb*, meaning the Valley of the Crime, with 'Ā'isha's camel in the forefront. A pack of dogs surrounded them and began to bark, and 'Ā'isha screamed: 'Take me back! Now I remember ... The Messenger of Allah, when once he was sitting with his wives, said, "I wish I knew which of you is the one at whom the dogs of *Hawb* will bark". Me! I am the woman of *Hawb*.' The dogs had reason to bark. For the first time Muslims were setting out to make war upon their fellow Muslims, led by the woman who had been so dear to the Prophet. A once luminous sky had turned dark, beauty was tainted and the bonds of brotherhood broken.

They met with the Caliph's forces near Basra and envoys went to and fro with much talk of right and wrong. There is little doubt that conflict could have been avoided, but this would not have suited the killers of 'Uthmān, who realized that peace might involve 'Alī's agreeing to punish them. They manipulated the situation so that each side believed itself treacherously attacked by the other, and battle was joined. It is said that seventy men perished at the bridle of 'Ā'isha's camel – this is therefore known as the Battle of the Camel – and her litter bristled with arrows like a porcupine with its quills raised, but she was unhurt. Appalled by the slaughter, Zubayr rode off in the direction of Mecca, but was caught and killed. Talha was wounded and died of his wound soon after, and 'Ā'isha surrendered. 'Alī visited her in her tent and congratulated her on being unharmed, adding reproachfully: 'The Lord pardon you for what has passed.' Not to be put down, she answered with her old spirit: 'And you!'

She was sent home in charge of his sons Hasan and Husayn, but before she departed 'Alī and his company gathered around to pay their respects to

---

[1] *The Sword of Islam*, Robert Payne (London: Robert Hale Ltd, 1959), p. 107.

one who was still, in spite of everything, the Mother of the Faithful. A curious little scene was enacted – one might almost suppose – for the benefit of posterity. 'Let us not entertain hard thoughts about each other,' she said, 'for truly, as regards 'Alī and myself, nothing occurred between us' – she was referring to the matter of the necklace – 'other than commonly happens between a wife and her husband's family, and indeed he was one of the best among those who entertained suspicions against me.' 'Alī replied solemnly: 'She speaks the truth!' and so they parted, never to meet again.

This matter had been dealt with, though at bitter cost, but the problem presented by Mu'āwiyah was more serious. In the spring of 657, 'Alī marched northwards and confronted the Syrian army on the plain of Siffin, close to the Euphrates river. The forces were almost equally matched and several days were passed in negotiation, 'Alī insisting upon the unity of the caliphate and Mu'āwiyah still demanding the punishment of 'Uthmān's killers. Fighting broke out, and it was soon clear that the advantage lay with 'Alī's people; Mu'āwiyah would have acknowledged defeat, but 'Amr – who was now in his service – suggested that the soldiers should be ordered to tie pages of the Qurān to their spears. This was done, and the cry was raised: 'The Book of Allah between you and us!' 'Alī would have ignored what was clearly no more than a trick to evade the judgement of battle, but he was persuaded to accept arbitration and left the field, weary of the whole business that had been put upon him. His only joy now in this sorry world was a small daughter from whom he could scarcely bear to be parted.

Others, however, were more passionately concerned with the ideal which they still hoped might be incorporated in worldly events and in a viable social structure, so there arose, out of the Battle of Siffin and the proposed arbitration, a movement of very particular significance in Islam, that of the Kharijites, the 'Dissenters' or 'Seceders' (the name derives from a verbal root meaning 'to come out'). 'Arbitration is God's alone!' they said, and then: 'No government but God's!' Their verdict upon both 'Alī and Mu'āwiyah was to cry in effect: 'A plague on both your houses'. Government, they said, should be in the hands of a council elected by the people, and they were able to draw on Bedouin support, since they expressed the nomad's resentment of the encroaching state, as well as the despair of many good Muslims watching their leaders at one another's throats. At the same time they represented a powerful current of puritanism which has, since their time, surfaced again and again in the history of Islam. Individuals or groups of believers have repeatedly 'come out' from the Muslim society of their day, anathematized it and called for a return to the 'true values' of Islam, as they were practised in Medina in the lifetime of the Prophet; many twentieth-century Muslim reformers might reasonably be described as neo-Kharijites, and although the movement died out as a specific sect (except for a small group in North Africa who call themselves by this name), its spirit marches on.

'Alī was now surrounded by conspiracies of one kind or another. He found life bitter, but there is no evidence to suggest that he became suspicious, as any other man might have done; he expected nothing from this world and could not therefore suffer disillusionment. As his enemies closed in on him he remained true to himself, mild, forebearing and conciliatory: some have blamed him for this, others still love him for it. Even Mu'āwiyah, who must by now have been strong enough to destroy him, seems to have had a grudging respect for a man he could never hope to understand; he agreed to an armistice, which left 'Alī free to deal with the Kharijites. This he did, effectively though unwillingly. Having established a base outside Kufa, they had marched on Ctesiphon and sacked the city with great bloodshed, since their puritanism excluded the spirit of mercy which is the essence of Islam. 'Alī caught up with them at an obscure village called Baghdad and destroyed their forces.

Frustrated in their hopes of military victory, as also in their expectation that 'Alī and Mu'āwiyah would clash in a campaign of mutual destruction, the Kharijites now planned the assassination of both men. A youth called, by a curious irony, 'Abdu'l-Rahmān ('Servant of the Merciful') was in love with a Kharijite girl whose father and brother had been killed in the battle of Baghdad, and he promised her the Caliph's head as a bridal gift if she would marry him. He travelled to Kufa in the month of Ramadan, the most sacred of all months, when mankind and nature itself should be inviolate, and on 24 January AD 661 seated himself in the mosque opposite the door through which the Caliph would enter.

Leaving his home for the dawn prayers, 'Alī was startled by the honking of geese. A servant was about to drive them away, but he said: 'Let them cry – they are crying for my funeral.' As he entered the mosque 'Abdu'l-Rahmān struck him on the head with a poisoned swordblade. He was carried home, in great agony, and lingered in this condition for three days. Before he died he begged his people to treat the assassin mercifully (in this matter they did not respect his wishes).

The tears shed for him in the centuries that have passed since his death would float many proud ships, and the love his memory evokes must have risen through all the heavens, even to the Throne of God.

So died the last of the *Rāshidūn*, the 'righly-guided' caliphs of Islam, just twenty-nine years after the death of the Prophet. Their example (or, for the Shī'a, the example of 'Alī alone) has been a decisive element in the shaping of the religion, and their troubles and misfortunes have been echoed in the living experience of the *Ummah*, Muhammad's people.

The fact that three of them died at the hands of their fellow-Muslims has introduced into the fabric of Islam a sadness which still casts its shadow over the joy inherent in lucid religious faith. Sometimes this sadness has given rise to anger, leading to further killing, and to acts of violence against a world which treated such men so cruelly. Ultimate Truth – the truth of the *Shahādah* – cannot be neatly fitted into the terrestrial dimensions and therefore finds expression in painful contradictions and through the interplay of opposites. If Truth is the principal business of religion – but for which all Faiths would be mere sentimentality and wishful thinking – then religion is inevitably stretched out upon the rack of contradiction, and only the unbeliever, in his little time and little place, is at peace in this world.

Chapter 8

THE WAY OF THE WORLD

Mu'āwiyah was wounded by the Kharijite sent to assassinate him, but he recovered from his wound. Now this Umayyad, the son of Abū Sufyān and Hind, was Caliph and there was no one to question his right. It has been questioned often enough since then, and to this day there are Muslims who speak of him in the way that Europeans speak of Adolf Hitler. This does him less than justice. He was beyond doubt a 'great man' as the term is commonly understood, and by no means a bad one, indeed – compared with some of those who came after him – he was an admirable ruler; one of those rare men who, almost by instinct, handle power with consummate skill and, for that very reason, have no need to play the tyrant.

But this is not the point. The son of the man who had been Islam's most dangerous enemy had stepped into the sandals of the Prophet, so far as worldly dominion and the care of the *Ummah* were concerned. The first four caliphs are described as 'rightly guided', not because all their successors were necessarily misguided, but because they had been close companions of the Prophet and were, in their different ways, like extensions of his being; they might stumble, but their feet were firmly planted on the path to which he had guided them. Mu'āwiyah was a man of this world. He said of himself once: 'Abū Bakr did not seek this world nor did it seek him – the world sought 'Umar even though he sought it not – but, as for us, we are sunk in it up to our waist.'

A tall man, handsome and fair-skinned, he possessed to a high degree the quality which the Arabs call *ḥilm* – leniency towards opponents, a readiness to accept insolence with affable indifference – yet he was a formidable man, and people seem to have sensed that his conciliatory behaviour and charm of manner were a matter of calculation rather than tenderness of heart. It suited him to disarm his enemies by generosity, and to someone who criticized this generosity he remarked that it cost far less than war. 'I have not used my sword when my whip would do,' he said, 'nor my whip when my tongue would do. Let a single hair still bind me to my people and I will not let it snap. When they slack, then I pull; when they pull, then I slack.' This seems a fair definition of statesmanship. Accessibility was – and to some extent still is – an obligation for an Arab ruler, and he was nothing if not an Arab. If a petitioner came to him when he was dining, he would invite the man to sit down and help himself, while a secretary read out his petition; his dinner parties, not surprisingly, were well attended.

But in one respect he broke with Arab tradition. In choosing servants of the state he paid no attention to their background or ancestry, or even to their religion (many of his senior officials, particularly in the key Ministry of Finance, were Christians, who seem to have had a nose for money). New men were chosen on merit, and perhaps the most prominent and effective of these was Zayyad Son-of-his-father. An Arab is often called *ibn* So-and-so, but what was one to call the son of a Meccan slave-girl who had distributed her favours so widely that she herself could not guess his paternity? The answer was simple, since every man – except Jesus – has had a father.

The Empire was consolidated and further extended. It was this same Zayyad who, as Viceroy of Iraq and Persia, led an army across the Oxus river and captured Bukhara; here, as in other cities of Central Asia, a magnificent culture blossomed and thrived, until the Muscovite hordes came out of the west and destroyed so much that was holy and beautiful. In AD 670 a Muslim general, setting out from his base at Qayrawān in what is now Tunisia, broke through the mountains into Morocco and reached the Atlantic; he rode triumphantly into the waves, calling upon God to witness that he had carried Islam to the extreme limits of the world. With military victories, internal peace and efficient government, Mu'āwiyah's twenty-year reign could be seen as a record of almost unblemished success. This is not how Muslims, with the advantage of hindsight, have seen it.

As the instrument of revelation Muhammad had brought mankind not only a spiritual doctrine – a means of approaching God – but also a social ethic and, in practice, a social system which neutralized many of the elements commonly considered 'natural' to man as a 'political animal'. In Medina he had moulded a sacred community, a brotherhood of the faithful, which was in the world but not of it. The first four caliphs had tried to the best of their ability to maintain this ideal. With the coming to power of the Umayyads the rot set in – or so it seems to Muslim historians – and there began a process of secularization which would never be entirely reversed from that day to this. Mu'āwiyah's achievements counted for nothing in the balance, because they were the achievements of a 'Caesar' – indeed, he has sometimes been called 'the Muslim Caesar'.

Even the change of capital from Medina, the City of the Prophet, to Damascus, the city of worldly grandeur, was significant. Piety did not emigrate from Medina to Damascus, and the process of secularization drove the spiritual forces out of the political arena. The last surviving companions withdrew from the public domain and their spiritual heirs did not return to it; yet, in compensation, their influence penetrated the mass of the people in the deserts, on the farms and in the teeming cities, and this influence, working as it were in the shadows, fostered the growth of faith and spirituality which is the true glory of Islam.

There is, however, a particular stain upon the Umayyad record which could never be erased and never has been erased: the killing of the Prophet's grandson, Husayn.

'Alī had two sons by Fātima, Hasan and Husayn. When his father died Hasan briefly laid claim to the caliphate, but he was easily persuaded to abandon it in return for a pension from Mu'āwiyah and the assurance of a peaceful life. 'I would not,' he said, 'have butchered for a mere kingdom's sake!' In any case, he had other interests. Even his closest friends lost count of how many women he married and divorced; some said ninety, others put the figure much higher, and 'Alī is supposed to have warned an associate: 'Never marry any of your daughters to my son Hasan; he will taste them and then put them aside.' Yet we are told that no woman he married could help loving him, such was the sweetness of his nature. Here, as so often in the Islamic context, a natural inclination served a spiritual purpose, shocking as this may seem to those nurtured in a quite different perspective. Because Hasan's seed was so munificently distributed, the Prophet's blood runs in the veins of a great multitude of Muslims, and in this physical heritage there is both nobility and grace.

It is thought that the agreement drawn up when Hasan resigned his claim included a provision that, after his death, the caliphate should revert to the descendants of 'Alī. When he did die (poisoned, some said, by an agent of Mu'āwiyah; surely a case of 'give a dog a bad name') the Caliph appointed his own son Yazid to succeed him, thus establishing a hereditary system in place of the elective one; on his death-bed he warned Yazid – a cheerful and luxury-loving young man whose mother was a Christian – that the people of Iraq would encourage Husayn to claim the caliphate. 'Defeat him,' he said, 'but then deal gently with him, for the blood of the Messenger of Allah runs in his veins.' Mu'āwiyah was right. No sooner had they received news of his death than the citizens of Kufa sent a message to Husayn urging him to accept the caliphate, whereupon he set out for Iraq with eighteen members of his household and some sixty others.

The Governor of Iraq dispatched a great army against him, and the people of Kufa, cowed and frightened, left Husayn to his fate. 'The heart of Kufa is with thee,' reported a messenger, 'but its sword is against thee.' On the plain of Karbala by the Euphrates river he drew up his little band in battle order, facing 4,000 troops. The Governor demanded unconditional surrender. He and his people resolved to die.

He fought as his father had fought when young, a lion-hearted man, dazzled by a vision in which ordinary mortals would be glad to share, brave beyond any common notion of courage. Early in the battle his ten-year-old nephew was struck by an arrow and died in his arms. In a short time two of his sons, four half-brothers, five nephews and five cousins fell; mortally wounded, he charged the enemy with such fury that they scattered on either side of him until he fell. Then they drove a spear into his back and cut off his head.

The martyrdom of the Prophet's beloved grandson at the hands of these Muslims had repercussions which still roll through the world like the waves which follow an earthquake on the sea-bed, and like Cain's murder of his brother Abel, it has burnt itself into the conscience of a great sector of mankind. Europeans, who are seldom emotionally involved in their own past history, and Americans who have little history in which to be involved, find it difficult to comprehend the immediacy – the timelessness

– of certain events in Islamic history so far as Muslims are concerned. Tens of thousands of young people have been ready to die – and have died – because Husayn came to such an end; in doing so they have hoped, whether consciously or not, in some way to redeem a humanity soiled by his death.

A young Iranian soldier of the 1980s, questioned by a Western newspaper correspondent regarding his attitude to death in battle, immediately recalls the martyrdom of Husayn. 'It is impossible,' he says, 'for you in the West to understand. We do not seek death but we regard death as a journey from one form of life to another, and to be martyred while opposing God's enemies brings us closer to God. There are two phases in martyrdom: we approach God, and we also remove the obstacles which exist between God and His people ... Becoming a martyr is not a passive think, like standing somewhere and waiting to be killed. It is an active thing. Imam Husayn ... killed as many of his enemies as possible before he was martyred ...'[1]

To this day Husayn's death is commemorated annually by Shi'a Muslims in Iran and in parts of Iraq, India and Pakistan – and nowhere more than at Karbala – by an outpouring of grief which leaves the Western observer appalled, and which profoundly shocks the Sunni Muslim (who sees in it something contrary to the spirit of sober resignation which, for him, is characteristic of Islam). But this grief has a universal significance. The Shi'a weep and wail not only for the death of this gallant, doomed man, but also for a world in which such things can happen, in which the good are put down while the wicked prosper. They lament this cruel world's destruction of so much that is beautiful, noble and precious. They grieve over the triumph of naked power and over the insult offered to bright hope.

Here the sense of tragedy, so familiar to the Christian tradition but, on the whole, alien to Sunni Islam in its decidedly matter-of-fact realism, asserts itself within the Islamic context. It may well be that this and other similar phenonema are necessary in the divine 'economy'; for if a religion is to be truly universal and offer shelter to every variety of human temperament, then other faiths – different perspectives – must in some way be reflected in it, though always in images which do not conflict with the basic doctrine.

The word 'Shi'a' means 'Party', in this case the 'Party of 'Alī' and of his descendants. It is often said by Sunni Muslims – the strict adherents of the *Sunnah* or 'tradition' of the Prophet, who make up ninety per cent of the Muslim *Ummah* – that the Shi'a have introduced a Christian element into Islam (a view which puzzles Christians, who do not see Imam Khomeini as a kind of pseudo-Christian); they accuse the Shi'a of giving 'Alī precedence over the Prophet himself and of treating him as a semi-divine being. This is a complex question, not to be over-simplified. All that need concern us here is the marked difference in spiritual and emotional 'climate' between Sunnism and Shi'ism, and the political consequences which flow from this difference.

[1] *The Times* (London), 7 April 1982.

With the coming of the Umayyads a political system and an imperial administration very different from that inaugurated by the Prophet in Medina had been introduced into Islam. 'The Sunnis,' says Frithjof Schuon, 'resign themselves to this fatality, whereas the Shi'ites enwrap themselves in the bitter memory of lost purity, which combines with the recollection of the drama of Karbala and, on the level of mystical life, with the noble sadness aroused by the awareness of our earthly exile – an exile which is then seen above all in its aspect of injustice, oppression and frustration as regards primitive virtue and divine rights.'[1] The 'divine rights' are those of the family of the Prophet, and therefore the descendants of 'Alī, while the refusal to accept that injustice and oppression are a part of the worldly scenario has made the Shi'a into political dissidents from the time of Husayn's death up to the present day.

The fatal step which leads to the destruction of a nation, a dynasty or an individual does not have to be taken deliberately. There is no reason to suppose that Yazid intended to disregard his father's advice and have Husayn killed. It is doubtful whether he gave the matter much thought, since his only interest seems to have been in hunting (he introduced the cheetah into the hunt in Arabia for the first time). Nevertheless, the Umayyads, although they held on to power for another seventy years, were probably doomed from the moment of Husayn's death.

The Shi'a were tireless, and conspiracy followed upon conspiracy. They worked on fertile ground. The Persians had been conquered and had embraced Islam almost as though this was what they had been waiting for from the beginning of time; but they had no love for their Arab rulers and no inclination to abandon their sense of superiority to these 'desert rats'. The Arabs, on the other hand, still felt that Islam belonged to them. They showed little interest in propagating the faith in the conquered territories, yet there were many conversions and this presented a problem. The Umayyads wondered how a 'foreigner' could be integrated into the privileged community of Islam and they hit upon a scheme which must have seemed both logical and practical. The prospective convert must first become an honorary Arab by attachment to a specific tribe as their 'client' (*mawlā*; plural *mawālī*); this provided him with an identity, a place in the scheme of things, after which he qualified as a fit person to become Muslim. As their numbers grew, however, the *mawālī* began to resent their situation as second-class citizens of the religious community and some at least must have felt that they were better Muslims than their masters. Here, too, there was ground for the Shi'a and other malcontents to cultivate.

The Umayyads, before they were destroyed root and branch, produced three outstanding rulers, no mean achievement in so short a period. Two were almost Napoleonic figures; the third was a saint.

Abdu'l-Malik, who reigned from AD 685 to 705, was called – though never to his face – 'Stone's Sweat' on account of his avarice. He was reading the Qurān when news came to him of his elevation to the caliphate. He closed the book and – so we are told – whispered, 'This is our

[1] *Islam and the Perennial Philosophy*, Frithjof Schuon (World of Islam Festival Publishing Co.), p. 95.

last time together!' It is said also that from that day on he was never seen to smile. He had little enough reason to do so. The Muslim lands were in revolt and half the Empire now acknowledged an anti-caliph, while the Byzantines had taken advantage of the situation to mount an attack in force. He drove them back, then destroyed the anti-caliph, crushed a revolt in Syria and restored order in North Africa. In all that he did, particularly in the combination of courage and ferocity which characterized his reign, he was a man of his time rather than a man embedded in the timeless tradition of Islam, a tradition preserved and nurtured among quiet men who took no part in such events, and whose names were never entered in the historical record. But there is one name never likely to be erased from that record: that of his principal lieutenant, Hajjaj.

This man was a former schoolmaster from Ta'if, and he represented a phenomenon seen occasionally in Christianity as also in Islam: one who bursts upon the world as a scourge, an 'incarnation' of wrath, perhaps to remind us that religion, though love and mercy flow through its structure, has none the less a cutting edge. When the Caliph called for a volunteer to govern Iraq, which was as usual in revolt, Hajjaj rose up and said: 'I am the man for that!' 'You are the hornet for it,' said the Caliph.

In Kufa, the Iraqi capital, the people murmured: 'If they could have found a worse they would have sent him;' but there was no one 'worse' to be found, and Kufa was soon quelled. The speech – one could hardly call it a sermon – which Hajjaj delivered in the city's chief mosque has been quoted numberless times, for no man ever threatened with more blood-thirsty eloquence than did Hajjaj; but perhaps the key to this strange character lies in the words he uttered when he staggered out from what had been thought to be his death-bed after a serious illness: 'Allah gave none of His creatures immortality save one, and that the vilest of them – Satan. I see every living thing dying. I see the withering of all that has sap. Every man must be heaved into his grave. Earth shall gnaw away his flesh, earth swallow his fluid and his blood. And the two things he loved most will soon divide: his beloved children and his beloved money.'

Islam is the religion of mercy; but it is also, and above all, the religion of truth, and truth is pitiless in that it cannot be other than it is. There is no way in which black can become white so as to appease the grief of a human soul. Not even God, for all His omnipotence, can choose to make error into truth. The relationship between truth and mercy is therefore the most complex relationship in the whole theatre of creation, and even beyond this theatre, in the principles which govern it. If a balance is possible it can be held steady only by the prophets, the sages and the saints; the rest go this way or that, to one extreme or the other. In the history of Christianity as in that of Islam there have been men for whom only truth mattered and who could not see that truth itself, when crystallized in earthly formulations and dogmas, may become relative and therefore subordinate to a higher wisdom or to the law of love and mercy. The Inquisition burned its heretics and Hajjaj slaughtered his rebels. But there have also been men – and they seem to predominate in contemporary Christian circles – who think only of love and mercy and would like to banish from religion the sword of discrimination, which divides truth from error; until eventually truth is compromised and, for this very reason, mercy becomes hollow and impotent, a sentimentality which has no roots in the heart's core, where truth eternally resides.

The voice of Hajjaj cannot be entirely silenced; we are not asked to like him and his kind, only to acknowledge that they have their place in the scheme of things, and that they remind us of what we would prefer to forget. It is none the less reassuring to find that so formidable a man could still be put down by a good woman. He continued to serve as Governor of Kufa under Abdu'l-Malik's son, Walīd, but the new Caliph's wife detested him. 'I do not like to see you alone with the Butcher of Creation!' she told her husband, and eventually she summoned Hajjaj to her presence. There is no record of what was said, but when he emerged from the audience, shaken and reduced in stature, he told the Caliph: 'She went on, by God, till I would rather have been beneath the ground than on it!'

Walīd was of a softer disposition than his father, who rebuked him from his death-bed for shedding a tear: 'Stop snivelling like a slave-girl!' An efficient administrator, he concerned himself with the education of orphans, assigned attendants to the disabled and guides to the blind, and settled regular pensions on the scholars of Medina who were learned in the religious law; he founded schools and hospitals, built roads and canals and established the first lunatic asylums; but his principal memorial is the great Umayyad Mosque in Damascus, one of the architectural wonders of the world. Amidst all this he presided over the final tremendous wave of Muslim expansion. One Arab army captured Ferghana and reached the Chinese frontier; another, commanded by the son-in-law of Hajjaj, conquered most of what is now Pakistan. In the west, a certain Tariq ibn Ziyyad crossed the narrow straits and took possession of the rock that still bears his name, *Jabal Ṭāriq* – Gibraltar – and then defeated an army of 25,000 under Roderick, the Visigothic King of Spain. 'These are not ordinary conquests,' the Governor of North Africa reported to Walīd; 'They are like the meeting of nations on the Day of Judgement;' and indeed the two great 'nations' of Islam and Western Christendom were now in full confrontation. Within three years the Muslims had crossed the Pyrenees. In AD 725 they took Nîmes, and in 732 Bordeaux; and in spite of their defeat at the hands of Charles Martel, they still held Arles six years later.

Walīd lived just long enough to receive at Court the first Spanish captives. He was succeeded by his brother Sulayman, who, after a brief reign, died of the plague and so made way for a third son of Abdu'l-Malik, 'Umar II. No son could have presented a greater contrast to his father, and his short reign of two and a half years was like a flash of light in the gathering darkness.

'Umar II had been schooled by pietists in Medina and, had the choice been his, would have chosen a life of asceticism, contemplation and good works. 'Are you glad or sorry to see me thus?' he asked a friend upon his accession.' 'Glad for the Muslims' sakes, sorry for yours.' 'I am afraid of being damned,' said the Caliph, and his friend replied: 'All will be well so long as you continue to *fear*. What I am afraid of on your account is that your fear will come to an end.' The advice of another friend set out succinctly the obligations of a Muslim ruler: 'You must see in every aged

Muslim your own father, in every young Muslim your brother, in every child your own child. As for your father – Rise up and visit him. As for your brother – Honour him. As for your child – Give love.'

He wore himself out trying to live up to this counsel. 'When I first saw him,' said a man, 'the waistband of his drawers could not be seen for the fat of his belly. I saw him later as Caliph, and I could have counted his ribs by eye.' He proved an unexpectedly good administrator, introduced sensible fiscal reforms and remedied many abuses; even more important, in relation to the future shape of Islam, was the fact that he treated religious scholars and jurists with a respect they had not previously enjoyed, recognizing that ultimately it was into the hands of these men that the Prophet had assigned the care of the Faith and of the faithful. Unlike his predecessors he encouraged conversions among the conquered peoples and, also for the first time, he gave pensions to the *mawālī* who had fought in the Arab armies. Had he lived longer it is just conceivable that the history of Islam might have taken a different course, for he had shown that it is possible, at least in very rare cases, to combine great power with virtue and integrity.

The last years of the Umayyad dynasty, however, were overshadowed by rebellion and conspiracy as the Shi'a faction became more desperate and the *mawālī* more resentful of their status. The key to successful revolution lay, so it seemed to the Shi'a, with the powerful and ambitious Abbasid clan, the descendants of Muhammad's uncle, al-'Abbās. A confederacy was formed, supported by the mass of the people, who were tired of what they saw as Arab paternalism and tired of paying taxes. Meanwhile the Kharijites, dreaming of a 'theocratic democracy' of perfect men and women from which all sin would be excluded, continued to harass the caliphate.

The disparate groups now united in opposition to the Umayyads were fired with the spirit of righteousness, or inflamed with the spirit of self-righteousness (we are free to choose which term seems the more appropriate). Everywhere – even in Mecca and Medina – they detected signs of a return to the licentiousness of pre-Islamic times, not least in what was later to be seen as one of the great cultural achievements of the Umayyad period: an intense and tragic love-poetry, which, after many generations and many transformations, took root in Christian soil and bore fruit in European romanticism. All agreed that their rulers had 'betrayed' Islam, but that as soon as power was in the hands of the Prophet's kin, a new era of freedom and justice would be established until the end of time. The Shi'a had their candidate, a certain Muhammad, known subsequently as 'the Pure Soul'. They discovered too late that the Abbasids had other ideas.

In spite of this unification of dissidents, the rebellion which broke out in AD 749 might have been no more successful than other such revolts – for the Umayyad Caliph Marwan II (known as 'the Wild Ass') was a formidable general — had it not been for a man of genius, a former slave of Persian extraction named Abū Muslim, who in that year raised the black standard of the Abbasids in the city of Merv. The Governor of the province sent repeated warnings to Marwan, sometimes in verse:

I see coals glowing among the embers, they want but little to
   burst into blaze.
Fire springs from the rubbing of sticks, and warfare springs
   from the wagging of tongues.
I cry in dismay: I wish I knew if the Umayyads are awake or
   asleep![1]

But Marwan was otherwise occupied, fighting the Kharijites in Iraq and
rebels in Syria.

Soon the whole of Persia was in Abū Muslim's hands and he advanced
upon Iraq. Marwan was encamped beside the Great Zab, an effluent of the
River Tigris. Watching the approach of the black banners borne by riders
on Bactrian camels, he described them as 'scraps of black storm-cloud';
then the storm came down upon him, his army was destroyed and he
himself fled to Egypt, where he was murdered soon afterwards. Three
hundred men of the Umayyad clan died that day. One escaped. He swam
the river with his younger brother, who responded to a shouted offer of
amnesty by swimming back and was promptly killed. But the survivor
went on, like a seed blown upon the wind.

This was Abdu'l-Rahmān, one of those singular figures who almost
reconcile us to the blood and turmoil of human history. Once across the
river, with one faithful servant for company, he set off through Palestine
and then across North Africa to seek refuge with his mother's Berber
relatives in Morocco. The journey took him five years, trudging by foot
from one tribal territory to the next, never once lying down to sleep with
any certainty of surviving the night, or awakening with any certainty that
he would live through the day. He reached his destination, however, and
soon afterwards crossed into Spain; there, with the support of a pro-
Umayyad faction, he was proclaimed *Amir* of Andalusia in Cordova in
756. During his long reign, and under the rule of his posterity over the next
three centuries, a European Islamic civilization flowered and bore fruit in
the arts, in philosophy and mysticism, and in a style of life which united
piety with sophistication in a unique combination. Christian Europe in the
so-called Dark Ages found light there and lit its candles of learning in the
great universities of Andalusia. However alien the more distant world of
Islam may seem to occidentals, Muslim Spain is an integral part of the
European heritage.

A just man and a firm believer in the Arab tradition of tribal democracy,
Abdu'l-Rahmān gave the people of Spain wise administration and a new,
equitable code of justice; he built aqueducts to bring pure water to the
cities and introduced the plants and fruits of Syria into the Iberian
peninsular. The Abbasids, though they had triumphed in the east, were in
no position to interfere at such a distance. Al-Mansūr, the second Abbasid
caliph (the first had died after a bloody reign of four years), even paid a
compliment to the Umayyad survivor, describing him as 'the Falcon of
Quraysh, who wandered alone through the deserts of Asia and Africa and
had the great heart to seek his destiny over the sea in an unknown land.'

[1]Quoted from *Muhammad's People*, Eric Schroeder (Portland, USA: The Bond
Wheelwright Co.), p. 256.

In any case al-Mansūr had more urgent problems on his mind. He had set himself to accomplish what is always the most urgent task for the successful revolutionary: the destruction of the architects of revolution. Abū Muslim – he who had planned and executed the whole campaign with such consummate skill – was invited to a great feast and murdered while he feasted. Such men are dangerous, as Stalin in our own age well knew. Surveying the dismembered body, al-Mansūr quoted a line from a poem: 'The traveller threw away his staff at last!' He then turned his attention to the Shi'a faction, whose idealism had been the motive force of the revolution to which he owed his caliphate. If they had thought themselves ill-treated by the Umayyads, they must now have looked back upon that time with nostalgia. The Umayyads, in their way, had been gentlemen; the Abbasid Caliph was restrained by no gentlemanly scruples.

For those with a taste for bloodshed it is a fortunate thing that revolutionary idealists never learn, however often history may attempt to teach them the lesson; they still advance with stars in their eyes to lay their heads on the chopping-block or bare their necks for a bullet, in the twentieth century as in the eighth. They never understand that revolution, which is by definition an act of destruction, must of necessity destroy its makers.

The 'lessons of history' may in many cases require interpretation. In this case they were spelt out in simple words and written in blood. A child could read them. The Abbasid revolution was supposed to restore primitive Islam, 'true' Islam; in great splendour and with many achievements to its credit, it did precisely the opposite. The Umayyads, with the exception of 'Umar II, may not have been good Muslims, but they were traditional Arab rulers, democratic in spirit. The new dynasty adopted the habits and practices of ancient Persian despotism. The Arab and Islamic principle of *Shūrā*, 'consultation', seemed to the Abbasids a waste of valuable time; now the headsman with his axe and leather mat stood beside the Caliph to deal with insolent or importunate petitioners.

The Umayyads had employed a number of Syrian *mawālī* in their service, and towards the end of their time the division between Arab and non-Arab Muslims was becoming blurred; but under the Abbasids it was the Persians who controlled the administration, and their outlook was quite different to that of the Syrians, who were for the most part converts from Christianity. The Persians, like the Arabs, achieved their apotheosis through Islam, and it was the marriage of the Persian genius with the Arab genius, both in their way incomparable – and yet so different – that made Islam the intellectual and imaginative marvel it eventually became. It was as though, through the preceding centuries of glory and disaster, this great people had been dreaming, albeit mighty in their dreams, and Islam was the magic wand that awakened them; but it was never a happy or easy marriage, and in the political sphere there was irreconcilable incompatibility. The gap between the Persians' long experience of centralized authority and the Arabs' equally long experience of freedom was too wide to be bridged by compromise.

As though to mark the change in 'climate' al-Mansūr decided to build himself a new capital and chose the site of the village of Baghdad, on account of its strategic position. The work was completed in four years, with the help of almost a hundred thousand craftsmen from every corner of the Empire. They built a great circular city with a double row of walls and the ruler's palace at the centre (as though the powers of this world had any claim to centrality). Surrounded by his guards, the Caliph was now isolated from his people; the days when it was a sin to construct a door were long past. The ruler had adopted an image which Westerners would recognize as that of an 'oriental potentate'. At the same time, with the move from Damascus to Baghdad, Islam now looked east rather than west, and the Mediterranean region – the old Roman world – became peripheral.

The Abbasids were a different breed of men in the exact sense of the term. For the Arabs, nobility derived as much from the mother as from the father (such skilled breeders of animals could hardly be unaware of this fact); but, for the new regime, woman was no more than an incubator for noble seed, and of all the Abbasid caliphs, over a period spanning some five hundred years, only three were born of free-born mothers. All the rest were the sons of slave-girls: Persian, European, Berber, Abyssinian, Slav, Turkish or Armenian, as the case might be. It is no wonder that Arab traditions meant little to them. They were surrounded by a corps of international civil servants headed, for the first fifty-three years of the Abbasid period, by members of the Barmak family – the so-called Barmecides – descended from a Buddhist priest; brilliant, ambitious men who used power like skilled chess-players, until they threatened to become more powerful than the Caliph himself, whereupon they were cut down.

The Abbasid dynasty produced some of the greatest rulers known to us and some of the worst. The history of Islam is a history of the clash of opposites and of the contrast between splendour and spiritual poverty, arrogance and humility, *Grand Guignol* wickedness and heroic virtue. It may be that these opposites were in some strange way combined in the only caliph whose name is familiar to the West, thanks to the popularity of the book of the *Thousand and One Nights* (or *Arabian Nights Entertainments*); Harūn al-Rashīd, who ruled from AD 786 to 809.

He came to the throne at the age of twenty-three through the machinations of the Barmecides: an elegant, civilized young man, who was so handsome that some said he should have been born a woman, and indeed he combined a certain feminine grace with the ruthless love of power inherited from his ancestors. It is said – but God knows best – that in the midst of such luxury as might suggest the sets for a Hollywood extravaganza, he prayed a hundred units of prayer each day, and each day gave generous alms to the poor; certainly he feared his Creator even as he defied Him, and it is little wonder that his nature was described as 'feverish', stretched as it was across the abyss which divides heaven from hell. He loved all that was rare and beautiful, yet the story is told of how once, dining with his brother, he was offered a platter of fish stew, and upon asking why the pieces were so small, was told that it was composed entirely of fishes' tongues. He asked the cost, which was more than a thousand dirhams; then, refusing to eat such food, he demanded an equivalent sum from his brother, which he at once gave out in alms to expiate 'this heathen folly'. Finally, he seized the priceless platter itself and ordered a servant to give it to the first beggar he met in the street.[1]

It is said that Harūn loved two people more than all others. The first was Ja'far the Barmecide, the son of his *Vizir* or Prime Minister, and he would often go out with him into the city disguised, seeking such adventures as might come their way. The other was his sister, Abbasa. One day, so the story goes, he said to Ja'far: 'I can no more do without you than I can do without my sister; when I am with her I miss you, and when I am with you I miss her. Now I have devised a way to enjoy both your loves together.' He ordered them to marry, but extracted from both a solemn vow that they would not have intercourse together. Prompted by Ja'far's ambitious mother, however, Abbasa crept one night into his bed when he was drunk, pretending to be a slave-girl. The result was a pregnancy which she managed to keep secret, and the baby, when it was born, was sent to foster-parents in Mecca. Eventually the Calph discovered what had happened and, in an uncontrollable rage, had his sister strangled and ordered Ja'far's execution.

Needless to say, modern historians are inclined to dismiss this story as 'legend' and to attribute the fall of the Barmecides to political and economic factors; certainly the family had become too powerful for the comfort of any ruler. Yet there is an element of probability in the tale. Harūn was in a position to live out his fantasies as are few men on earth. Who has not longed for those he loves to love each other, yet feared that this very love of theirs might exclude him? And who has never once in his life felt murderous impulses towards those closest to him? For an Abbasid caliph, to desire the death of a man or woman, even momentarily, was to bring about that death on the instant.

Whatever the truth of the matter, Harūn's last years were overshadowed by melancholy and perhaps by a touch of paranoia, and the circumstances of his death from stomach cancer must haunt the imagination of anyone sensitive to such things. He sent one day for his doctor and told him that he had dreamed the previous night of a man holding out in the palm of his hand a little red earth and saying to him: 'This is the soil of the place where you are buried.' He had asked in his dream where this place was, and the voice answered: 'Tus.' The physician, of course, assured him that this dream was the product of a disordered digestion and prescribed a purgative.

Revolt broke out in Khurasan, and Harūn left Baghdad to deal with the rebels. He had reached the outskirts of the town of Tus when he fell ill. An unlabelled sample of his urine was given to a doctor in the town, and the reply came: 'Tell the man whose water this is that he should make his will — there is no cure for him.' He then ordered an attendant to bring him soil from the area, and the man returned with a little garden soil in his open palm. Harūn cried out: 'That's the hand! That's the arm! That's the red earth!' and for a little while he sobbed like a child; then he chose his shroud and recited the verse: 'My wealth has not availed me; my power is gone from me!'

---

[1]*Muhammad's People*, Schroeder, pp. 298–299.

Men have hesitated to judge Harūn, for only one who has enjoyed (or suffered) the possession of absolute power, combined with great talents and all that physical beauty and charm of person can add to this, endowed by God with titanic appetites, but also with that heart's fever which is passionate love, given also piety and generosity and longings which shatter the soul and stretch all human limits to breaking point – only such a one could judge such a man or understand the terrors and the temptations of his destiny; and men of this calibre do not tell their judgement.

In this, as in the fall of the Barmecides, the Muslim discovers many lessons regarding the nature of the world and much to remind him of human mortality: 'The world's soft to the touch; so is the adder, sudden in venom.' A man said: 'I had business one day at the Treasury Office, and as my eye ran over one of the ledgers that lay open I noticed the entry: One Dress of Honour and Governor's Insignia (Ja'far ibn Yahya): dinars 400,000. It did not seem so very long after that I was in the Office again and saw this item entered on the current page: Naptha and wood-shavings for burning body (Ja'far ibn Yahya): kirats 10.'[1] A few pennies sufficed Ja'far at the end.

There were those in Baghdad who said that life was a perpetual festival in Harūn's time. The power and splendour of the Empire had reached its zenith, and Baghdad was the magnet which drew both treasure and talent to itself. In the port were ships laden with furs and ivory, delicate porcelain and silks from China, jewels and perfumes; while overland came gold from Khurasan, marble from Syria, lapis lazuli from beyond the Oxus and turquoise from Nishapur. The houses of the wealthy, with their magnificent furnishings, were cooled by imported ice in the hot summer months, and it is said that the city had 27,000 public baths within its perimeter; its first hospital was built by Harūn, soon to be followed by many others, with teaching facilities for medical students and free treatment for the poor. Schools and colleges were open to everyone, and in the great academies work had begun on translating the books of Greek philosophy and science into Arabic. The scholar and the poet could live at ease, for there was no shortage of patrons, and learning was valued more highly than wealth or noble blood.

Women dictated fashion and exerted their influence over the affairs of state, and the beauty of many of them was legendary. There was no role in such a setting for the uncultivated; they belonged in the provinces. A slave-girl or concubine who expected to take her place in this glittering society had to spend some time in a school of manners, mastering the Arabic and Persian classics, learning to recite and improvise poetry and to play on a musical instrument, and sharpening her wits at chess; attired in brocade and tastefully bejewelled she could then regard the great ladies of any other city as dowdy provincials.

Yet amidst all this splendour something of the Arab heritage – inescapable in Islam – remained; one may marvel, writes Sir John Glubb, 'at the extraordinary diffusion throughout the whole Empire of the spirit of the old Arab conquerors. Their code of chivalry, devotion to poetry, their

[1] *Muhammad's People*, Schroeder, p. 336.

romantic attitude to sexual love, their princely hospitality and generosity, was spread over the whole Empire from Spain to India and China.'[1]

Behind the walls of the great houses there may have been licence, but there was also piety and a sense of obligation to the poor. The chroniclers tell of a rich merchant who, each spring, sold off his stoves, his woollen garments and his winter furniture and gave the money away, doing likewise in autumn with his brocades, his precious tissues, summer matting and water-coolers. Warned by his steward that he would bankrupt himself and advised to keep such things for the next season, he said: 'No, I will not have that! These are the things Allah has permitted me to enjoy through the summer – or through the winter – and He has brought me safely to a time when I can do without them. It is possible that I have offended Allah either in getting them or using them, and I would rather sell these things and put the money to this purpose ...'

Baghdad's decline from the splendour of its zenith was gradual (the decline of the institution of the caliphate occurred more swiftly), although a civil war between two of Harūn's sons immediately after his death caused widespread damage and great suffering. The victor, the Caliph Ma'mūn, proved to be one of the most effective of the Abbasid rulers. Far more important, however, for the future direction of Islam than any internecine quarrels was a spiritual and intellectual conflict which took place at this time.

Ma'mūn continued and expanded his father's policy of encouraging the translation of foreign books into Arabic. He established a Hall of Wisdom, which included an astronomical observatory, and he set up a College of Translation, employing a team of scholars to work not only on Greek texts but also on Sanskrit and Syriac texts. A Christian scholar who translated Plato's *Republic* and Aristotle's *Categories* was paid in gold the weight of the books he compiled (a practice which modern governments would do well to emulate). Here, amidst the intellectual ferment of Ma'mūn's Baghdad, were sown the seeds of the European Renaissance.

The impact of 'Greek knowledge' – Islam's ambiguous gift to the West – upon Christian Europe was shattering and transforming. For a time, seven centuries earlier, it had threatened to have an equally decisive impact upon Islam. A sect or movement called the *Mu'tazilah* had already arisen in Harūn's time, and under Ma'mūn its doctrines were adopted by the state. The Mu'tazilites were 'rationalists' and their principal aim was to integrate Semitic monotheism into the alien structure of Greek thought; many of their arguments run parallel to Christian debate regarding the nature of the *logos*. It was one particular aspect of their teaching, however, which appealed to the Caliph. In opposition to the orthodox, who maintained that the Qurān is eternal and 'uncreated', they said that the sacred Book is a created object, like anything else we see or handle in the universe.

The modern mind is impatient of theology, which is absurd since this mind has been formed by the theologies of the past and their remote echoes in popular thought. In any case, the doctrine of the 'createdness' of the Qurān had immediate practical implications; it meant that the Book could

[1] *A Short History of the Arab Peoples*, Sir John Glubb (Hodder and Stoughton, 1969), p. 110.

be adapted to the circumstances of the time and to political exigencies. This would have the effect of an immense increase in the power of the ruler and of the state. Like the French revolutionaries almost a thousand years later, Ma'mūn realized that rationalism is the key to absolute power and to the ruthless manipulation of the people. Once 'religious prejudice' and 'superstition' have been swept aside, there are no limits to what can be done; and for a caliph of Islam, hitherto shackled by the religious Law, this represented total liberation from all constraints. For the first and last time in the history of Islam, an 'Inquisition' was established, the *mihnah*, demonstrating – if any demonstration were necessary – that rationalism can be as bigoted as any manifestation of religious faith. Those who did not acknowledge the 'createdness' of the Qurān were persecuted, and the greatest religious jurist of the time, ibn Hanbal, was imprisoned and savagely beaten. Others were put to death.

The 'Inquisition' lasted only for some twenty years, and the orthodox view of the Qurān prevailed; but Mu'tazilism was not annihilated. It was absorbed by a religion which has a unique capacity for absorption and it enriched the mainstream of Islamic thought. The most influential of all Muslim theologians, al-'Ashari, whose school represents 'orthodoxy', in so far as there can be said to exist an orthodox theology in Islam, started his life as a Mu'tazilite and – like an ex-communist putting down Marxists – was able to use Greek dialectic against the champions of Greek thought. What was usable in Mu'tazilite doctrine was used to reinforce orthodoxy; the rest withered away.

This reinforcement was, to say the least, timely, for central authority was now in the process of dissolution and the once unified Empire was breaking up into its separate parts. The caliphate, having failed in the attempt to strengthen its position through an ideology, now sought safety in the armed protection of a corps of élite guards. Ma'mūn's brother Mu'tasim, who succeeded him on the throne, surrounded himself with a Turkish bodyguard, which he could trust not to involve itself in local intrigues and to be loyal to him alone. The Turks soon became so unpopular, riding wildly through the bazaars and knocking people over as they passed, that he determined to deprive Baghdad of the pleasure of his royal presence and, at huge expense, had a new city built for him at Samarra some seventy miles distant.

In this way the Abbasid dynasty brought down upon itself a grim and peculiarly ironic judgement. Before long the caliphs found themselves the prisoners of their guards, who played with them as they liked, and when they grew tired of the game, killed them. The Abbasids had, so it seemed – and still seems – to many Muslims, robbed the descendants of the Prophet of their rightful heritage, temporal power over the *Ummah*. One might be tempted to say that this was just as well, considering what we have seen of the way of the world. A day came when a certain *sharīf* (a descendant of the Prophet), passing by the principal mosque in Baghdad, recognized a ragged beggar squatting in the dust. This was the Caliph of the time, who had escaped from his Turkish guards after they had put out his eyes and imprisoned him. The *sharīf* took him home, fed him and gave him shelter, reflecting perhaps that rulership is not always an unmixed blessing.

It no longer mattered. The fate of caliphs, divisions within the Empire and all the drama of great events, though these might provide the material for a thousand historical romances, had become irrelevant, no more than froth on the surface of a great river.

Western historians have often been blamed – and rightly so – for placing a full stop after the destruction of Baghdad by the Mongol hordes in AD 1258, as though all that mattered in the history of Islam ended there. This was indeed no more than the conclusion of one episode in a continuing story. Islam is a living religion, the Muslim *Ummah* is a living community and its history is open-ended, today's news as much as yesterday's. But we are not concerned here with history for its own sake. Up to Harūn's time, and that of his sons, the story of the caliphate was at least to some extent the story of Islam and had its influence upon the shaping of the religion. The point had now come when the divorce between dynastic and political history on the one hand and the life of the *Ummah* on the other was made absolute. Sunni Islam had crystallized in a definitive pattern, and the legal and social framework within which the community lived, generation after generation, changed very little in the next thousand years. The full implications of the Qurān and of the *hadīth* had been worked out by men who laboured quietly, indifferent to what happened at Court. The *Ummah* had taken on a life of its own and had become spiritually and socially self-sustaining.[1] If the entire structure of government and administration were to disappear overnight in any occidental country, chaos would ensue; if this were to happen – even today – in any reasonably typical Muslim country, we might find that it made very little difference to the life of the people, and in earlier times the only contact most citizens are likely to have had with government was in the person of the local tax-collector. They went one way, their 'rulers' another.

It is only too easy, when reading of the men who played their part on the stage of history, to suppose that those were dangerous times in which to live and, thinking of the executioner's axe, to finger one's throat. But no one was obliged to come on stage. If a man – or a woman – chose to do so, then the opportunities were tremendous, the possible rewards immense, and the perils incalculable. Glory one day and, the next, the axe. Those were the rules of the game, and the maxim was: play if you dare. It is sometimes startling, when one places some famous Muslim poet, philosopher, mystic or architect in his historical context, to realize how little he seems to have been affected by events which, in retrospect, appear so violent and so disastrous. In fact such men were prizes for any caliph or any sultan in the divided Empire and could name their own price: there was no prouder boast for a ruler than to be able to say, 'My philosopher can put down yours any day' or, 'My poet's verses put your poet's jingles in the shade'.

---

[1] 'For a long time, in fact since the ninth century, mainly despotic rulers were obeyed but kept at a safe distance, partly because Muslims had developed a comfortable social order based on an intricate network of personal and group loyalties and obligations.' The rulers may have been usurpers; 'what counted, however, is that the social order was legitimate because it was governed by the law of God.' P. J. Vatikiotis in *Arab and Regional Politics in the Middle East* (Croom Helm, 1984).

Contemporary Muslims, however, often feel ashamed of their own history. It is little comfort to tell them that the story of other peoples and other cultures – not least that of Christendom – was equally violent, for this was not just any community, not just any culture: this was the *Ummah*, of which only the best could be expected. And since, for the Muslim, nothing exists without a purpose, one has a right to ask for what purpose the Abbasid caliphs and their like existed. In the first place, it is reasonable to maintain that the spectacle of human nature extended to its uttermost limits has much to teach us about ourselves and is therefore, after its fashion, a 'sign for those who understand'.

According to a famous *ḥadīth* of the Prophet, Adam was created 'in the image of God'; and we are Adam's progeny, 'the tribe of Adam', as the Qurān has it. There is something in man, precisely because the One-without-associate, the Independent, the Self-sufficient is in some mysterious way reflected in his nature, which demands such freedom from constraint as only an absolute ruler has. But because man is not God this opportunity to extend himself limitlessly leads to destruction; in the desire for great power and in its exercise there are certainly elements of greed and arrogance, but there may also be an element of nobility striving for a supreme mode of self-expression. These men we have been considering revealed human nature, stripped to the bone, in all its grandeur, its instability and its ferocity; and those who find such men totally alien know very little about themselves.

Secondly there are lessons to be learned concerning the encounter between religion and politics, piety and worldly efficacy, as also concerning the encounter, in the life of Everyman, between intention and act, the pattern dreamed-of and the pattern realized in the recalcitrant materials of this earth.

The pietists were for ever calling down curses upon the heads of the Caliphs, and their successors today can find no spark of pity in their hearts for men of power who are less pure than they are; but it is never as simple as that. The saying of Jesus that 'Offences must needs come, but woe to him through whom the offence cometh' is amongst the most daunting statements in the Gospels, for sometimes it is only through 'offences' that religion is preserved. Had it not been for formidable rulers who, from impure motives and with dirty hands, exercised their trade in the only effective way it could be exercised, there might have been no space left in this world for the pious, nor any school in which they could learn piety. Such contradictions are by no means confined to Islam; they are universal and arise wherever the spiritual and the worldly confront each other. Precisely because this earth is not Paradise and cannot be Paradise, it is condemned – at least from a certain point of view – to being a 'Theatre of the Absurd'.

Given the fragility of every religion at birth and in its early years, it may be that there are really only two questions to be asked. Did Islam survive? Did it spread across the world? The answer to both questions is in the affirmative. After that the history books may be closed.

PART III

The Fruits of the Faith

Chapter 9

THE RULE OF LAW

During the period of decolonization in the 1950s and early 1960s the question as to which territories were – or were not – fit for self-government was seriously debated. No one raised the more fundamental question as to whether any nation on earth is fit for self-government. Then as now, the Swiss were said to manage their affairs competently and Costa Rica was well spoken of; but elsewhere it was difficult then, and remains difficult today, to suggest any model which a newly created national entity might reasonably seek to imitate. One is obliged to ask whether there may not be something basically unworkable in the very concept of government as the term is currently understood.

In the past the tribal system, functioning like an extended family, may have come as close to perfection as any human society can hope to come, not only in ancient Arabia but also in Africa before the slave-trade, in North America before the coming of the white man, in Central Asia and in the Pacific islands; but wherever mass societies emerged, requiring systematic organization, 'government' was – until recently – accepted along with plague, famine and taxation as among the unavoidable evils to which fallen humanity is exposed.

Acceptance of a necessary evil, however, does not imply any willingness to see it grow and expand; the aim must always be to reduce it to a minimum, but minimal government requires, as its complement, the self-regulating community, since men and women cannot live reasonably under conditions of anarchy. Such a community can function and endure only within the framework of a revealed or pre-determined Law, which in effect takes the place occupied by instinct in the life of animals.

The Qurān, which is the 'constitution' of any truly Islamic community, itself validates this comparison, for it assures us that God has laid down for every species and for every group of created things a Law and a Way; but whereas the inanimate universe, together with all living creatures unendowed with Intellect, is governed by laws inherent in its very structure, man, precisely because he possesses Intellect and a relatively free will, is required to follow the Law of his own being voluntarily and with understanding. Stones cannot know why they fall nor birds why they migrate. Man is by definition a knower and by destiny a chooser; but, in the Islamic view, he does not have the capacity to make laws for the conduct of society.

The belief that God is the sole Legislator flows directly from the Muslim confession of faith, *lā ilāha illa 'Llāh*, which, in this context, can be interpreted as meaning that 'there is no legislator but the Legislator'. The message embodied in the Qurān – and the laws derived from it and from the *Sunnah* of the Prophet – bind the community together; no exterior pressure is required to make this binding effective. True sovereignty resides neither in the ruler nor in government nor in a statistical majority; it belongs to God, but is in a certain sense delegated to His 'rightly-guided' community; and the Law, precisely because it is a 'reminder' of the laws inherent in our own created nature, should not in principle require the apparatus of the state, officials and policemen, to make it effective. Whatever place the contemporary Westerner may give to religion in his personal and social life, this is still only 'a place'; it is seen as one element in the total structure of human life, but it is not itself that totality. For Islam, on the other hand, the social order is a part of the religion and cannot be separated from it.

The function of the ruler (or 'government' as such) within this system is strictly limited. Islamic society is theocentric rather than theocratic. Were it the latter, there would be a need for a semi-divine ruler, the representative of God on earth and the interpreter of His will; but in the context of a theocentric society the ruler occupies a peripheral rather than a central role. Despite certain idealistic theories arising from nostalgia for the time of the *Rāshidūn*, the first four caliphs, the Muslims have on the whole taken a very pragmatic view of the ruler's function. He is not expected to be a saint or a sage or even a good man in the usual sense of the term, and his private vices may be overlooked so long as they are kept private.

What is required of him is that he should have a strong right arm with which to defend the community against its enemies and to maintain the Law. It is often said that Muslims prefer a strong and even ruthless ruler to a gentle and conciliatory one. If this is so, it is because a ruthless man is likely to be more effective in fulfilling the function allotted to him in the Islamic system. Most human communities throughout history have lived precariously, surrounded by enemies on every side (our situation today is no less precarious), and they cannot give proper attention to the worship of God, or get on with the business of living, unless they are able to rely upon an effective protector. One of the great problems of the Muslims in the twentieth century is that their readiness to tolerate a ruthless ruler, which could be justified so long as government had a short arm and interfered very little in the life of the people, becomes a source of danger as soon as political theories, supported by modern techniques, extend the role of government into every street and every household.

Pious Muslims have always regarded power as a fearful thing, even as a one-way ticket to hell; profiting from the protection afforded them by the ruler and from the good order he establishes in the city, they thank God that someone else bears this burden and walks this tightrope over the abyss. They suspect that there must be a profound flaw in the character of anyone who deliberately seeks to expose himself to the dangers and temptations of power.

It is significant that the Prophet, who spoke of so many things – down to the smallest details of daily life – had little to say about government as such and showed no interest in political theorizing. There is, however, a particular *ḥadīth* which has far-reaching implications in this context. At a time of rapid expansion in Arabia, one of the companions came to him and asked to be made governor of a recently conquered territory. 'No,' he said. 'If you wish to rule, then you are unfit!'[1] If power is thrust upon a man, he may be forgiven much; but if he chooses to put a noose around his own neck, he is likely to hang by it. If, today, we look around us at the various systems of government existing in the world, we find that all – with one notable exception – have this feature in common; the rulers, whether they are democratic politicians, party functionaries or military dictators, hold power because they deliberately sought power and believed themselves fit to wield it. The one exception, of course, is hereditary monarchy. The implication, however unpalatable it may be to Muslim intellectuals and political theorists in our time, is suggestive.

Sunni Islam has always set great store by political stability, even if this involves tolerating corrupt government, for revolt against constituted authority involves splitting the community, and the unity of the community is the paramount consideration; moreover, what the religion requires for its full practice is not ideal government, efficient administration or even 'social justice', but a stable environment, a house with solid walls in which the furnishings stay in place. Ibn 'Abbās reported God's Messenger as saying: 'If anyone sees in his ruler what he dislikes he should show patience, for no one separates a span's distance from the community and [then] dies without his dying like the people of pre-Islamic times.'

At least in earlier times, it was only at the two opposite extremes of the Islamic spectrum that revolt against an unjust ruler was fully sanctioned. The Shi'ites dreamed of a charismatic ruler appointed from among the descendants of the Prophet – no other could be considered legitimate – while the Kharijites (and their political heirs) dreamed of a charismatic community of righteous men and women which could never submit to anything that savoured of secular rule. Both were able to justify revolution in terms of their particular doctrine. It was partly in reaction against such recipes for instability that Sunni jurists emphasized the duty of obedience to authority.

Their views had much in common with those expressed by the British historian and political philosopher of the late eighteenth century, Edmund Burke. For the Sunni jurists, as for Burke, the social disruption caused by revolt or revolution outweighs, in its long-term effects, any advantages that might be gained by replacing a bad government with a slightly better one. Their opinion was based upon a realistic assessment of the human situation, taking account of the fact that few people, when faced with a major – or minor – decision in the course of their lives, sit down and weigh the moral factors involved in the light of ultimate principles. For the most part, people act in accordance with ingrained habits, in terms of custom and within the limits established by their social framework. They do what comes naturally to them.

To destroy the framework – and to tear the delicate net of social

[1] 'Do not ask for rulership,' he said (according to another *ḥadīth* recorded by Bukhari and Muslim), 'for if you are given power as a result of asking for it you will be left to deal with it on your own; but if you are given it without your asking, then you will be helped in exercising it.'

relationships – in however good a cause is to cut at the roots of custom, overturn tradition and disturb habits, leaving the individual under an obligation to make moral choices at every twist and turn of his life. This he will not do. It is far more likely that, as soon as all familiar restraints are removed, something comparable to the force of gravity will lead him on a downward path. Society can then be kept in order only by force, which is why tyranny follows revolution as the night follows the day. A corrupt ruler may have been replaced by a man of high principles, or a bad and incompetent government by a more professional and responsible one, but in the course of this upheaval society has been atomized and people have lost their bearings; all must now be regimented if order is to be maintained and grandiose plans for social improvement implemented.

The stability of Islamic society over a period of at least a thousand years, unaffected by almost unceasing turmoil at the 'political' level, was the stability of a society which refuses to make changes in the framework of communal and individual life or, if compelled by circumstances to make minor adjustments, keeps these to the absolute minimum. Writing of medieval Islam, von Grünebaum says: 'The Muslim possesses a quality of repose, of dignity and poise, which could develop only as a result of a static conception of the ideal world and the ideal society. The West is ready to sacrifice the present for the future ... We recognize the supreme value of change because we are afraid of stagnation ... The Muslim's world is at rest, and he is at rest within it. His immediacy to God and his acceptance of the divine order were never, during the Middle Ages, seriously disturbed,'[1] Von Grünebaum was writing almost forty years ago and it is doubtful whether the West is any longer so eager to 'recognize the supreme value of change', but it remains true that the changelessness of Muslim society over so many centuries represents a way of life almost unimaginable to the Westerner, for whom the lives of people only a hundred years ago seem as alien as those of the ancient Etruscans. For the Muslims, from the ninth century until the nineteenth, time stood still and the world was stayed on its centrifugal course. One thing alone made this possible: the adherence of society as a whole – or of a whole chain of societies – to the *Sharī'ah*, the religious Law of Islam.

The word *Sharī'ah* means 'road' or 'highway', but its derivation refers to the beaten track by which wild animals come down to drink at their watering-place. It is the road which leads to where the waters of life flow inexhaustibly.

Christians are puzzled when told that jurisprudence, not theology, is the principal religious science in Islam and that the *'ālim*, the learned religious scholar, is primarily a jurist who tells people what to do rather than what to believe. But for the Muslim there is no problem in knowing what to believe; his concern is with what to do under all circumstances in order to conform to the Word of God and to walk without stumbling on the road which leads to Paradise. The word *fiqh*, usually translated as 'jurisprudence', comes from the verb *faqiha*, which means neither more nor less

[1] *Medieval Islam*, Gustave von Grünebaum (University of Chicago Press), p. 346.

than 'he understood'. *Fiqh*, then, has to do with understanding the divine commands and their ramifications in the fabric of daily life. For the occidental, jurisprudence is a dull and sterile topic of little interest (unless one becomes involved with the police), which is hardly surprising since secular law is a web of man-made complexities; a solicitor's office is not a place where the Christian is likely to seek his soul's salvation.

But for the Muslim, the crystallization of the Quranic message and the Prophet's example into a body of livable law has been the supreme adventure. Islam is 'submission' to the Will of God, and the study of this miraculously revealed Will is seen as the most important study open to man as a creature endowed with intellect and reason. Law, moreover, has to do with the art of living together. In its broadest sense it is the science of human relationships. The Islamic revelation came at a moment in the history of Arabia when men had lost their bearings; with the development of city life – civilization – in Mecca and Medina the tribal structure was disintegrating and the moral principles which guaranteed the tribe's survival as a social entity were dissolving. This situation posed a simple and urgent question: how are people to live together in community? As the Muslim sees it, God provided the answer to this question in the Qurān and in the example of the Prophet, but He left the necessary work of elaboration to the believers. Over the next two centuries they laboured to construct, from these basic materials, a solid, comprehensive and enduring structure of Law.

It is not, therefore, strictly accurate to describe the *Sharī'ah* as a body of revealed Law. Human effort and rational judgement played their part in its development, but the Muslim considers that this effort was inspired and this judgement enlightened by divine aid. Only a small proportion of the Qurān deals with legal matters, 'commands and prohibitions', and this would not suffice were it not amply supplemented by the recorded sayings and actions of the Prophet, the collections of *ḥadīth*. In assessing the authenticity or otherwise of this record, human judgement necessarily intervenes, so the earliest architects of the Law were the *mutaḥadi-thūn*, the 'scholars of *ḥadīth*'.

The method by which the authenticity of a particular *ḥadīth* was established has nothing in common with the methods of occidental scholarship, but is none the worse for that. It was, in any case, the only practical method of assessment under the circumstances. If we are told by an informant that a friend told him that his uncle had said that his cousin had told him that his grandfather had been told by a friend that his own grandfather had heard So-and-so make a certain remark, then – assuming that this is a matter of great importance – our concern will be with the reliability of the chain of informants, the 'transmitters' as they are called in Islam. Nothing could be of greater importance for a Muslim than what the Prophet actually said in guiding the new community. For the scholars of the second and third centuries of the Islamic era, the authenticity of a *ḥadīth* depended upon the human value of each named individual in the chain of transmission; one weak link – immoral, perhaps, and therefore probably a liar – broke the chain. In so tight a society, in which everyone knew everyone else's business, it was by no means impossible to assess all the characters involved; and on this basis, as also through the consensus of the scholars, a *ḥadīth* could be classified as sound, good, less certain or, finally, unsound; or it could be rejected altogether.

Those who undertook this task were like men who search for gems in a mine or pan for gold in a river; but they were professionals, and their eagerness to discover precious stones or precious metal was balanced by a pious conscience and an acute critical sense.

Western academics, schooled in the techniques of 'historical criticism' as it has been applied to the Bible, have taken pleasure in casting doubt upon the *ḥadīth* literature as a whole. They may be left to their own devices. It is a little late in the day to raise such questions, almost fourteen centuries after the Prophet's death. We cannot know with 'scientific' certainty that a particular *ḥadīth* is authentic beyond all possible doubt; but we have no right to demand such certainties in this life. Moreover, if this *ḥadīth* has been accepted by pious men over the centuries and has been a building-block in the divinely willed structure of Islam, then it is beyond the reach of human criticism. God can do as He chooses with 'facts', and His choice is to use them for our spiritual benefit. When the truth is spoken, the question as to who it was who spoke it is of secondary importance. Ultimately truth is spoken by One alone and by no other, though there are many mouthpieces. The people of our time are so unsure of themselves that they ask for each utterance to be labelled and authenticated, just as they must know the name of the artist before they can judge whether a painting is beautiful. This atmosphere of doubt and this craving for proof and assurance are foreign to the world of Islam and to the mentality of the Muslim.

The establishment of a canon of *ḥadīth* was, however, only the first step in a long and complex process. Legal provisions drawn directly from the Qurān and the *Sunnah* could not be expected to cover every contingency, nor could rules of conduct adequate to the simple life of Medina serve to regulate the life of a great empire and its teeming cities. The means had to be found to develop a body of Law which would cover every imaginable circumstance, without ever losing contact with its sacred and unimpeachable sources. To achieve this, three principal methods were evolved: 'consensus' (*ijmāʿ*), 'analogy' (*qiyās*) and 'intellectual effort' (*ijtihād*).

The Prophet had said: 'My community will never agree upon an error.' This guaranteed the soundness of any consensus reached among the people as a whole, but it would have been unreasonable to give to the opinion of a shepherd or an artisan, unschooled in the Qurān and *ḥadīth*, the same weight as that given to the considered judgement of the learned men, the *ʿulama*. On the other hand, these learned men were members of the larger community, and the opinions of the latter could not be ignored. There were cases – for the most part minor ones – when the community as such overruled the learned élite, as when coffee was first introduced into Arabia: the *ʿulama* pronounced it a prohibited beverage, but the mass of the people disagreed and, in due course, their view was legitimized. The stability of the system depends upon maintaining the delicate balance between rigidity and flexibility.

Ijma' could never, of course, supersede the documentary sources, but it served to legitimize the implications and conclusions drawn by the learned men from these sources, either by the use of analogy or by individual effort. This consensus, however, was not a matter of majority opinion statistically assessed; to be valid it had to be so close to unanimity that no counting of heads was necessary. 'After God and the Prophet, the Community,' says Kenneth Cragg. 'They may be reasonably accepted as a frame of reference, a court of appeal, for the validation or otherwise of what is truly and authentically Islamic. This, it should be clear, is not democracy as such ... It is the attainment of a common mind on a particular point, the legal recognition of an existing state of affairs – or of opinion – which has come to be in the community in an area of former silence.'[1]

The points upon which consensus is reached are likely to have been the outcome of *ijtihād*, 'effort' or 'initiative' on the part of individual scholars. As Cragg points out, a *mujtahid* – one who is judged capable of such initiatives – qualifies only after prolonged legal, theological and grammatical training, and then struggles through long days and nights to reach conclusions which may commend themselves to consensus in the course of time. It goes without saying that they should never contradict anything that is clearly expressed in the sacred texts, and the whole process is surrounded by safeguards to avoid the danger of 'innovation'.

According to the opinion accepted, until recently, in Sunni Islam (but not amongst the Shi'a), the 'Gate of *ijtihād*' was closed in the eleventh or twelfth century of the Christian era. There were two reasons for this. In the first place, it was considered that every conceivable contingency had been covered and the *Sharī'ah* was therefore complete, with no areas of ambiguity remaining. Secondly, the learned men were under constant pressure to give legal rulings in accordance with the wishes of the ruler – the caliph, sultan or amir. In many cases their very lives must have depended on their being able to tell him, with great respect, that they no longer had the power to do so: 'Great Sultan, I know you to be the wisest of rulers and most virtuous of men and nothing would make me happier than to give a ruling in your favour, but alas – the Gate of Personal Judgement has been closed.'

Over the past two centuries, the 'Gate' appears to have been re-opened, in practice if not in principle. It was closed at a time when no one could have anticipated any fundamental change in the conditions of human life or in the structure of Muslim society. The impossible has now happened, and this has brought into question the finality and immutability of the four 'Schools of Law' (*madhāhib*), which determine the life-pattern of the Sunni Muslim.

All four arose in the eighth to ninth centuries of the Christian era and are named after their founders: Abū Hanīfa (d.767), Malik ibn Anas (d.795), Ibn Idrīs ash-Shafi'i (d.819), and Ahmad ibn Hanbal (d.855), who have been described as the 'grammarians of the divine Word'. But these grammarians were not confined to the study or the library. Abū Hanīfa died in prison, having been condemned for refusing to accept a judgeship;

[1] *The Call of the Minaret*, Kenneth Cragg (Oxford University Press, 1956).

ibn Hanbal was imprisoned for denying the doctrine of the 'createdness' of the Qurān; and Malik had his shoulder-bones broken when he was beaten by the Caliph's guards. Far from representing the power of the state, they were shields between the community and the ruler – as were the best among the *'ulamā'* over many centuries – and asserted with uncompromising firmness the dignity and independence of the Law, its precedence over the edicts and interests of the temporal power.

From them flowed four streams of Law, but the water is the same in each. The differences between these schools, sometimes quite wrongly described as 'sects', are of a minor nature, as might be expected from the fact that ash-Shafi'i had been a pupil of Malik, and ibn Hanbal had been a student of ash-Shafi'i. Some are stricter than others regarding what is or is not 'obligatory' for the Muslim. The Hanbalites are 'literalists', distrusting 'personal opinion' (*ra'y*) and anything that savours of allegorical interpretation of the Qurān. There are differences between them regarding the omissions (in word or act) which invalidate the ritual prayer and concerning ablution; but only when these differences are exaggerated by narrow-minded people do they threaten the unity of Sunni Law as such.

There has, however, been a reaction in recent times, not only against making any distinction between the four 'schools', but even against the *Sharī'ah* as it was formulated by the great medieval jurists. Here, as so often, extremes meet. On the one hand, the 'modernists' dismiss all such formulations as 'out of date'; on the other, those who may for convenience be described as 'fundamentalists' would like to go back to the Qurān and the *Sunnah* in their pristine purity, ignoring all subsequent interpretations. They seem to forget that interpretation comes about in answer to a real need for it, and they are unwilling to admit that the men whose work they so lightly dismiss were probably both better and wiser than they are.

It must be admitted none the less that the legal mind runs readily to excess, dotting every 'i' and crossing every 't' with meticulous care, creating complications when the matter is simple, and striving laboriously to find answers to questions that have not been asked. The Qurān tells us: 'O Believers, do not ask concerning matters which, if they were made known to you, would trouble you ...' (Q.5.101); and the Prophet said, 'Do not ask me about matters which I leave unspoken, for truly there were people before you who went to their doom because they put too many questions to their messengers and thereupon disagreed.' It is indeed possible that too many questions have been asked by people who might have done better to rely upon conscience and common sense, but the Muslim who is certain of his faith and serene in this certainty is not easily troubled; he goes his way and leaves others to go theirs, knowing that the answers to all questions and the solution to all differences of opinion will be made evident soon enough.

The occidental tends to see the *Sharī'ah* as a straitjacket rather than as a framework, unaware that it has within it adequate space for free movement (and for individual differences), and unwilling to accept the psychological implications of the fact that a physical body disintegrates when placed in a vacuum. The Law, says Seyyed Hossein Nasr, 'places before man many paths according to his nature and needs within a universal pattern which pertains to everyone. Human initiative comes in selecting what is in conformity with one's needs and living according to the Divine norm as indicated by the *Sharī'ah*. Initiative does not come only in rebelling against the Truth, which is an easy task since stones fall by nature; initiative and creativity come most of all in seeking to live in conformity with the Truth and in applying its principles to the conditions which destiny has placed before man. To integrate all of one's tendencies and activities within a divinely ordained pattern requires all the initiative and creative energy which man is capable of giving.'[1]

Immersed in our individual subjectivities -- which, by their very nature, distort every perspective – we need objective standards if we are not either to sink into insanity or, alternatively, rampage through the world as though no one else really existed. In Islam it is the immutable Law which provides the objective criteria that pull us up in mid-course, and if we try to ignore it, then there are penalties to remind us that the Law is an objective reality, a rock which is not eroded by the stream of time nor melted by the heat of subjective desires.

The harsh punishments imposed under Islamic Law (though less harsh than those prevailing in Europe until comparatively recently) are the expression of principles which cannot be changed to suit our convenience; what matters, however, is not that the punishment should be inflicted whenever appropriate but that the principle should remain intact. The Prophet told his people to 'avert penalties by doubts', and any stratagem which averts the penalty without impugning the Law is legitimate. The tale is told of a lawyer in Harūn's time who rose to wealth and eminence after devising a subtle legal argument which saved the Caliph from having to charge his own son with adultery. The Westerner might say that this cunning lawyer earned himself a fortune by twisting the law to suit his master; the Muslim, on the other hand, approves his conduct in that he found a way for the Caliph to show mercy without offending against the majesty of the Law.

The severity of the punishment for adultery marks the gravity of this offence against a society based upon the integrity of the family and its delicate web of relationships. The existence of the penalty makes the necessary point, but its application is made almost impossible – except in cases of voluntary confession – by the proviso that four unimpeachable witnesses must have observed the act in detail and must submit to being flogged for perjury if the case is still not proved. Flogging is specified as the penalty for a number of offences, but the Law does not specify what instrument is to be used, and in the early days of Islam it was often nothing more damaging than a light sandal or the hem of a garment; this was still technically a 'flogging', the point was made and the Law was upheld. A thief may have his hand cut off, but not if he stole from genuine need or because his family was hungry, or if he stole the property of the state.[2]

---

[1] *Ideals and Realities of Islam*, Seyyed Hossein Nasr (London: Allen & Unwin Ltd., 1966), p. 98.

[2] Unlike contemporary advocates of 'nationalization', the Muslim jurists of ancient times maintained – with perfect logic – that public property is indeed 'public' and therefore quite different to private property. Each citizen is part-owner of whatever belongs to the state, and a man cannot steal from himself.

Perjury, even in a civil case, is an offence of the utmost gravity since it is an offence against the Law itself, and forensic skill employed in an unjust cause is condemned. 'You people bring disputes to me,' said the Prophet; 'but it may be that some of you are better able to put their case than others. I have to decide on the evidence before me. If I happen to expropriate the right of anyone in favour of his brother, let not the latter take it, for in that case I have given him a piece of hell-fire.'

The position of a judge, like that of a ruler, is unenviable. We are told by the chroniclers about a certain pietist in Abbasid times who stormed into the Caliph's audience-chamber and denounced him to his face for tyranny and injustice ('The best *jihād*,' the Prophet said once, 'is a true word in the presence of a tyrant'). The man had gone by the time the Caliph could devise a punishment sufficiently cruel to meet his case: this was that he should be appointed a judge, and an edict issued to the effect that no judgement of his should be overruled by any Court of Appeal. Soldiers were sent to bring him back for condemnation, but he was never found.

In Islam the rigour of *Sharī'h* Law is always overshadowed by the Law of Mercy, but never to the extent of undermining the abiding principles which are its basis. A certain man in Medina came to the Prophet to confess a sin and receive whatever punishment was due to him (for it is, according to a *ḥadīth*, 'better to blush in this world than in the hereafter'). He was asked if he could free a slave, but he could not. He was asked if he could fast for two months, but he replied that he could not. Finally he was asked if he could provide food for the poor. When he replied that he could not, he was told to wait while the Prophet considered the matter. At this point someone came in with a large basket of dates as a gift for the Prophet, who then presented them to the waiting man and instructed him to give them as *sadaqa* (a gift to the needy). 'Am I to give them to someone poorer than myself, Messenger of Allah?' asked the man; 'I swear by Allah there is no poorer family than mine between the two lava plains of Medina!' The Prophet laughed until – it is said – 'his eye-teeth were visible' and told the sinner: 'Then give them to your family to eat.'

The community sheltered and ordered by the *Sharī'ah* is the 'rightly-guided' community and membership of it is, for the Muslim, 'a part of faith'. To leave the community is to come perilously close to leaving the Faith. Mankind, says Montgomery Watt, 'needs a religious community which is charismatic, and Islam more than any other great religion has realized in actual life the idea of the charismatic community.'[1]

Islam being theocentric, the community owes its cohesion primarily to the Faith, not to government and not to its religious leaders. Each individual Muslim is personally responsible for the well-being of his fellows, his 'brothers' and his 'sisters', to aid them in poverty, to comfort them in distress and to put them right when they go astray (though always in a spirit of kindness); at least in principle, each member of the community, however humble, has a duty – when he sees something wrong or out of place – to correct it either with his hand or with his tongue, or, if he

[1] *Islam and the Integration of Society*, W. Montgomery Watt, p. 234.

does not have the power to do this, then to correct it within his own heart. His duty does not, however, extend to sending for the police or reporting the matter to the authorities, for – as a Muslim – he embodies the Law in himself; there is no question of handing over his responsibility to the impersonal state.

As has been suggested by a number of writers, including Frithjof Schuon, the nearest equivalent we can find in the West to a society of this type is a monastic community, and the fact that in this case the 'monks' are married and have children in no way vitiates the comparison.

United by a common belief in a transcendent Reality and in a specific revelation of the divine Will, in laws and a code of conduct which are religious – not social – in origin, the hours of each day marked by the sacred offices (the canonical prayers) and the round of the year marked by religious festivals, the members of the community are held together by the ordinances of the Faith rather than by civic duty. The atheist and the agnostic have no place here, nor have the adherents of alien political ideologies such as Marxism; there must surely be, somewhere in the world, a desert in which they can make themselves a home while they await their entry into the fire, for Islam cannot tolerate subversion within its house. The Christians and the Jews, on the other hand, and all who 'believe in God and the Last Day', have rooms set aside for them where they may follow their own dispensations in peace.

In a quaintly phrased but none the less telling comparison, François Bonjean, writing of the holy cities of Islam and comparing them to monastic communities, remarks that the 'ordinary artisans and administrators and merchants' recall 'the mien and manners of our ecclesiastics';[1] they seem, in other words, more like priests than laymen. 'If monasticism is defined as a "withdrawal for God",' says Schuon, 'and if its universal and inter-religious character is recognized on the grounds that the thirst for the supernatural is in the nature of normal man, how can this definition be applied in the case of spiritual men who are Muslims and do not withdraw from society? ... To that the answer must be that one of the *raisons d'être* of Islam is precisely the possibility of a "monastery-society", if the expression be allowable: that is to say that Islam aims to carry the contemplative life into the very framework as a whole; it succeeds in realizing within that framework conditions of structure and of behaviour that permit of contemplative isolation in the very midst of the activities of the world ... The famous "no monasticism in Islam" really means, not that contemplatives must not withdraw from the world, but on the contrary that the world must not be withdrawn from contemplatives ...'[2]

This is the crux of the matter. One of the things that Christians and occidentals in general seldom understand is this mighty effort, this *jihād*, waged to prevent any element of earthly life from escaping and taking on a separate existence of its own, or flying off, as though gripped by centrifugal force, into the empty space which we call the secular or profane realm. The Muslim who sits quietly in the mosque facing the *qiblah* and invoking

---

[1]Quoted from an article by Francois Bonjean published in *Les Cahiers du Sud*, 1947.
[2]*Light on the Ancient Worlds*, Frithjof Schuon (London: Perennial Books, 1965).

his Lord has not left the world to go its own way; he is not only a contemplative, he is also a warrior, and the world is his prisoner of war. From the corner of his eye he watches to see that it does not evade him.

In the same context, Seyyed Hossein Nasr says: 'The unitary principle of Islam, however, could not permit this contemplative way to become crystallized as a separate social organization outside the matrix moulded by the injunctions of the divine Law or *Sharī'ah*. It had to remain as an inner dimension of that Law and, institutionally, as an organization integrated into the Islamic social pattern and inseparable from it.'[1]

Even men and women quite lacking in natural piety are, through integration into this theocentric community, carried along the road which leads to salvation, their daily lives penetrated by a transcendent perspective which, as individuals, they may be incapable of perceiving, let alone of understanding. Like little fish in the vastness of the ocean, they would soon perish if they swam alone, but, in the midst of a great shoal, they swim safely in the right direction.

At the same time, the members of this community have not chosen the holy life as their vocation but have been born into it, and to expect too much of them would be contrary to the realism inherent in the Islamic perspective. The 'consensus' decisively rejected the Kharijite view that the 'sinner', since he imperils the community, must either be put to death or expelled into the outer wastes. Their view was to some extent inherited from tribal society, since the very survival of the Arab tribe in the desert depended upon rigid conformity to the rules imposed by the harsh environment. This was not the Prophet's way, and he said on a number of occasions that he had not been sent 'to make your religion difficult for you'. He demanded of his people, not superhuman virtue, but an honest effort to do their best even if it did not amount to very much. He detested unnecessary 'fuss' over small matters since he had an infallible sense of priorities. A trivial example will serve to illustrate this point. Abu Huraira reported that on a certain occasion a desert Arab who was in the mosque in Medina got up and passed water where he stood. The people seized him in fury, but the Prophet said to them: 'Leave him alone and pour a bucket of water over what he has passed, for you have been sent only to make things easy and not to make things difficult.'

The Faith and the Law, however, are not the only binding factors which have given Islamic communities their tremendous power of endurance. It might have been expected that loyalty to the *Ummah* would replace all 'natural' loyalties, and it did indeed replace loyalty to the tribe, but the ties of relationship which link human beings one to another are the basis of the whole structure. Islam works with nature, not against it.

The threads which compose the great web of relationships within which each individual is situated are knitted together through marriage (which is no doubt one reason why the Prophet said that 'marriage is half the religion') and extend on the one hand through the issue (and their marriages), and on the other through the blood-ties of the partners and the further ties contracted by those to whom they are related. Polygamy

[1] *Islam and the Plight of Modern Man*, Seyyed Hossein Nasr (London: Longman, 1975), p. 73.

further increases these relationships, and each 'extended family' is linked with a number of others so that there is no break in the web, which is complementary to the close-knit communal life of the city.

Despite the importance of the nomads in the early history of the religion, it is the traditional Islamic city which best expressed its particular genius. What was best in the structure and in the customs of the nomadic tribe was transformed but not destroyed in accordance with the needs of the new society.

Central to any Muslim community is the communal prayer, the *Ummah* assembled in the act of worship, which is also the fountain-head of their social life. The life of the city was focused upon the Great Mosque, that of each district upon its local mosque, every family close enough to hear the call of the mu'ezzin summoning them to prayer, summoning them to unity as a sacred community, summoning them to Paradise, which is also a place of meeting. If the Great Mosque was the heart of the city, its stomach was the market (also, in its way, sacred, since the good things we use and the food which nourishes us are from God), and its brain the schools and colleges where knowledge, the most precious of all commodities, is exchanged.

There was nothing outwardly splendid about such cities – here we are far removed from Roman splendour – with their narrow alleys contrasting with the inward space devoted to worship and to family life. Islam has no taste for 'Promethean' grandeur or for any kind of pretentiousness. A seventeenth-century French traveller visiting Egypt remarked that there is 'not a single fine street in Cairo, but a mass of little ones turning hither and thither, which clearly demonstrates that all the houses are built without design, each choosing that place which it pleases him to build on without considering whether he stop up a street or no . . .'[1] This 'warren' preserved the organic cohesion and independence so essential to the life of the Muslim, keeping the impersonal forces of the state at bay – there were no wide avenues to encourage military parades. The order which governed the life of the people was more inward than outward.[2]

Trade was the economic life-blood of the city, but it also served to forge further ties of relationship. The good things given by God, worthy to be enjoyed, become the source of further good when they provide subsistence for those who trade in them and, at the same time, encourage intercourse in acts of barter and exchange. The very act of meeting between 'believers' carries its own special blessing. 'Two Muslims will not meet and shake hands,' said the Prophet, 'without having their sins forgiven them before they separate'; and one of his companions, ibn 'Abbās, remarked that, 'Satan weeps every time he hears a Muslim give the greeting of peace to his

[1] Quoted from *The Cambridge History of Islam*, Vol. 2, p. 456.

[2] The fact that one is obliged to use the past tense in writing of the 'Islamic city' may provide a clue to the spiritual and psychological malaise afflicting so many Muslims today. Except for Fez and Sana'a, there remain few if any cities which could be said to exteriorize the spirit of the Faith and, in this way, provide an environment in which the Muslim can feel truly at home. Only too often he feels a stranger in his own birthplace, and nothing in his surroundings reminds him of God, nothing is designed to facilitate the performance of his religious duties, and nothing provides him with the sense of continuity so essential to his spiritual life.

brother Muslim, and Satan says, "Woe is me! They will not separate until Allah has forgiven them both".'

In a sense the business transaction is of secondary importance compared with the act of meeting. The host offers coffee or some other beverage to those with whom he is negotiating and thereby reinforces the tie between them. He knows that God is present, approves the establishment of such relationships and is pleased when the steaming kettle passes between those assembled. The profit or loss of the interested parties belongs to time, but the act of meeting partakes of eternity.

'Satan has despaired of being worshipped by those who engage in prayer,' said the Prophet, 'but he has hopes of setting them against one another,' and amongst the gravest sins mentioned in the Qurān is that of 'severing ties of relationship'; ties of family, of friendship, of community or of co-workers in an enterprise, all of which contribute to spinning a web of unity in a fragmented world, and but for which people would be atoms incessantly colliding. The reinforcement of such ties may expiate many sins. A man came to the Prophet and said: 'I have committed a serious sin. Can I do any act of penance?' The Prophet asked him if his mother was alive, and when he replied that she was dead, asked if he had a maternal aunt. He said that he had, so the Prophet told him: 'Then do her a kindness!'

According to another *hadīth*, God will say on the Day of Resurrection: 'Where are those who have mutual love for My sake? Today I shall shelter them in My shade, when there is no shade but Mine.' And the Prophet said: 'You see the believers in their mutual pity, love and affection, like one body. When one member has a complaint, the rest of the body is united with it in wakefulness and fever.' It is in the context of such sayings as this – and there are many of them – that we may measure the gravity of offences which undermine the community, break bonds and sever ties of relationship; and these usually begin with the wagging of tongues. 'If anyone guarantees me what is between his jaws and what is between his legs, I will guarantee him Paradise,' the Prophet said. He asked some people once if they knew what defamation was, and when they replied that God and His Messenger knew best, told them that it was 'saying something about your brother that he would dislike'. A man asked him how the matter stood if what he said about his brother was true, and he replied: 'If what you have said is true you have defamed him, and if it is not true you have slandered him.'

The Qurān tells us: 'Truly, those who love that scandal should be spread concerning those who believe – grievous suffering awaits them in the world and in the hereafter; for Allah knows [the truth] and you know not' (Q.24.19). And again: 'O Believers! Let not people deride other people, who may be better than themselves ... neither defame one another nor insult one another with epithets; evil is the imputation of iniquity after [attainment to] faith ... O Believers! Shun most suspicion, for indeed suspicion is in some cases a sin. And spy not [upon one another], neither backbite [one another]. Would any of you like to eat the flesh of his dead brother? You would abhor it! So be conscious of Allah. Truly Allah is Relenting, Merciful' (Q.49.11/12).

The past sins of men and women are indeed 'dead flesh', not to be picked over or discussed with prurient interest, and there are frequent references in the *ḥadīth* literature to the fact that, if we wish God to overlook our sins, it is for us to conceal the sins of our neighbour, and if we are in a position to reprove him, to do so privately: 'Never does a believer draw a veil over the nakedness of another believer without Allah drawing a veil over *his* nakedness on the Day of Resurrection'; and again, 'Do not hurt those who believe, and do not impute evil to them, and do not try to uncover their nakedness [i.e. their faults); for, truly, if anyone tries to uncover his brother's nakedness, Allah will uncover *his* nakedness on the Day of Judgement.'

Such counsels of concealment, discretion and delicacy are quite contrary to the contemporary Western preference for 'bringing things into the open' or – to use a current phrase which is expressive in this context – for 'letting everything hang out'. Even less in tune with contemporary principles is the idea that we ought, if we can, to hide our own sins and weaknesses, in accordance with the saying: 'Better a hundred sins in the sight of God than one in the sight of men'. In a well-authenticated *ḥadīth* reported by Abū Huraira the Prophet said: 'All my people will be kept safe except for those who publish their own wrongdoing. It is a kind of impudence for a man to commit an act of disobedience during the night and then, when Allah has concealed it for him, to tell someone in the morning that he had done this or that during the night. His Lord had concealed it in the night, yet he – in the morning – exposes what Allah had concealed!'

Our contemporaries, at least in the Anglo-Saxon sector of the world, can only see this as an inducement to hypocrisy. The cult of 'honesty' has now gone so far that many people believe that nothing they do matters so long as they are honest and open about it and never pretend to be better than they are; moreover, to conceal what one has done suggests that one is ashamed of oneself, and how could this be in an age in which the 'self' is a god – possibly the only god there is? The motive – at least on the surface – is a reaction against Victorian 'hypocrisy', although what was really blameworthy in the people of the nineteenth century was not their secretiveness but their self-righteousness; but, at a deeper level, however paradoxical this may seem, the passion for self-exposure betrays a desire for reassurance and for social approval. If I confess my sin quite shamelessly – putting upon it whatever gloss I choose – and my friends do not think less of me, then all is well and I need not feel troubled.

For the Muslim, every infringement of the Law, every sin, has two quite separate aspects. In the first place, it relates to the individual's situation *vis-à-vis* his Creator, whom he knows to be ever ready to forgive, provided the sinner repents and resolves to do better, if he can, in the future. Secondly, if this sin is made public, it is an encouragement to others to do likewise; and this, from the point of view of the community – the rightly-guided community – is the more serious aspect of the matter. We all know how ready most people are to copy each other and to justify what they do in terms of what others have done. A bad example held up before the public gaze is therefore a wound inflicted upon the community, undermining the Law and loosening ties of relationship. For this offence, forgiveness is less likely.

There are, however, more profound reasons for protecting the 'nakedness' of others and for concealing our own. As was suggested earlier, few personalities are unified and all of a piece. For a man to try to cover and inhibit those elements within himself which he would like to overcome and to bring forward those which he would like to see triumphant is not 'hypocrisy'. If he would like to be better than he is, then he deserves to be encouraged in this aim, and there is something very peculiar about the contemporary tendency to regard a person's worst qualities as representing his 'true' self, although it goes hand in hand with the common belief that ugliness is in some strange way more 'real' than beauty and that to discover a shameful secret is to discover the truth. Perhaps a saner point of view is suggested by a story which Muslims tell about Jesus. It is said that he was walking one day with his disciples when they passed the carcass of a dog. 'How it stinks!' said the disciples; but Jesus said: 'How white its teeth are!'

No one was ever damned for thinking too well of people. It is said that his fellow monks once called St Thomas Aquinas to the refectory window, crying: 'Brother Thomas, come quickly and see a flying ox!' He heaved his considerable bulk out of the chair and went to the window. Seeing nothing, he returned amidst mocking laughter and sat down again, saying: 'Better to believe in a flying ox than in a lying monk!'

We are, by nature, poor judges of anyone and anything, and most factual evidence is partial if not conflicting. Ultimately, there is a simple moral choice: to believe the best or to believe the worst, to have faith or to shrink back from this leap in the dark and whimper in a corner until death takes us.

To return, however, to the question of presenting one's best face to the world, we might consider the case of a man who is without any innate dignity of character or of natural bearing: if he attempts to appear dignified for the sake of impressing the people around him or for material gain, then he is indeed a hypocrite; but if he does so from love of the quality of dignity, its beauty and its honour, and from a desire to be more worthy of his Creator despite his own inadequacies, then what do we call him? If we could foresee the fate of souls when they come to the final Judgement we might be surprised by the verdict upon him, and in any case it is none of our business to pull away his mask and expose the raw and disfigured features in the name of some abstract notion of 'honesty'.

The quality of personal dignity – not least dignity of deportment – was certainly highly valued in Islam in the past and, in spite of certain appearances today (due to the influence of modern Western manners), is still highly valued among more traditionally minded Muslims. This, together with what is often referred to as the 'cult of politeness', does indeed give rise to accusations of 'hypocrisy'; but in so tight-knit a society good manners are essential to maintain a certain distance between people, a certain privacy. Life would be intolerable in such a society if everyone spoke his mind.

Bonjean, whose reference to the 'ecclesiastical mien' of ordinary

Muslims was quoted earlier, remarks that the 'politeness' – or 'impoliteness' – of a people *is* that people, it demonstrates the very essence of their character and their conception of human life; and he asks, 'Who is the truly polite Muslim?' and concludes that this is the Muslim who has the firmest hold on his own tradition, who under all circumstances succeeds in making it 'living and active' within himself and among other people, and 'who is judged the least unworthy of serving as a model for his children, for his relatives, for his neighbours, for the inhabitants of his quarter, for his city, or for simple passers-by and for travellers, for the whole of humanity'. Another way of putting this would be to say that this is the Muslim who comes closest to following the example of the Prophet, and Bonjean himself adds that 'at the end of all the avenues of Muslim politeness' is the affirmation *lā ilāha illa 'Llāh*. He says also that an element in this 'cult of politeness' is the awareness that this world is of little consequence, and adds that the Muslim does not permit his glance to linger upon the 'wretchedness and vulgarity' inseparable from our littleness; 'the believer must not lose hold on the thought of God even for a moment'.[1]

Bonjean further discusses the significance of the Arabic term *ḥishmah*, variously translated as 'modesty', 'reserve', 'discretion' or 'decorum', which has been an essential and typical quality of traditional Muslim life and which forbids loud talk, unruly behaviour, displays of anger or excitement and, in short, all those modes of behaviour which we see practised fairly widely in Muslim countries today. Nowhere does he mention the famous 'egalitarianism' which is supposed to be among the essential features of Islam, unless one acknowledges that to treat others with politeness, regardless of their social position, is in effect to treat them as equals.

In this case, as in so many others, a term in common use becomes misleading when applied across a cultural frontier, and the egalitarianism preached by left-wing Muslims today provides yet another example of how the body of Islam may be poisoned by secular ideologies which seem, superficially, to resemble certain Islamic principles and therefore slip undetected across the frontier.

Modern egalitarianism, as we know it in the occidental world, has its roots in rebellion and in a belief in man's power to mould his own destiny and overcome 'unregenerate' nature. It is also one of the logical conclusions of atheism, for if there is nothing beyond this life – no possible righting of wrongs or compensation for loss – then he who does not receive his fair share in this world is a once-and-for-all loser. The poor man who, for Islam as for Christianity, is amongst God's favoured creatures – already 'blessed' – is, from this point of view, eternally poor. The French Revolution, which brought egalitarian doctrine on to the stage of history, was not only a revolt against an aristocracy that had become degenerate; it was a revolt against religion and, ultimately, against the 'nature of things'.

There are undoubtedly circumstances under which all men are equal. They are equal in a prison or a brothel, and they are equal in a monastery. Occidental egalitarianism (as a principle, for it has never been achieved in

[1]François Bonjean, in *Les Cahiers du Sud*.

practice) is that of the prison or the brothel. Muslim egalitarianism is that of the monastery, of a religious élite which is in itself a kind of aristocracy. What Islam does recognize as an article of faith is the relativity of all earthly differences and the impossibility of assessing the true value of any man or woman in terms of their social or economic position here. Moreover, the power and the splendour of God reduce all that appears to be other-than-Him to dust. 'You are all the children of Adam,' the Prophet said, 'and Adam was dust.' In the full light of the sun, a beacon is no brighter than a candle; they are equal. But when the sun is not shining – when God veils His face, as He does in this life – their difference becomes apparent.

There is equality not only in an élite but also among the poor, and the Qurān tells us: 'You are the poor, He is the Rich' (Q.35.15). Muslim 'egalitarianism' takes account of both points of view; there is a certain equality between all Muslims because they form an élite, the 'best of people', and because they are dust, because – before God – they are 'the poor', with no power, no rights, no possessions (since 'all is His'). They are not dogs, to quarrel over bones; and the advantages of this world are – under the divine Light – no more than dry bones in the desert.

Yet here and now: 'He it is who hath placed you as Viceroys on earth and hath raised some of you in rank above others, that He may test you by that which He hath given you. Indeed, thy Lord is swift in punishment, and He is indeed the Forgiving, the Merciful' (Q.6.165). One aspect of this 'testing' is that we should not envy those 'raised in rank' above us, or those more favoured than ourselves in the good things of this earth: 'And never turn thine eyes [in longing] towards such splendour of the life of the world as We may have allotted to others ...' (Q.20.131). No vice is more implacably condemned in the Islamic perspective than the vice of envy; and envy, precisely, is the motor which drives – into fury and bloodshed – the egalitarian doctrines of the post-Christian world. Envy, the Prophet said, 'devours good deeds just as fire devours fuel'.

The social idea of Islam is a community in which each individual lives within his or her allotted role under the rule of law, filling out the mould provided by the circumstances of this world – while ever conscious of living each moment of life in the sight of God – within a secure web of human relationships, walking on a straight and well-trodden path towards a goal which lies beyond the gateway of bodily death. The fact that a human society – or a great network of human societies – lived out this ideal, seeing no reason to change it for another, for a thousand years suggests both a lesson and a warning for today's world.

Chapter 10

THE HUMAN PARADOX

It is time to speak again of Adam, primordial or archetypal Man; and to speak also of Eve, without whom the first creation would have been imperfect and incomplete. Christians have long debated as to whether the Biblical account of our human origin is to be taken literally or allegorically. This debate is not foreign to Islam, in relation to the Qurān, but on the whole Muslims have been less troubled by the question, knowing – if they are wise – that both points of view may lie safely within the great circle of truth.

The Qurān describes the 'Adamic' creation and the fall of the first couple and, for the Muslim, the Qurān is infallibly true; whether this truth is factual in the historical sense or allegorical is a matter of perspective and does not affect its substance. The distinction is less sharp than it appears to the Western mind, since both historical fact and allegory are among the tools of God. He teaches us and informs us through the Qurān (as also through 'facts'), and He does so in the manner best adapted to our needs, our mode of understanding and our intellectual and imaginative capacity; so the Quranic account of the creation of Adam serves the divine purpose, and there is no occasion here for breaking heads in argument. What matters is the meaning transferred from That which infinitely transcends us to the human mind, with all its limitations; surely a miraculous transference. This meaning relates, not only to an event remote in time, but also to ourselves, for we are all 'the children of Adam', forged 'from one soul': that is our identity, fit to be entered on our passports.

'And when thy Lord said unto the angels: Truly I shall place on earth a Viceregent. They said: Wilt Thou place upon it one who will make mischief therein and will shed blood? While, as for us, we celebrate Thy glory and extol Thy holiness. He said: Indeed I know what ye know not!

'And He taught Adam the names of all things, then placed them before the angels, saying: Tell Me the names of these, if ye are truthful. They said: Glorified art Thou! No knowledge have we save that which Thou has taught us. Thou indeed art the All-Knowing, the Wise. He said: O Adam! Inform them of the names of these [things]; and when [Adam] had informed them of the names, He said: Did I not say to you that I know the secrets of the heavens and the earth; and I know what you show and what you hide?

'And when We said unto the angels: Prostrate yourselves before Adam, then all fell prostrate, except for Iblīs. He refused through pride, and was thus among the unbelievers. And We said: O Adam! Dwell thou and thy wife in the Garden, and eat freely [of the fruits] thereof where ye will, but approach not this tree lest ye become wrongdoers. But the Satan caused them to depart from this and expelled them from the state in which they were ...' (Q.2.30–36).

In another *Sūrah* we are told that God asked Iblīs why he had not prostrated himself when commanded to do so, and he replied: 'I am better than he! Thou didst create me from fire and him from clay' (Q.7.12). And we are told also that in tempting Adam he whispered to him: 'Shall I show thee the tree of immortality and a kingdom that wasteth not away?' (Q.20.120).

The chroniclers and commentators,[1] relying sometimes upon what the Prophet himself said of these matters and sometimes upon inspired imagination, have filled out this narrative framework and coloured it in rich colours. With their love of precise detail they tell us that the colour of Eve's hair was auburn (*shahla*, a shade in which blue and red are mixed), and her locks were so long that you could actually hear them rustling. She was so plump that her thighs chafed when she walked, and God spoke to Adam saying: 'This is My handmaiden, and thou art my servant, O Adam! Nothing I have created is dearer to me than ye twain, so long as ye obey Me.' So much did He love them that He and none other performed the marriage ceremony, the archangel Gabriel acting as the groom's friend and the assembled angels as witnesses, which is why the Muslim is commanded to make public his wedding ceremony, following in the footsteps of our father Adam. All of which reminds us that the first human creation was a dual creation – 'Glory to Him who created the pairs ...' (Q.36.36) – but that duality as such is divisive and that two must again be oned in their act of union or in a dynamic unity constantly renewed. Is not marriage 'half the religion'?

The commentators tell us the order of precedence in which the archangels came to do obeisance to Adam; they tell us also that he knew not only the names of all things, but every language, even the languages of fish and frogs. They describe how the angels bore him on their shoulders, so that he towered above them, and carried him thus through the paths of heaven. Others stood all about, rank upon rank, and as he passed them he greeted them with the greeting of peace, to which they replied: 'And upon thee be peace and the mercy of Allah and His blessing, O Chosen of Allah, His preferred one, the masterpiece of His creation!'

How to impress the pre-eminence of Adam upon dull human minds? This is the traditional way: it is said that a pulpit was set up for him and that all the inhabitants of heaven were summoned, rank upon rank, before him and that he was endowed with a voice which reached them all. That day he was clothed in a garment of brocade light as air, with two jewel-encrusted girdles anointed with musk and ambergris. On his head was a golden crown which had four corner-points, each set with a great pearl so luminous – or so transparent to the divine radiance – that its brightness would have put out the light of the sun and the moon. Around his waist, encircling his very being, was the belt of God's 'Good Pleasure' (*ridwān*),

[1]See in particular the *Qiṣaṣ al-Anbiyā'* by al-Kisā'ī, extracts translated in *A Reader on Islam*, ed. Arthur Jeffery (Mouton & Co., 1962).

and the light which came from it penetrated into every one of the chambers of Paradise. Adam stood upright before the celestial assembly and greeted them. Then God said: 'O Adam! For this [saying] did I create thee, and this greeting of Peace shall be your greeting and that of your descendants until the end of time.'

When he came down from the pulpit his radiance was even greater than it had been before. A bunch of grapes was brought to him and he ate of it. This was the first celestial food he had tasted, and when he had satisfied himself he said: 'Praise be to Allah!' And his Creator said: 'O Adam! For this [saying] did I create thee, and it shall be customary for thee and thy descendants until the end of time.' But when Iblīs, the satanic personification, heard that Adam had taken food, he murmured: 'Now I shall be able to seduce him!'

But this shadow had not yet materialized to mar the splendour of the occasion, nor had its consequences – consequences in the midst of which we live out our lives – and a great procession traversed the heavens in unshadowed light, primordial Man mounted on his mighty steed and, beside him, primordial Woman riding her noble she-camel. Even in our twilight world we may glimpse that radiance, for it is timeless, and shadows – when all is said and done – are no more than shadows; but only on condition that we are true to our contract, for a covenant was then made between God and man, sanctioned and witnessed by the hosts of heaven, so that it could never be put aside and so that the descendants of Adam and Eve could never escape from its obligations, to which, as seeds within Adam's loins, they freely assented. By this covenant humankind acknowledged their Lord with a resounding 'Yes!' and committed themselves to perpetual affirmation.

The fall into relativity – 'the Fall' – could not change this commitment, of which mankind has been reminded by means of consecutive revelations, nor could all trace of Paradise be removed either from human memory or from the earth. It is said that when Adam fell he brought with him a little of the scented air of Paradise, which clung thereafter to the trees and valleys and filled all the place with perfume (the perfumes known to us are derived from that scented air). With him too came the Black Stone, which was then whiter than snow, and Moses' rod of celestial myrtle-wood; and Adam spoke to his Lord, saying: 'O my Lord! I was a near neighbour to Thee in Thy dwelling-place. I had no other Lord but Thee. There did I feed in luxury and there did I dwell wheresoever I pleased, but Thou didst cast me down ... Even then I still heard the voices of the angels and saw how they went around Thy throne, and I still perceived the breezes and scent of the Garden. But Thou hast cast me to the earth and reduced me to a height of sixty cubits, cutting me off from that hearing and that seeing ...'[1] And it was then, so we are told, that God made to Adam and to his progeny the promise that they would never be left without guidance through the darkness of the land and the sea.

---

[1] Quoted from the *Kitāb at-Ṭabaqāt al-Kubra* of Ibn Sa'd (d. AD 845).

Such was Adam's rank and stature and that of Eve, his wife. Yet 'Adam was dust'. Man, as such, is the 'Viceregent of Allah on earth', but when he forgets that he is only dust he loses this function and becomes the 'lowest of the low' (Q.95.5). As creature he is all *and* nothing; in practice he is obliged to choose between being all *or* nothing. Created, according to a saying of the Prophet, in the image of God – a theomorphic being, his nature reflecting as in a mirror the 'Names' or attributes of his Lord – he is none the less a creature of flesh and blood, fashioned out of the earth upon which, for a short while, he walks, and condemned to fall back into it; a wayward creature filled with unappeasable longings and constantly tempted to satisfy them at the lowest level, to live beneath himself. This is the paradox which underlies the human situation.

There are a number of different ways in which the Quranic insistence upon Adam's superiority to the angels may be explained, and none of them exhausts its full significance. So fundamental a truth could not be confined to one revelation – one religion only – and the Christians are familiar with it; according to St Gregory Palamas, 'Though in many things the angels are superior to us, yet in a certain way they are none the less inferior ... they are so, for example, in respect of existence according to the image of the Creator, for in this sense we are created more perfectly conformable to the image of God ...'

This explanation, familiar also to a number of Muslim philosophers, turns upon the fact that the angels, for all their splendour, are 'peripheral' beings, in the sense that each represents a particular aspect of the divine Plenitude; no single one among them reflects in his nature the totality of God's attributes. The Perfect Man, on the other hand, though far distant from the Light of heaven, stands, as it were, directly beneath the divine axis and mirrors Totality. This is why man, when his nature is fully developed and perfectly balanced, is described as a 'central' being, and this is why it is possible for him to be the '*Khalīfah* of Allah on earth', the Viceregent.

Moreover, the angels are incapable of disobedience and therefore of 'sin' in any sense of the term; as passive tools of the divine Will they are without responsibility or the power of choice. We have then a further paradox: the fact that only a being capable of choice and, for that very reason, capable of sin can 'represent' God in His earthly domain. Neither the angels nor the animals are able to disobey their Creator; man has that option, for it is a necessary aspect of his delegated responsibility and his privileged situation.

It is precisely this situation – man's 'centrality' – that offers him the possibility of committing monstrous crimes (it is absurd to speak of a criminal as 'behaving like an animal'; animals do not commit crimes). The more exalted the creature, the deeper the abyss into which he is capable of falling. The teaching of certain Muslim philosophers that all the divine Names (or 'attributes') are reflected in the human heart offers a key to this paradox. A generous man is so because he reflects the qualities expressed in the divine Name *al-Karīm*, 'the Generous'. The man who has beauty of character or the woman who has physical beauty reflects something of *al-Jamīl*, and the strong man would have no strength were it not for *al-Qawī*, 'the Strong', and *al-Qahhār*, 'the All-Compelling'. But *Allāh* is also and, indeed, essentially *al-Aḥad*, 'the One'; One alone, One who has no partner, the unique, the incomparable. From this Name is derived the relative uniqueness of each human being and the fact that each is – at least potentially – a microcosm, a totality.

It is commonplace in England to remind a child who is too demanding that he is 'not the only pebble on the beach'. The problem is that every one of us, in his innermost identity, is – though in an entirely relative sense – the 'only pebble'. Each is, in virtuality, not only a man or a woman, but Man, Woman. When this spiritual quality is appropriated by the mortal ego, man makes himself a god beside God; the Viceregent usurps the place of the King. He is then alone in creation and all other creatures are either toys to play with or obstructions blocking his way; at the same time, he feels that they have no real existence apart from him; for, indeed, creatures have no existence apart from God. Man is the only creature who kills his own kind as a matter of course,[1] who punishes them because they do not fit the pattern of righteousness which seems to him unquestionable, and who lusts for a power and a dominion which will prove that he is truly one alone, without equal, totally himself. The greatest sin, in other words, is simply the obverse side of the supreme privilege which man enjoys; and lesser vices also are the shadows of the virtues which reflect the divine Perfection, bearing witness, in a perverse way, to the grandeur of our state. Animals have a safe passage through this world, but man is always balancing on the edge of an abyss, and it is little wonder that the angels should have foreseen that this new creation would 'make mischief in the earth'.

But the Quranic account of the creation of Adam and the command to the angels to prostrate themselves before him singles out one particular point for emphasis. He had been given a knowledge which the angels do not possess. He had been taught 'the names of all things'. This too is an aspect of his theomorphic nature, for as *al-Khāliq*, 'the Creator', God defines or singles out – by 'naming' them – the possibilities which have it in them to appear outside the divine treasury in the theatre (*maẓhar*) of this world. As *al-Bārī* He produces them and as *al-Muṣawwir* He shapes their earthly form, but the first step is the supreme creative act of 'naming'.

Islam is commonly regarded as the religion of Law, but it is above all the religion of Knowledge; not that there is any contradiction here. As was mentioned earlier, the Arabic word for 'Law' has the primary meaning of 'understanding' and therefore relates to knowledge. To know the 'name' of something is to possess it in our understanding and to perceive it with the eyes of our intelligence. The Prophet said that 'Allah has created nothing more noble than intelligence'; and he said also that 'the superiority of the learned man over the ordinary worshipper is like the superiority of the full moon over the stars'. According to the Qurān, He who is the All-Knowing 'grants wisdom to whom He pleases, and whomsoever has been granted wisdom has indeed been given abundant wealth' (Q.2.269). 'Are those who *know* and those who are ignorant to be deemed equal?' (Q.39.9). For Islam, knowledge, intelligence and understanding define

---

[1] One of the 'ninety-nine Names' of God is *al-Mumīt*, 'He who slays'.

man as such. We cannot define him as a creature who is good or who is strong, or even as one who is loving; but we can define him as one who understands – or is capable of understanding.

Lest we should suppose, even for one moment, that knowledge can be ours to possess and to hoard, the Qurān reminds us that 'He knoweth; ye know not' (Q.24.19). Adam was taught the names of all things by God, and Adam was – according to the Islamic perspective – a Prophet; Muhammad received the Qurān from the same source, the only source from which true knowledge may be derived, and he was the last of the Prophets to follow in Adam's footsteps. If the Muslim is to tap that same source and become 'one who understands', he has no choice but to model himself upon this 'perfect exemplar', imitating Muhammad so far as he is able, both in his character and in his mode of action. Since the Prophet is 'closer to the believers than their [own] selves' (Q.33.6), it can be said that he is the believer's *alter ego* or – to take this a step further – more truly 'oneself' than the collection of fragments and contrary impulses which we commonly identify as the 'self'.

This is why the *hadīth* literature is of such immense importance in the everyday life of the Muslim; and the record is so extensive that it is always possible, even among learned people, for someone to astonish and delight his friends by quoting to them a 'Prophet story', or a saying of which they had not previously heard. The intimate knowledge we have of Muhammad's life (much of which we owe to 'Ā'isha) is, from a practical point of view, just as important as his religious teaching and the example he set in affairs of greater consequence. The believer feels close to him in life and hopes to be closer still after death, loving him not only as master and as guide but also as brother-man. It is in the light of this relationship that we may understand parts of the record which often appear trivial to the occidental, such as 'Ā'isha's meticulous account of the manner in which they washed from a single bowl after making love, and her added comment, 'he would get ahead of me and I used to say, "Give me a chance, give me a chance!"'

It is often from quite minor incidents that we get the clearest impression of his style, particularly of his unfailing common sense. A woman who had barely escaped with her life from some raiders by making off on one of the Prophet's camels told him: 'I vowed that I would sacrifice the camel to Allah if he saved me by means of her.' 'That is a poor reward,' he said. 'Allah saved you by means of her and now you want to kill her. Leave the animal alone!' adding – one supposes as an afterthought – 'Besides, she happens to be my property.' One is immediately warned against a certain kind of 'piety' which readily sacrifices other people's interests to prove itself. His dislike for interfering in private matters was also an essential aspect of his style as leader of the community. A woman who had developed a dislike for her husband drove him out of the house, although he loved her deeply ('I can still picture him,' said Ibn 'Abbās, who told the story, 'following behind her in the streets of Medina with the tears running down his beard)'. The Prophet asked her if she would not take her husband back. She inquired whether he was giving her a command, and he said he was simply interceding for the man. 'In that case,' she said, 'I have no need of him!' In the Muslim perspective such incidents are not necessarily different in essence, or any less wonderful, than Adam's preaching to the multitude of angels; and this is something that the occidental has particular difficulty in grasping.

Al-Ghazzalī (d. AD 1111), who is one of the most widely accepted authorities, wrote of the true Muslim as one who 'imitates the Messenger of Allah in his goings out and his comings in, his movements and his times of rest, the manner of his eating, his deportment, his sleep and his speech'. So a man should sit while putting on his trousers and stand while putting on his turban, start with the right foot when putting on his shoes and, when cutting his nails, begin with the forefinger of the right hand; and al-Ghazzalī mentions the case of a pious man who never dared eat a melon, much as he wished to do so, because he could not discover the precise manner in which God's Messenger ate melons. Did he cut them into segments? Did he perhaps scoop the flesh out with a spoon? We shall never know. But this outward observance is, of course, meaningless unless it both reflects and engenders a profound inward conformity to the perfect exemplar, given us by God as 'a mercy to mankind', a conformity of the believer's soul to the soul of Muhammad.

There are certain plants and shrubs which need to grow on a trellis or support of some kind if they are to grow to perfection; otherwise they sprawl on the ground, without direction, their leaves consumed by snails and slugs, their purpose unfulfilled. Man is a 'climber' too, and we do not need to seek far afield for examples of the human incapacity to grow – or even to function in a truly human way – without a support, a framework, a model.

The *Sunnah* of the Prophet provides not only a framework but also, as it were, a network of channels into which the believer's will enters and through which it flows smoothly, both guided and guarded. It is not his way, the Muslim's way, to cut new channels for his volitive life through the recalcitrant materials of this world, against the grain of things. At first sight one might expect this to produce a tedious uniformity. All the evidence indicates that it does nothing of the kind; and anyone who has had close contact with good and pious Muslims will know that, although they live within a shared pattern of belief and behaviour, they are often more sharply differentiated one from another than are profane people, their characters stronger and their individualities more clearly delineated. They have modelled themselves upon a transcendent norm of inexhaustible richness, whereas profane people have taken as their model the fashions of the time. To put it another way: the great virtues – and it is the Prophet's virtues that the believer strives to imitate – can, it seems, be expressed through human nature in countless different ways, whereas worldly fashion induces uniformity. In media advertisements one 'fashion model' looks very much like another.

None the less, occidentals see in all this an absence of 'spontaneity' and a process of 'depersonalization'. The word 'spontaneity', which, by its derivation, refers to action springing from the deepest source of our being, has been much misused in recent times. It has come to mean thoughtless and unconsidered reaction in response to outward stimuli, although the dictionary still defines it as action 'occurring without external cause', which is the very opposite to this. The Muslim way of life certainly discourages automatic reactions to the events which impinge upon us – as does the Muslim code of manners – but it is this, precisely, that makes possible the exercise of true spontaneity. This recalls a *ḥadīth* quoted earlier concerning the virtue of 'slowness' and the satanic nature of 'haste'. Spontaneous action comes, not from the surface personality but from the deepest source of our being, and it is at that level that the Prophet is 'closer to the believers than their own selves'.

A number of orientalists have claimed that Islam, as they see it, 'depersonalize' man by its demand that he should model himself upon another rather than 'be himself'. The same could be said of any religion, not least Christianity; but 'being oneself' is an ambiguous phrase which means one thing to the believer and quite another to the agnostic. The sacrifice (or transmutation) of the empirical selfhood is one of the basic requirements of spirituality, whether Muslim, Christian, Hindu or Buddhist, but since this outward selfhood or ego is situated in a world of things which change and die, its sacrifice merely hastens the inevitable (the Prophet is reported to have said: 'Die before you die!'). Meanwhile, the question is not whether we should 'lose ourselves' – since all do so in one way or another – but where we lose ourselves: in light or in darkness, in good dreams or in nightmares, in truth or in falsehood.

Curiously enough, it is only since many people have come to see the human person as a meaningless accident in a meaningless universe (in accordance with what they suppose to be the 'scientific' view) that they have attached such importance to the empirical selfhood, and resented so bitterly whatever savours of the 'impersonal' in traditional religion. They are obliged therefore to put their faith in a fiction and to cling to it in the coldness of space and the devouring fire of time. For who is this 'person'? Is he myself as a baby or as a child, as a youth caught in the net of joy, middle-aged, senile or at the moment of death? We cannot locate him with any certainty. All we know is that there exists, between the aged man and his childhood self, a causal relationship, together with a fragile link of memory; we are obliged to admit that he is not, in any practical sense, the same person.

What was said earlier regarding the human personality as a city of many factions – 'my name is legion' – is relevant here. On the one hand we are subject to constant change in the course of time; on the other we are not even 'all of one piece' in any given moment of time. If we are in search of a 'real self', then we must seek it elsewhere; in unity (*tawḥīd*), in religion (which, according to its Latin derivation, means 'binding'). Unity of the outward and the inward, binding of the outward to the inward. If we envisage the outward personality as the changing expression or projection of an unchanging nucleus or centre, then we may begin to glimpse an answer to the perennial question: 'Who am I?' But we cannot stop here; there is one more step to be taken before the question is finally resolved. This centre, called by Muslims (though not by Muslims alone) the 'heart', is indeed the central point to which our outward personality corresponds as periphery, but although it is 'within' us, it is not 'ours'. It belongs to

God, and it is eternally present with Him; and yet, since it is also 'within' us, it is the place where He is present, immanent. In other words, if we penetrate sufficiently deeply into ourselves – through all the layers of dreams and of darkness – we come out into the open and find everything there; hence the saying of the Prophet: *man 'arafa nafsahu 'arafa rabbahu,* 'he who knows himself knows his Lord'.

Muslim mystics refer to the 'heart' as the *barzakh,* which means 'isthmus'; on the one side is the sea of this world, subject to wind and weather; on the other, the ocean of the Beyond, the celestial ocean. An isthmus divides two bodies of water, but it is also the link between them. On this side you step into the sea of change, but if you cross that little strip of land, you may plunge into the great ocean. The isthmus belongs to both, just as the 'heart', the centre, is ours and yet not ours.

We are reminded of the intimate link between awareness of God on the one hand and self-knowledge on the other in a Quranic verse: 'Be not as those who forgot Allah so that He caused them to forget their own selves (*anfusahum*)' (Q.59.19); and according to a *hadīth qudsī*: 'Neither in the earth nor in the heavens is there space for Me, but in the heart of my believing servant there is space for Me.' There are some who have questioned the authenticity of this *hadīth,* but it has been the inspiration of a number of profoundly important spiritual teachings within Islam and it is echoed in Christianity; not only by Angelus Silesius (who may have been influenced by Islamic teachings), when he wrote that 'the Most High is absolutely without measure, and yet a human heart can enclose Him entirely'; but also by Meister Eckhardt, when he said: 'God might make numberless heavens and earths, yet these ... would be of less extent than a needle's point compared with the standpoint of a soul attuned to God.' If there is space in the believer's heart for the Creator Himself, then there is certainly space in his soul for creation. Man contains the universe within himself more surely than the universe contains him.

Here we have a further indication of his function as the Viceregent of God on earth. The human heart – the central point of his being – is where the 'two seas' meet, the link between what is above and what is beneath, and it is said to be by means of the 'Eye of the Heart' that God sees us and that we 'see' Him. In the words of a contemporary Muslim writer: 'If the earth be likened to a windowless house, then man is a watch-tower in the house, and the Eye of the Heart is as a single window in that watch-tower, to which all the dwellers in the house look up for their light.[1] Without this Eye man ceases to fulfil his essential function, having fallen from his true nature; but with this Eye he is the sole earthly receptacle of the spiritual light, of which he is the dispenser among his fellow creatures, so that ... though he does not possess the Heavens, yet the Heavens of themselves lean down to touch the earth in him, its highest point.'[2]

It is clear that if we are to fulfil our true function, we must first identify and then *become* our true selves; the man alienated from his own centre is

[1]'The house without a window is hell,' says Rūmi, adding: 'The function of religion is to make a window' (*Mathnawī,* III. 2404).
[2]*The Book of Certainty,* Abu Bakr Siraj Ed-Din (New York: Samuel Weiser Inc.), pp. 30–31.

alienated from all things, not only a stranger to himself but also a stranger in the universe. Yet he cannot find the centre nor can be 'become himself' without help. For the Muslim, the Prophet not only shows us the way to the centre but, in a certain sense, is himself the way, since it is by taking him as our model, or by entering into the mould of his personality, that we are best able to travel to our destination. Action which springs from our own true centre – 'without external cause', as the dictionary has it – is the only truly 'spontaneous' action, and it is therefore in imitating him that we achieve spontaneity.

But what of those who do not accept the guidance of a divine messenger or follow in his footsteps? What of those who never fulfil their function? We are told that even their good actions are without substance and count for nothing in the scales of justice, and this is a hard thing for the modern agnostic – or even the 'liberal' Christian – to understand.

The Qurān, however, is quite explicit on this point. After asking, 'Who are the greatest losers by their works?' it gives the answer: 'Those whose effort goes astray in the present life although they reckon that they are doing good deeds' (Q.18.103–104); and as for 'the likeness of those who disbelieve in their Lord, their works are as ashes which the wind blows away on a stormy day' (Q.14.18). Or again, 'their deeds are as a mirage in a desert which the thirsty man supposes to be water, until he comes to it and finds it is naught, and finds, in its place, Allah ...' (Q.24.39). So far as the actions of those who 'desire the life of the world and its glamour' are concerned, 'what they contrive here is vain, and void are their works' (Q.11.15).[1]

Here the issue is not one of morality, nor can it be reduced – as the agnostic might suppose – to a question of 'punishment' for unbelief. It is much wider than that and much more profound, for it has to do with the nature of reality, or perhaps one should say with the nature of unreality. The outward personality, when it loses all connection with its Creator, the source of its being, and is cut off from its own centre, has a shadowy quality, and the works of shadows can have no substance. It is a basic principle of Islam that all good – and all that is positive – originates with God. If a man has no centre, then he has no enduring identity to which good deeds might adhere so as to be counted in his favour when he comes to judgement. Living amidst mirages, he is a stranger to reality until the day when, his illusions stripped away, he finally comes face to face with the Real, *Allāh*, his hands empty and his past life meaningless.[2]

---

[1]According to a *ḥadīth* recorded by both Bukhari and Muslim, Abu Huraira reported God's Messenger as saying, 'None of you will be rescued by his works', and adding, 'but if you keep to the straight path, are moderate, pray morning and evening and part of the night, and earnestly practise moderation, then you will reach [the goal].'

[2]Many contemporary Christians find this doctrine cruel and therefore untenable. They like to believe that 'nice' people – even nice Marxists – go to heaven effortlessly. Yet Christianity, both Roman and Protestant, holds basically the same view although from a different perspective (that of 'original sin'). For Luther, in particular, works without faith can do nothing whatsoever to save a soul from damnation; a lifetime spent in selfless service to humanity counts for nothing if faith is lacking. It should hardly be necessary to add that no one – no theologian, Muslim or Christian – can presume to set limits to the torrential,

Sins may be punished or they may be forgiven at the time of reckoning, but a fundamental error concerning the nature of reality is comparable to blindness, and we are told that, 'Whosoever is blind here will be blind in the hereafter and even further astray' (Q.17.72). To the major errors of *kufr* ('unbelief' or the denial of truth) and *shirk* (the association of other 'gods' with God), Islam adds a third, ingratitude; but this is so closely bound up with unbelief that the same word serves for both and it is the context that indicates the precise meaning. Ingratitude, however, also partakes of the error of *shirk*, since it involves attributing to ourselves what should rightly be attributed solely to God and, in this way, supposing ourselves to be 'gods'.

'This [punishment] We awarded them because of their ingratitude,' says the Qurān; 'Do We punish any save the ungrateful?' (Q.34.17). The reason is plain: 'And it is Allah who brought you forth from your mothers' wombs knowing nothing, and He gave you hearing and sight and hearts that you might give thanks' (Q.16.78); and again: 'It is Allah who made for you the night that you may rest therein, and the day for seeing, indeed Allah is bountiful to mankind but most men give not thanks ... It is Allah who made for you the earth as a dwelling and the heavens as a canopy, and fashioned you and shaped you well, and hath provided you with good things. Such is Allah, your Lord, the Creator of all things, so glorified be Allah, the Lord of the worlds. He is the Living, there is no god save Him. Call, then, unto Him, making religion sincere for Him. Praise be to Allah the Lord of the worlds!' (Q.40.61/64–65).

God gave to Adam and to his descendants the gift of intelligence, asking in return, not for blind praise, but for a lucid and joyful understanding of the nature of all things and their source. It is therefore incumbent upon us to recognize the facts of our situation, which is one of total dependence, total indebtedness.

Such a state of dependence seems to the modern occidental intolerable, though it cannot be so to the genuine Christian. Since the Renaissance Western man has prided himself upon his independence, if upon nothing else, and this independence is closely bound up with a spirit of rebellion against God, against destiny and against the very nature of things. Prometheus stole fire from heaven; he did not wait to be given it, and Prometheus is the model. The Muslim, being profoundly practical, sees this not as heroism but as foolishness. Facts, he says, are facts. We are totally dependent upon God, and that is that.

The evidence is all around us. There are a thousand ways in which our existence may be terminated between one moment and the next; a simple drug will transform the most intelligent among us into an idiot, or the bravest among us into a coward; and we know from our reading if not from experience that techniques of torture, more widely practised today than at any time in the past, can destroy every vestige of human dignity in a very short time. Such human dignity as we may have – and the Viceregent

---

all-encompassing mercy of God; but, equally, no one can presume to take this mercy for granted either in his own case or in the case of others who have failed in their primary human obligation.

of God is indeed a figure of great dignity – is a robe loaned to us, just as a woman's beauty is loaned to her, just as our skills, whether hereditary or acquired, are on loan, as are our strengths and our virtues. We can claim nothing as being truly ours except for our weaknesses and our vices, together with the ill we do in the world; for the Qurān assures us that all good comes from God, all ill from man. We do not even control the breath of life within us, and: 'No soul knoweth what it will earn tomorrow nor doth any soul know in what land it will die. Truly Allah is the Knower, the Aware!' (Q.31.34).

Existence is pure gift. Consciousness is pure gift. Our eyes and ears, our hands and our feet are gifts, as are our sexual organs. Mountains and rivers and the blue sea are gifts, as is the air we breathe; so too is light, and the darkness given us for rest. The nourishment which comes from the earth, or which – by a very special concession to our weakness – we are permitted to take from the bodies of the animal creation and from the fish of the sea, is a gift. But above all, the awareness which brings these together in consciousness and in enjoyment, and the power we are given to acknowledge their source and to give praise, are divine gifts.

To be ungrateful is to close ourselves off from the supreme gift, greater than all these; the gift of the divine Mercy and, ultimately, of Paradise, where all such gifts are incalculably magnified. In a mortal body and in a dying world, we praise and give thanks. It is for this, says the Muslim, that we were created.

Occidental man does not deny this dependence in principle. If he is a Christian, he knows himself to be a wretched sinner, fit only for damnation unless redeemed by Christ's blood. If he is an agnostic and believes that 'scientific' theories are a comprehensive form of knowledge, he sees himself as a chance agglomeration of particles and energies – monkey, son of monkey – and certainly of no account. Yet still, even in raging darkness, he has his stubborn pride; he thinks himself the conqueror of nature and there-fore, ultimately, of the God in whom he does not necessarily believe. This indeed is the Promethean heritage, a sickness that has come down through the centuries from a Graeco-Roman world which had lost its soul. There are some very strange skeletons in the cupboard of the occidental mind.

But gratitude on a fine day in a happy family is one thing, gratitude in the face of loss and suffering is quite another. Suffering has been with us for a long time, to say the least, but the 'problem of suffering' as the dominant theme of religious and philosophical debate is of fairly recent origin. It becomes a problem on this scale only when a great number of people begin to feel that it should not exist and that human beings have some kind of right to perpetual happiness. There are still good Christians who, in the face of bitter loss, are able to say, 'The Lord giveth and the Lord taketh away, blessed be the name of the Lord!', rejoicing in the gift and accepting the loss, but they are in a minority; for most people in the West today, a God who allows us to suffer is not a God in whom it is easy to believe.

The Muslim view is based upon an awareness that all we have or enjoy is a gift or a loan, and upon an acceptance of the destiny willed by God for each individual soul. On the one hand: 'Allah asketh naught of any soul save that which He hath given it' (Q.65.7), 'He it is who causeth you to laugh and causeth you to weep, and He it is who giveth death and giveth life' (Q.53.43–44), and 'To Allah we belong and unto Him we return' (Q.2.156); and, on the other, 'No affliction befalleth in the earth or within yourselves but it is in a Record before We bring it into being – indeed that is easy for Allah! – that you may not grieve over what escapes you nor rejoice over what comes to you' (Q.57.22–23).

The knowledge that God is the sole Owner of ourselves and of all that exists does not preclude human emotions, which are themselves God-given. Once, when the Prophet was occupied with some people, one of his daughters sent him a message that her little son was dying; he told the messenger to return and remind her that, 'What Allah takes belongs to Him, what He gives belongs to Him, and He has an appointed time for everyone ...' His daughter then sent the messenger back asking him to come to her, and he went to her house with some of his companions. The child was now on the point of death, and tears flowed from the Prophet's eyes. 'What is this?' one of the people asked him. 'This,' he said, 'is compassion, which Allah has placed in the hearts of His servants. Allah shows compassion only to those of His servants who are compassionate.'

How is this to be reconciled with the Quranic command not to grieve? The point, clearly, is that our natural feelings must never be taken out of their proper sphere and elevated to the rank of philosophical principles. The fact that I am sad does not mean that the world is out of kilter, the fact that I have been hurt does not mean that God is unjust, and the fact that my personal life may have been darkened by tragedy does not mean that no sun shines upon creation. It is when emotion is transposed to a different dimension that we have a 'problem of suffering' and this, precisely, is what has happened in our time.

When misfortune strikes profane people they suffer on two levels and their pain is doubled. On the one hand, there is the misfortune as such and the pain they feel; on the other, there is the belief that it should never have happened and that its happening proves something very bitter and very ugly about the nature of the world (and if they bring God into it, then about the nature of God). They suffer because 'something is wrong'; and then they suffer again because 'everything is wrong'. At the end of this particular road is the abyss which we call despair, a grave 'sin' for the Muslim, as it is for the Catholic Christian, for now a wound which may initially have been clean and simple has suppurated and poisoned the bloodstream.

Since no one can live or function in constant pain which feeds upon itself, and in an empty universe without mercy and without meaning, a third evil – the greatest of all – joins itself to the other two, and this is hardening of the heart. The pious Muslim endures, as does the pious Christian, because he is assured that a stream of light flows deep beneath the dark land he now inhabits, even if he can neither see it nor sense it. But there is little virtue – indeed, there is much vice – in an endurance based upon the desensitizing of all those faculties through which we respond to God, to nature and to our fellows. Anything is preferable to this, even the most abject breakdown, since there can be no hope for those who are spiritually dead, slain by their own hand. An endurance unaccompanied by hardening of the heart can exist only on a religious basis, because it can exist only where there is a sense of proportion, which amounts to saying that suffering is bearable only when it is understood, even if this understanding is obscure and unformulated.

The Muslim says 'Yes' to everything that comes to him – or tries to say 'Yes', which is enough, since, according to a *ḥadīth*, 'acts are judged by their intentions' – because he knows whence it comes. At the same time, he knows that it is better to be purified here than hereafter. The Arabic word *tazkīyah* has a double meaning which is of great significance: it can be translated either as 'purification' or as 'growth'. To take only one of several possible examples, the words *Qad a'flaha man tazakka* in *Sūrah* 87 are rendered by some translators of the Qurān as 'he is successful who purifieth himself', and by others as 'he is successful who groweth'. The English language cannot accommodate both meanings together, and yet a whole philosophy is comprised in the apparent ambiguity of the world *tazkīyah*.

According to the ancient Chinese philosopher Mencius: 'Grief and trouble bring life, whereas prosperity and pleasure bring death.' This has been restated often enough since his time, and the Qurān tells us that 'with hardship cometh ease', while the Prophet said that 'Paradise is surrounded by things that you dislike'. If we wish to grow and to mature – and this must be the Muslim's ambition, since he believes that his life is only a preparation for what comes after – then, however much misfortune is disliked, it cannot be seen as merely negative, which is precisely the way the profane person sees it. The Muslim, because he believes in Paradise, does not expect this world to be a paradise, and he is thereby saved from much bitterness and from the doubling or trebling of grief.

Philippe Guibertau, one of a number of Frenchmen who in some measure compensated for their country's colonial record by their appreciation of Islam, an appreciation which reinforced rather than undermined their own faith, observed: 'I have seen sick people, whether men, women or children, on Islamic soil both in the Hejaz and in Morocco; indeed they complain when they suffer too much, but never is there a word of recrimination against Providence, never do they blame God for having made them suffer: they are even disengaged from their "ego" to such an extent that they never ask whether they will take long to get well or even if they will ever get well. On the other hand ... sick people in the West, even among those who pass for Catholic, are indignant over being touched by sickness; "How could such a thing have happened to me!" ...'[1]

It is hardly surprising that Guiberteau should have added: 'It is on North African soil that many Europeans have rediscovered the sense of the supernatural', soil upon which they have come face to face with 'a people who have such faith in the incommensurable transcendence of God that they are dying of it, so much do they despise that which – precisely – is not God'. 'Dying' or 'living'; in this case the words are interchangeable according to one's perspective, not least because eternal life is, in terms of our worldly experience, a death. Totality is the death of the partial and the fragmentary; the candle's flame is lost in the sun.

---

[1] *Islam, Occident et Chrétieneté*, Philippe Guiberteau (Cahiers du Sud).

For those who see themselves only as isolated fragments, the experience of suffering is an experience of alienation and therefore an intolerable invasion. For the Muslim his personal identity and his destiny are one; nothing that enters his experience can be considered a 'foreign body'. 'Why, when an affliction came upon you ... did you ask, "How is this?" Say [unto them]: It is from yourselves' (Q.3.165). The word *maktūb*, 'it is written' or 'fated', means that whatever happens to us was inscribed upon our individual essence from the beginning of time. To wish that something else had happened to us is to wish ourselves other than ourselves, which is a perverse self-denial and, indirectly, a denial of our Creator who gave us what He gave us. Abū Huraira reported the Prophet as saying: 'So far as good things are concerned, be eager for what benefits you, seek help from Allah and do not be too weak to do so. [But] if some affliction comes to you do not say, "Had I done such-and-such this would never have happened", but say, "Allah decrees, and He does what He wishes"; for "Had I done ..." provides an opening for the devil's action.'

The advocates of 'determinisim' and the advocates of 'free will' have argued as fiercely in the Islamic world as elsewhere, and both have found appropriate texts in the Qurān and in the *hadīth* literature to support superficially opposite points of view. They have done so despite another report originating with Abū Huraira, who said: 'The Messenger of Allah came to us when we were arguing about [the nature of] *Allah's decree*. He was angry, and his face became so red that it was as though a pomegranate seed had burst open on his cheeks. He said: "Is this what you were commanded to do, or was it for this that I was sent to you? Your predecessors perished only when they asked about this matter. I warn you, I warn you, not to argue about it!"'

Two things are certain, and we must reconcile them as best we can or leave their reconciliation to a greater wisdom. In the first place, the concept of the divine omniscience would be empty if we did not acknowledge that God knows not only all that has ever happened but also all that will ever happen, and that the 'future' is therefore, in a certain sense, already 'past'. In the words of the Bible: 'That which hath been *is* now; and that which is to be hath already been.'[1] One could not look for a clearer statement of something universally known if not universally understood. Secondly, since as human beings we are subject to time and cannot see the future, we have an experience of free choice which is perfectly valid on its own level and reflects – on this level – the total freedom which is God's alone. We make our choice and act accordingly; only when the act is past and the day is done can we say *maktūb*, 'it was written' – 'it was decreed for us from the beginning of time'. But by then another day has dawned and other choices are to be made, and we do not, if we are Muslim, waste time considering what 'might have been' but could, in fact, never have been.

Here, as so often, we have to face the fact that the distinction between believer and unbeliever is a distinction between different universes of thought and of feeling. Told that the 'divine decree' is unalterable, the agnostic – if he is really such – sees himself as a trapped animal caged by an

[1]Ecclesiastes, 3.15.

alien and impersonal force. The believer, on the other hand, though exiled from the earthly Paradise, is never exiled from the divine Presence and is no stranger to the One by whose decree he lives and dies. It is said that the Arabic word for 'man', *ins*, is directly related to the word for 'intimacy', *uns*, and this is one way of indicating his unique privilege of intimacy with the Divine, and at least of hinting at the reciprocity which is at the heart of man's intercourse with God, God's intercourse with man. It is in terms of this reciprocity that we may best understand the nature of prayer and the place which prayer occupies in the life of the Muslim.

Christians who are aware of the master/slave imagery which is central to the Islamic perspective and who see the religion as 'impersonal' compared with their own faith, frequently ask whether the Muslim envisages any kind of personal, reciprocal relationship with his Creator. The Muslim, on the other hand, emphasizes the total self-sufficiency of God and is shocked by the Christian's belief that God in some mysterious way 'needs' man. The difference is real enough but it is also, to some extent, a matter of presentation. For Islam, reciprocity between Creator and creature, with its implication of mutual need, comes about, not on account of some apparent insufficiency in the Godhead, but because the Creator chooses to act in this way. In other words this reciprocity arises from need on our side and from overflowing generosity on His.

The Quranic condemnation of 'forgetfulness' – 'They forgot Allah, so He hath forgotten them' (Q.9.67) – and of 'indifference' (*ghaflah*) is balanced by constant emphasis upon awareness, expressed sometimes in terms of *taqwa*, translated either as 'fear of God' or as 'consciousness of God', and sometimes in terms of *dhikr*, a key word in Islam, which may be rendered either as 'remembrance' or as 'mention': 'Remember Me, I shall remember you' (Q.2.152). It is in this awareness, this remembrance, this bringing to mind, that 'hearts find rest' (Q.13.28). Prayer itself is defined as 'remembrance', and indeed all awareness of God is a form of prayer, for to think of Him and keep Him in mind is already to pray to Him; and it is in this way that the outer man and the inner man, hardened by their experience of life in this world, are melted and made receptive – 'Their skins and their hearts soften at the remembrance of Allah' (Q.39.23). Those whose love of the world has carried them out of earshot are lost: 'Then woe to those whose hearts are hardened against the remembrance of Allah' (Q.39.22); and as for him 'who turneth away from the remembrance of Me, his will be a constricted life, and I shall bring him blind to the gathering on the Day of Resurrection' (Q.20.124).

The Qurān tells us that mankind was created for one purpose, and that purpose is 'worship', but it tells us also that this worship evokes an immediate response: 'Call upon Me, and I will answer!' (Q.40.60). There is, therefore, a dialogue in prayer, but man alone is capable of a dialogue with God; the rest of creation 'prays' and 'praises' but does so, as it were, unconsciously, simply by being what it is. 'The seven heavens and the earth and all that is therein glorify Him, and there is not a [single] thing that does not celebrate His praise; but ye understand not their praise' (Q.17.44). According to a text attributed to Jalāluddin Rūmi: 'The darkness of the night and the brightness of the day, the beams of the sun and the light of the moon, the murmuring of the waters and the whispering of the leaves, the stars of the sky and the dust of the earth, the stones of the mountain, the sands of the desert and the waves of the oceans, the animals of water and land praise Thee.' Yet their praise is inarticulate, whereas man has been given the supreme gift of speech, together with the intelligence which makes speech coherent and therefore opens up the possibility of dialogue.

'Man prays and prayer fashions man. The saint has himself become prayer, the meeting-place of earth and heaven; and thus he contains the universe and the universe prays with him. He is everywhere where nature prays, and he prays with and in her; in the peaks which touch the void and eternity, in a flower which scatters itself or in the abandoned song of a bird.'[1] This is the function of the *Khalīfah*, the Viceregent; this is what he was made for, and in fulfilling his function he is shaped by it. It is said that the Prophet's grandson Hasan was asked once how it was that people who spent much of the night in prayer looked 'so beautiful'; he explained that it was because 'they have been alone with the All-Merciful, who covers them with light from His Light.'

For the human being, at once privileged and yet exposed to the most fearful danger, living is a movement of the perishable and the unstable towards the permanent and the absolute; or else it is a movement towards disintegration. According to al-Ghazzalī there are, in the 'invisible' world, 'wonders in relation to which this visible world is seen to be of no account. He who does not ascend to that world ... is but a brute beast, since the beasts are not given the wings with which to take flight thither. Know that the visible is, to the invisible, as the husk to the kernel, as the form and body are to the spirit, as darkness to light ... He who is in that world above is with Allah and has the keys of the Unseen.'[2]

Here again we meet with a paradox: man as a creature of two worlds or – to put the same thing another way – as a creature with two identities in a single body, the one perishable, the other immortal. It is difficult to conceive of a dialogue between God and His slave; it is far less difficult to conceive of one between God and His chosen Viceregent. It is in the *hadīth qudsī*, those recorded sayings of the Prophet in which God spoke directly through him, that we find the most striking references to the reciprocity which is the basis of dialogue.

'I am with [My servant] when he makes mention of me' – or 'when he remembers Me' – 'If he makes mention of Me to himself, I make mention of him to Myself ... And if he draws near to Me a hand's span, I draw near to him an arm's length; and if he draws near to Me an arm's length, I draw near to him a fathom's length. And if he comes to Me walking, I go to him speedily.' Here the response to prayer or, indeed, to the simple act of bringing God to mind, is of incomparable magnitude, for the divine presence is obviously greater than any other imaginable gift. As for human supplication, this is not only heard, it is awaited: 'Our Lord who is blessed and exalted descends each night to the lowest heaven, when two-thirds of the night have passed, and asks, "Who supplicates Me that I may answer

---

[1]*Spiritual Perspectives and Human Facts*, Frithjof Schuon (Faber & Faber), p. 213.
[2]Quoted from *al-Mishkāt al-anwār* of al-Ghazzalī.

him? Who asks of Me that I may give to him? Who begs for My forgiveness so that I may forgive him?"'

Even in this poor world, according to another *hadīth*, 'Allah has angels who travel on the roads seeking those who remember Allah, and when they find people doing this they call to one another, "Come to what you are seeking!" and surround them with their wings up to the lowest heaven.' Their Lord asks them ('although He is best informed') what these worshippers are saying, and the angels answer that they are glorifying Him, though they have never seen Him; they are asking for Paradise, though they have never seen it; and they are seeking refuge from hell, though they have never seen it. Their Lord then says to His angels: 'I call you to witness that I have forgiven them!'

Not everyone – to say the least – seeks communion, dialogue with God; most of those who turn towards the heavens in prayer do so from desire or from fear, and those who do so from fear are in search of forgiveness. We are told that God does not greatly care about the motive so long as people do turn to Him and thereby establish the essential link. This is brought out in an astonishing *hadīth* which might have been considered doubtful had it not been recorded by one of the most highly respected of *mutahadithūn*: 'By Him in whose hand is my soul, had you not sinned Allah would have removed you and brought a people who sin, then ask for Allah's forgiveness and are forgiven.' According to a *hadīth qudsī*, 'Allah has said: O son of Adam, so long as you call upon Me and ask of Me, I shall forgive you what you have done and I shall not care. O son of Adam, though your sins reached the clouds in the sky, if you were then to ask for My forgiveness I would forgive you. O son of Adam, were you to come to Me with sins almost as great as the earth [itself] and then face Me, ascribing to Me no "partner", I would bring you forgiveness in like measure.'

These texts and sayings relate in prayer in general and, perhaps above all, to the *dhikr*, the 'remembrance', which is the essence of all prayer. But Muslims make a sharp distinction between private or extempore prayer, called *du'ā'*, and the ritual prayer which is obligatory five times each day, *salāh*. The effectiveness of the latter does not depend upon individual circumstances, feelings or inclinations. It is a rite, a God-given framework, and so all the human creature has to do is, so to speak, to step into it. It is preceded by the ablution which washes away accumulated grime, by orientation (that is to say, by the worshipper turning to face Mecca), and by the intention to perform such-and-such a prayer or to participate in it.

As we have seen, Islam and Christianity interpret the consequences of Adam's 'fall' differently, and Islam does not accept that any 'sin' – any 'fall' – could determine the inmost essence of the human creature. Man cannot, according to this perspective, lose his theomorphism, his likeness to the divine image, however deeply this likeness may be covered in filth. Not even the most corrosive acid could ever destroy the divine imprint. By means of the ritual ablution this primordial purity, the purity of the creature as he first issued from the hand of God, is temporarily restored and he is made fit to stand upright before his Creator.

The past clings to us; past sins, past errors. God's forgiveness washes these away or, under His name *al-'Afū*, He effaces them as though they had never happened (or, to be more precise, as though they had never attached themselves to our substance), for He alone can break the chain of cause and effect. The ritual washing in ablution is an image of this forgiveness or this effacement. Yesterday's grime is removed from the skin and the grime of the past is removed from the soul, and the substance used for this purpose is that same substance from which we were first created: 'And He it is who from water hath created man' (Q.25.54).

'Uthmān (the third Caliph) reported that the Prophet said: 'If anyone performs the ablution well, his sins will come out from his body, coming out even from under his nails'; and Abū Huraira reported his saying: 'When a believer washes his face in the course of ablution, every sin he contemplated with his eyes will fall away from his face together with the water, or with the last drop of water; when he washes his hands, every sin they did will fall away from his hands with the water, or with the last drop of water; and when he washes his feet, every sin towards which his feet walked will fall away with the water, or with the last drop of water, with the result that he comes forth purified from sin.' In Islam 'purity' might almost be defined as a synonym for objectivity, since it means, above all, to be free of the subjective distortions and self-interest which most closely bind us. To say that something is 'pure' means that it is unmixed with extraneous elements and is wholly itself, like pure gold.

Restored to himself, the worshipper stands up to pray. He stands facing the Ka'ba in Mecca, however distant he may be from it. 'Whencesoever thou comest forth, turn thy face towards the sacred Mosque, and where-soever ye may be turn your faces toward it . . .' (Q.2.150). Books of Islamic Law compiled before the compass was in general use go into immense detail regarding the means by which a traveller may discover the correct orientation, but they never overlook the fact that 'acts are judged by their intentions'. If the worshipper faces in the wrong direction through an una-voidable error, and does not discover his mistake until the time for the prayer in question is past, then his prayer is accepted by God. He intended to face the Ka'ba, and that is what matters.

Orientation, both in the simple physical sense and symbolically, is of immense importance in Islam.[1] The Ka'ba is, for the Muslim, the centre of the world; it is also the symbol of his own inward centre, the 'heart', where all things come together. To face in the right direction is to be well on the way to achieving personal integration. It is to be already on the 'straight path' upon which, in his prayer, the Muslim will ask God to lead him, except that in the first case the path is, so to speak, on the horizontal – leading to Mecca – whereas in the second it is vertical and leads to 'the Lord of this House', the Lord of the Ka'ba, God Himself. The horizontal journey is like a projection of the vertical one on to a flat surface; in other words, the former is a symbol of the latter and, at the same time, its precursor.

---

[1] Not only in Islam. According to an American psychiatrist, William Sheldon, who had – very probably – barely heard of the religion of Islam: 'Continued observations in clinical psychological practice lead almost inevitably to the conclusion that deeper and more fundamental than sexuality, deeper than the craving for social power, deeper even than the desire for possessions, there is a still more generalized and universal craving in the human make-up. It is the craving for knowledge of the right direction – for orientation.'

So *ṣalāh*, the ritual prayer, is 'established'. 'When entering on prayer you should come into the Presence of Allah as you would on the Day of Resurrection, when you will stand before Him with no mediator between you, for He welcomes you and you are in confidential talk with Him, and you know in whose Presence you are standing, for He is the King of Kings. When you have lifted your hands and said: "God is most Great", then let nothing remain in your heart save glorification, and let nothing be in your mind at the time of glorification but the glory of God most High, so that you forget this world and the next while glorifying Him. When a man bows in prayer, it is fitting that he should afterwards raise himself, then bow again to make intercession until every joint of his body is directed towards the throne of God . . . and he thinks so little of himself that he feels himself to be less than a mote of dust.'[1]

This ritual prayer is, according to the Prophet, 'the key to Paradise', and he said to his companions: 'Tell me, if there were a river at someone's door in which he washed five times daily, would any dirt remain upon him?' When they replied that none would remain, he said: 'That is like the five times of prayer by which Allah obliterates sins.' If only people knew what blessing lies in the Dawn prayer, he told them, 'they would come [to the prayer] even if they had to crawl to do so'. It is little wonder that when the Call to Prayer is made, 'the devil turns his back and breaks wind, so as not to hear the Call being made . . .' That is the devil's way of evading reality; but men and women, if they are whole and sane, respond. A man came to the Prophet saying: 'Messenger of Allah, I have done something which merits punishment, so appoint [a punishment] for me!' The Prophet said nothing, and when the time for prayer came, the man prayed with him, then repeated his request for punishment. 'Did you not pray with us?' the Prophet asked him. He agreed that he had done so. 'Well then, Allah has forgiven your offence.'

The ritual prayer has two focal points: one has to do with understanding and relates to the mind, the other is existential and has to do with the body. The first is the recitation of the *Fātiḥah*, the short *Sūrah* placed at the beginning of the Qurān, in every single unit of prayer (together with the recitation of other passages from the Qurān in the first two units), and this is done while the worshipper is standing, as is his right when he prays as God's Viceregent on earth; the second is the prostration of the body, with the forehead touching the ground, folded up in the foetal position and obliterated beneath the splendour of the divine Majesty. These two focal points are the two poles of human experience, human reality.

The *Fātiḥah* begins, not with the words 'I praise Allah', but with 'The praise is to Allah', because the Viceregent is praying on behalf of all creation. Just as water comes down from above as blessing and rises again to the heavens as steam or vapour, so the divine gifts are, as it were, transmuted into praise, which returns to the 'Lord of the worlds', who is then qualified as 'the Merciful, the Compassionate', and after that, as 'King of the Day of Judgement', since He stands at the end of every road and everything comes finally to Him to be 'judged' and allotted its proper

[1]Kharrāz, quoted from *Readings from the Mystics of Islam*, Margaret Smith, no. 26.

place according to its nature. After defining the relationship of creation to the Creator, God's Viceregent, speaking in the plural on behalf of his province, says: 'Thee do we worship and in Thee do we seek refuge' (or 'from Thee do we seek help'), and he goes on to voice the universal hope: 'Lead us on the straight way,[1] the way of those upon whom is Thy grace, not of those upon whom is Thine anger, nor of those who stray.'

This is the *Fātiḥah*, 'the Opening', which the Muslim – assuming that he prays – recites a minimum of seventeen times each day, and far more often if he also prays what are called the *Sunnah* prayers, in accordance with the practice of the Prophet. He bows after his recitation so that the upper part of his body is horizontal, and in this position he glorifies God as 'the Immense', 'the Vast' or the 'the Infinite', the God whose power extends beyond all imaginable extension on the horizontal. Then he prostrates himself and glorifies God 'the Most High', 'the Transcendent', who is unimaginably above and beyond all things; he has made himself so small that he can do this, for any merely human extension, such as the extension of his body in height or in breadth – vertical or horizontal – would be like a denial of that transcendence.

The Viceroy who recites the revealed words of the Qurān does not live in the same land as the King, though he speaks to him; it is in the prostration that he is most certainly in the royal presence, and if he speaks now it is the speech of total intimacy. The lady 'Ā'isha said: 'One night I missed the Messenger of Allah from our bed, and when I sought him my hand came to the soles of his feet while he was in the act of prostration with them raised, and he was saying: "O Allah, I seek refuge in Thy Good Pleasure from Thy anger, and in Thy forgiveness from Thy punishment, and I seek refuge in Thee from Thyself. I cannot reckon Thy praise" ...'

The ritual prayer, in all its dimensions of height, breadth and profundity, is an act of concentrated 'remembrance' (*dhikr*), and even the busiest man is recalled five times a day from his straying to acknowledge his dependence and to bring into awareness the Reality which infinitely transcends him, yet which bends down to him in mercy. But wise men have said that all the Five Pillars of Islam were instituted only for the sake of the 'remembrance' of Allah.

This is obvious in the case of the first, the witnessing to the divine Unity, and of the second, prayer. The third pillar is *zakāh*, the giving of alms, the sharing of wealth, which – quite apart from its social function – compels us to recognize that other human beings are as we are, equally unique, and that their existence is as much a miracle as our own; only in the context of 'remembrance', which puts everything in its place, can this recognition become a reality that is experienced, rather than a simple duty. The whole point of the Fast of Ramadan, which is the fourth pillar, is the achievement of a state of detachment from the world, as also from the ego and its desires, which creates a space for the 'remembrance' of Allah and even for His presence; and the fifth, the Pilgrimage, brings us back physically as well as spiritually to the centre, the place where 'remembrance' becomes meeting and actuality.

[1]This could also be translated as 'the ascending Path'.

This 'remembrance', this constant awareness, is combined with *taqwa*, the awe-struck consciousness of God as the supreme Reality, invoked, as the Qurān puts it, 'in fear and in hope'.

Since the creation of Adam, who was shaped from dust and made glorious, paradox has been piled on paradox, not least when this creature of dust stands upright and brings to earth something of heaven. The scented breezes of Paradise may now be preserved only in bottles – they no longer circulate with the winds – but their perfume clings to works of art and of craftsmanship, whereby things of beauty are fashioned for use, as it does to the lives of certain men and women who have followed beauty to its source and made of their own human substance an open door between what is above and what is beneath; for these are the supreme artists.

Chapter 11

ART, ENVIRONMENT AND MYSTICISM

It is sometimes said that there is no such thing as 'Islamic Culture', and if we limit the term 'culture' to its modern connotation this is true enough. There are no secular, profane arts in Islam (nor do we find them in any traditional civilization), and this follows directly from the principle of *tawḥīd*, the principle of unity, enunciated in the Confession of Faith: *Lā ilāha illa 'Llāh*.

Traditional Islamic civilization and all its varied manifestations are dominated by this principle, discoverable whichever way you turn, just as the divine Unity expressed in the Name *al-Waḥīd* (from which the term *tawḥīd* is derived) may be uncovered wherever any contingent surface is scratched or penetrated to reveal what lies beneath. God is everywhere present and He can be found everywhere, which is why the whole world is the Muslims' 'mosque' or place of prayer. Oneness is the substratum of existence.

There is an approach to religion (and to the metaphysical doctrines but for which religion would be invertebrate) through sacred art – particularly through sacred architecture and the crafts which serve men's daily needs – which, for many people, leads more directly to the core than does any verbal and discursive expression of the essential message. Through this art and through these crafts faith is made tangible on the level of the senses, and sense-impressions have an immediacy which is lacking in mental concepts and moral prescriptions. Whoever has seen the Great Mosque of Kairouan has seen Islam,[1] and whoever has handled authentic products of Muslim craftsmanship has touched Islam; those who have seen and touched the Ka'ba have penetrated even more deeply into the substratum of the Faith and made contact with a reality that is universal.

Islamic art, says Seyyed Hossein Nasr, 'is the earthly crystallization of the spirit of the Islamic revelation, as well as a reflection of the heavenly realities on earth, a reflection with the help of which the Muslim makes his journey through the terrestrial environment and beyond to the Divine Presence itself, to the Reality which is the origin and the end of his art.'[2] At

---

[1] A teacher in an English comprehensive school in a poor area of the Midlands recently took a party of her pupils to Tunisia. Emerging from the Mosque of Kairouan, the toughest boy in the class said to her: 'Miss, I never knew religion could be beautiful!'
[2] Quoted from the Introduction to *The Art of Islam* by Titus Burckhardt.

the same time it reminds us constantly of 'the open', the space in which creatures breathe freely; fresh air, sweet water and virgin nature. Revelation by its very nature reverberates long after its lightning flash has penetrated this world and 'crystallized', reverberates not only in human hearts through successive generations but also in earthly forms, century after century; or one might say that the lightning remains latent in these forms, ready to burst forth under the right conditions even when certain other aspects of the religion have been eroded by time.

This, of course, applies to all sacred art, and if the Muslim does not specifically describe his art as 'sacred', it is because an art completely divorced from religion is inconceivable to him, and he has therefore no need to make the distinction which the West makes between sacred and profane. His determination to exclude from his life everything that savours of the profane and the secular frequently shocks the Westerner, whose concern is almost exclusively with the latter and who, within the secular realm, makes a sharp distinction between, say, a novel by Kafka and a 'James Bond' novel, between Beethoven and 'pop' music, and between a Dutch master and an advertising poster. So far as the Muslim is concerned these distinctions have little meaning once a particular activity or aspect of life has been divorced from the Faith; they amount to little more than the differences between one kind of mud and another. It is hardly surprising under the circumstances if he shows what the Westerner sees as a lamentable lack of taste and discrimination when dealing with the products of Western culture and technology.

At the same time Islamic 'culture' – giving this term its widest possible sense – is concerned exclusively with what is useful, either for our life in the world or for our final ends. There is nothing particularly unusual in this. The same could be said of medieval Christian civilization, and, from the historical point of view, it is only during very brief and exceptional periods that people have had either the opportunity or the inclination to devote their best energies to the superfluous, or enjoyed 'art for art's sake'. Necessity has usually dictated an overriding concern for our livelihood, while faith has required, at the very least, an equal concern for whatever serves our final ends, our 'salvation'. Yet even this implies a division which is alien to Islam, and the successful Muslim is he who is blessed with good both in this world and in the hereafter.

The two supreme arts of Islam are calligraphy (combined with illumination) and architecture, the one having to do with the revealed Word, the other with the human environment. It could perhaps be said that calligraphy relates to the first part of the *Shahādah*, the attestation to the divine Unity, upon which the Qurān is a vast commentary, while architecture is governed by the second part of the *Shahādah*, the attestation to the prophethood of Muhammad, in that the Islamic environment is designed to enable men and women to live in accordance with his *sunnah*.

It could almost be said that the Arabic script was created for the sake of the Qurān and to serve it. The Arabs of pre-Islamic times possessed a primitive script, but they tended to distrust writing as a medium which imprisoned the free spirit of their poetry. The spoken word was all-powerful; in comparison with this living splendour, the written word seemed to them desiccated, like a pressed flower. It was essential, however, that the Qurān should be recorded in writing, lest any word of the Revelation be lost or changed as the words of other scriptures had been changed; it was no less essential that a script should be developed which matched in nobility the nobility of its content.

The massive lettering of the Kufic style satisfied this need. 'This grave procession of hieroglyphs,' says Martin Lings, 'some simple and others compounded of more than one element, ... (is) suggestive of inevitable necessity, as if its letters were intended to express the decisiveness of the Divine decree from which the Revelation sprang, or as if to proclaim that the message they bear is irrevocable and immutable. At the same time there is something solemnly cryptic and reserved about this style which seems to withhold more than it gives, as if fearful of divulging secrets ...'[1]

Words are gradually spelt out, as though the calligrapher suffered the pain of giving birth, and the individual letters are often far removed from each other, 'as if to warn us' – as Martin Lings says – 'that the contents are too tremendous to be lightly and easily unfolded'. One is sometimes reminded of a particularly long-drawn-out style of Quranic recitation,[2] in which the reciter pauses after a verse or even after a few words, like a climber pausing to catch his breath on a mountain ascent, or as though overwhelmed by the majesty of sound, while at the same time allowing his listeners to absorb this sound so that it reverberates within them.

The Qurān, however, exists to be understood. The deciphering of Kufic is a laborious task, and in due course scripts developed which are far easier to read and which flow, some like molten lava and others as delicate tracery. They are beautiful and expressive in themselves, and at the same time lend themselves to ornamentation, usually in connection with vegetable motifs which remind us of the correspondence between the *ayāt* (verses) of the Book and the *ayāt* ('signs') in nature. There is another correspondence, no less important: God is 'the Light of the heavens and the earth', and His Self-revelation is a manifestation of Light. It is through Quranic illumination, with its use of the solar colour, gold, and the celestial colour, blue, that we are reminded of this aspect of the Book.

Here the Muslim faces a problem. Illumination is an 'art-form', and forms by their very nature imprison their content in the very act of making it accessible to our senses and our intelligence. Islam refuses to confine deity in any formulation, for to do so would be to limit Reality and thereby falsify it. 'It is a function of sacred art,' says Martin Lings, 'to be a vehicle of the Divine Presence'; but the Muslim artist 'will conceive this function not as a "capturing" of the Presence but rather as a liberation of its mysterious Totality from the deceptive prison of appearance. Islam is particularly averse to any idea of circumscribing or localizing the Divine ...'[3] How can 'the open' be confined within the margins of a page? The Muslim artist solved this problem on the one hand by the use of designs

---

[1] *The Quranic Art of Calligraphy and Illumination*, Martin Lings (World of Islam Festival Trust), p. 16.

[2] There are seven different styles of Quranic recitation, governed by the strict rules of the art or science of *tajwīd*.

[3] *The Quranic Art of Calligraphy and Illumination*, Martin Lings, p. 72.

such as the palmette (the stylized 'little Tree'), which point outwards to what lies beyond the page, and on the other by repetitive patterns which are, as it were, cut short by the margin but which, in the mind's eye, may be extended indefinitely in every direction, 'for ever and ever'. In this way the human imagination is invited to supply what the graphic image can only suggest.

The decoration of mosques (which, of course, includes Quranic inscriptions) is dominated by the same principle, the art of the unconfined or of limitlessness, exemplified in the arabesque with its rhythmic interlacements. For the Muslim artist, says Titus Burckhardt, geometrical interlacement 'is an extremely direct expression of the idea of the Divine Unity underlying the inexhaustible variety of the world. True, Divine Unity as such is beyond all representation because its nature, which is total, lets nothing remain outside itself ... Nevertheless, it is through harmony that it is reflected in the world, harmony being nothing other than "unity in multiplicity" (*al-waḥdah fi'l-kathrah*) and "multiplicity in unity" (*al-kathrah fi'l-waḥdah*). Interlacement expresses the one aspect and the other.'[1]

The Christian, when he enters a church, is stepping out of the profane world into a sacred enclosure; but for the Muslim the whole earth is his 'place of prayer'. A mosque, therefore, is not a consecrated building; it is a small area of the earth that has been walled for convenience so that the faithful can pray there without distraction. The Christian church is centred upon the altar, the locus of the divine Presence and of the priest's attention, and its orientation is towards the point on the horizon at which the sun rises at Easter, so that the axes of all churches, wherever they may be, run parallel to one another. The mosque, on the other hand, is a space for prayer, and as such, does not have its centre within the enclosing walls; its orientation is towards the Ka'ba, so that all the mosques in the world form a great circle around Mecca (assuming that we envisage the earth as it is represented on a flat surface).

The church is, in a certain sense, a place of aspiration and of dynamic tension, looking towards the risen Christ in breathless hope, seeking union and implying the incompleteness of the human soul until that union is achieved. The mosque is at peace, because for the Muslim the divine Unity is here and now, present everywhere and needing only to be recognized for what it is. Islamic architecture possesses its fullness in every place, recalling the *ḥadīth*, 'All is well with the believers under all circumstances'; it reminds us that, in the divine Knowledge, all *is* well, all is complete: *consumatum est*. Aspiration is, by its nature, uneasy, seeking easement, but that which is complete in itself is already at ease, like a still pool reflecting the sun.

The first mosque of Islam was simply the courtyard into which the Prophet's apartment and the apartments of his family opened out. In the course of time mosque architecture developed in terms of ethnic genius – the mosques of West Africa are very different in appearance to those of Arabia, as they are to the mosques of south-east Asia – and individual

[1] *Art of Islam: Language and Meaning*, Titus Burckhardt (World of Islam Festival Trust), p. 63.

inspiration, but the basic principles are the same, the 'atmosphere' is the same and the purpose is the same. The dome replaced the open sky, but the dome is an image of the sky above; minarets jutted upwards, an attestation to the divine Unity, like the first Arabic letter of the name *Allāh*, or like the pointing index finger of the Muslim when he bears witness to this Unity in the course of prayer. At the same time the 'place of prostration' (which is the literal meaning of the word 'mosque') was embellished because 'Allah is beautiful and He loves beauty', and it was suffused with light because 'Allah is the Light of the heavens and the earth'.

Titus Burckhardt speaks of the Muslim architect transforming stone into a vibration of light, and anyone who has seen the Court of Lions in the Alhambra Palace in Granada will know exactly what he means and just how miraculous this transformation is. The divine Light brings things out of nothingness into being; to be visible is to be. For Islam, light is the most adequate – or least inadequate – symbol of the Divinity, but light as such is dazzling and human weakness requires that it should be broken down into the colours of the spectrum which, as it were, both analyse and express its nature. In the decorative tiling of mosques, as in Quranic illumination, the language of colour is employed to reveal the secrets hidden within the splendour of light, in the same way that the 'beautiful Names' are employed in the Qurān to reveal something of the nature of God, who is in Himself too dazzling to be conceived.

Nowhere in the mosque, or in other manifestations of normal Sunni Muslim art, do we find any representation of human figures, which might draw us into earthly drama; nor do we find representations of animals, for 'there is no animal on earth, nor a flying creature borne on two wings, but they are communities like yourselves' (Q.6.38); or, as an alternative and more literal translation, we might say 'made in your image', opening up a line of thought which cannot be pursued here. The immediate reason for the 'aniconism' of Islam is the prohibition of idolatry in any form and a precaution against the possibility of idolatry, but it is also a precautionary measure against human pretension; we cannot create life – 'You cannot create even a fly' (Q.22.73) – and to make an image of a living creature suggests to the Muslim that the artist is attempting this blasphemous task. He must be stopped before he begins to see himself as a little god.

Beyond this there is the question of respect for the 'secret' contained in every living creature, a 'secret' which cannot be represented in earthly forms. The higher the creature the further we are from any possibility of representing his essence, his meaning. From this point of view, a representation of the Prophet could only be an empty shell and, as such, not merely displeasing but actually dangerous; for who knows what influences may creep into an empty shell or what phantasmagoria may be projected into the vacuum presented by an 'idol'? As for the ordinary man, his potentiality as the Viceregent of God is something ungraspable and certainly beyond any possibility of representation, unless by means of a symbolism which is necessarily abstract in form. The human person cannot be reduced to his or her terrestrial modalities.

Prohibitions, however, can never be absolute, since they relate to a world, a state of existence, which is not in itself absolute, and every rule requires exceptions. Both people and animals are lovingly delineated in Persian miniatures; but they are not the people of this earth nor the animals of this earth. They exist in a different dimension. They are shadows cast on to a flat surface from elsewhere and then coloured in the colours of our locality. As Burckhardt says, the miniature does not seek 'to portray the outward world as it commonly presents itself to the senses, with all its disharmonies and accidentalities; what it is indirectly describing is the "immutable essences" (*al-a'yān ath-thābitah*) of things'; it is like a 'clear and translucent dream, as if illumined from within'.[1] The absence of perspective adds to the quality of objectivity which goes with this 'translucence', since perspective always implies the presence – even the intervention – of an individual subject observing the scene from his particular viewpoint. These pictures exist in their own world and their world is free from the distortions which affect our earthly vision.

Moreover, the human figures within the landscape do not dominate it. Arnold Hottinger draws a parallel between this treatment of the human figure and other aspects of Islamic art, including the manner in which human characters are treated in Arabic and Persian literature: 'This character of *pure opening*, of the abstract and the crystalline, which is possessed by the great works of Islamic architecture goes along with the coordination of different objects in the miniatures, as in a garden, with the spontaneous sequences of individual illuminations in the poems and with Firdausi's nimble and luminous figures refusing to be confined within one system. We find it again in the infinite, free flow of the tales in the *Thousand-and-one Nights*, a mixture of humans, animals, demons, commonness and beauty ...'[2] This is a long way from any humanistic theory or practice of art in terms of which one little centre of misery, one suffering creature in a picture or a story, can cancel out a whole landscape of joy and peace; and Hottinger draws attention to the quality of 'detachment' which characterizes this art. The world is what it is, and in the miniature the artist refuses to let his human figures say more about what he is trying to convey than the rest of the picture, which is like a mirror reflecting the inner harmony that is – or should be – the normal state of being.

Hottinger quotes a curious but revealing passage written by the nineteenth-century 'romantic' Hofmannsthal on the subject of the *Thousand-and-One Nights* (or *Arabian Nights Entertainments*, as this collection of stories is sometimes called): 'Here we have infinite adventures, dreams, wise speeches, pranks, indecencies, mysteries; here we have the boldest spirituality and the most complete sensuality woven into one. There is no sense of ours which is not moved, from the highest to the lowest ... We see that this whole is interwoven with poetic spirituality in which we progress with lively ecstasy from first perception to complete understanding. All these sensual things are covered by a presentiment, a presence of God which is indescribable. Over this maze of what is human, animal and demonic, there is always stretched the shining canopy of the sky or the sacred starry heavens. And like a gentle, pure and strong wind, eternal, simple, holy sentiments blow through the whole ...' What we have here, as

[1]*Art of Islam*, Titus Burckhardt, p. 31.
[2]*The Arabs*, Arnold Hottinger, p. 77.

elsewhere in the Islamic cosmos, is the presence of 'the open'; desert and steppe, unbounded horizons.

Where, then, are we to find a specifically 'human' art? No art is closer to us both physically and psychologically than that of dress, and if the human figure is excluded – or enters only as an element in the design – elsewhere, it is none the less clothed in splendour at the centre of the Islamic environment. 'No art', says Titus Burckhardt, 'has a more telling effect upon a man's soul than that of clothing, for a man instinctively identifies himself with the clothes he wears.' He also dresses in accordance with his idea of himself and of his role in the scheme of things. Burckhardt identifies modern occidental dress as representing 'a turning away from a life entirely dominated by contemplative values, with its bearings fixed on the hereafter'; the lesson implicit in the traditional dress of Islam, however much it has varied from one region to another, is that the human body is among the 'signs of Allah', and to veil it, as Burckhardt says, 'is not to deny it, but to withdraw it, like gold, into the domain of things concealed from the eyes of the crowd'.[1]

It is common enough in the West to dress chimpanzees in human clothing, either for the amusement of children visiting a zoo or to advertise products on television, and contemporary Western tailoring looks very well on monkeys; it looks less well on human beings and absurdly inappropriate on Muslims at prayer; but it is the badge of 'civilization' and worn as such. A soldier knows that he is truly in the army when he puts on his uniform and a monk is assured of his vocation when he dons the robes of his order; both Kamal Ataturk and Mao Tzetung, when they wished to make a complete break with the past and create a new kind of Turk and a new kind of Chinese, started by changing their people's mode of dress, and it is interesting to note how quick Catholic priests are to adopt secular clothing when they lose confidence in their priestly function.

Those who think of themselves as clever monkeys will dress as clever monkeys, while those who believe themselves to be the 'Viceregents of Allah on earth' will also dress accordingly. Sometimes we are more concerned with peripheral threats than with the threat closest to us; many Muslims are deeply concerned about the threat to their way of life represented by such Western customs as dancing and 'dating', but only a few are aware that not merely their way of life, but their very identity as Muslims might be undermined by a mode of dress totally alien to the Islamic concept of man's role in creation.[2]

The argument one hears only too frequently is that 'outward things' do not matter; all that matters is 'what you have in your heart'. This argument is, to say the least, naive. What we have in our hearts is constantly influenced – and eventually changed – by our immediate environment, and the environment closest to us is the robe, suit or dress we wear; after that comes the home, and after the home, the city.

Just as the way in which people dress indicates their idea of themselves, so the way in which they build indicates their idea of society and of the

[1]*Art of Islam*, Titus Burckhardt, pp. 99–100.
[2]According to a *ḥadīth*, classified under the heading 'Clothing': 'He who copies any people is one of them.'

purpose of life. Occidental architecture in this century is an open book in which the ideologies of our time may be studied. Traditional Islamic architecture, despite a tremendous variety of styles, bears the unmistakable stamp of Islam; the traditional home and the traditional city were precisely matched to the lives of people who, in all their activities, followed the *sunnah* of the Prophet, and for this very reason they facilitated the following of the *sunnah*, just as Arab dress facilitates the performance of the ablution and the movements of the ritual prayer.

The bulldozers have been at work, however, in the name of 'modernization', and the new towns built on the ravaged land, with their third-rate imitation of all that is worst in occidental architecture and their shoddy workmanship, offer suitable accommodation only for *shayātīn*, 'satans'. The Westerner who observes this and deplores it invites the accusation that he wants to keep the Muslim world 'backward' and 'picturesque' the better to dominate it, though his accusers are likely to be the very people who condemn the West for its 'decadence', while rushing to adopt the complete infrastructure of this same decadence (it is tempting to add that at least the West knows how to be decadent stylishly).

But what is at issue here is not a matter of taste or of preferring the decorative to the utilitarian; it is a matter of spiritual laws as inexorable as any law of nature and, at the same time, a matter of human psychology. Speaking of the distrust of anything that might be described as 'romantic' or 'picturesque' which is so common in our time, Frithjof Schuon remarks that 'the "romantic" worlds are precisely those in which God is still probable; when people want to get rid of Heaven it is logical to start by creating an atmosphere in which spiritual things appear out of place; in order to declare successfully that God is unreal they have to construct around man a false reality, a reality that is inevitably inhuman because only the inhuman can exclude God. What is involved is a falsification of the imagination and so its destruction ...'[1] The Muslims today are constructing around themselves an environment in which faith can only seem out of place, prayer superfluous and the *sharī'ah* an inconvenience.

The human soul and body are capable of adapting themselves to inhospitable conditions, provided the worsening of the environment takes place gradually. Europeans and Americans have a certain immunity to the malign influences of the modern environment, and familiarity with it enables them to make value-judgements regarding the products of technology. People elsewhere have no such immunity and their past experience of life – in hand-made rather than machine-made environments – gave them no opportunity to develop standards of taste applicable to these products. The outcome of this situation is exactly what one would expect; people who, only a generation ago, lived amongst things that were beautiful and entirely fitting to the Islamic way of life now live amidst trash which they cannot even recognize for what it is. In most cases it is only the European who, when he contrasts, say, a contemporary Egyptian home with a traditional Arab house (furnished with the products of Islamic craftsmen), sees what they have lost and fears for their sanity. The

---

[1] *Understanding Islam*, Frithjof Schuon (London: Allen & Unwin, 1963), p. 37.

influence upon them of an environment totally alien to Islam is all the more dangerous for being unperceived.

It is sometimes maintained that the difference between a tool and a machine is only one of degree, but nobody could seriously deny that the difference between a traditional craftsman and a worker who presses buttons in an automated factory is fundamental.

The essentially sacred character of the crafts was almost universally recognized in the past by the most diverse peoples in every part of the world. The crafts were taught to mankind, according to some, by the 'gods' or, according to others, by 'spirits', and the craftsman prepared himself ritually for work that was, in its way, priestly. For Muslims, the crafts were divinely revealed through successive messengers of God, and the act of making, from raw materials, an object both useful and comely was, until recently, recognized as a form of prayer. The products of a sacred activity carry with them a blessing, a *barakah*, which encourages the user to 'remember' God and brings him closer to God. No traditional civilization could have accepted the notion that there are things which serve only our physical well-being; every activity and every object must relate to the whole man, who is spirit, soul and body, and Islam – the religion of unity – is the religion of 'wholeness'.

In his book on the Moroccan city of Fez, *Fas: Stadt des Islam*,[1] Titus Burckhardt describes a meeting with an old craftsman who still followed the traditional ways. 'I knew a comb-maker who worked in the street of his guild. He was called 'Abd al-Azīz ... He obtained the horn for his combs from ox skulls, which he bought from butchers. He dried the horned skulls at a rented place, removed the horns, opened them lengthwise and straightened them over a fire, a procedure that had to be done with the greatest care lest they should break. From this raw material he cut combs and turned boxes for antimony (used as an eye decoration) on a simple lathe ... As he worked he chanted Quranic *surahs* in a humming tone.

'I learned that, as a result of an eye disease which is common in Africa, he was already half-blind and that, in view of long practice, he was able to "feel" his work rather than see it. One day he complained to me that the importation of plastic combs was diminishing his business. "It is only a pity that today, solely on account of price, poor quality combs from a factory are preferred to much more durable horn combs," he said, "it is also senseless that people should stand by a machine and mindlessly repeat the same movement, while an old craft like mine falls into oblivion.

'"My work may seem crude to you, but it harbours a subtle meaning which cannot be conveyed in words. I myself acquired it only after many long years and, even if I wanted to, I could not automatically pass it on to my son if he himself did not wish to acquire it – and I think he would rather take up another occupation. This craft can be traced back from apprentice to master until one reaches our Lord Seth, the son of Adam. It was he who first taught it to men, and what a Prophet brings – and Seth was a Prophet –

---

[1]This book, which succeeds in conveying the 'feel' of traditional Islam – its spirit and its substance – more effectively and more powerfully than the vast majority of books which have attempted this difficult task, has now been translated into English by William Stoddart.

must clearly have a special purpose, both outwardly and inwardly. I gradually came to understand that there is nothing fortuitous about this craft, that each movement and each procedure is the bearer of an element of wisdom. Not everyone can understand this. But even if one does not know this, it is still stupid and reprehensible to rob men of the inheritance of Prophets and to put them in front of a machine where, day in and day out, they must perform a meaningless task".'

The old comb-maker has said all that needs to be said, and those who do not understand him will never understand anything about the human situation or about the demand God makes upon us to sanctify our activities, something that we cannot do unless these activities are inherently capable of sanctification. To regret the passing of this old man and of others like him has nothing to do with sentimentality. It has to do with fear, the fear that once we have become quite useless – totally unsanctified and unsanctifiable – we shall be fit only for the bonfire which awaits the debris of a ruined world.

The discipline of the craftsman whose tools are so simple that he must rely upon wisdom, competence and manual skill to produce objects which are, in their way, perfect is very similar to the discipline of the mystic, whose raw material is not clay, wood or bone, but his own soul. Islamic mysticism, called *taṣawwuf* in Arabic and commonly referred to as Sufism, is a vast and complex subject, and one which contains many traps for the unwary, but it cannot be ignored in any general study of the religion in the way that Christian mysticism might be ignored by a writer on Christianity. We cannot, as Seyyed Hossein Nasr remarks, 'do justice to the wholeness of the Islamic tradition and its immensely rich spiritual possibilities by putting aside its inner dimension. In speaking about Sufism, therefore, in reality we shall be speaking about the Islamic tradition in its most inward and universal aspect.'[1]

Among the orientalists there have been some who readily acknowledge the tremendous deepening and intensification of religious experience brought about by Sufism. 'What was to remain in other civilizations an activity confined to outsiders, ascetics, monks, nuns and divines,' says Arnold Hottinger, 'struck deep roots into the masses of ordinary Muslims and indeed became the most important social link, holding Muslim society together for centuries.'[2] Others, it has been suggested, have deliberately minimized the importance of the mystical dimension in order to strengthen the Christian position, on the assumption that an Islam cut off from this dimension cannot compete with Christianity or claim adequately to answer the spiritual needs of mankind. Be this as it may, there are certainly a number of books purporting to give a comprehensive view of Islam which present a misleadingly superficial picture of the religion and leave the Western reader wondering how anyone who asks of his faith something more than a rule of conduct for daily life could be a Muslim, let alone become a Muslim from deliberate choice.

The fact is that many Westerners, particularly those who have lived for a

[1] *Islam and the Plight of Modern Man*, Seyyed Hossein Nasr (Longman Ltd, 1975), p. 49.
[2] Arnold Hottinger, *The Arabs*, p. 96.

time in Muslim countries, find it almost inconceivable that there could be any common ground between exoteric, legalistic Islam and the broad sweep of Sufism, with its daring leaps into the spiritual heights and its daring plunges into the depths of the ocean of Being, its emphasis upon the presence of God within the heart of man and its claim to draw knowledge of things divine from the very source of Knowledge itself. They may well have been confirmed in their opinion by Muslims who have told them that Sufism is 'unorthodox', or even that it is an 'innovation', and their own experience in the Christian world may have led them to regard mysticism as a somewhat peripheral aspect of religion. They feel justified in their opinion that Islam is little more than a 'Boy Scout religion', with rather unpleasant undertones of violence and bigotry.

Before considering the objections which certain Muslims raise against the mystical dimension of their religion, it is important to stress that Sufism takes different forms in accordance with the very different temperaments of those who are drawn to it. The *ṭuruq* (plural of *ṭarīqah*, which means 'path' or, in this case, 'spiritual path') do not differ in essentials – all have grown from the same root – but they do differ markedly in their methods and disciplines, as do Christian monastic orders. No neat classification is possible, but there is an obvious distinction between those Sufis who are 'drunken' and those who are 'sober': the former, drunk on the 'wine' of gnosis or on the 'wine' of divine Love – or on both together – do not behave as other men do, but are seized by ecstasy and care nothing for the conventions of ordinary life; the latter contain their ecstasy within themselves, keeping it under strict control, avoiding scandal even when they reel inwardly under the divine touch, and maintaining discretion as to their spiritual state. The ideal, as it was expressed by a great Sufi Master of the present century, Ahmad al-ʿAlawī, is to be 'inwardly drunken' and 'outwardly sober'.[1]

A further distinction might be made between those *ṭuruq* which are 'devotional' and those which are 'intellectual' or 'gnostic', following a way of Knowledge (*maʾrifah*, that is to say 'divine Knowledge') rather than a way of Love, although the two often merge into each other and Love is a kind of Knowledge, albeit indirect, just as Knowledge is conjoined with Love in mystical experience; what we love is known to us,[2] and what is known to us cannot but be loved. It is a question therefore of emphasis rather than of any fundamental difference.

Alternatively, we may distinguish between, on the one hand, a Sufi way based upon a deepened sense of the meaning of the common rites of the religion (ritual prayer, the Fast and so on) and upon meticulous observance of the *Sharīʿah*; and, on the other, a way which gives priority to the practice of *dhikr* (the 'remembrance of God') in its technical sense. For obvious reasons, those Muslims who regard Sufism with suspicion will always prefer the 'sober' Sufi to the 'drunken', the 'devotional' to the 'gnostic', and the meticulous adherent of the *Sharīʿah* to the Sufi whose adherence to outward observances is confined to what may be necessary to avoid scandal.

[1] See *A Sufi Saint of the Twentieth Century*, Martin Lings (Allen & Unwin Ltd., 1961).
[2] Cp. the Biblical term for sexual intercourse: 'He knew her'.

Mysticism, particularly in its metaphysical dimension, breaks through the boundaries which protect the simple faith of the ordinary believer and carries us into an unconfined region in which there are very real dangers of going astray, especially if the human ego has not first been brought to order. At the same time it tends to 'relativize' the formal religion which is its springboard but which it has, in a certain sense, outdistanced. Dogmas and prescriptions which the ordinary believer sees as absolute are interpreted allegorically, or used as points of reference which may eventually be transcended. Particularly shocking to the exoteric 'Establishment' is the fact that the mystic often claims – if only by implication – an authority derived directly from God and a knowledge given from above rather than learned in the schools.

The mystic has his rights – which are the rights of Truth itself – but so has the ordinary believer, whose faith in a few simple principles (which are none the less adequate for his salvation) may be undermined by teachings which seem to him to call these principles into question. This is why many spiritual Masters have observed great discretion in their outward teaching, reserving the essence of their doctrine for those few who are qualified to receive it; and this is also why the exoteric authorities have regarded mysticism with a certain suspicion. At the very least they have seen a need to control it lest it threaten the whole structure of authoritarian faith.

So far as the Catholic Church was concerned (in the Christian context), this presented no real problem, since the majority of Christian mystics, with a few notable exceptions, have been monks or nuns living under a strict rule and subject to the authority of their Superiors. The position in Islam is very different. It is true that every Sufi is under the authority of his Sheikh (a term which, in this particular context, may be translated as 'spiritual Master' or 'Director'), but there is no higher authority in Islam which could appoint or depose the Sheikhs, or prevent them from going their own way. This has led, on occasion, to excesses and heterodox practices which have done more than anything else to give Sufism a bad name in certain circles.

Control has, however, been exercised, and it has been exercised partly by public opinion – the 'consensus' of the *Ummah* – and partly by means of a kind of dynamic tension, maintained through the centuries between the exoteric religious authorities on the one hand and the Sufi Sheikhs on the other. An undercurrent of opposition to Sufism within sections of the Islamic community has served as a necessary curb on the mystics, without this undercurrent having ever been strong enough to prevent those who have had a genuine vocation for a Sufi path from following their destiny. In this way a healthy balance has been maintained between the esoteric and the exoteric dimensions of the religion.

It is important none the less to emphasize that the division or boundary line between the two has never been as clear-cut as this might suggest. Many of the *'ulamā'* (religious scholars) and *fuqahā'* (jurists) who make up the official Establishment in Islam have themselves been – and are today – members of Sufi brotherhoods, while Sufis of great spiritual eminence have held important positions in the Establishment, a recent example being the late Sheikh Abdul-Halīm Mahmūd, Rector of al-Azhar (the most ancient and the most important university in the Sunni Muslim world) until his death in 1978, and one of the most widely respected figures in contemporary Islam.

Three particular watersheds in the history of the complex relationship between the inward and the outward dimensions of the religion deserve mention here. The first concerns the life and teachings of Ibn Mansūr al-Hallāj (d. AD 922), one of the three or four outstanding Sufis whose names are familiar to Westerners interested in mysticism.[1]

Al-Hallāj was executed in Baghdad for expressing himself too freely – in the manner of the 'drunken' mystics – although there may also have been political factors involved in his condemnation. His statement *Anā'l Haqq*, unveiled as a naked assertion – without qualification and without explanation – was clear heresy so far as the religious authorities were concerned. This statement, 'I am the Truth', means in effect 'I am God'. Whatever the 'I' in question might be for al-Hallāj – and so far as he was concerned it was God Himself, not the mortal man, who spoke these words through him[2] – the 'I' is, for most of humanity, including the majority of believers, the human ego, and for the ego to say 'I am God' is the ultimate sin or the root of all sin. His contemporary, Junayd, a pillar of 'sober' mysticism, never contested his spiritual stature but said none the less, when al-Hallāj wished to join his circle, 'I do not take madmen as companions; companionship demands sanity. Sobriety is the mark of a sound spiritual state; drunkenness is the mark of too much longing.'

He could not be other than he was or do otherwise than he did, but he himself was fully aware of the ambiguity of his statements and of the danger that they would lead people astray. In spite of this, he could not restrain himself: 'The man who would reveal the secret of Allah to His creatures,' he said, 'feels a suffering beyond human power to endure'; but to a group of learned men who had come to question him he said: 'What questions could you ask of me? For I see only too well how right you are and how wrong I am!' When he was condemned to die, he said, 'My death will preserve the sanctions of the Law,' well knowing that for the ordinary believer to lose all fear of God – as he had done – is to embark upon the road to disaster.

When he was finally brought to the gallows, after long delay (for there were many who tried to save him), he prayed: 'These Thy servants who are gathered to slay me out of zeal for Thy religion – forgive them, Lord, have mercy upon them. Surely, hadst Thou shown them what Thou hast shown me, they would never have done what they have done; and hadst Thou kept from me what Thou has kept from them, I should not have suffered this tribulation. Whatsoever Thou doest, I praise Thee.' He died praising,

---

[1]See *La Passion d'al-Husayn al-Hallāj, Martyr mystique de l'Islam*, Louis Massignon (Paris, 1922), and other works by the same author.

[2]In this context Jalāluddīn Rūmī remarked to his disciples: 'Take the famous utterance, "I am God". Some men reckon it as a great pretension; but "I am God" is in fact a great humility. The man who says "I am the servant of God" asserts that two exist, one himself and the other God. But he who says "I am God" has naughted himself and cast himself to the winds. He says, "I am God": that is, "I am not, He is all, nothing has existence but God, I am pure non-entity, I am nothing". In this the humility is greater.' (*Discourses of Rumi*, translated by A. J. Arberry, John Murray, p. 55).

having written earlier in a poem: 'I am my Love, my Love is I; two spirits this body occupy. If you see me, He it is whom you see; when you see Him you will see me.' In the union of lover and Beloved all questions are answered and all ambiguities resolved.

So far as ambiguities are concered, they were – at least to a great extent – resolved in the eleventh century AD by Abu Hamīd al-Ghazzālī, regarded by many as the most significant and influential figure in medieval Islam. Appointed at an early age as a professor of religious Law in the great Nizāmiyya College in Baghdad, he came gradually to question the bases of his own faith, resigned his post and sought among different schools of thought for a solution to his doubts. He found it in Sufi teaching and became, after many years of travel and solitary meditation, an incomparably effective bridge-builder between the two contrasting dimensions of Islam. No one could rival him either in his knowledge or his practice of the *Sharī'ah*, nor – in his own time – had he any equal as an exponent of Sufi doctrine. It could be said that he 'legitimized' Sufism, and his greatest work, the *Ihyā 'ulūm ad-dīn* (the 'Revivification of the Religious Sciences'), was a synthesis which covered every aspect of the believer's life, from the correct manner of eating and drinking and the conduct of marital relations to the disciplines and rewards of the mystical path.

No less important than al-Hallāj and al-Ghazzālī in the development of Sufi doctrine was the Andalusian mystic, Muhyīddīn ibn 'Arabī (d. AD 1240), called by those who approve of him *ash-Sheikh al-akbar* ('the supreme spiritual Master'), and regarded by those who disapprove of him as a heretic. He remains a centre of controversy to this day; his writings are banned in Saudi Arabia, and in 1980 the Egyptian Parliament stopped publication of his collected works in Cairo (a decision that was rescinded soon afterwards). And yet his influence has been inescapable over the past seven centuries, and a great number of Muslims have found in his complex and sometimes obscure doctrines an invaluable key to the inner mysteries of their faith.

The legitimate opponents of Sufism, that is to say, those among the *'ulamā'* who consider that mysticism weakens the hold of the Law on ordinary believers, or that it ventures into forbidden regions of thought and experience, have been joined more recently by two other groups with far less claim to legitimacy. The first of these might be described – although without any malicious intent – as the 'snobs'. It is a curious feature of Sufism that it has caught in its net the two extremes of the social spectrum, the intellectual élite and the masses. The middle classes have been rather less involved, and the prosperous lawyer or businessmen who gives his servants an evening off to attend the *hadrah* of their order will refer to Sufism with slightly contempuous indulgence as 'popular superstition'. His attitude has much in common with that of the eighteenth-century Church of England parson to 'religious enthusiasm'.

The second group includes modernists, revolutionaries and all those whose interest in their religion is limited to its usefulness as a political weapon. They equate Sufism with 'quietism' and 'fatalism' and blame it for all the ills suffered by Islam since European power became dominant in the world. Sufism, they say, castrated a dynamic religion which would otherwise have conquered the world. They are lamentably ignorant about their own history, or else wilfully obtuse.

However praiseworthy the record of many of the *'ulamā'* – particularly the outstanding religious scholars of the early period – in standing up against tyranny, there exists a natural affinity between the religious authorities and the authority of the state. It was the Sufis who were most often prepared to speak their minds and risk their necks. Subsequently, the Muslim world was too bewildered by the onslaught of the West – and too divided – to put up any very effective resistance to it, and the Amīr Abdu'l-Qādir, who fought the French in Algeria in the 1830s, was possibly the only Muslim since the Middle Ages who might be compared in courage, magnanimity and greatness of heart to Salāhu'd-Dīn ('Saladin', as he is called in the West). Abdu'l-Qādir was a Sufi and, in his enforced exile in Damascus, he devoted the rest of his life to studying and commenting upon the works of Ibn 'Arabī.

Shamyl, who held the armies of the Tsar at bay from 1834 to 1859, fighting one of the most extraordinary campaigns in military history, was a Sheikh of the Naqshbandi order. 'The Lion of Daghestan', as the British press of that time called him, is remembered today by the Muslims of the Caucasus, whose quiet but implacable resistance to the Soviet regime is inspired and led by Sheikhs of the same order. Political activists in the Middle East must show what, if anything, they are capable of in the way of fidelity, courage and effectiveness before they criticize the Sufis.

There is, in any case, a certain irrelevance in such criticism, whatever its motives or its religious basis, for Sufism is in the bloodstream of the *Ummah* and lends its flavour, not only to every aspect of Muslim art, but also to the everyday life of the believer. Even those who think themselves totally opposed to it and entirely free from its influence cannot avoid speaking in terms derived from Sufism when they speak of their Faith, and it is impossible to imagine a global religion of Islam deprived of this dimension. The Turks were converted by Sufi preachers, traders and travellers, as were the people of the Indonesian archipelago and many of the peoples of the Indian subcontinent. History is inescapable, and the history of Islam is bound up with that of the Sufi orders, just as the outward religion is penetrated by the inward and vivified by it.

The Sufi Sheikhs have shown a certain impatience when asked to give a precise and definitive definition of *taṣawwuf*. Talking with Dr Carret, the Sheikh al-'Alawī mentioned that 'above the religion there is the doctrine'. Dr Carret asked what this doctrine was, and he answered, 'The means of attaining to God Himself'. Dr Carret then inquired what these means were, and the Sheikh answered with a smile: 'Why should I tell you, since you are not disposed to make use of them? If you came to me as my disciple I could give you an answer. But what would be the good of satisfying an idle curiosity?'[1] Those who wish to see the landscape must make their way to the look-out point; if they are not prepared to do this, it may be assumed that their interest is merely that of a dilettante or, as the Oxford Dictionary

[1] *A Sufi Saint of the Twentieth Century*, Martin Lings (Allen & Unwin Ltd., 1961), pp. 26–27.

rather aptly puts it, a 'smatterer, one who toys with the subject'. One does not toy with the 'means of attaining to God'.

Definitions do, however, exist. Sufism, it has been said, is 'to love nothing that your Beloved does not love'. According to Junayd, it is simply that 'Allah makes thee die to thyself and be resurrected in Him', and one of his disciples explained that the Sufis are those who have 'fled from all that is other-than-He, possessing nothing and possessed by nothing'; according to Bayazid of Bistham, they are 'generous like the ocean, good like the sun, humble like the earth'. Sufism, we are told, is 'sincerity', and this equates it with *ihsān*. The Prophet spoke of three degrees in religion: *islām*, submission; *īmān*, faith; and *ihsān*, which is the perfection of submission and faith and is usually translated as 'excellence'. Sufism, according to this definition, is the means of bringing both submission to God and faith in God to their logical conclusion, or simply of drawing from the Confession of Faith – *lā ilāha illa 'Llāh* – its ultimate significance. It is a matter of going to the end of the road. 'Is it not face to face with the Truth that our riders dismount?' asked the Sheikh al-'Alawī in one of his poems.

The ordinary believer is said to be stationary, though the vehicle in which he sits – the religion as such – carries him forward; the Sufi is described as a 'traveller' or one who 'races forward': 'Race [one another] towards forgiveness from your Lord and a Garden whereof the breadth is as the breadth of the heavens and the earth, which is established for those who believe in Allah and His messengers. Such is the bounty of Allah, which He bestoweth upon whom He will, and the bounty of Allah is inexhaustible' (Q.57.21).

Martin Lings speaks of the particular 'affinity' which the Sufis have with the Qurān as that which distinguishes them from other Muslims, 'namely that the choice they have deliberately and irrevocably made of the Eternal in preference to the ephemeral is not merely theoretic or mental but so totally sincere that it has shaken them to the depth of their being and set them in motion upon the path. The Qur'ān itself is a crystallization of this choice, for it insists without respite on the immense disparity between this lower world and the transcendent world of the Spirit.' Who else, he asks, except for their counterparts in other religions, 'can possibly compare with Sufis for putting first things first and second things second?'[1]

Sufism, according to some authorities, may be defined quite simply as *dhawq* ('taste'), and this is of particular interest if one remembers that the English word 'sapience' – a little-used synonym for 'wisdom' – comes from a Latin root meaning 'to taste'; to be wise, therefore, is not so much to keep the truth in mind as to experience it existentially, in other words to taste it.

The immediacy of the knowledge of celestial realities – or of Reality as such – which the mystic enjoys, or hopes to enjoy, corresponds more closely to the immediacy of sense-perception than it does to the indirect knowledge which the mind has of ideas or phenomena and is equally exempt from doubt and uncertainty. In other words, that aspect of Sufism which has to do with knowledge – it has other aspects as well – might be defined as 'making concrete' what, for most people, is 'abstract', until

---

[1] *What is Sufism?*, Martin Lings (Allen & Unwin Ltd., 1975), p. 30.

spiritual perceptions possess the same quality of self-evidence which we normally associate with the seen, heard, felt and tasted world of physical objects surrounding us.

No one would deny that there exist many opportunities for self-deception in this field. Every human activity comprises certain risks, and the higher the activity the greater the risks, while those who crawl on their bellies need not fear falling. But this is precisely why no man or woman may legitimately embark on the Sufi path without first being initiated into an authentic *ṭarīqah* (which, so to speak, integrates them into the company of 'travellers') and then placing themselves under the watchful guidance of a spiritual Director who has already traversed the path upon which they now set foot.

It is not then their business to seek or expect visions, experiences, or perceptions beyond the common limits of human existence, but simply to devote themselves to the practices of their order in obedience and humility. What is to come to them will come, God willing, in its own way and in its own good time, and no man can set limits to it. 'It is obviously absurd,' says Frithjof Schuon, 'to want to impose limits upon knowledge; the retina of the eye catches the rays of infinitely distant stars, it does so without passion or pretension, and no one has the right or the power to hinder it.'[1]

The idea of *dhawq* – the idea that one can actually know the ultimate truths in personal experience – has considerable appeal for questioning modern minds, and there is no doubt that many people in the contemporary world can only approach religion through mysticism. They are not prepared, as their forefathers were, to accept these truths on 'hearsay' or on the authority of those better and wiser than themselves; they must 'taste' them. Perhaps this is no more than a polite way of saying that they are 'men of little faith', and it could also be said that those who refuse to believe without actually seeing the object of their belief do not really deserve to see. But this is the nature of our time, and one can only operate in terms of the given situation; and it is not only in the West that this situation exists. An increasing number of born Muslims – 'passport Muslims' – whose faith has been undermined by a modern education are finding their way back to Islam through its Sufi dimension.

This is not, however, an easy solution to anybody's difficulties. Those who seek tangible proof of religious truth seek it, at least in the first instance, for their own satisfaction; they seek knowledge as a personal acquisition and spiritual development as a personal achievement. They are likely to be disappointed. Sufism, in common with every authentic mysticism, says with implacable firmness, 'Not I!': 'Not I, Lord, but Thou and Thou alone!' The first phase of the path is not towards self-aggrandisement but towards self-extinction, called in Islam *fanā*, in accordance with the Quranic verse: 'Everyone therein [in the created worlds] is extinguished, and there remaineth the Face of thy Lord, the possessor of Majesty and Bounty' (Q.55.26–27). Death precedes resurrection; the plant's leaves wither, it dies and its seed is buried in the earth, until there comes about a new growth in the light of the sun. The Sufi is obliged to let

---

[1]*Logic and Transcendence*, Frithjof Schuon (New York: Harper & Row, 1975), p. 216.

go of everything and lose himself before he can hope to find himself in God and so achieve the condition known as *baqā'*, 'subsistence' or, in Martin Lings' phrase, 'eternality'. That which subsists and endures is not the person we were – the person we valued above all else on earth – before we came this way.

Westerners when they look for the first time into the writings of the great exponents of Sufism expect to find marvellous accounts of spiritual experiences and ecstasies. They will find this but, often to their surprise, they will find a great deal more about the virtues, the 'slaying of the *nafs* (the selfhood)', obedience to the divine Commands and the training of character.[1] These books deal in considerable detail with the duties of the human condition: fear of the Lord, trust in God, detachment and, above all, spiritual povery (*faqr*); indeed, the follower of this path is usually called a *faqīr*, a 'poor man', rather than a 'Sufi'. What comes to us – or may come to us – is a gift from God which is adjusted to our receptivity, but is none the less out of all proportion to our deserts. Our principal task is to make ourselves ready. What is offered is clear and simple but, faced even with the possibility of this gift, we find ourselves to be a mass of contradictions, not merely unfit to receive it but incapable of taking it in.

The profane man's selfhood is a debris of memories and dreams, false hopes and lingering guilts, or hard little pebbles of self-concern, desire and fear. This is the 'hardened heart' of which the Qurān speaks so often. A vessel must be emptied before it can be refilled, and only someone who has expelled this debris from the centre of his being can hope that something of the divine plenitude may flow into him. There is not room in the human heart for two, as the mystics have said on a number of occasions.

Other images may help to illustrate this point. In our unregenerate state we are, as it were, enclosed behind a wall of ice which shuts us off from 'the open'. Ice has a certain transparency, which is why anyone who uses his eyes may sometimes glimpse what lies beyond. The mystic sets himself to melt this wall of ice or, very occasionally (as in the practices of Zen Buddhism), to shatter it. Or again, we can speak of the 'mirror of the heart', a mirror designed to reflect celestial realities, but in most cases too grimy or – since ancient mirrors were made of metal – too rusty to do so. 'How can the heart be illuminated while the forms of creatures are reflected in its mirror? . . . Or how can it desire to enter the Presence of God until it has wiped from itself the stain of forgetfulness?'[2]

The Prophet said: 'There is a polish for everything to remove rust, and the polish of the heart is the remembrance of Allah!' The very basis of Sufi practice is invocation, 'remembrance', or 'mention' (*dhikr*) of God's holy Name, or of a formula dominated by the Name, such as *Allāhu akbar*! And we are assured that God is present in His Name, or makes Himself present, when our lips move in pronouncing it (or when we mention it silently in

---

[1]Titus Burckhardt reported that Mulay 'Ālī (grandson of the founder of the Darqāwī order), whom he came to know well while living in Fez in the early 1930s, always declined to speak of the 'inward states' of the Sufis, saying: 'These are fruits that grow of themselves on the tree of divine service; let us rather speak of how to care for the tree and how to water it, and not of its fruits before they are ripe.'

[2]Quoted from the *Kitāb al-Hikam* of Ibn 'Atā'illāh.

our hearts). For the Sufis, constant invocation, constant 'remembrance', is the key to every lock – is there any lock that is proof against the power of the All-Powerful? – and it is also the very essence of prayer, for after mentioning prayer as such, the Qurān tells us: *wa la dhikru 'Llāhi akbar* ('and indeed the remembrance of God is greater').

The whole art or science of Sufism consists in perfecting the *dhikr* and in making it perpetual (so that even in the midst of activity it continues to sing in the heart). This is equivalent to an uninterrupted awareness of the divine Presence; but it must not, of course, be supposed that God can be 'summoned' by some human act. He is always present – 'If you dissect the heart of any atom you will behold a sun within it,' said a Persian poet – but we are inclined to wander, and we have again and again to return to the point where we began, here and now, in the present and in the Presence.

Ultimately, as the Sufis understand the matter, the heart that has been emptied of debris through purification and by means of the *dhikr* is fit to become the seat of Him whose Throne encompasses all things, and they quote in this context a *hadīth qudsī*: 'My slave ceases not to draw near unto Me through voluntary devotions until I love him; and when I love him, then I am the hearing wherewith he hears and the sight wherewith he sees and the hand wherewith he fights and the foot by which he walks.' One who has come to this emptiness and thereby to this plenitude, when asked how he fares, may reply:

> I fare as one by whose majestic will
> The world revolves, floods rise and rivers flow,
> Stars in their courses move; yea, death and life
> Hang on his nod and fly to the ends of the earth,
> His ministers of mourning or of joy.[1]

We are now in a region beyond confessional divergencies, a region in which the distinctions we observe in our daily life no longer make sense or contribute to understanding, a region in which *seeing* merges into *being*. The 'Eye of the Heart' with which the accomplished Sufi sees his Lord (and with which his Lord sees him) – that same 'Eye' of which St Paul wrote in his Epistle to the Ephesians, and in reference to which a North-American Indian sage is recorded as saying: 'I am blind and see not the things of this world; but when Light comes from On High it illuminates my heart and I can see, for the Eye of my heart sees all things'[2] – this Eye becomes a gate through which the being passes to become what in essence he always was, uniting with the eternal identity which is his in the Presence of God.

He can never attain to this goal through his own efforts, but he can never attain to it without effort. 'What separates man from divine Reality is the slightest of barriers: God is infinitely close to man, but man is infinitely far from God. This barrier is, for man, a mountain; he stands

---

[1]Quoted from *The Mystics of Islam*, Reynold A. Nicholson (Routledge & Kegan Paul).
[2]See *L'Oeil du Coeur*, Frithjof Schuon (Paris: Gallimard, 1950), p. 22.

before a mountain which he must remove with his own hands. He digs away the earth, but in vain; the mountain remains. Man, however, goes on digging, in the name of God. And the mountain vanishes. It was never there.'[1]

[1]*Stations of Wisdom*, Frithjof Schuon (London: John Murray, 1961), p. 157.

Chapter 12

OTHER DIMENSIONS

It is not only the mystics who are concerned with the problem of making the 'abstract' concrete, that is to say, with extending the sense of reality which every sane man and woman possesses to include realities which are not within the grasp of our physical senses. They may press further into the 'unknown' than their less adventurous companions – the 'true journey', according to Ibn Atā'illāh, is towards a state of awareness in which 'you see the hereafter closer to you than your own self' – but the problem exists for every believer.

For Islam as for Christianity this life is a preparation for what is to come, but no one will seriously prepare himself for something that appears to him unreal, a fantasy, a dream. It is difficult enough for the young to grasp in an entirely concrete manner the fact that – assuming they survive – they will eventually be old people. How much more difficult, then, for the human creature, young or old, to understand that divine Judgement, heaven and hell will come as surely as tomorrow's dawn, or yet more surely, since that dawn cannot come unless God so wills, whereas the advent of physical death and all that follows upon it represents the only infallible prediction we can make concerning our own future.

It is by no means easy for those whose whole attention is focused upon the massive apparent reality of this world to accept the fact that it can at any moment, and will at some moment, disappear like a puff of smoke. Yet the Qurān assures us that the *akhīrā*, the hereafter, is 'better and more lasting', and this suggests that it is more real than any 'reality' we experience here. Terminology presents a problem in this context: terms such as 'the hereafter' and, to an even greater extent, 'the afterlife' can be misleading if they are taken to suggest something that is little more than a shadowy reflection of what came before, or a disembodied continuation of the life we experience here, and this is what they do suggest to many people in our time. Unfortunately no alternative terminology is available; none, at least, that would bring out the essential point, which is that our experience in the *dunyā*, the world, is qualitatively less real than our 'experience' in the *akhīrā*. Nor is there any word to suggest the limitless possibilities which are open to the spirit when it has passed through the gateway of physical death.

Imagination, however, can go some way to filling the gap. Let us compare our situation here and now to that of a group of people confined to a single room in a great house and unable to remember anything outside this room. The house has many other rooms, and beyond it stretches a vast park, beyond which are the hills, valleys and rivers of the land in which it is situated. This land is but one sector of the planet, and the planet itself is hardly more than a speck of dust in the total cosmos.

How do we describe to the people confined in one room all that lies outside its four walls? Do we speak of other rooms in the house, some incomparably more splendid, others no more than squalid attics or fetid dungeons? Do we describe the park, with its ornamental lake, or perhaps invite our captive audience to extend their imaginations even further and visualize the lands beyond the park? Do we dare speak of the planet's fiery interior? Finally, is it advisable to draw these people still further into the unknown and tell them of stars and galaxies?

The different 'rooms', the 'park', the 'lands' and the 'galaxies' are in other dimensions of being to those with which most of us are acquainted, some so intensely real that our human life would seem, in comparison, like a dream, others no more than what we ourselves would call 'dreaming' in comparison with waking life. This story has no end, such is the extent of the 'hereafter' in relation to the theatre in which our human experience unfolds, and to attempt to describe it to worldlings is to invite them to use a faculty that has become atrophied from lack of use.

Revelation allows for this incapacity. Both Islam and Christianity offer a highly synthetic, condensed view of the 'hereafter'. The simple alternative, Heaven/hell, provides the ordinary believer with as much information as he needs for his salvation. It is obvious that any given state of experience elsewhere must be either 'better' or 'worse' than the life we experience here, and it is sufficient that men and women should seek the 'better' and strive to avoid the 'worse'. But these doctrines also employ a symbolism which, if it is understood by those who have a need to understand, extends the horizon beyond the images of heavenly joy and infernal fires, particularly when it is co-ordinated with the symbolism of other religious and mythological traditions. The language of myth and symbol is the only universal language.

Only in the modern age has it become necessary, at least in one sector of humanity, to speak of the complexities – the extended horizons – beyond the simple images. In earlier times the hope of Heaven and the fear of hell were overwhelmingly real to Christians, even if they frequently acted as though these dimensions did not exist (just as the young frequently act as though they would never grow old). The loss of this hope and this fear has been a decisive factor in shaping the culture and the climate of opinion in the midst of which we now live.

The Muslim, on the whole, remains intensely aware of what is to come. The Qurān, although it defines the *kāfirūn* primarily as those who actively deny God and His Self-revelation, defines them also as those who disbelieve in the 'Hereafter' and in the Judgement which precedes its unfolding. Faith in God cannot be separated from the conviction that we shall one day 'stand' before Him, and this conviction virtually guarantees salvation. The tale is told of a man whose life had been so wicked that, when he was dying, he ordered his son to have his body burned and the ashes scattered so far afield that not even God would be able to reassemble him. When, none the less, he was brought before the supreme Judge he was – so we are told – forgiven his sins, because the greatness of his fear testified to great faith.

On one occasion when the Prophet was addressing the people from the pulpit, he quoted the Quranic verse, 'And for him who fears the standing before his Lord there are two Gardens' (Q.55.46), and a certain Abū Dardā called out, 'Even if he commits fornication and steals, Messenger of Allah?' The Prophet repeated the verse and Abū Dardā repeated his question. After this had happened a third time and the Prophet again said, 'And for him who fears the standing before his Lord there are two Gardens,' he added, 'in spite of Abū Dardā!'

The three monotheistic religions (unlike Hinduism, for example) are not altogether happy with the imagery of 'dreaming' as applied to our present state of existence, although this imagery is by no means foreign either to Islam or to Christianity. It is often misundersood, since people readily take it to mean that life is 'less real' than we take it to be, whereas the intention is to indicate that there are other possible states of experience so intense that, in relation to our everyday experience of this world, they may be compared to wakefulness in relation to dreaming. There is a *ḥadīth* recorded by Muslim which can scarcely be interpreted in any other terms. The man who had the pleasantest life in the world, so we are told, will be dipped momentarily into hell on the Day of Resurrection. He will then be asked, 'Son of Adam, did you ever experience any good? Did anything pleasant ever come your way?' and he will reply, 'No, my Lord, I swear it!' Then the man who, of all men, had the most miserable life on earth will be dipped momentarily into Paradise. He will then be brought before his Lord and asked, 'Son of Adam, did you ever have any misfortune? Did any distress ever come your way?' and he will reply, 'No, my Lord, I swear it! No misfortune has ever come to me and I have never known distress.'

It would be difficult to find a simpler or more striking illustration of the difference between degrees of reality as experienced by a consciousness transposed from a lower one to a higher one. At the same time it offers, at least to those who are prepared to accept the possibility that there may be states of experience 'more real' than anything we live through here, one answer to the question as to how God can allow the innocent to suffer in this world. If anyone were to awaken from a bad dream, full of fear and torment, to find himself at home beside his beloved, sunlight streaming through the window, a prospect of golden days before him and all his deepest longings satisfied, for how long would he remember the pain of his dream? On the other hand, if he were to awaken from a dream of delight to find himself in an all too familiar prison cell, awaiting the next session of torture at the hands of merciless inquisitors and quite without hope, dream-pleasure would melt away in moments. Whether it be sweet or sour, reality takes precedence over dreaming, and the greater reality takes precedence over the lesser.

A delicate balance has to be maintained between two extremes: on the one hand a view of human life which attributes absolute reality to the world of the senses, on the other a view which dismisses this world as 'unreal'. Islam, as the religion of the 'middle way', has maintained this balance with great care, however often individual Muslims may have veered to one extreme or the other. To treat the barriers – or 'veils' – which separate different degrees of reality as solid and opaque is to condemn our world to barren isolation; to pretend that they do not exist is to abolish the world, or since we cannot in fact do this, to lost contact with the lesser reality as it impinges on us in our earthly life. What Islam teaches, in effect, is that the veils exist by the will of God, and that they are an aspect of His mercy, since we could not play the games we play here and now were we not veiled from a Light which – were it fully revealed – would burn up all existence in a moment;[1] even the irruption into our world of the angelic dimension in its full splendour would bring everything to an end. 'They say: Why hath not an angel been sent down unto him? If We sent down an angel, then the matter would be judged, no further time would be allowed them' (Q.6.8).

It is related that on one occasion the Prophet asked the archangel Gabriel to show himself in the 'mighty form' in which God created him. 'O Beloved of God,' said Gabriel, 'I have a terrifying form such as no one could look upon without being rapt from himself.' The Prophet insisted none the less, and Gabriel finally agreed to allow his angelic dimension to encompass earthly vision. There was a great rush of sound, as of a hurricane in full spate, and Gabriel appeared in his earth-crushing splendour so that his form blotted out the horizon. The Prophet fainted under the impact of this vision, whereupon the archangel resumed his earthly disguise, embraced the fallen man and kissed him, saying: 'Be not afraid, O Beloved of God, for I am thy brother Gabriel!' but he added: 'What would it have been like if you had seen Isrāfīl (he who summons to the Last Judgement), for then my own form would have seemed to you a small and puny thing.'

The veils exist, but they are at least semi-transparent; the greater realities still shine through – though veiled – upon the lesser ones, just as angels may appear to men but only in disguise. 'Paradise is closer to you than the thong of your sandal,' said the Prophet, 'and the same applies to the Fire.' On a certain occasion the people saw him apparently reach out for something and then draw suddenly back. They asked him the reason for this, and he replied: 'I saw Paradise, and I reached out for a bunch of its grapes. Had I taken it, you would have eaten from it for as long as the world endures. I also saw hell. No more terrible sight have I ever seen ...'

The thread of Being runs through all possible states of existence, all the dimensions, as does the thread of Mercy; this is already implicit in the basic doctrine of *tawḥīd*, for the One cannot be cut up into separate pieces, nor can the different degrees of Reality be shut off from each other by impenetrable partitions. For the terms Being and Mercy we might substitute beauty and goodness, which overflow from their single Source to reach the furthest limits of existence. According to a *ḥadīth* quoted previously, God is beautiful and He loves beauty, the same beauty through which we in our distant place perceive something of the Divine and scent the fragrance of Paradise; and, according to another *ḥadīth*, He rewards any good that we do a hundredfold, because 'He has reserved for Himself

[1] According to a *ḥadīth* recorded by both Muslim and Ibn Hanbal, 'Light is his veil; were He to remove it, the glory of His face would burn all who attained unto it.'

ninety-nine-hundredths of all goodness, and – by virtue of the hundredth part left on earth – all His creatures are animated by love and the horse lifts up its hoof for fear of hurting the child.'

Moreover, if heaven and hell are so close to us – as the Prophet said they are – then, at least in a certain sense, we already live in these dimensions, though for the most part unaware of them, and no more than a thin membrane separates us from the Joy and from the Fire. It is said often enough that 'we are all human', and so we are; but it might be added that our outward 'humanity' is no more than a veneer covering a deeper identity. Here and now, in our daily lives, we already rub shoulders with 'the people of Paradise' and 'the people of the Fire.'

Even in the physical environment which surrounds us, these extra-terrestrial dimensions are perceptible to those gifted with sharp sight, and Islam is certainly not alone in making this point; according to the Christian writer, William Law, 'There cannot be the smallest thing or the smallest quality of anything in this world, but it is a quality of Heaven or of hell, discovered under a temporal form.'

It is in terms of this perspective, with its clear implication that beauty – far from being a luxury – is a means of salvation, and ugliness a way to damnation, that we may judge the importance of the environment which people make for themselves and in the midst of which they prefer to live; and it is in the same terms that we may judge the significance of the cult of ugliness (usually called 'realism') which overshadows a good deal of contemporary thought and contemporary art. There is a common assumption today that the ugly is in some curious way 'more real' than the beautiful, and this amounts to saying that hell is closer to us than heaven (as well it may be in this age). Modern art provides the most terrifying evidence for this. An art critic, for example, describes a painting by Lucien Freud in these words: ' A young man with long fairish hair lies completely naked on a chaise-longue, his legs drawn up and splayed apart. In his left hand he holds a small black rat with beady eyes; its long, snake-like tail lies across his right thigh near his penis. The young man stares up at the ceiling. His expression is of one who has seen horror or some profound emptiness . . .'[1] It might not be easy to find, at least on public view, a contemporary painting which bears witness to the closeness of Paradise as powerfully as does this to the closeness of hell.

Since God is both our origin and our end and is present with us in each moment of time, these reflections of His Beauty and of His Wrath are always at hand, but it is His Presence as such which dominates every possible dimension. Those who do not in some measure find Him in this life or, at the very least, turn towards Him 'though they see Him not', are those who, according to the Qurān, will be raised up blind when the only alternatives, stark and simple, are light or darkness, presence or absence. People forget the relativity of time and the fact that it is a purely local condition. Here and now we are what we will be.

Even if we know this in theory, we fall very easily into the habit of looking no further than our bodily senses can reach and treating this world

[1] *The Times* (London), 2 March 1978.

of experience as though it were a closed and self-sufficient system. The theology of Islam takes measures to correct this habit and does so by means of what might be described as radical surgery. It severs the link between cause and effect which is the basis for our rational understanding of the world.

Theology never assumed in Islam the importance it has had in Christianity. Practice, not theory, was what mattered, and there was no obligation to provide answers to questions which should not have been asked in the first place. The traveller need know little of the country through which he is passing, provided he has been told the direct route to the right point of exit, and the Prophet had said, 'Be in this world as though you were a stranger or a traveller ...' Yet the Qurān commands the believer to 'think', to 'consider', to use his intelligence; and people do ask questions, to which they expect answers. It occurred to certain pious men that it might be better to deal with these questions in a manner that would reinforce piety, rather than leave the questioner to find answers which might undermine faith.

In the later part of the eleventh century of the Christian era, Sunni Islam finally accepted as an 'official' and agreed formulation of the articles of faith the theology of al-Ash'arī (d.AD 935) and his school of thought. He himself had started his career as a Mu'tazilite, a 'rationalist', and was able to use the tools of Greek dialectic against rationalism and against all similar attempts to explain the world solely in terms of its own limited categories.

Ash'arite theology is particularly identified with two theories, both of which bear striking witness to the unflinching unitarianism of the Islamic perspective and its intense awareness of divine omnipotence. The first is that of 'acquisition' according to which all our actions are created by God but are subsequently 'acquired' by the human being, who is thereafter responsible for them. The second is the doctrine commonly known as 'occasionalism' according to which every event that occurs in this world is new-minted, unconnected with its predecessor, in other worlds with its cause. God alone is the cause of each event and He creates the world anew at every moment. This theory was taken up by the Sufis in terms of the 'renewal of creation at each breath' (*tajdīd al-khalq bi'l-anfās*). God is the Creator not only at the beginning of time but now, in this instant, and forever; He creates a new world in each infinitesimal moment of time. Phenomena cannot be the cause of other phenomena, events cannot beget events, for then they would be 'gods' beside God. Shadows do not cast shadows. Quicker than the eye can perceive or the mind grasp, the world with all that it contains disappears into nothingness as though it had never been; no less swiftly, a new world is created in its place – if God so wills.

Until the present century this must have been a difficult theory to grasp. Today any child could understand it. We have, in cinematography, an exact illustration of what the Ash'arites were saying. The audience watching a movie sees a smooth sequence of cause-and-effect operating in time, but in fact the successive frames on the film passing through the projector do not have any such relationship. A single frame is flashed on the screen; there is then a moment of darkness, imperceptible to the human eye, after which another frame appears. The film editor controls the order in which these frames are shown. The audience sees a stone strike a window whereupon the glass shatters, but the frames which show the stone being thrown did not 'cause' those which show the breakage. The editor could have removed the latter or inserted others in their place, or he could have reversed the order in which they were projected. The editor can do as he pleases in the cutting-room, just as God 'does as He pleases', and since – for the Muslim – it is unthinkable that God could be under any compulsion whatsoever, it follows that He is not obliged to allow a particular effect to follow a particular cause.

According to the Ash'arite theologian Fudālī, it is not fire that causes burning in a piece of wood – how could something as humble as fire be the cause of anything? – but it is God alone who causes burning in the object seized by the flame. We have here, says Frithjof Schuon, 'a striking example of the spirit of rigorous alternatives characteristic of the Semitic and Western mentalities; in order to be able to affirm one essential aspect of the truth, other aspects must be denied, although they would in no way derogate from the principle to be demonstrated.'[1] To admit that fire burns, adding that it does so because God created it for this purpose, would do nothing to undermine the divine omnipotence; but Fudālī believes that it might do so and, in terms of the psychology of the Semite and of Western man, he may not have been entirely wrong.

The requirements of piety and the rights of objective truth do not always coincide on the level of theology, as Schuon has pointed out in a detailed critique of the Ash'arite position.[2] At this level, piety takes precedence over objectivity, and Al-Ash'arī's principal concern is to remind us constantly that God is present and active in all things and to suggest that – but for this Presence – the world would be no more than a discontinuous chaos. He succeeds, but at a price. 'From the metaphysical point of view,' says Schuon, 'this is an unnecessary luxury, since the intellect has other resources than pious absurdity ...' But, from the psychological point of view, the Ash'arite theory of creation achieves its object, and it does so in a way that is characteristic of Islam. God is never absent and never inactive; everything must be attributed to Him as its source, even if this involves denying that He acts through the instrumentality of secondary causes and in accordance with discernible 'laws of nature', and a refusal to admit that, in Schuon's words, 'if God creates an apple tree it is to produce apples and not figs'. Just as the Muslim is forbidden to make images of living things, lest he worship them as idols, so he is prevented from attributing effects to earthly causes, lest he imagine that these causes are independent of the divine omnipotence.

Modern science is based upon this attribution and does indeed exclude God from the chain of causality; it is only in the discipline of physics that certain contemporary scientists detect the presence of something outside their terms of reference, but physics has become so abstruse a science that it has little influence on current 'mythology'. In so far as atheistic scientism

---

[1]*Stations of Wisdom*, Frithjof Schuon (London: John Murray, 1961), p. 70.
[2]See 'Dilemmas within Ash'arite Theology' in *Islam and the Perennial Philosophy*, Frithjof Schuon (World of Islam Festival Co., 1976).

denies transcendent causes and isolates the world of appearances from reality, al-Ashʿarī has — as Schuon says — replied to it in advance by his denial of physical causality. This is a matter, not of introducing modifications into the scientific view of the world, but of taking a sledge-hammer to the foundations upon which this view has been constructed; the whole house comes down.

Contemporary Muslim intellectuals — those, at least, whose voices are most often heard — seek scapegoats for the fact that Islam never developed the means of destroying the world and dehumanizing man. They have been maimed by their sense of inferiority *vis-à-vis* Western technological achievements. Some blame the rigidity of the *'ulamā'*; some blame Sufism and others Ashʿarism. Islam, they point out, gave science to Europe and then fell asleep, while Europe picked the ball up and raced with it towards the goal of power and imperial domination.

It is true enough that Islam passed on to Western Europe the 'Greek virus' (to use Arnold Hottinger's phrase), an organism to which it had proved immune but to which Christendom succumbed; but the Muslims of our own time must be the only people on earth who have ever complained of their ancestors' immunity to disease. They refuse to admit that neither the science they admire nor the technology they covet could ever have arisen in a truly Islamic climate; the former depends upon an attitude towards God and the latter upon an attitude towards nature (and towards human vocations) neither of which are compatible with the Muslim's unitarian faith, and both depend upon the isolation of this world from other dimensions.

Islamic science — in the great age of spiritual and intellectual adventuring — was concerned on the one hand with discerning the 'signs of Allah' in natural phenomena, and on the other with observing the forces and laws of nature the better to co-operate with them, so that the human family might be the more comfortably fitted into its God-given environment. Until the whole pattern of his existence was thrown out of balance in recent times, it was never the Muslim's way to work — as it were — against the grain of the wood, to force the natural world out of shape or to abuse its riches. His world was regulated in accordance with human proportions; he built nothing that might overwhelm him in terms of its size or grandeur, he never became the servant of his own tools, and so long as he obeyed the command to 'walk gently upon the earth' — he and his horses, his camels and his cattle — it seems unlikely that he could ever have designed bulldozers to rip it up.

His 'pure' science was the knowledge of essences rather than of phenomena as such. Stars and stones, mountains and the earth's vegetation, the waves of the ocean and the clouds in the sky were not a random collection of objects but a sequence of pictures contained in a single volume. These pictures, these 'signs', were all the more comprehensible for being simple, free from the complexities and distortions which human inventiveness introduces into the phenomena of the natural world. If modern science has destroyed the normal human capacity to think in terms of symbols, it is also true that modern technology has obscured the symbolism inherent in the natural environment and therefore made comprehension more difficult.

'Allah is the Light of the heavens and the earth; the likeness of His Light is as a niche wherein is a lamp, the lamp is in a glass, the glass as it were a shining star. [The lamp is] kindled from a blessed tree, an olive neither of the East nor of the West, whose oil would well-nigh shine though no fire touched it. Light upon light!' (Q.24.35). An arc lamp or a neon strip are sources of light, but who can doubt that they lend themselves less well to such symbolism than does a simple oil lamp? Our technological inventions have had a certain stunning and stupefying effect upon us, and it has become increasingly difficult to perceive – or even to believe in – the 'transparency' of natural phenomena. Not only is the world around us drained of meaning, but the problems inherent in any attempt to describe other dimensions of experience in the imagery of things found here become almost insurmountable.

The question as to how celestial realities may be communicated to the human mind has been touched on several times in this book. We are obliged to return to it again and again because this is the field upon which the most important battles are fought, particularly in the present age. Blind and unquestioning faith is becoming increasingly rare. The agnostic finds scriptural and traditional accounts of divine Judgement, Heaven and hell either improbable or absurd. The believers quarrel among themselves as to whether such descriptions are to be taken literally or allegorically.

The fact is that we are ungrateful people. We want – naturally enough – to know what (if anything) happens to us after death. God is not deaf to this demand. We are offered a vast selection of images, hints and indications which, if we are prepared to use our powers of intelligence and imagination, provide an adequate answer. We then complain of contradictions in this imagery, obscurity in these hints and lack of precision in these indications.

Any description of the posthumous states of being would be suspect if it contained no contradictions in terms of our experience here. It is impossible that states so different to our own should fit neatly into the categories of this world or conform to our local conditions. The laws which govern time are unlikely to apply to other forms of duration, and the laws which govern space are unlikely to apply to other forms of extension; but, because time is one of the possible forms of duration, and space is one of the possible forms of extension, images taken from time and space may be transposed to other dimensions. We have five senses in this world. We might have five hundred elsewhere, each one as different from the other as are sight and hearing in our present experience, but we are still obliged to speak of these things in terms of 'seeing', 'hearing', 'touching', 'smelling' and 'tasting'.

On the other hand, if the hereafter were totally unimaginable, this would mean that different levels of reality are sealed off from each other, without connection, which would be contrary to the doctrine of *tawḥīd* and, indeed, contrary to common sense. Were this so, we would have no reason to take an interest in what happens to us elsewhere since, whatever it might be, it would bear no relation to our knowledge, our hopes, our needs and our desires as creatures of the earth.

The necessary connection between experience here and experience elsewhere is emphasized by the Qurān: 'Give glad tidings to those who believe and do good; for them are Gardens beneath which rivers flow. Whenever they are given sustenance from the fruit thereof, they say: This is what we were given aforetime. And they are given it in the likeness of that' (Q.2.25). The treasures of Paradise and the bounties of earth must have something in common since they flow from a single source. And yet: 'No soul can know what joy of the eyes is hidden from them; a reward for what they have done' (Q.32.17). It is axiomatic in religious terms that God never gives less than He promises. He never disappoints expectations which He has Himself aroused. But he does – we are assured – give more than He promises, and it is this 'more' that is indecipherable or that exceeds the reach of the human imagination; and this it is that, in the last resort, over- whelms the simple images people have of a 'happy afterlife', just as a great light overwhelms a lesser one. 'Therein they have all that they desire, yet with Us there is more' (Q.50.35).

All human enjoyment is limited. Paradise is by definition boundless, for it opens out on to the Infinite. On the human level this can be suggested only in numerical terms – we shall have a thousand joys, ten thousand, a million and so on – or in terms of increase without end, but without repetition. Erotic love, for example, will have all the wonder and all the freshness of 'first love' (the 'perpetually renewed virginity' of the 'Houris', which causes so much amusement to Western students of Islam, is an obvious reference to this). Every drink is like the first drink of a thirsty man, though none thirst in Paradise, and every taste of food is like the first taste taken by a starving man, though none starve there, and every meeting is true friendship discovered for the first time, and there is nothing in Paradise that is not newly minted and to be enjoyed with the appetite of youth.

All this is logical, however difficult it may be to imagine, for it is impos- sible that a state of experience defined in terms of 'more and yet more' could be static. Boundlessness indicates no discoverable end to a movement towards what is better and then better still, and after that, even better, with no limits set to increase in joy, in beauty and in discovery. The greatest marvel is always overtaken by a greater marvel, the sweetest com- panionship is for ever growing sweeter, and love – though from the very start it seems perfectly consummated – still grows limitlessly. The people of Paradise are constantly surprised, for every time they think that they hold perfection in their hands, and that there can be nothing better than this, they find before them something better still. 'The lowest place of any of you in Paradise,' said the Prophet, 'is that in which Allah will tell him to make a wish, and he will wish and wish again. Allah will then ask him if he has expressed his wish and, when he replies that he has, He will tell him that he is to have what he wished for together with as much again.'

Yet the problem remains. In referring to erotic love, food and drink, should we have placed them cautiously between inverted commas or can they be left to stand as they are? This is really a matter of expediency, since either course of action could be justified. The things of Paradise (and of hell) are 'like' the things of earth because of the interconnection between all possible states of experience; they are 'unlike' them because of the incom- mensurability between different dimensions or levels of reality.

On account of 'likeness' we are free to say that there are indeed food and drink in the hereafter (delicious in Paradise and abominable in hell); on account of 'unlikeness' we have every right to adopt the opposite point of view, but those who do so must then suggest other means of expressing what is to be expressed. It is easy enough to say that all such images should be understood allegorically, but the average man will then ask of what use 'allegorical' food and drink are to him. Not only Islam but also the other world religions have always preferred the concrete imagery leaving the faithful to make what they will of it in accordance with their intelligence and their imaginative powers. We have to accept the fact that some good but simple people will go through life with very crude notions of the hereafter, while others, less good and much less simple, will dismiss heaven and – even more readily – hell because of the apparent crudity of the images employed.

It is with these considerations in mind, and without any irrevocable commitment either to the 'literal' or the 'allegorical' interpretation of sacred imagery, that we must consider what the Muslim believes – in the light of Qurān and *ḥadīth* – about the Last Judgement, the joys of Paradise and the pains of hell.

None escape judgement. Every human creature has lived in a condition of veiling – subject to every kind of self-deception – and is obliged, when the veils are removed, to face the naked truth. 'Thou wast heedless of this. Now have We removed from thee thy covering, and piercing is thy sight this day' (Q.50.22), and 'whosoever has done an atom's weight of good shall see it, and whosoever has done an atom's weight of evil shall see it' (Q.99.7–8); for '*There* will every soul become aware [of the significance] of what they did, brought back to Allah, their true Master; and all that they devised will have forsaken them' (Q.10.30).

While the consequences of everything he ever did now seem to take on a life of their own, each soul is quite alone: 'Now indeed have you come unto Us solitary as We created you in the first instance and you have left behind you everything We gave you, and We see not beside you those – your intercessors – who you thought were partners with you...' (Q.6.94). Each bears his burden, for no created thing can share it with him or bear even a small part of it: 'No burdened soul can bear another's burden, and though one weighed down with his load calls [for help] with it, naught will be lifted even if he [to whom he calls] be near of kin' (Q.35.18).[1] In Frithjof Schuon's words: 'At death all assurance and all competence fall away like a garment and the being who remains is impotent and like a lost child; nothing is left but a substance we have ourselves woven which may either fall heavily or, on the contrary, let itself be drawn up by Heaven like a rising star.'[2] All familiar landmarks have disappeared except for those of

---

[1] There is, however, an important exception to this rule. Anyone who kills a man or woman without adequate justification (as, for example, in self-defence or following due legal process) bears the added burden of all the sins his victim may have committed and will have to answer for them (cf. Q.5.29 and other passages). The victim has, as it were, shifted all responsibility for the sins of a lifetime to his murderer. By extension, one may assume that the same applies

[2] *Understanding Islam*, Frithjof Schuon, p. 84.

faith and prayer, and he who was without faith and never entered upon prayer finds himself in darkness upon 'a vast abysmal sea': 'There covereth him a wave, above which is a wave, above which is a cloud; layer upon layer of darkness. When he holdeth out his hand he can scarcely see it. And for him for whom Allah hath not appointed light, there is no light' (Q.24.40). No light of his own, that is to say; for he emerges out of this roaring, chaotic darkness into a light that is – for him – terrible beyond imagining.

The Islamic vision of Judgement is dominated by the idea of 'exposure'. Nothing whatsoever is hidden from Him who, according to the poet Sanā'ī, 'feels the touch of an ant's foot as it moves in darkness over a rock'. On that Day there is no shade but His, no refuge from Him unless it be with Him: 'And when the trumpet sounds a single blast and the earth, with the mountains, is lifted up and crushed with one blow ... On that Day will ye be exposed, not a secret of yours hidden' (Q.69.13–14, 18). Since there is no covering to be found, mankind will be assembled on that Day naked and barefoot. When the Prophet said this, the lady 'Ā'isha, who never failed to ask what others might have thought but hesitated to ask, inquired whether men and women would be together, looking at one another. 'The matter will be too serious, 'Ā'isha, for them to look at one another,' he said.

As though this exposure were not enough, there will be a host of witnesses present. The animals will be there to testify. According to a *ḥadīth*, a prostitute was (or will be) forgiven because, coming upon a dog that was dying of thirst, she took off her shoe, tied it with her head-covering, lowered it into a well and brought out water for the animal to drink. And the Prophet said also that 'a woman was punished on account of a cat which she kept shut up till it died of hunger'. The ambiguity of tense may be noted: an event taking place beyond time as we know it may be referred to as past although, for us, it lies in the future. The relativity of time in this context is emphasized by the fact that, according to the Qurān, the 'Day of Quaking', the 'Day of Arousing', the 'Day which will turn the hair of children grey' (Q.73.17), the Day upon which 'each nursing mother will forget her nursling and each pregnant woman will be delivered of her burden, and thou wilt see mankind as drunken, though they will not be drunk' (Q.22.2), will last for fifty thousand years, yet – according to a *ḥadīth* – it will pass for the sincere believer 'like the passing of a single hour'.

The gentle earth itself will, as it were, find a voice and bear witness: 'on that Day will she relate her tidings, for her Lord will have inspired her' (Q.99.4–5); and whatever has been done on land or sea – or 'in the heavens' – 'though it be but the weight of a mustard-seed and though it be in a rock' will be brought forth (Q.31.16). The encounter with absolute Truth leaves nothing hidden.

More significant still, man bears witness against himself and cannot do otherwise. He comes to Judgement with a 'driver' and a 'witness' who have been with him throughout his life, and the powers within the divided city

---

to cases of 'execution' by the state if the extreme penalty is not in accordance with the religious Law, or if grounds for clemency have not been exhaustively explored.

which was his earthly personality have much to say, yet he himself – the self which might devise excuses and justifications – is silenced: 'This Day We seal up their mouths, and their hands speak to Us and their feet bear witness as to what they earned' (Q.36.65). It could therefore be said that the soul judges itself, for now – at last – it knows itself fully, knows itself in relation to the Norm to which it may have conformed or from which it may have departed. Each finds his way infallibly to the only niche into which he will fit, whether this be above or below, and the Qurān reminds us constantly that God is never unjust; He allows us to go where by nature we belong.

The soul's substance, which had, in this life, a certain fluidity, is as it were fixed or crystallized when life is over; it cannot change, however much it might wish to do so. 'If each soul that hath done ill possessed all that is in the earth, it would seek to ransom itself therewith, and they feel remorseful when they see the penalty; but it has been judged between them in justice and they are not wronged' (Q.10.54). This world is the place of mercy, where we need only ask in order to receive; on the Day, pure objectivity rules, and we are what we are or what we have made of ourselves. 'Say: O My servants who have wronged their own souls, despair not of the mercy of Allah, who forgiveth all sins. Indeed He is the Forgiving, the Merciful. And turn unto your Lord in repentance and submit to Him before there cometh unto you the penalty. Then ye will not be helped' (Q.39.53–54).

We read in a *ḥadīth* of a bridge that is to be crossed, the same bridge mentioned in many traditions and mythologies throughout the world, thin as a hair and razor-sharp, stretched over the abysmal depths. Each soul must cross by this perilous way if it is to come to Paradise, and some – it is said – cross like lightning and others like the wind, some as a bird might fly, some at the speed of a fine horse and others like a man running, until one comes 'walking on the big toes of his two feet' and the bridge shakes him off, as it does so many others, to fall headlong into the Fire. This too is an aspect of the Judgement, exposing the soul's fitness or lack of fitness for the celestial Garden.

The abyss into which those tumble who are unfit for anything better is a place of raging fire which, according to the traditional accounts, was stoked for a thousand years till it became red, for another thousand till it became white, and then for another thousand till it became black as a starless night; and the Qurān tells us that as they approach it, 'they will hear its crackling and its raging sigh as it spies them from afar; and when they are flung, chained together, into a narrow place therein, they plead for immediate destruction. Plead not on that day for a single destruction, [but] plead for oft-repeated destruction!' (Q.25.12–14).

There, 'in the shadow of black smoke', they must eat the deadly fruit of the tree called Zaqqūm, said by some to be the fruit of the evil they did during their lives on earth, and their drink is 'pus', which 'they can scarcely swallow' (Q.14.16–17). According to the *ḥadīth* literature, they meet there with scorpions as big as mules and huge snakes which flay them from scalp to toe-nails; when they put on their sandals of fire their brains boil as though in a copper cauldron, their molar teeth glow like live coals and their entrails melt and flow. Their voices, when they cry out, are like the voice of the ass, which begins with a sound of panting and ends with a braying. It is said that were the smallest fraction of the fire's heat to come our way, it would burn up all the inhabitants of earth, and if one of the garments of the people of hell were hung above us, the stench and the heat combined would kill every last one of us.

Death comes upon the damned from every quarter, yet – according to the Qurān – 'they cannot die' and suffering therefore stretches ahead of them indefinitely. 'As often as their skins are consumed [by the fire], We replace them with new skins that they may taste the torment' (Q.4.56); for here there can be no relief through numbing of the senses, and the damned never grow accustomed to their condition. 'That which is within them, and their skins too, are melted' (Q.22.20), and this is particularly significant if we remember all that is said in the Qurān about hardness of heart, as also about impermeability to the divine mercy and the divine message.

There is little in the Muslim imagery of the infernal regions that could seem alien to the Western imagination. Whether Dante 'borrowed' the imagery of his *Inferno* from Islamic sources or whether it occurred to him more or less spontaneously is unimportant; the fact remains that it accords very closely with the Muslim vision of the realm of the damned, and both lend themselves readily enough to allegorical interpretation, of which the great Quranic commentary of Fakhr ad-Dīn ar-Rāzī (d. AD 1209) provides an interesting example.

According to Rāzī, the 'chains' or 'fetters' mentioned in a number of verses 'are a symbol of the soul's remaining shackled to its (erstwhile) physical attachments and bodily pleasures ... and now that their realization has become impossible those fetters and shackles prevent the resurrected personality (*an nafs*) from attaining to the realm of the spirit...' Subsequently these 'shackles' generate spiritual 'fires', since frustrated desire gives rise to an intense sensation of burning, which according to Rāzī is the meaning of the 'blazing fire' (*al-jahīm*). The sinner tries to swallow the choking agony of deprivation and the pain of separation from all that he longs for, hence the references to 'the food that chokes'.[1] It must be admitted that interpretations of this kind have rather less impact than does the stark and terrible imagery of Qurān and *hadīth*, and they are therefore less effective in shocking the human soul into a sense of reality.

The most important and controversial question, however, is whether the Muslim hell is 'eternal', and here – as so often – we encounter problems of terminology. Coomaraswamy and others have stressed the essential difference between 'eternity' (beyond any form of time or duration) and 'perpetuity' (indefinite duration). If we accept these definitions, it can be said that God alone is eternal because He alone is Absolute Reality, and the Qurān certainly supports this view. Perpetuity might seem to go on 'for ever and ever', but there is an escape from it upwards, towards the eternal, just as there is an escape from dreaming in waking. The damned may see no end to their suffering, but God sees an end to it. Moreover, His mercy

[1]See Muhammad Asad's *The Message of the Qurān*, in particular p. 904.

'takes precedence over His wrath', and to suggest that it could be entirely absent from hell would be to suggest that hell has an independent and self-sufficient existence, beyond the reach of His all-pervading mercy, and this is unacceptable to the Muslim.

It is hardly surprising, therefore, that we read in the traditional sources that a 'green tree' (or, in other versions, 'water-cress') will grow in the fields of hell as time draws to its close; and indeed the imagery of 'scouring' and 'melting' employed in the Qurān implies a process of purification, rather than punishment for punishment's sake. All this suggests, in Christian terms, Purgatory rather than a hell in which all hope is to be abandoned, although no lesser an authority than St Thomas Aquinas said that there is no true eternity in hell, but only time; and time must have a stop.

Equally significant is the fact that intercession still operates. According to a *hadīth* recorded by both Bukhari and Muslim, the two most respected authorities, the believers who have come safely to Paradise will plead for their brethren in hell and will be allowed to bring out those they recognize. Their faces will be protected from the Fire, and they will bring out a great number of people. They will then be told by their Lord to go back and bring out any 'in whose hearts you find so much as a *dīnār* of good'. They will do so, but will be commanded to return a third time and bring out any 'in whose hearts you find so much as an atom of good', and this they will do, though the angels and the prophets will already have rescued an incalculable number from the Fire. Then God will say: 'The angels have interceded, the prophets have interceded, the believers have interceded, and only the Most Merciful of the merciful now remains'; and He Himself will bring out a 'handful' – and there is nothing that could ever fill His 'hand' – of people who never did any good and who have been turned into charcoal. He will cast them into a river called the River of Life, and they will emerge like seeds from rubbish that is carried away in a flood, and they will emerge 'like pearls'. After this we may be allowed to wonder how many remain in hell till the bitter end.

In another *hadīth* from the same sources we are told that the very last man to be brought out of hell, when God has given him all that he wished for and more – although not without some argument between them – finds his way to his dwelling in Paradise 'more easily than he did to the dwelling he owned in the world'. After a lifetime on earth, after the trauma of death and after the seemingly endless torments of the Fire (which turned him to charcoal), he has come home and recognizes his home without a moment's hesitation.

It is almost as though he had never been away.

We can draw but one conclusion. Wherever it may find itself and however far it may wander, the human soul is at home only in Paradise. Elsewhere it is in exile. And yet it must not be forgotten that what was brought out from the 'rubbish', or from the charred remains, was a 'seed' (which then 'sprouted' in the water of Life). The nucleus within us which seeks Paradise and is at home there is not the outward personality busy with the affairs of this world and separated from its essence, although that too, in its way and unwittingly, is in search of a consummation it can never

find here; it is the innermost essence of each being – the 'spirit' – that longs
for home-coming and can never be satisfied until it reaches home. Whatever there may be in our nature that does not accord with our essence is
dross to be burned away; and whosoever believes that this dross is himself
– his 'true self' – will be burned with it.

With the entry into Paradise time is redeemed and everything falls into
place. Were it possible for the blessed to retain a single unhappy memory
this would not be the perfection promised them, yet it cannot be said that
they forget anything, since Paradise is the place where everything is clearly
seen; what they see, then, is the total perfection of creation, in which all
disharmonies are resolved. Nothing there is lost, for the smallest loss
would be an impermissible imperfection, a stain on the glass; and the very
fact that we love something on this earth is sufficient proof that it is a
reflection of what exists there in an incomparably more beautiful form.

There can be no return to the shadows and ambiguities of this world, or
of any other world, once the command has been given: 'Enter, ye and your
wives, into the Garden to be made happy ... therein is all that souls desire
and all that eyes delight in, and there shall ye remain' (Q.43.70–71); for
these it is 'whom We reward in accordance with the best they ever did,
overlooking their evil deeds; [these are] among the companions of the
Garden' (Q.46.16).

These, the people of Paradise, 'this day have joy in all that they do, they
and their companions, in gentle shade, on couches reclining; theirs the
fruit [of delight] and theirs whatsoever they desire. The word from the
Lord of Mercy is [for them]: Peace!' (Q.23.55-58). From a slightly
different angle, we see a distinction made between 'the foremost' and the
'people of the right hand', for although none here find less than they desire
– all, indeed, find more – the blessed differ in substance or in capacity for
joy and there are gradations even in Paradise. The 'foremost' are the
muqarrabūn, the 'close ones' (close, that is, to God Himself), and in the
Sūrah 'Wāqi'ah', the Qurān describes their condition in a rich yet concise
symbolism which has lent itself to voluminous interpretation. They recline
upon 'inlaid thrones' and are waited upon by 'immortal youths', who
bring them a drink from a 'pure spring' (could this be the Water of Life
itself?); they recline 'face to face' in perfect communion and feed on the
'flesh of birds', an angelic food free of the weight and coarseness of earthly
things; and with them are the fair ones, wide and dark of eye, the *ḥūr*, who
are like 'hidden pearls', so secret, so delicate, so beautiful; and the word
that resounds in their ears is 'Peace, peace!'.

Those 'on the right hand' are no less happy, since they have all the
happiness they can bear, 'among fruit-bearing lote-trees and flowering
acacias and spreading shade and gushing water and fruit in plenty,
never-failing and never out of reach'. God, who need only say to anything
'Be!' and it *is*, has made for them 'a new creation', maidens 'perfectly
matched' to them, loving, companionable. In our world, desire and its
object, need and its satisfaction, are separated, sometimes by great distances or by an impassable gulf; but Paradise participates more closely in
the divine Unity than does our present state of experience. In Paradise the
gap is closed.

Eschatology is always at the mercy of pedants who take the symbolism which is its necessary language even more literally than does the most unimaginative believer. But perhaps part of the problem is that they study eschatological imagery from the wrong angle. What matters is not the means whereby joy is said to be created but the fact that joy exists, not the objects which are said to satisfy desire – 'fruit' and 'pure drink' and 'the flesh of birds' – but desire as such and its perfect satisfaction.

A man who obviously considered that a heaven without camels would be no heaven at all asked the Prophet whether he would find camels in Paradise. 'If Allah brings you into Paradise,' said the Prophet, 'you will have what your soul desires and what your eye delights in.' Whether the man's profound need, which in this world found its satisfaction in the ownership of fine beasts, would still require camels for its satisfaction in Paradise may be left as an open question.

The question of the *ḥūr* ('Houris'), the wide-eyed maidens who are the companions of the blessed, has – to say the least – attracted the attention of Christians over many centuries, and although the notion of celestial eroticism no longer shocks as it once did, contemporary Westerners remain fascinated by it and seldom fail to ask why similar provision is not made for women among the blessed when, after surviving Judgement, they reach their true home.

It will be obvious from what was said earlier on the subject of sexuality and, indeed, from all that has been said about the Islamic perspective, that nothing so central to our life on earth could be excluded from Paradise; this would represent an unaccountable gap in the very fabric of felicity. If lesser joys and other beauties we taste here are taken to reflect what exists more perfectly elsewhere, then sexual delight must have its place in the matrix of Reality, and the beauty of women must be a particularly direct reminder of the eternal Beauty, manifested even more directly in Paradise. This Beauty shines through the *ḥūr* who, as personifications of the richness of the divine gifts, represent bounty, loving-kindness and all the gentle virtues; and union with them, in such close proximity to God Himself, must have an even more intense significance than does sexual intercourse in the earthly context.

There is, in fact, a double symbolism here: in the first place, that of joy, union (the sexes exist for the sake of union) and completion; secondly, that of Beauty, partially visible on earth, everywhere visible in Paradise, brought to life – tactile, warm and intimate – in the *ḥūr*. Beyond this is a still deeper symbolism with which the mystics concern themselves. The divine Essence, the 'reality of Reality', which is beyond all possible conceptualization ('The eye,' it is said, 'cannot see the eye'), is described in Arabic by the feminine word *dhāt*, and because it is 'dark' to our understanding, it is sometimes represented as 'Night', *Layla*, which is also the name of the heroine of many Muslim tales and poems. Through the beauty, innocence and mystery of a young girl the deepest secret of all things, manifest and unmanifest, is sensed and loved.

Just as hell is a place of separation – for although the damned are chained together, they hate one another – so Paradise is the place of full and perfect communion, and Islam sees nothing amiss in representing this in erotic terms. According to a *ḥadīth*, each man will see his own face reflected in that of his companion and also in her body, and she will see her face in his and in his body, as though, in such perfect union, they merged, although without losing their respective identities; it is also said that the marrow is visible, running like 'luminous honey', in each maiden's bones (so transparent are they), and this is the very essence of Beauty made visible. Forms, which in this world seem so solid and so opaque, do not – in Paradise – conceal the divine Light which has projected them. And these forms are infinitely changeable. No one will understand this unless he can rid himself of purely earthly habits of thought, according to which each thing is isolated in its opaque solidity and each spirit irrevocably attached to a particular psycho-physical form; yet if he remembers that the word 'personality' derives from the Latin *persona*, meaning an actor's mask, he will realize that masks are not usually glued to faces and will draw from this fact certain logical conclusions.

In Paradise, we are told, the blessed – both men and women – will be provided with seventy garments, every one of which will change its colour seventy times each hour. If we bear in mind that, in this world, the body and the personality are 'garments' of the spirit, the significance of this *ḥadīth* is clear enough. It is said also that there is in Paradise a market 'in which there is no buying or selling, but only the forms of men and women'; the spirits of the blessed enter into whatever form they will, for they could scarcely be content with any lesser freedom of expression, and this is the Place of Contentment.

Under the circumstances, it may be that the question as to why there are no male equivalents to the *ḥūr* becomes redundant. But it will still be asked whether the 'average Muslim' actually thinks in terms of such complex symbolism, in which case the answer must be that such things do not need to be spelt out analytically in order to be understood (though not necessarily conceptualized) by those whose minds, imagination and sensibility have been shaped by Islam. Only when certain questions are asked does it become necessary to spin out words in explanation, and the 'average Muslim' does not ask these questions, but knows that all will be well in Paradise; and this is enough.

But for how long? If God alone is eternal in the precise meaning of the word and if, when all is done, a green tree grows in the ground of hell, how can He promise the blessed that they will never have to leave Paradise (Q.15.48)? In the first place, there is no equivalence whatsoever between Paradise and hell (any more than there is between the divine Mercy and the divine Wrath). The one is open, the other closed, the one is boundless, the other limited. Good and evil, though we habitually speak of them as a pair, do not belong to the same order or the same degree of reality, which is why we are promised that a good deed will be rewarded tenfold – or a hundredfold (or with any augmentation one cares to imagine) – whereas the evil deed receives only its equivalent in punishment and no more than that (good is fertile, evil is barren).

Secondly, Paradise is 'open' in a very special sense; it opens out on to the Divine, and in the Presence of Him who is both eternal and infinite, there can be no end to anything. 'Allah has promised to the believers – men and women – Gardens beneath which rivers flow, wherein they will abide, blessed Gardens of inexhaustible delight; and, greater still, the *riḍwān* of Allah – this is the supreme triumph' (Q.9.72). *Riḍwān* is usually translated as 'acceptance' or 'good pleasure'; for its verbal root *raḍiya*, the dictionary offers such meanings as 'to be satisfied', 'to consent', 'to approve', but no translation can convey the force and significance of a word which describes something greater than Paradise itself, if only because Paradise is difficult enough to imagine without our having to imagine what is beyond it. We can only cling to the idea of 'openness', which is itself ungraspable in purely human terms of reference.

The Prophet said that a moment will come when God asks the blessed if they are content, and they will reply, 'How should we not be content, Lord, when Thou has given us what Thou didst not give to any of Thy creatures?' Then He will say, 'Shall I give you something more excellent than this?' and they will ask what could be more excellent. He will reply: 'I shall cause My *riḍwān* to alight upon you . . .' And the Prophet said also: 'While the people of Paradise are in their enjoyment a light will shine upon them and, raising their heads, they will see that their Lord has looked down upon them from above. He will say: "Peace be upon you, O people of Paradise!" . . . He will then look at them and they will look at Him, and they will not turn aside to any of their enjoyment so long as they are looking at Him until He veils Himself from them, though His Light remains.'

And again, the Prophet said: 'By Him in whose hand is my soul, no gift of His is more precious than this looking upon Him!' and when the vision fades, and they have come back to themselves and return to their celestial household, their companions in delight observe that they are now 'more beautiful than they were before'. This is journey's end and landfall for those who prayed during their earthly lives: 'My Lord, cause me to land at a blessed landing-place, for Thou art the best of those who bring to landfall' (Q.23.29).

There is here a perfect matching. If we translate *riḍwān* as 'acceptance' on the part of God, then *islām* may be translated as 'acceptance' on man's part; he 'accepts' God, with all that this implies, and 'accepts' his destiny, with all the distress it may contain, and he takes the 'straight path' which leads to Paradise and, beyond, to the beatific vision; and, because of this, God 'accepts' him and gives him 'Light upon light'.

When, in accordance with the first Pillar of his religion, the Muslim makes the Confession of Faith he attaches himself to the essential and puts aside all that is – in appearance – other-than-God, and he acknowledges the truth brought by the messengers. When, in accordance with the second Pillar, he prays – whether in a mosque or on the desert sands, in a Western city or in the polar regions – he places himself at the centre of all possible worlds, for God has promised that He will be present wherever His name is mentioned, and the place where He is present is necessarily central in every dimension.

When, in accordance with the third Pillar, this Muslim pays the poor-due and observes the obligation of loving-kindness towards his fellows, he acknowledges the rights of other creatures – made in the same image as himself – and recognizes that God, who is close to him, is close also to them. When he fasts, in accordance with the fourth Pillar, he detaches himself from the locality in which he is temporarily housed, the better to prepare himself for his everlasting home.

And when, as a pilgrim, he stands before the Ka'ba in Mecca (after circling it seven times), the centrality already prefigured by his orientation when he prayed far off is made actual. Clothed only in two pieces of plain, unsewn cloth, he has left behind him the characteristics which identified him in this world, his race, his nationality, his status; he is no longer so-and-so from such-and-such a place, but simply a pilgrim.

Beneath his bare feet, like mother-of-pearl, is the pale marble of this amphitheatre at the centre of the world, and although he is commanded to lower his eyes when praying elsewhere, he is now permitted to raise them and look upon the Ka'ba, which is the earthly shadow of the Pole or Pivot around which circle the starry heavens. Although Paradise may still seem far distant, he has already come home.

الحمد لله رب العالمين

Praise is (due only) to Allah, Lord of the Worlds.

Printed in the United States
55213LVS00006B/1-117